TAKAHAMA   MAISONNEUVE   PAVLOWITCH

EMMA
DREAMS
OF STARS
INSIDE *THE* GOURMET GUIDE

STORY BY: EMMANUELLE MAISONNEUVE AND JULIA PAVLOWITCH
ART BY: KAN TAKAHAMA

Emma Dreams of Stars:
Inside *the* Gourmet Guide

A VERTICAL Book

Editor: Michelle Lin
Translation: Eamon Fogarty
Production: Grace Lu
Anthony Quintessenza
Proofreading: Micah Q. Allen

First published in France in 2018 by Les Arènes, Paris.
Kan Takahama is represented by le Bureau des Copyrights Français in Tokyo, Japan.
English language version produced by Kodansha USA Publishing, LLC, 2021

Originally published in French as *Le Goût d'Emma* by Les Arènes.

This is a work of fiction.

ISBN: 978-1-64729-057-3

Printed in Canada

First Edition

Kodansha USA Publishing, LLC
451 Park Avenue South
7th Floor
New York, NY 10016
www.kodansha.us

KODANSHA

T his is the story of a young woman with a passion for food. Emma had been on track to attend hotel school in Toulouse, but she took a different route and chose instead to study law, public relations, and later, journalism. She traveled across continents and explored the fascinating richness of the world's cuisines in all their varieties and combinations of flavors.

Fresh from these experiences, she decided to devote herself to the cult of a certain little red guidebook. She applied on a whim, then waited. Her motivation and initiative earned her a place as the only woman on *The Michelin Guide*'s all-male team of restaurant and hotel inspectors.

Over the course of four years, she rambled alone down the roads of France and frequently flirted with indigestion, eating nine restaurant meals a week and spending every night in a different hotel. Visiting the businesses referenced in the Guide was an all-day affair of assembly-line style inspections allowing for only thirty minutes per location before dashing off to the next. Inspecting by day and editing by night to work for *The Michelin Guide* was, above all else, to never let the exhaustion get the best of you...

Emma dreamt of epic feasts, palaces, and stars, but the reality she encountered was much leaner and less glamorous. In small restaurants, she discovered the hardscrabble day-to-day life of impassioned restaurateurs. She also came across a few unclassifiable gems hiding just at the margins of the Guide's strict rating system.

Out of these experiences came *Emma Dreams of Stars*, a healthy forkful of life raised to the stars!

This story is my story.

Emmanuelle Maisonneuve

For my (grand)parents,
who taught me about cooking from the heart.

EM

CONTENTS

CHAPTER 1

LE VIOLON D'INGRES

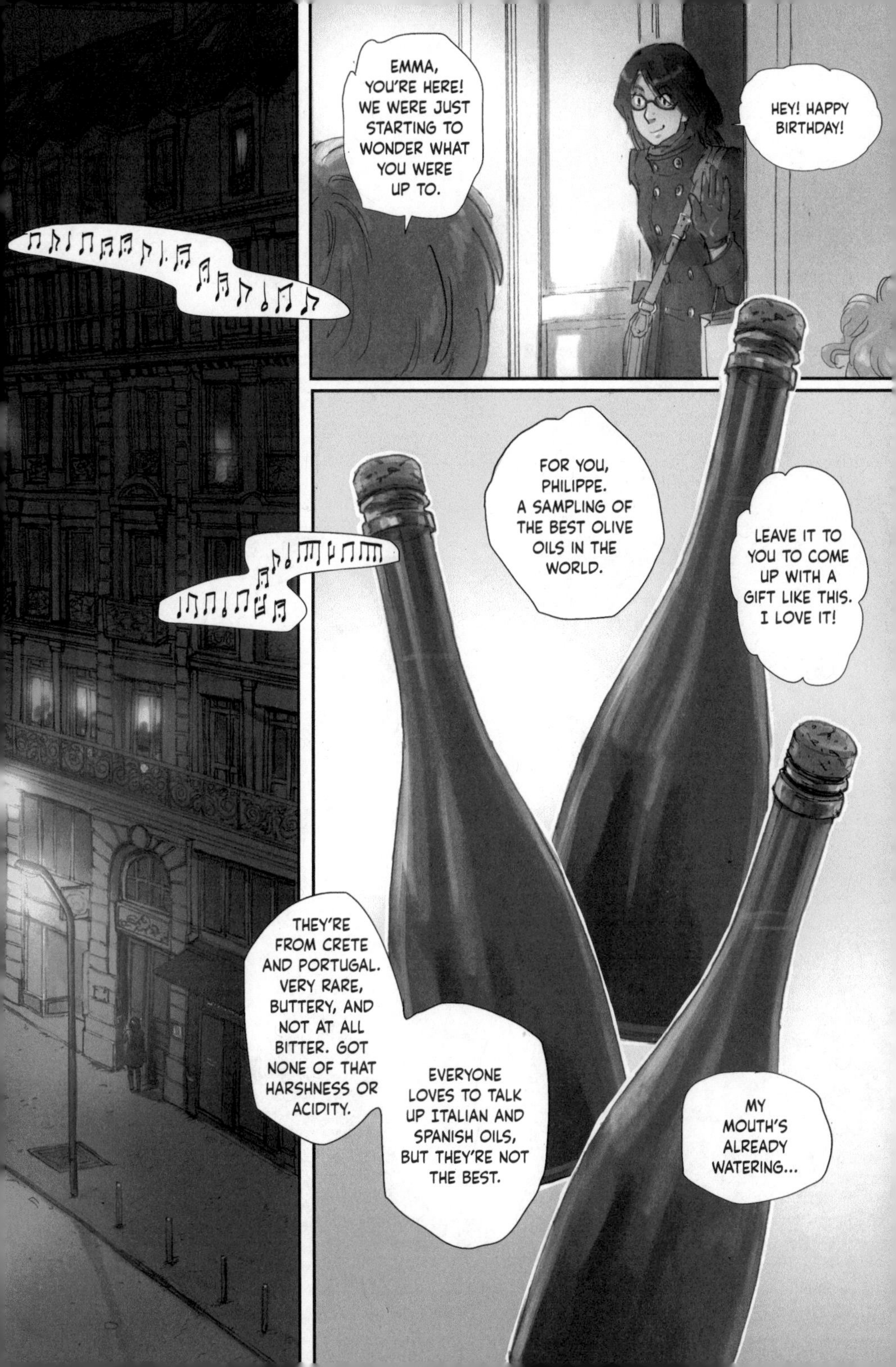

EMMA, YOU'RE HERE! WE WERE JUST STARTING TO WONDER WHAT YOU WERE UP TO.
HEY! HAPPY BIRTHDAY!
FOR YOU, PHILIPPE. A SAMPLING OF THE BEST OLIVE OILS IN THE WORLD.
LEAVE IT TO YOU TO COME UP WITH A GIFT LIKE THIS. I LOVE IT!
THEY'RE FROM CRETE AND PORTUGAL. VERY RARE, BUTTERY, AND NOT AT ALL BITTER. GOT NONE OF THAT HARSHNESS OR ACIDITY.
EVERYONE LOVES TO TALK UP ITALIAN AND SPANISH OILS, BUT THEY'RE NOT THE BEST.
MY MOUTH'S ALREADY WATERING...

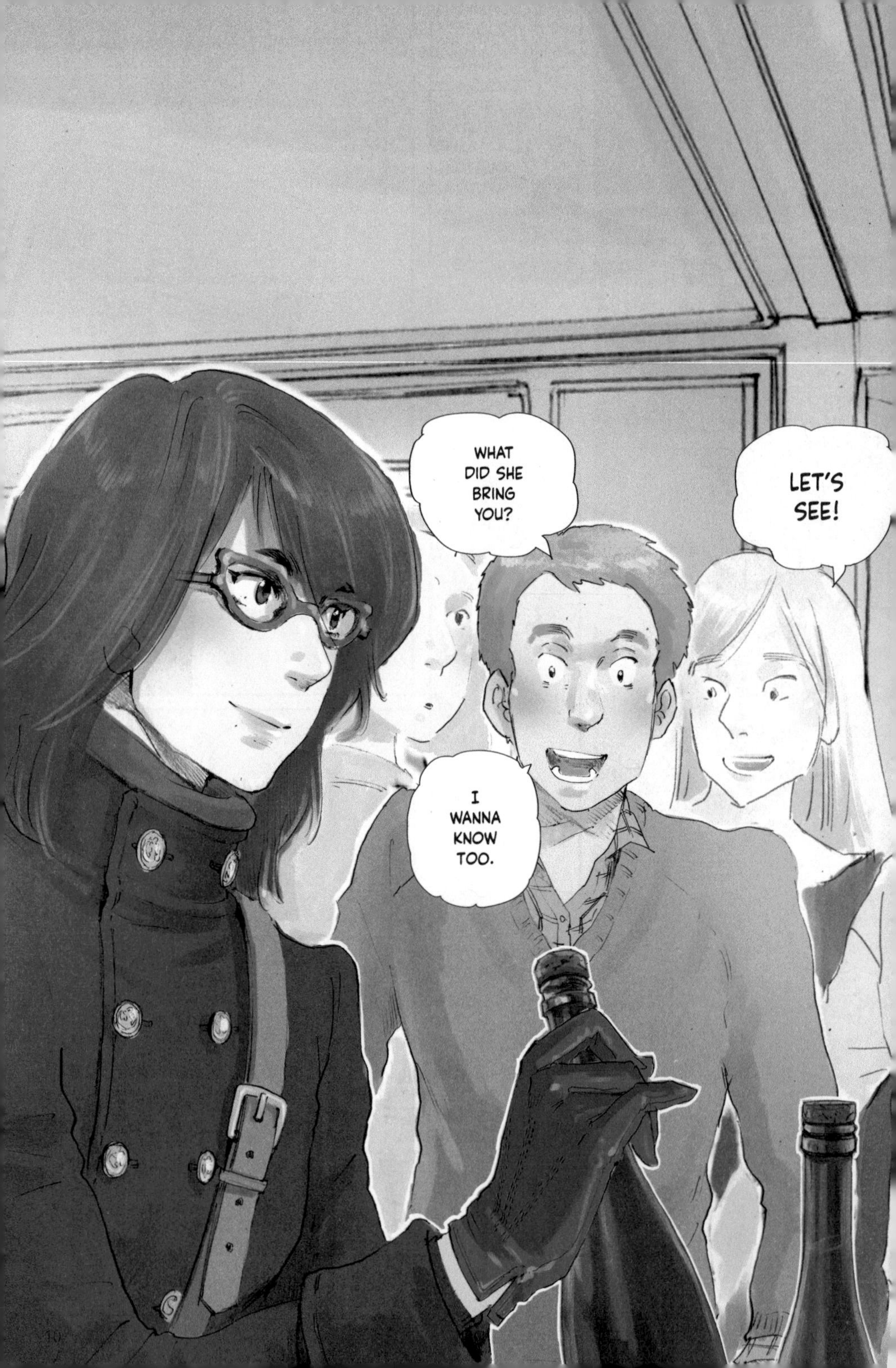
WHAT DID SHE BRING YOU?
LET'S SEE!
I WANNA KNOW TOO.

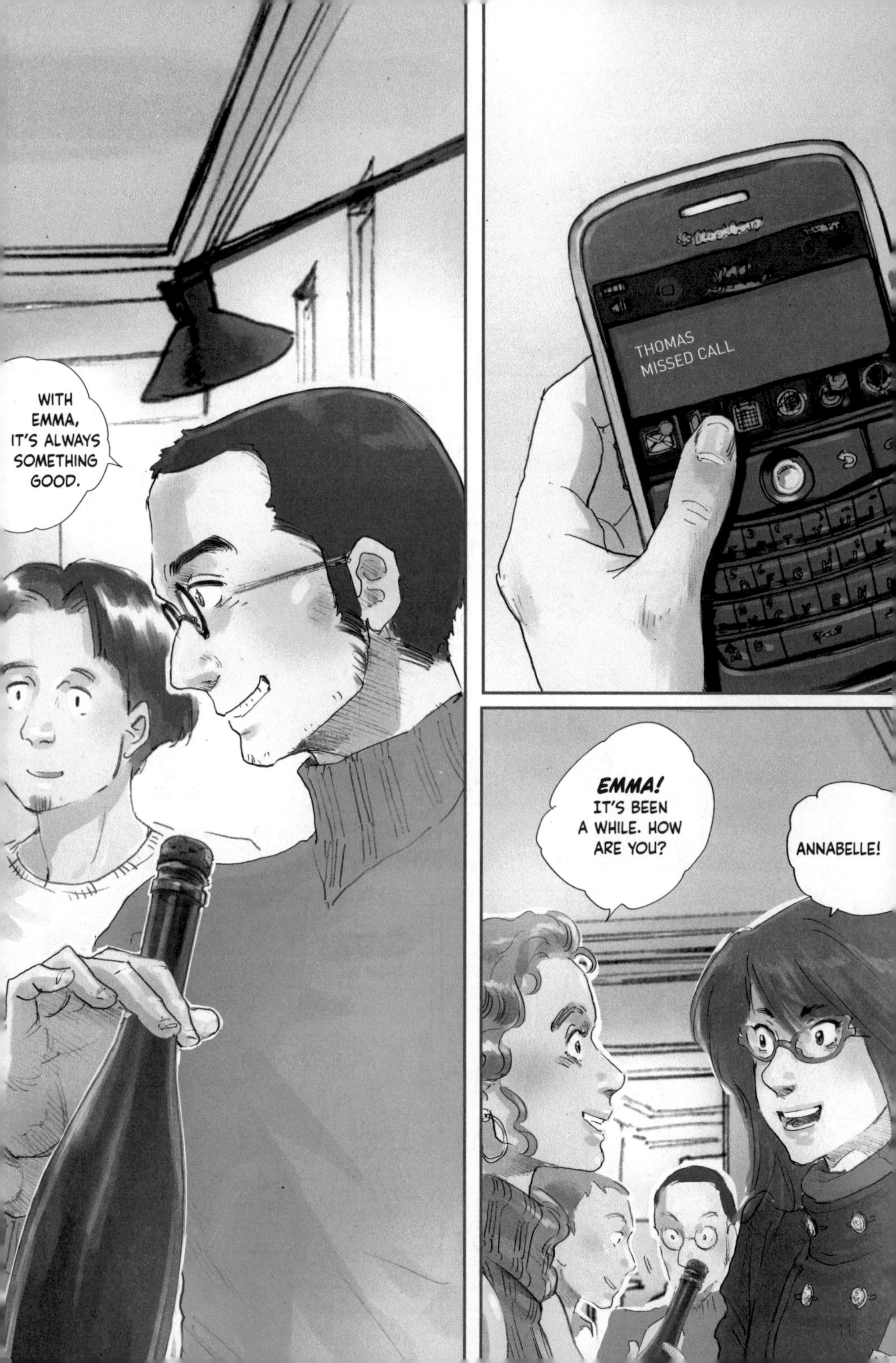
WITH EMMA, IT'S ALWAYS SOMETHING GOOD.
THOMAS
MISSED CALL
EMMA! IT'S BEEN A WHILE. HOW ARE YOU?
ANNABELLE!

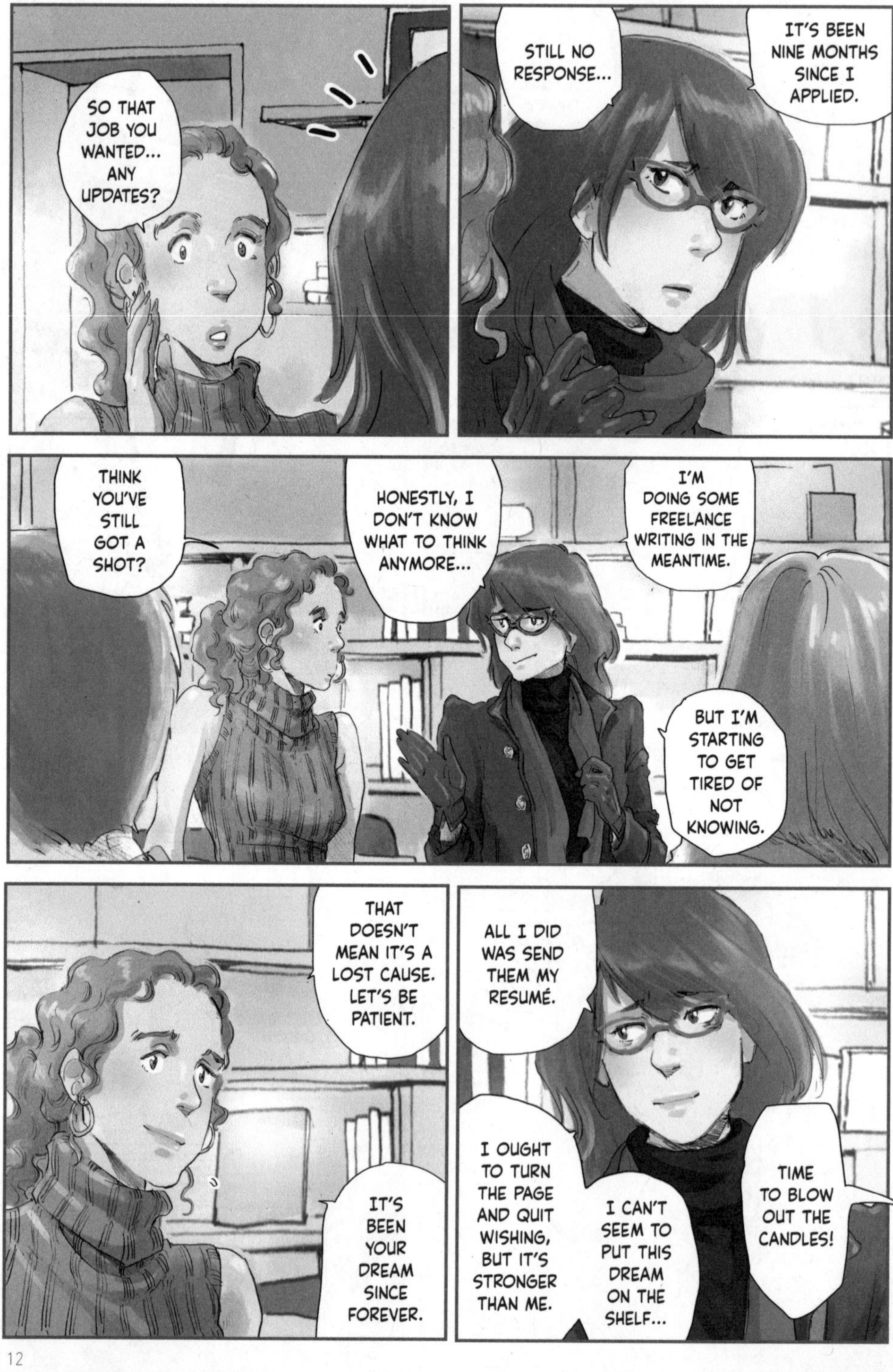
SO THAT JOB YOU WANTED... ANY UPDATES?
STILL NO RESPONSE...
IT'S BEEN NINE MONTHS SINCE I APPLIED.
THINK YOU'VE STILL GOT A SHOT?
HONESTLY, I DON'T KNOW WHAT TO THINK ANYMORE...
I'M DOING SOME FREELANCE WRITING IN THE MEANTIME.
BUT I'M STARTING TO GET TIRED OF NOT KNOWING.
THAT DOESN'T MEAN IT'S A LOST CAUSE. LET'S BE PATIENT.
IT'S BEEN YOUR DREAM SINCE FOREVER.
ALL I DID WAS SEND THEM MY RESUMÉ.
I OUGHT TO TURN THE PAGE AND QUIT WISHING, BUT IT'S STRONGER THAN ME.
I CAN'T SEEM TO PUT THIS DREAM ON THE SHELF...
TIME TO BLOW OUT THE CANDLES!

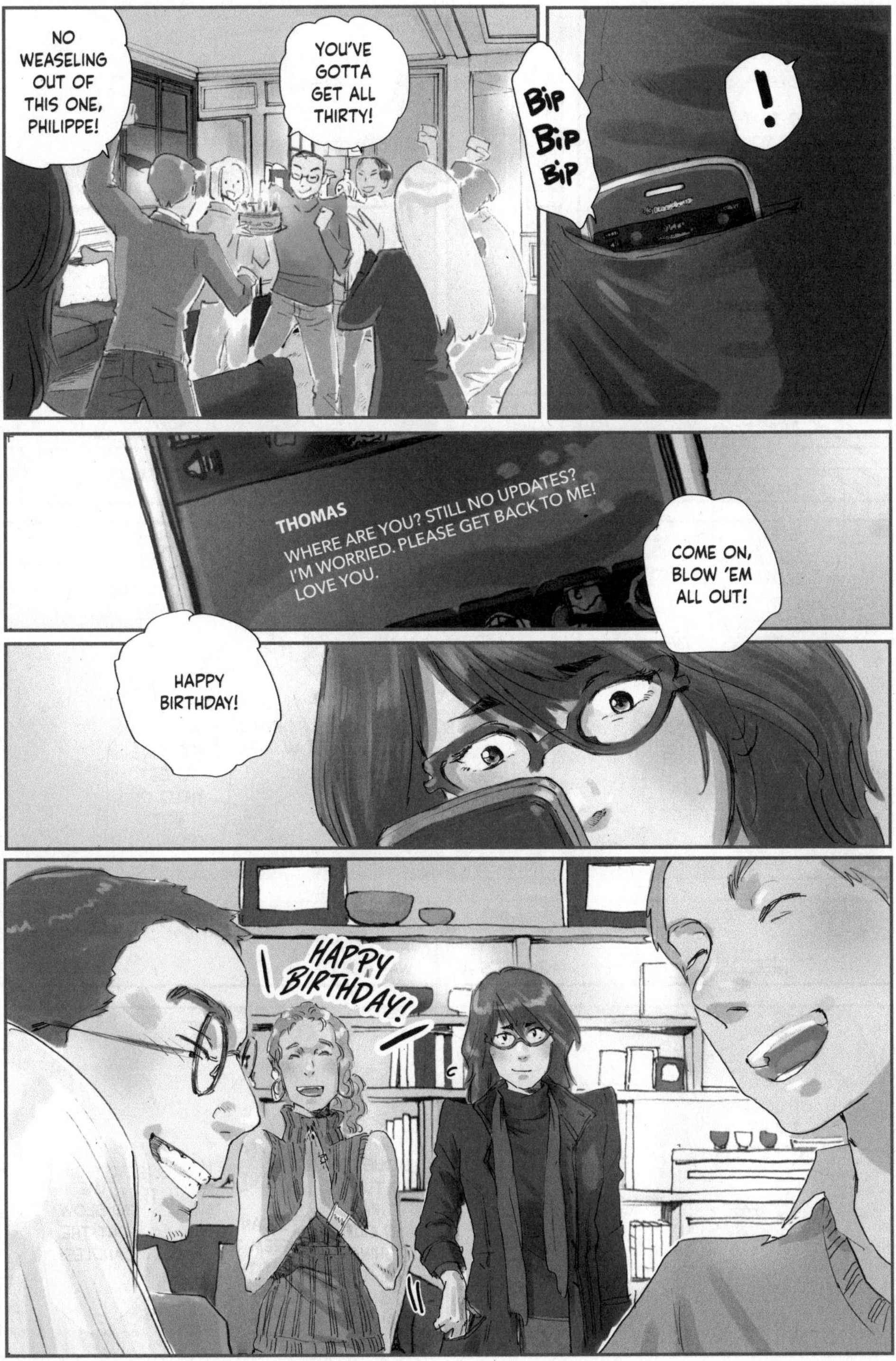
NO WEASELING OUT OF THIS ONE, PHILIPPE!
YOU'VE GOTTA GET ALL THIRTY!
Bip Bip Bip
!
THOMAS
WHERE ARE YOU? STILL NO UPDATES? I'M WORRIED. PLEASE GET BACK TO ME! LOVE YOU.
COME ON, BLOW 'EM ALL OUT!
HAPPY BIRTHDAY!
HAPPY BIRTHDAY!

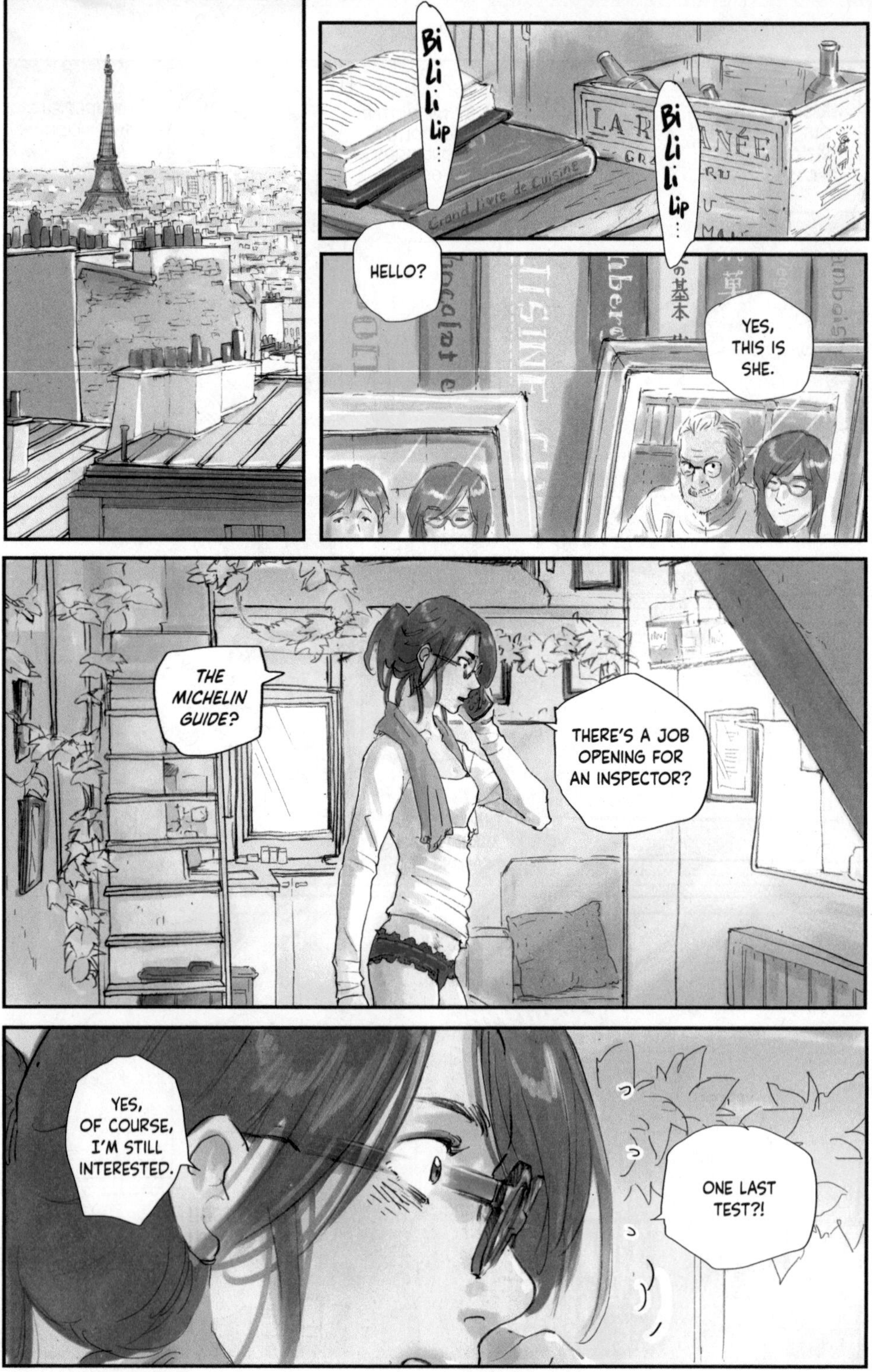
Bi Li Li Lip...
Grand livre de Cuisine
Bi Li Li Lip...
HELLO?
YES, THIS IS SHE.
THE MICHELIN GUIDE?
THERE'S A JOB OPENING FOR AN INSPECTOR?
YES, OF COURSE, I'M STILL INTERESTED.
ONE LAST TEST?!

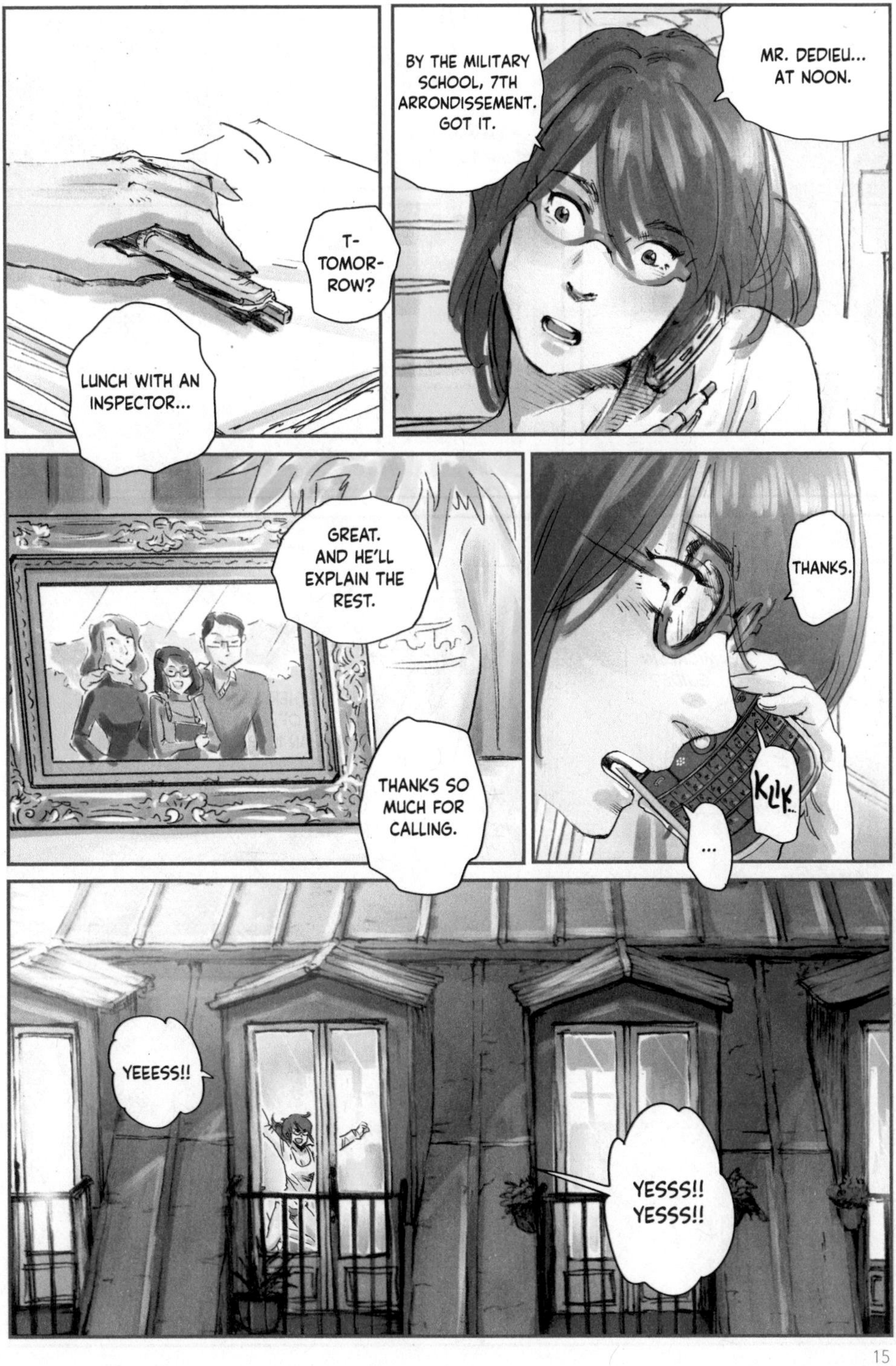
T-
TOMOR-
ROW?
LUNCH WITH AN
INSPECTOR...
BY THE MILITARY
SCHOOL, 7TH
ARRONDISSEMENT.
GOT IT.
MR. DEDIEU...
AT NOON.
GREAT.
AND HE'LL
EXPLAIN THE
REST.
THANKS SO
MUCH FOR
CALLING.
THANKS.
KLIK...
...
YEEESS!!
YESSS!!
YESSS!!

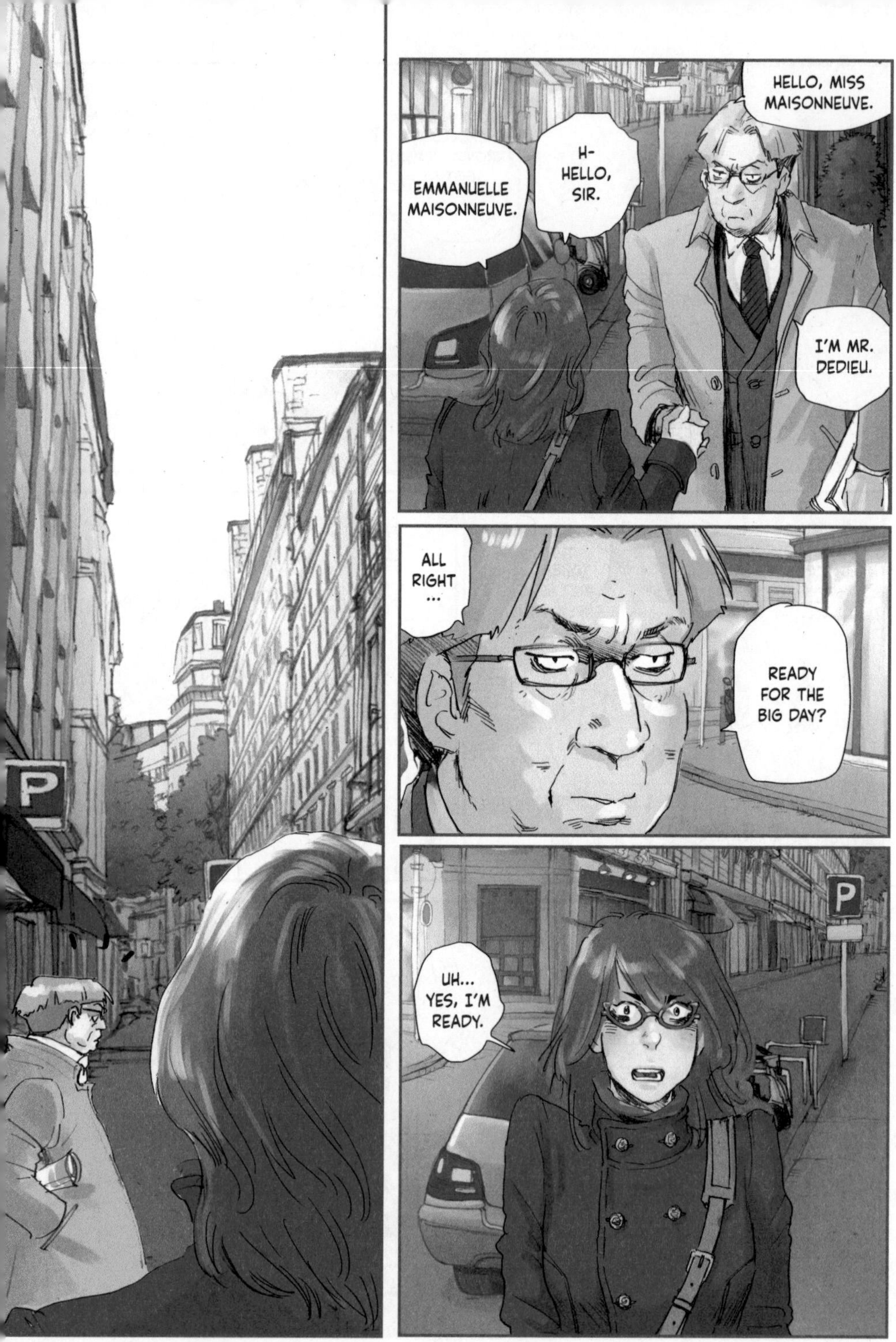
HELLO, MISS MAISONNEUVE.
H- HELLO, SIR.
EMMANUELLE MAISONNEUVE.
I'M MR. DEDIEU.
ALL RIGHT ...
READY FOR THE BIG DAY?
UH... YES, I'M READY.

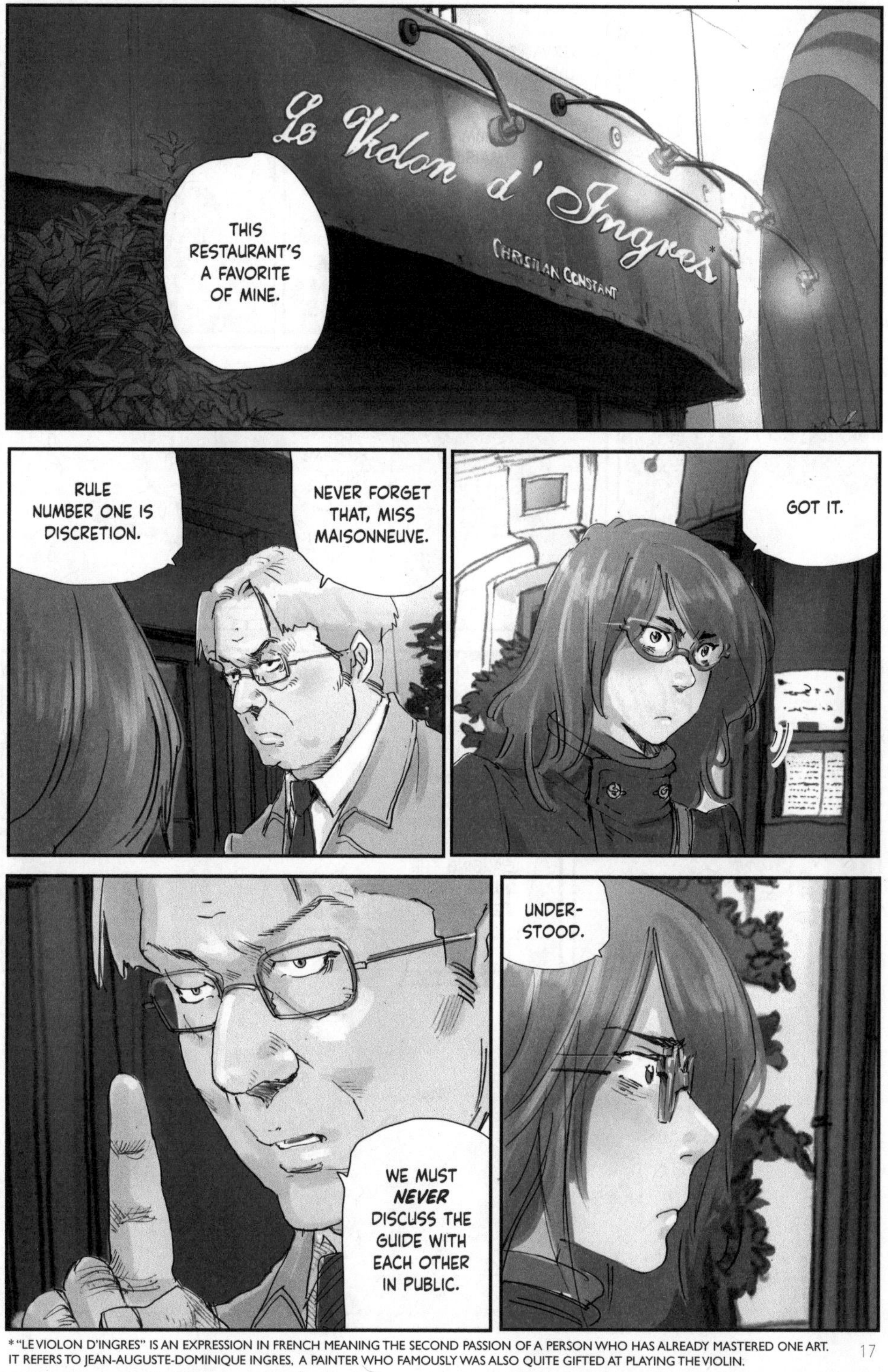
Le Violon d' Ingres*
CHRISTIAN CONSTANT
THIS RESTAURANT'S A FAVORITE OF MINE.
RULE NUMBER ONE IS DISCRETION.
NEVER FORGET THAT, MISS MAISONNEUVE.
GOT IT.
WE MUST ***NEVER*** DISCUSS THE GUIDE WITH EACH OTHER IN PUBLIC.
UNDER-STOOD.

* "LE VIOLON D'INGRES" IS AN EXPRESSION IN FRENCH MEANING THE SECOND PASSION OF A PERSON WHO HAS ALREADY MASTERED ONE ART. IT REFERS TO JEAN-AUGUSTE-DOMINIQUE INGRES, A PAINTER WHO FAMOUSLY WAS ALSO QUITE GIFTED AT PLAYING THE VIOLIN.

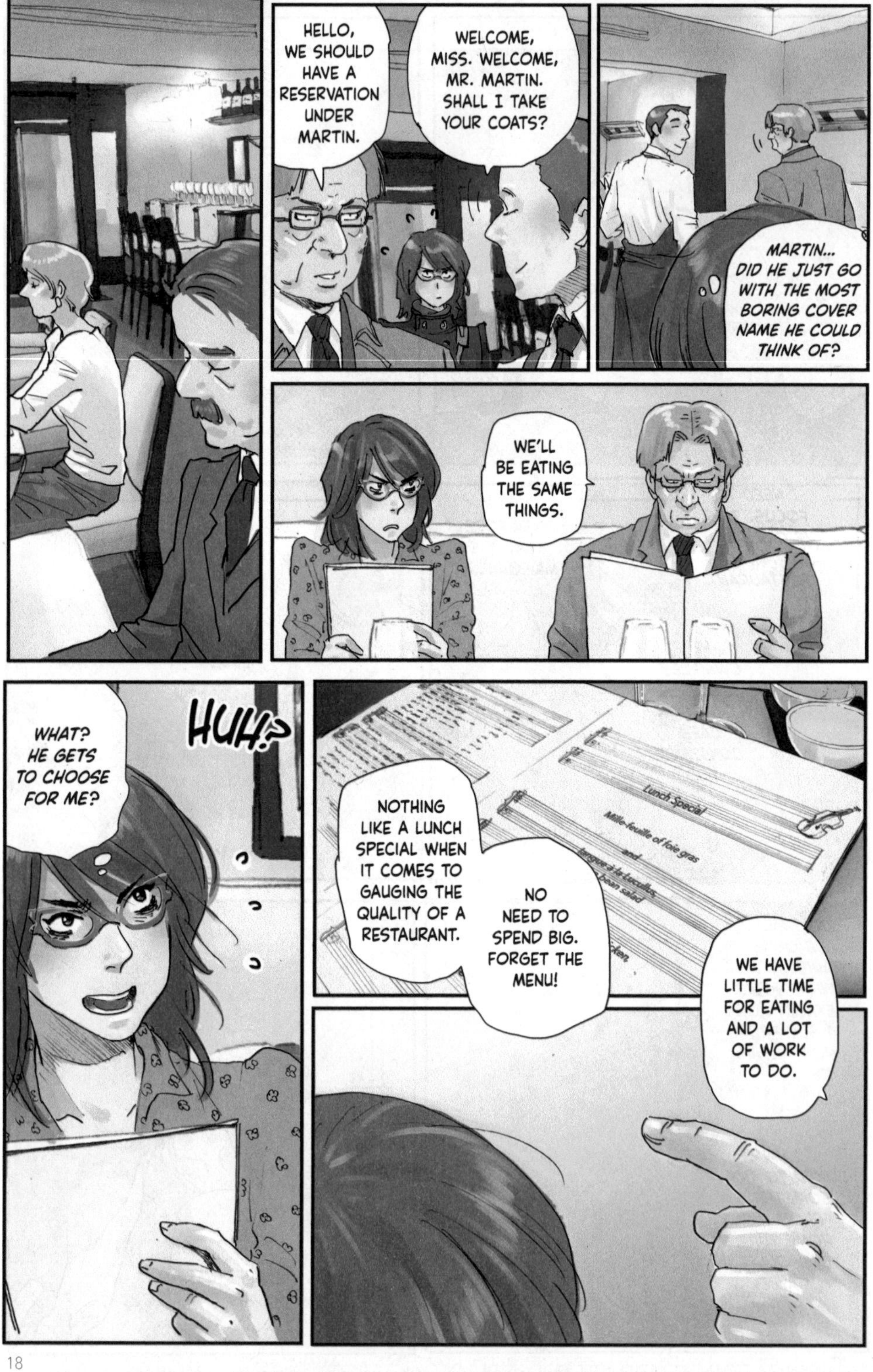
HELLO, WE SHOULD HAVE A RESERVATION UNDER MARTIN.
WELCOME, MISS. WELCOME, MR. MARTIN. SHALL I TAKE YOUR COATS?
MARTIN... DID HE JUST GO WITH THE MOST BORING COVER NAME HE COULD THINK OF?
WE'LL BE EATING THE SAME THINGS.
WHAT? HE GETS TO CHOOSE FOR ME?
HUH!?
Lunch Special
Mille-feuille of foie gras
and
langue à la Lucullus
NOTHING LIKE A LUNCH SPECIAL WHEN IT COMES TO GAUGING THE QUALITY OF A RESTAURANT.
NO NEED TO SPEND BIG. FORGET THE MENU!
WE HAVE LITTLE TIME FOR EATING AND A LOT OF WORK TO DO.

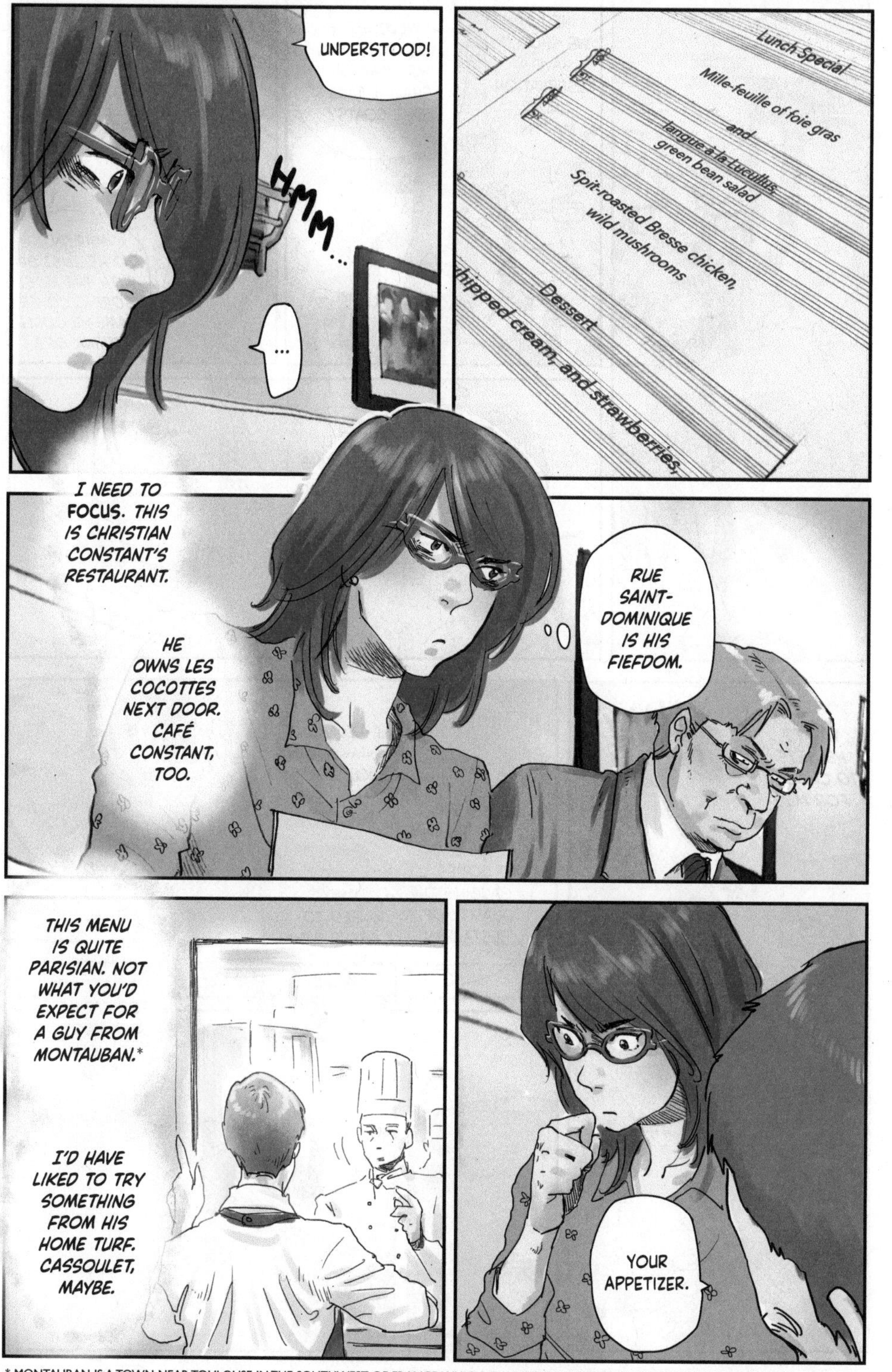
UNDERSTOOD!
HMM...
...
Lunch Special
Mille-feuille of foie gras
and
langue à la Lucullus,
green bean salad
Spit-roasted Bresse chicken,
wild mushrooms
Dessert
whipped cream, and strawberries,
I NEED TO FOCUS. THIS IS CHRISTIAN CONSTANT'S RESTAURANT.
HE OWNS LES COCOTTES NEXT DOOR. CAFÉ CONSTANT, TOO.
RUE SAINT-DOMINIQUE IS HIS FIEFDOM.
THIS MENU IS QUITE PARISIAN. NOT WHAT YOU'D EXPECT FOR A GUY FROM MONTAUBAN.*
I'D HAVE LIKED TO TRY SOMETHING FROM HIS HOME TURF. CASSOULET, MAYBE.
YOUR APPETIZER.

* MONTAUBAN IS A TOWN NEAR TOULOUSE IN THE SOUTHWEST OF FRANCE, WHICH IS ALSO THE HOMETOWN OF THE RESTAURANT'S NAMESAKE.

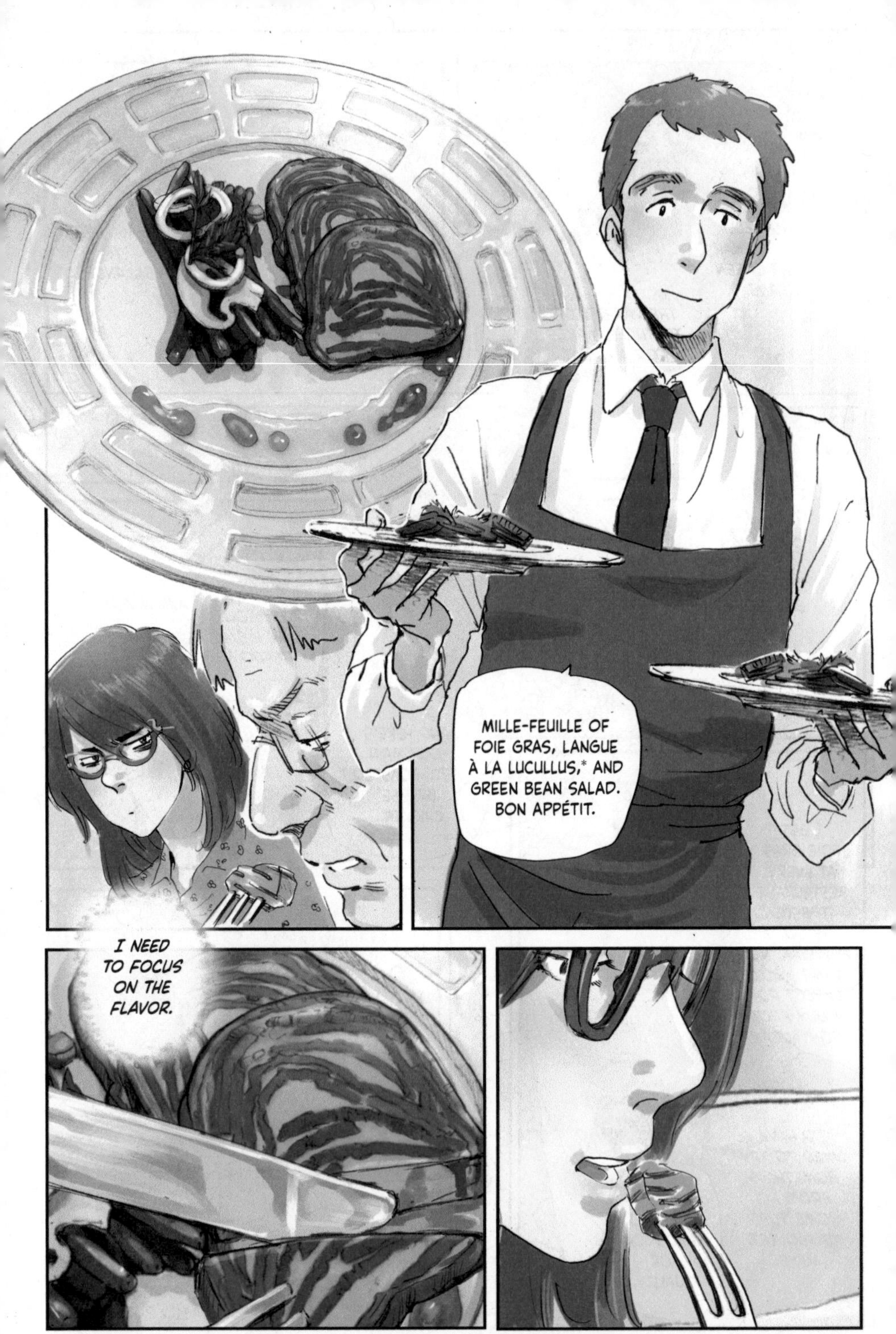
MILLE-FEUILLE OF FOIE GRAS, LANGUE À LA LUCULLUS,* AND GREEN BEAN SALAD. BON APPÉTIT.
I NEED TO FOCUS ON THE FLAVOR.

* A REGIONAL SPECIALTY FROM VALENCIENNES IN THE NORTH OF FRANCE, LANGUE À LA LUCULLUS IS A TERRINE BUILT FROM ALTERNATING LAYERS OF SMOKED BEEF TONGUE AND FOIE GRAS.

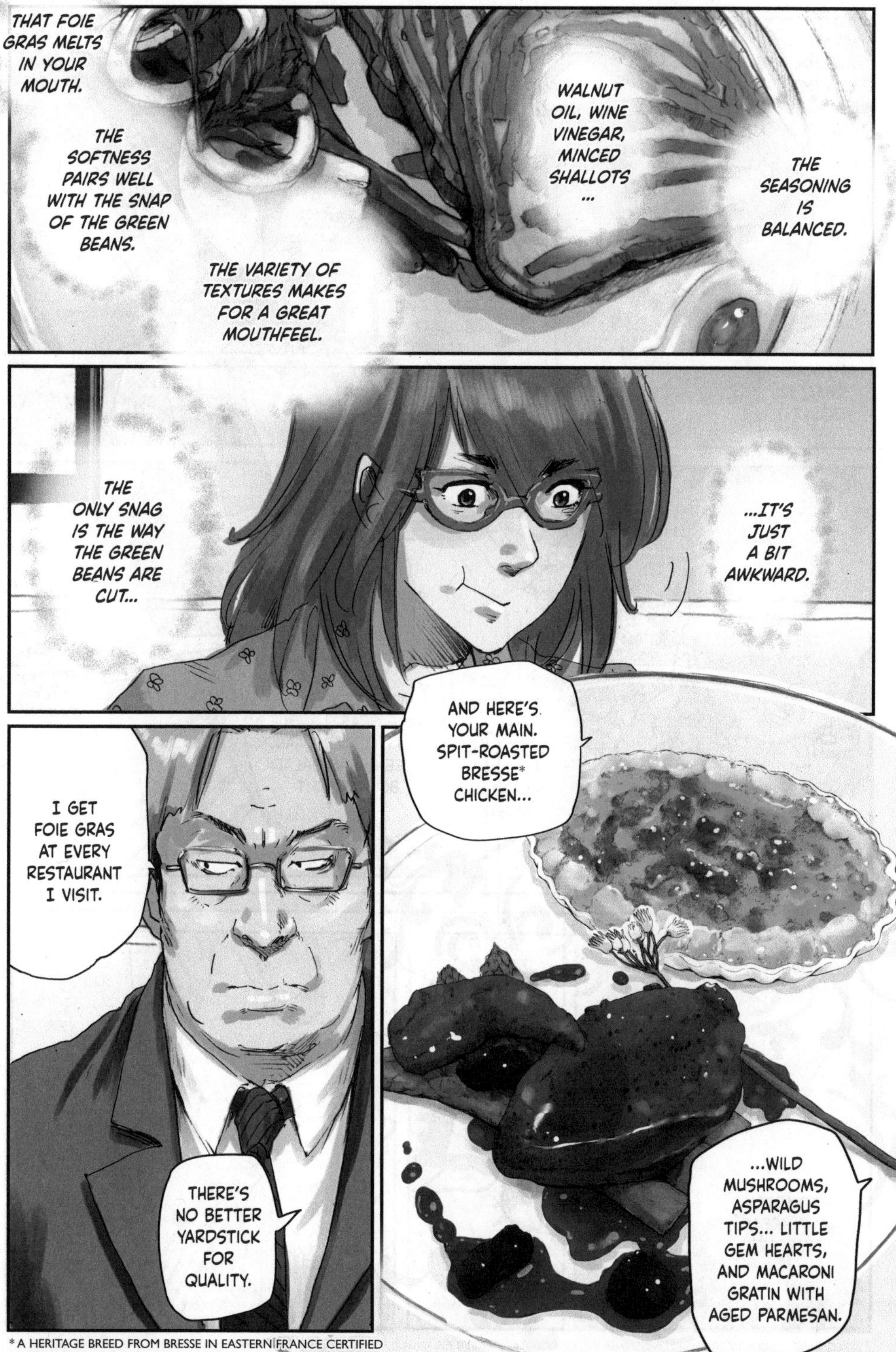
THAT FOIE GRAS MELTS IN YOUR MOUTH.
THE SOFTNESS PAIRS WELL WITH THE SNAP OF THE GREEN BEANS.
THE VARIETY OF TEXTURES MAKES FOR A GREAT MOUTHFEEL.
WALNUT OIL, WINE VINEGAR, MINCED SHALLOTS ...
THE SEASONING IS BALANCED.
THE ONLY SNAG IS THE WAY THE GREEN BEANS ARE CUT...
...IT'S JUST A BIT AWKWARD.
I GET FOIE GRAS AT EVERY RESTAURANT I VISIT.
THERE'S NO BETTER YARDSTICK FOR QUALITY.
AND HERE'S YOUR MAIN. SPIT-ROASTED BRESSE* CHICKEN...
...WILD MUSHROOMS, ASPARAGUS TIPS... LITTLE GEM HEARTS, AND MACARONI GRATIN WITH AGED PARMESAN.

* A HERITAGE BREED FROM BRESSE IN EASTERN FRANCE CERTIFIED THROUGH FRANCE'S "APPELLATION D'ORIGINE CONTRÔLÉE" SYSTEM.

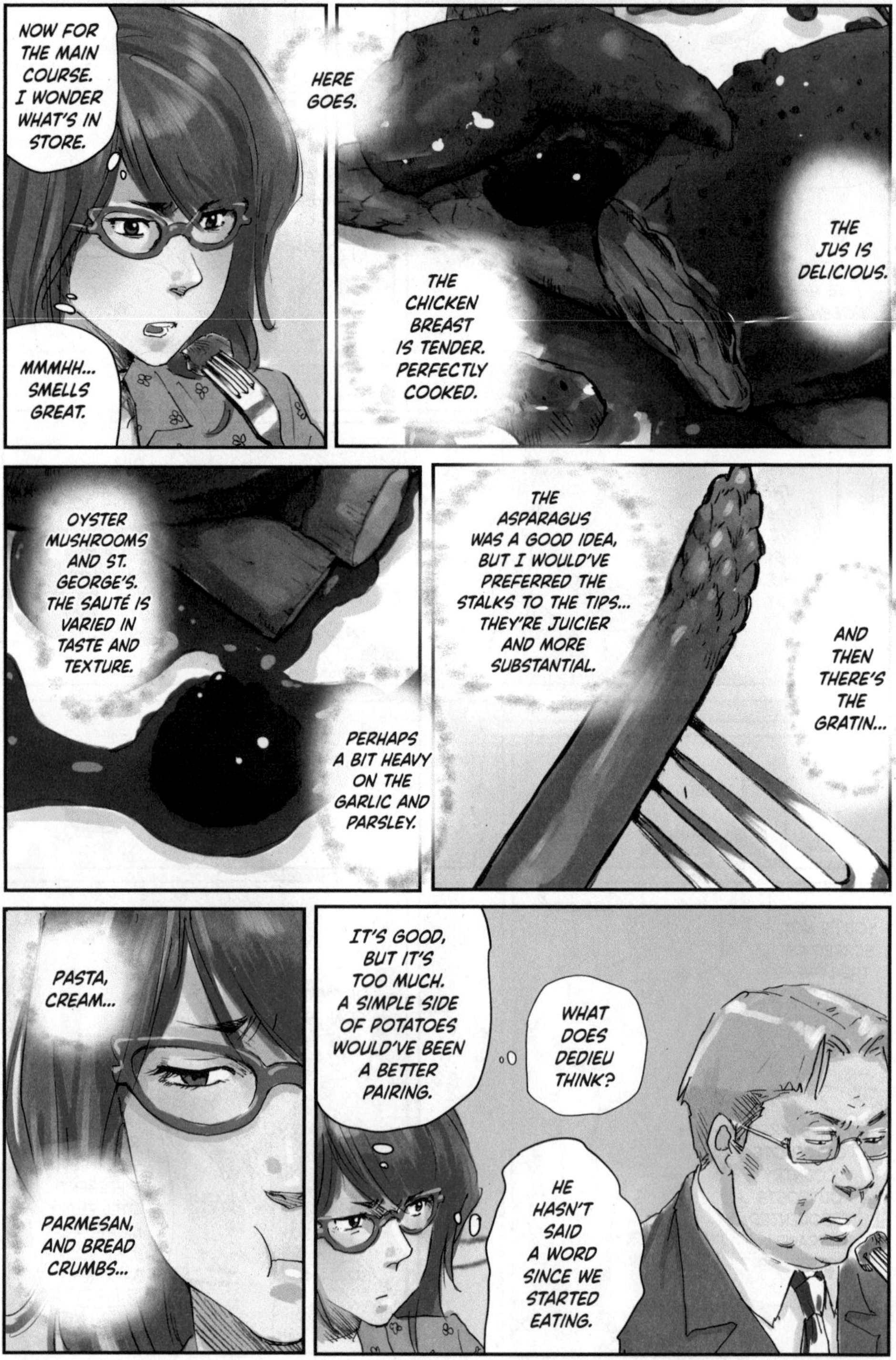
NOW FOR THE MAIN COURSE. I WONDER WHAT'S IN STORE.
MMMHH... SMELLS GREAT.
HERE GOES.
THE CHICKEN BREAST IS TENDER. PERFECTLY COOKED.
THE JUS IS DELICIOUS.
OYSTER MUSHROOMS AND ST. GEORGE'S. THE SAUTÉ IS VARIED IN TASTE AND TEXTURE.
PERHAPS A BIT HEAVY ON THE GARLIC AND PARSLEY.
THE ASPARAGUS WAS A GOOD IDEA, BUT I WOULD'VE PREFERRED THE STALKS TO THE TIPS... THEY'RE JUICIER AND MORE SUBSTANTIAL.
AND THEN THERE'S THE GRATIN...
PASTA, CREAM...
PARMESAN, AND BREAD CRUMBS...
IT'S GOOD, BUT IT'S TOO MUCH. A SIMPLE SIDE OF POTATOES WOULD'VE BEEN A BETTER PAIRING.
WHAT DOES DEDIEU THINK?
HE HASN'T SAID A WORD SINCE WE STARTED EATING.

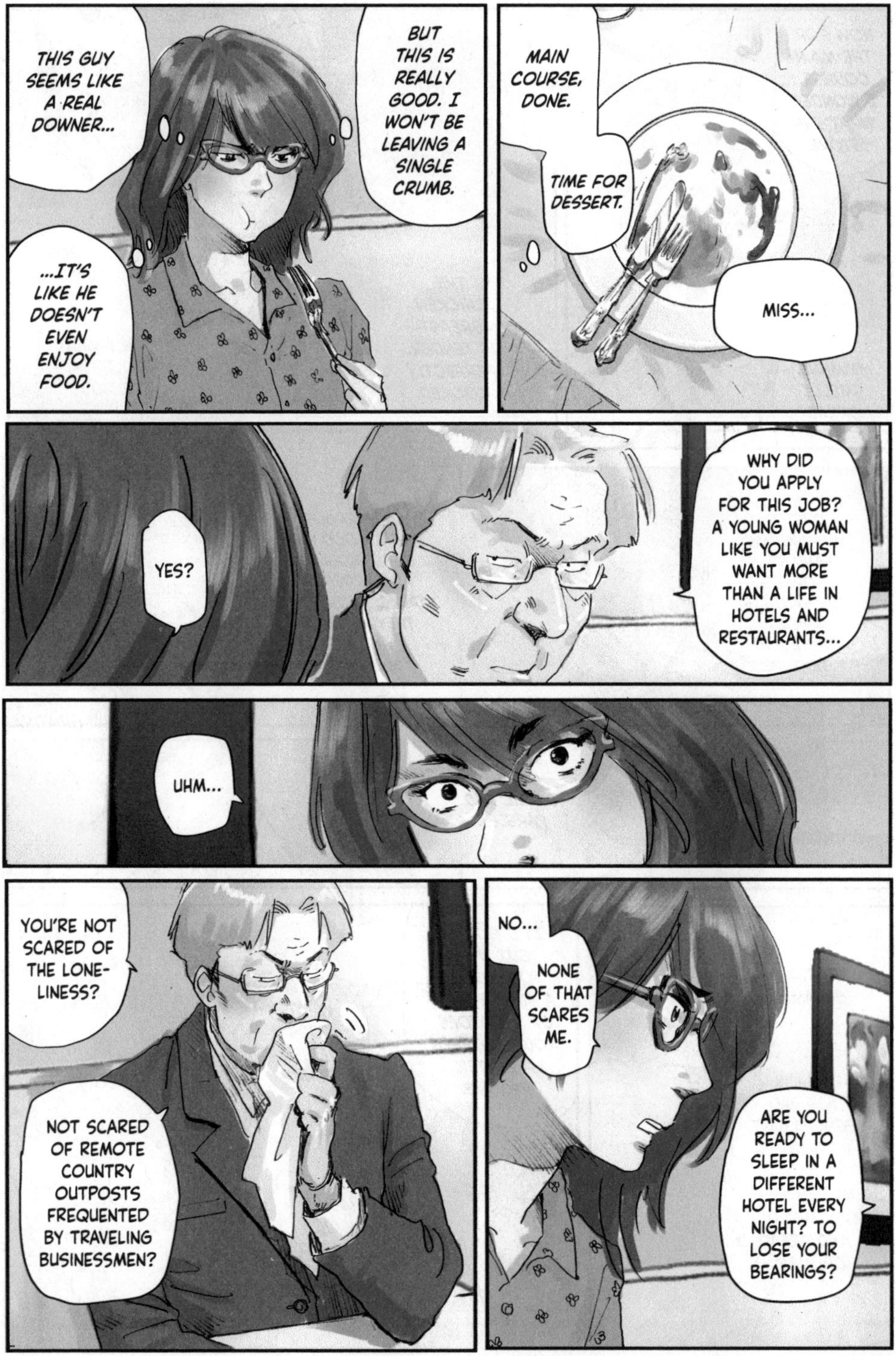
THIS GUY SEEMS LIKE A REAL DOWNER...
BUT THIS IS REALLY GOOD. I WON'T BE LEAVING A SINGLE CRUMB.
...IT'S LIKE HE DOESN'T EVEN ENJOY FOOD.
MAIN COURSE, DONE.
TIME FOR DESSERT.
MISS...
YES?
WHY DID YOU APPLY FOR THIS JOB? A YOUNG WOMAN LIKE YOU MUST WANT MORE THAN A LIFE IN HOTELS AND RESTAURANTS...
UHM...
YOU'RE NOT SCARED OF THE LONE-LINESS?
NOT SCARED OF REMOTE COUNTRY OUTPOSTS FREQUENTED BY TRAVELING BUSINESSMEN?
NO...
NONE OF THAT SCARES ME.
ARE YOU READY TO SLEEP IN A DIFFERENT HOTEL EVERY NIGHT? TO LOSE YOUR BEARINGS?

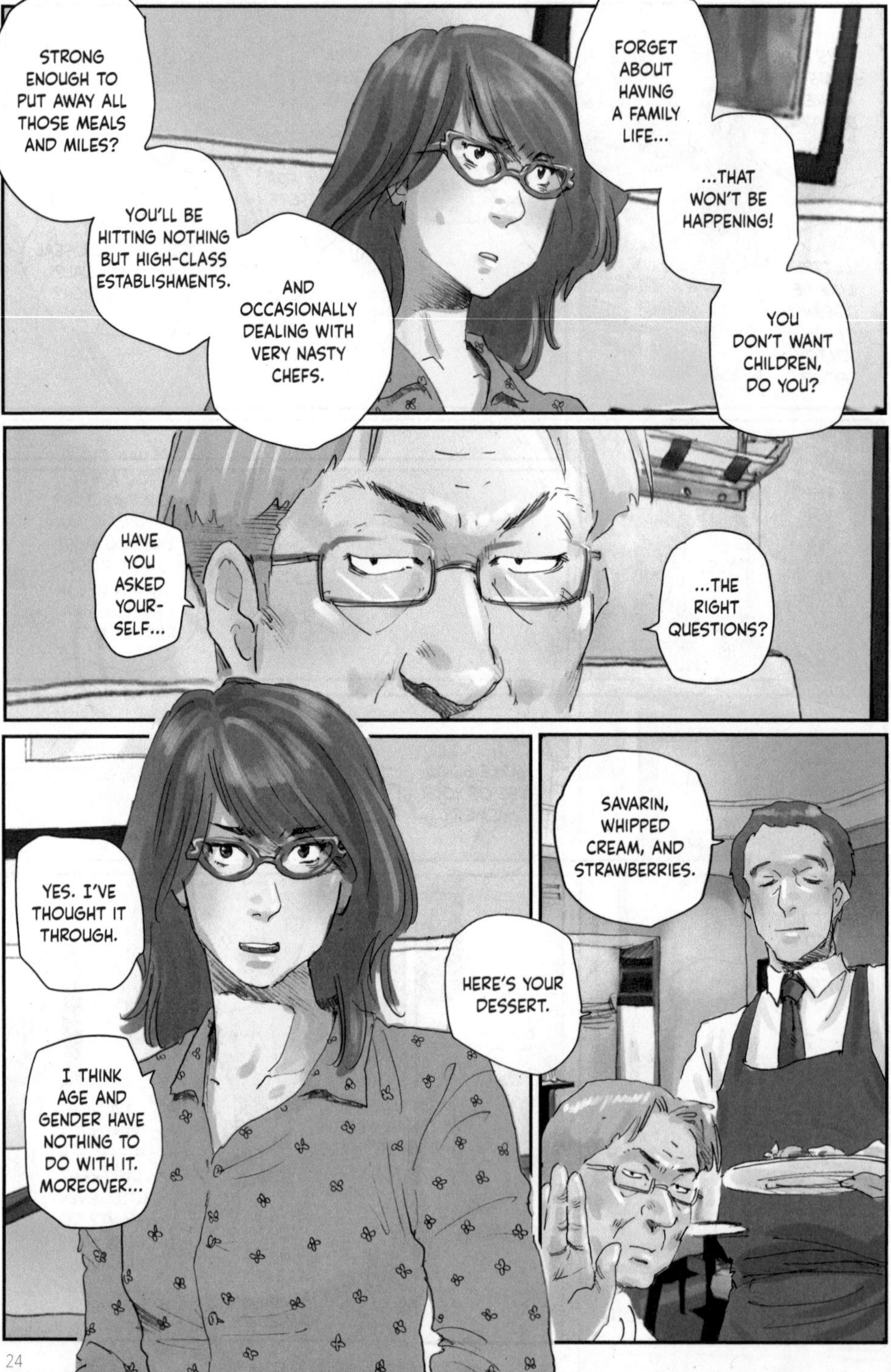
STRONG ENOUGH TO PUT AWAY ALL THOSE MEALS AND MILES?
YOU'LL BE HITTING NOTHING BUT HIGH-CLASS ESTABLISHMENTS.
AND OCCASIONALLY DEALING WITH VERY NASTY CHEFS.
FORGET ABOUT HAVING A FAMILY LIFE...
...THAT WON'T BE HAPPENING!
YOU DON'T WANT CHILDREN, DO YOU?
HAVE YOU ASKED YOUR-SELF...
...THE RIGHT QUESTIONS?
YES. I'VE THOUGHT IT THROUGH.
I THINK AGE AND GENDER HAVE NOTHING TO DO WITH IT. MOREOVER...
SAVARIN, WHIPPED CREAM, AND STRAWBERRIES.
HERE'S YOUR DESSERT.

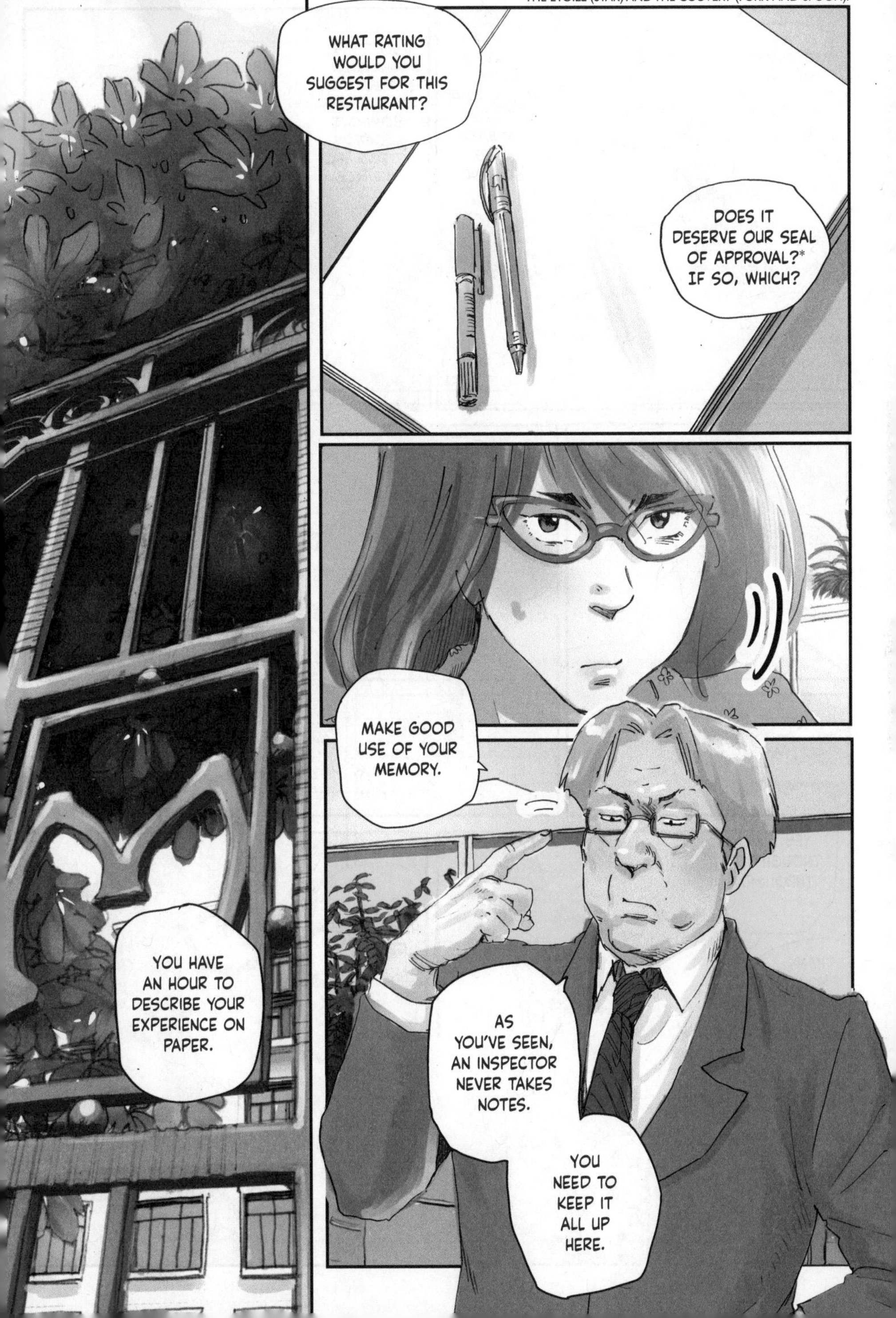

YOU HAVE AN HOUR TO DESCRIBE YOUR EXPERIENCE ON PAPER.
WHAT RATING WOULD YOU SUGGEST FOR THIS RESTAURANT?
DOES IT DESERVE OUR SEAL OF APPROVAL?* IF SO, WHICH?
MAKE GOOD USE OF YOUR MEMORY.
AS YOU'VE SEEN, AN INSPECTOR NEVER TAKES NOTES.
YOU NEED TO KEEP IT ALL UP HERE.

* *THE MICHELIN GUIDE* HAS TWO SYMBOLS FOR RATING RESTAURANTS: THE ÉTOILE (STAR) AND THE COUVERT (FORK-AND-SPOON).

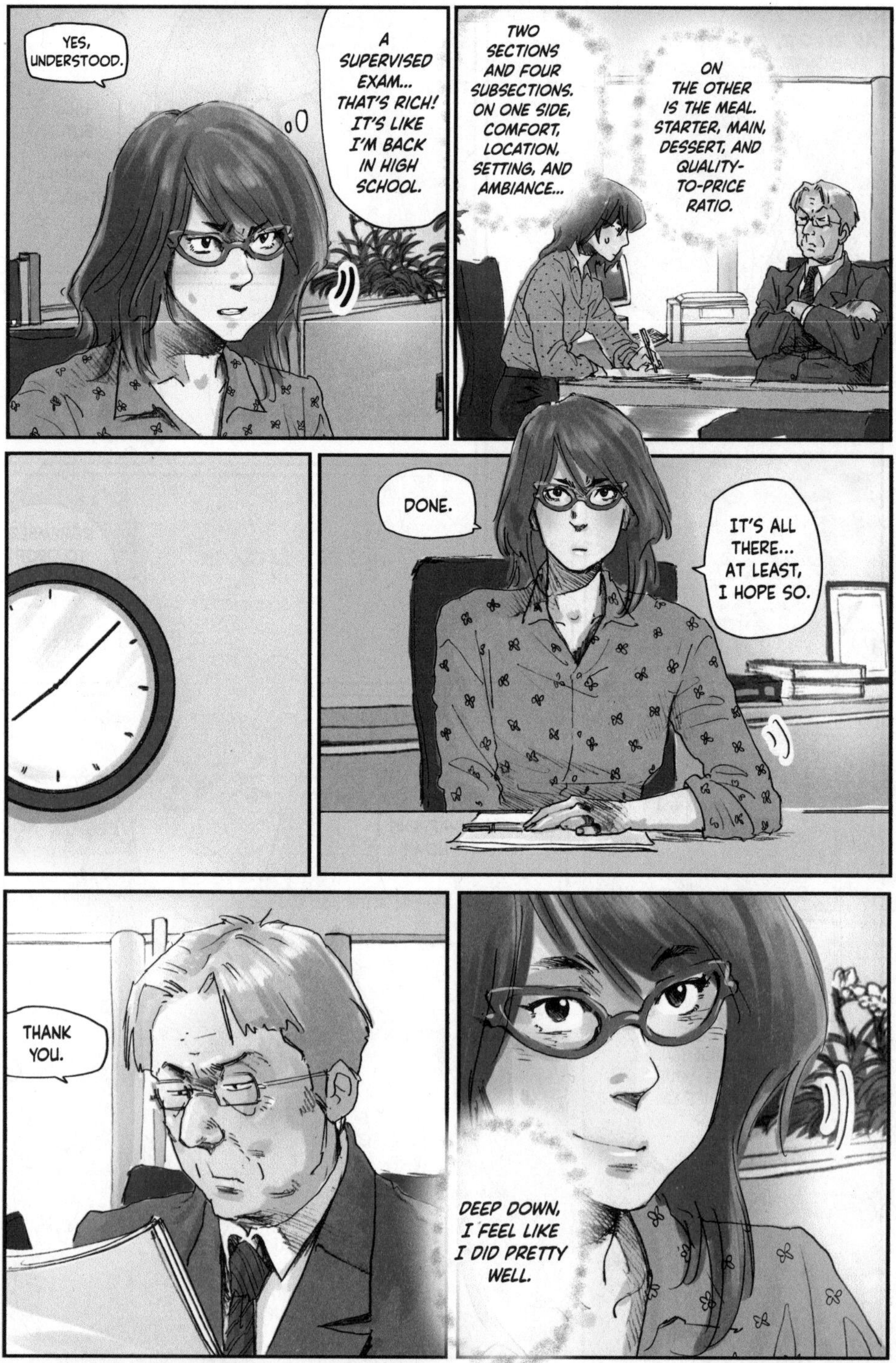
YES, UNDERSTOOD.
A SUPERVISED EXAM... THAT'S RICH! IT'S LIKE I'M BACK IN HIGH SCHOOL.
TWO SECTIONS AND FOUR SUBSECTIONS. ON ONE SIDE, COMFORT, LOCATION, SETTING, AND AMBIANCE...
ON THE OTHER IS THE MEAL. STARTER, MAIN, DESSERT, AND QUALITY-TO-PRICE RATIO.
DONE.
IT'S ALL THERE... AT LEAST, I HOPE SO.
THANK YOU.
DEEP DOWN, I FEEL LIKE I DID PRETTY WELL.

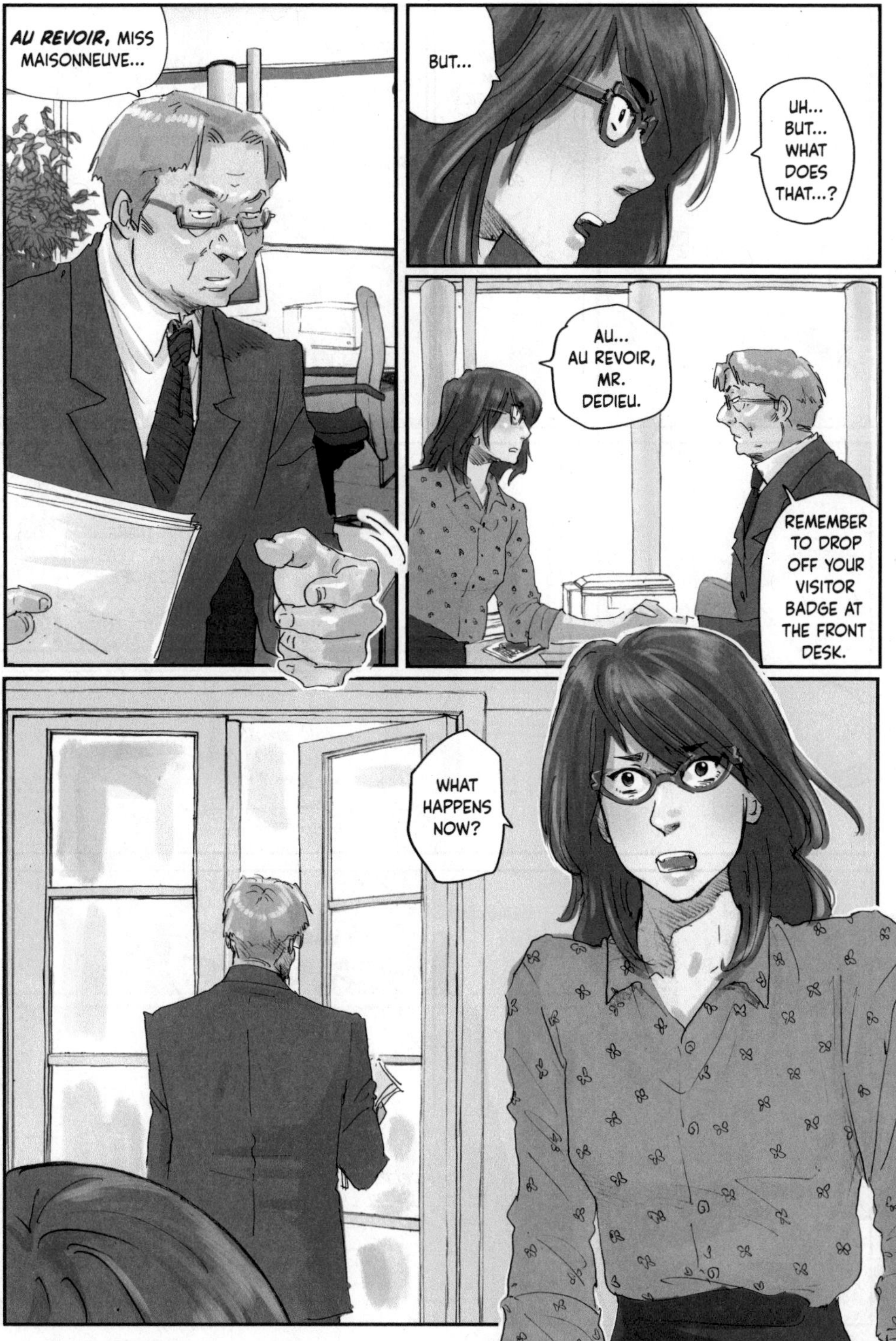
AU REVOIR, MISS MAISONNEUVE...
BUT...
UH... BUT... WHAT DOES THAT...?
AU... AU REVOIR, MR. DEDIEU.
REMEMBER TO DROP OFF YOUR VISITOR BADGE AT THE FRONT DESK.
WHAT HAPPENS NOW?

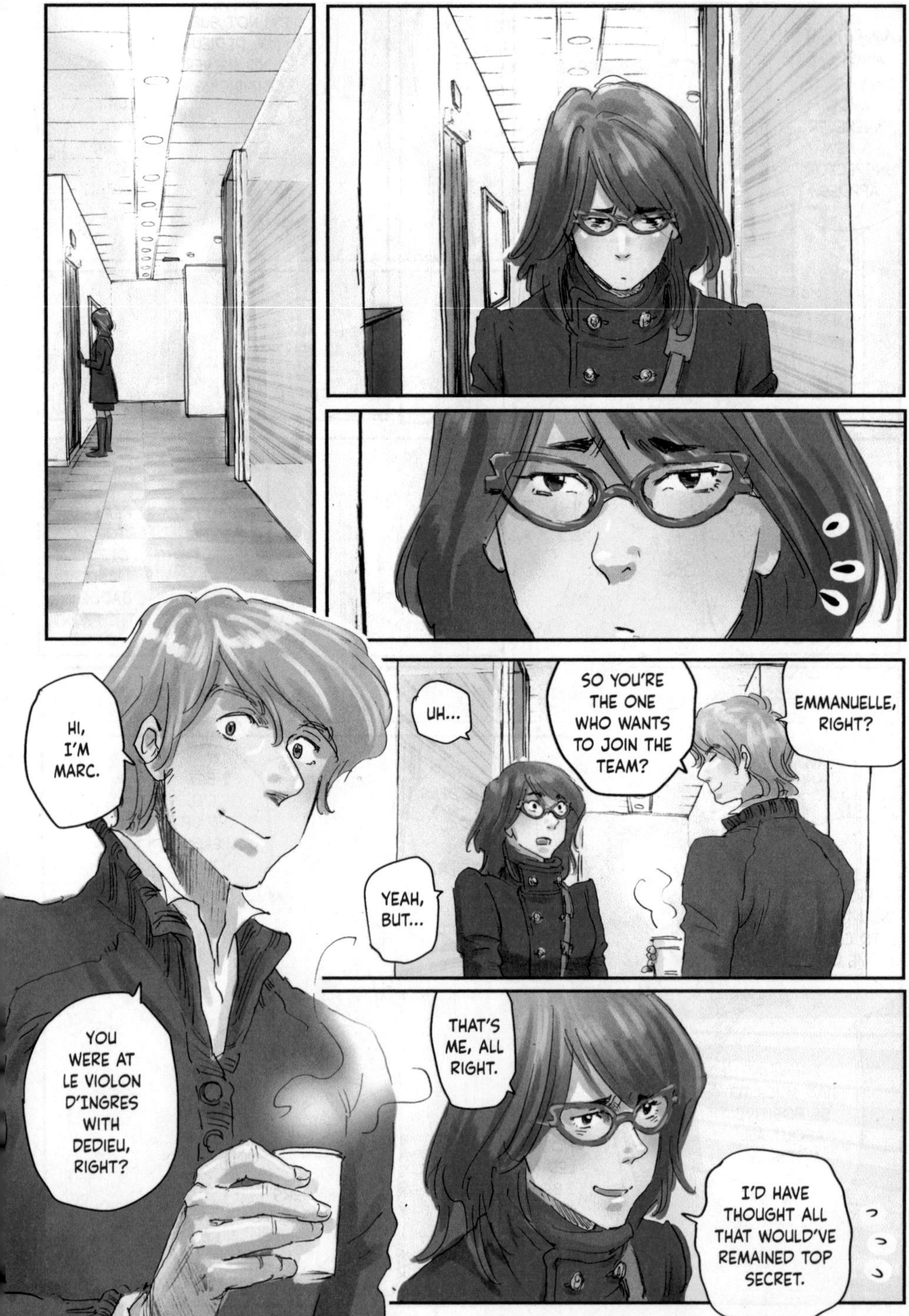
HI, I'M MARC.
UH...
SO YOU'RE THE ONE WHO WANTS TO JOIN THE TEAM?
EMMANUELLE, RIGHT?
YEAH, BUT...
YOU WERE AT LE VIOLON D'INGRES WITH DEDIEU, RIGHT?
THAT'S ME, ALL RIGHT.
I'D HAVE THOUGHT ALL THAT WOULD'VE REMAINED TOP SECRET.

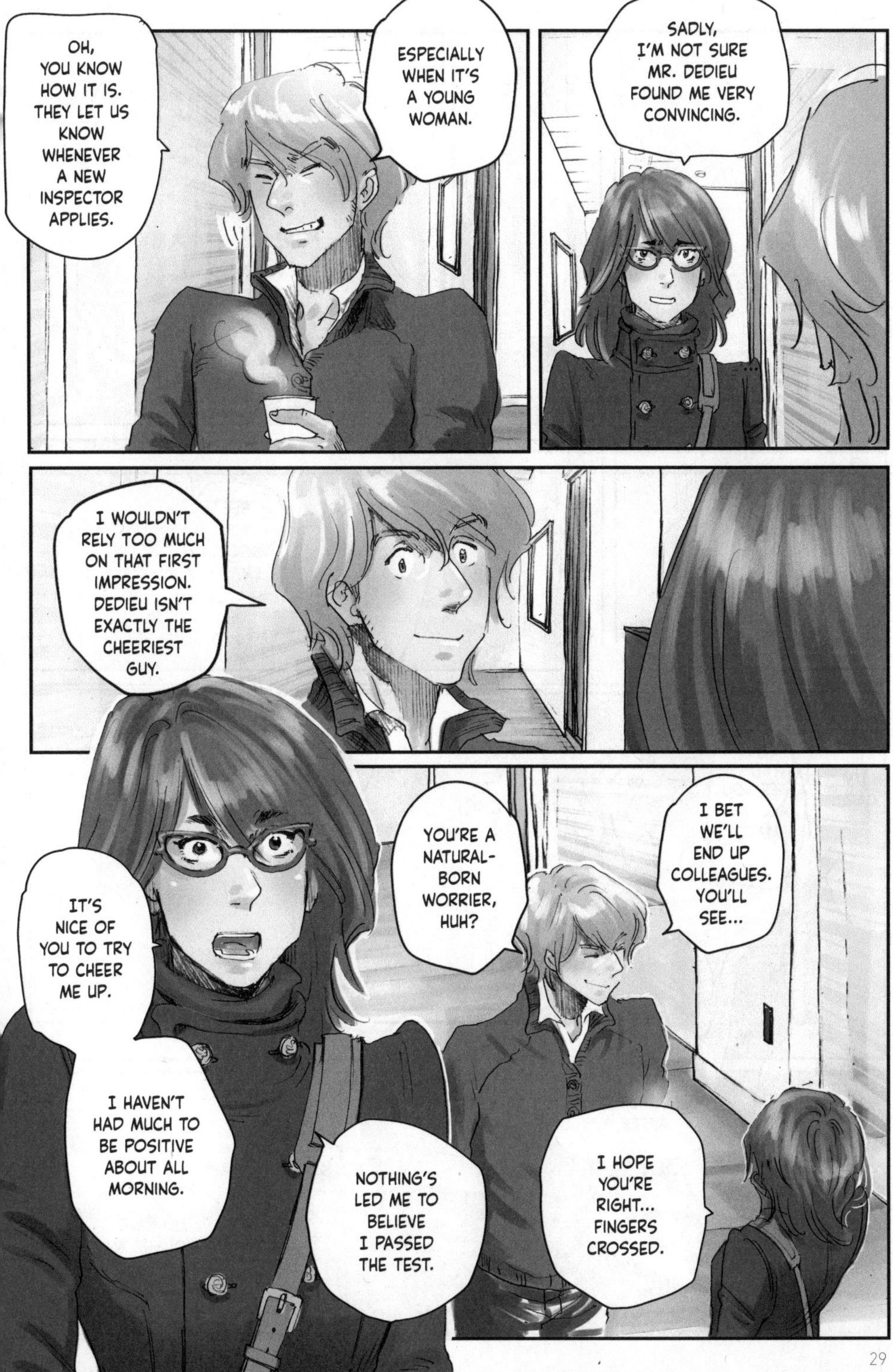

OH, YOU KNOW HOW IT IS. THEY LET US KNOW WHENEVER A NEW INSPECTOR APPLIES.
ESPECIALLY WHEN IT'S A YOUNG WOMAN.
SADLY, I'M NOT SURE MR. DEDIEU FOUND ME VERY CONVINCING.
I WOULDN'T RELY TOO MUCH ON THAT FIRST IMPRESSION. DEDIEU ISN'T EXACTLY THE CHEERIEST GUY.
IT'S NICE OF YOU TO TRY TO CHEER ME UP.
I HAVEN'T HAD MUCH TO BE POSITIVE ABOUT ALL MORNING.
NOTHING'S LED ME TO BELIEVE I PASSED THE TEST.
YOU'RE A NATURAL-BORN WORRIER, HUH?
I BET WE'LL END UP COLLEAGUES. YOU'LL SEE...
I HOPE YOU'RE RIGHT... FINGERS CROSSED.

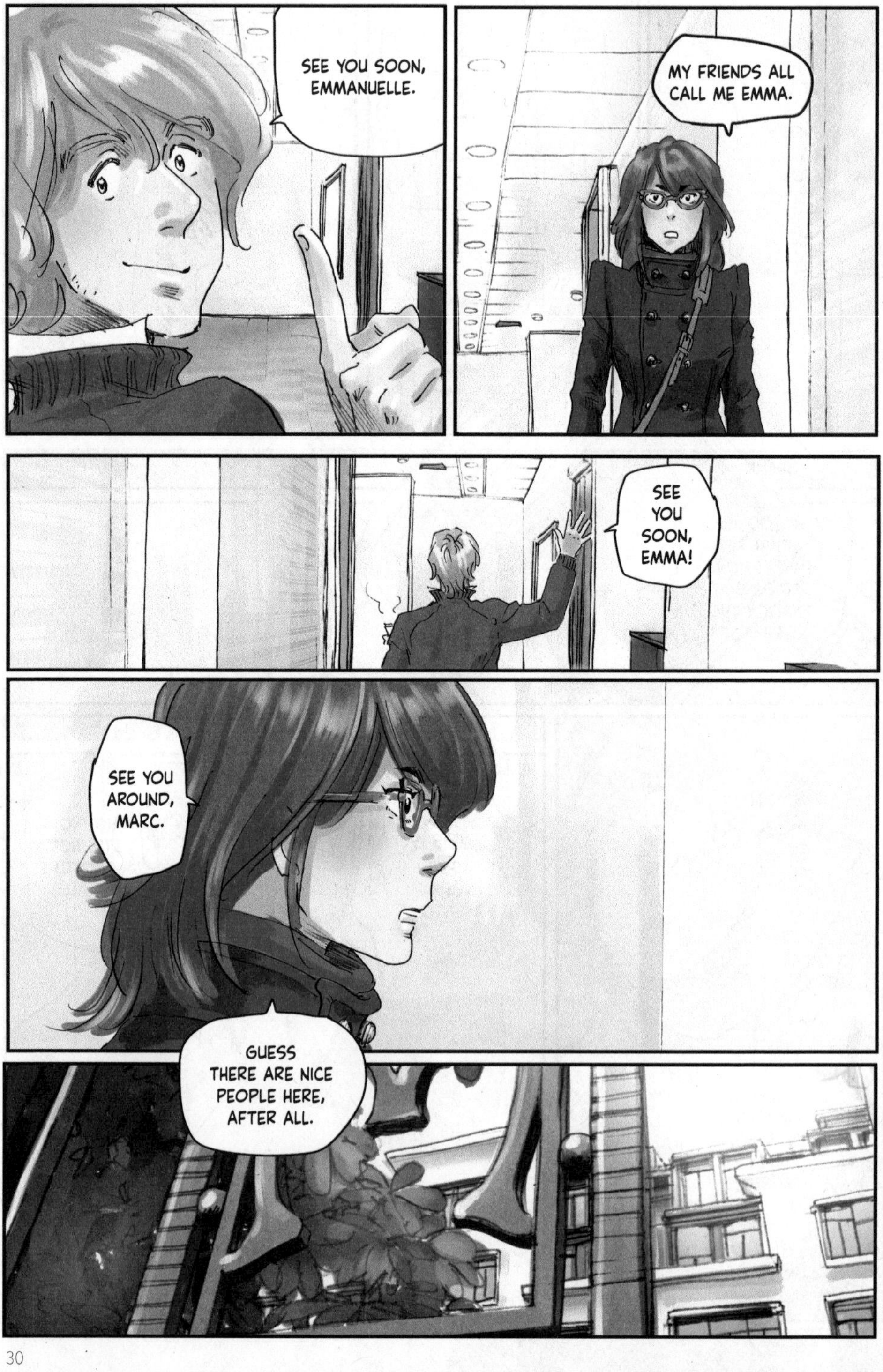
SEE YOU SOON, EMMANUELLE.
MY FRIENDS ALL CALL ME EMMA.
SEE YOU SOON, EMMA!
SEE YOU AROUND, MARC.
GUESS THERE ARE NICE PEOPLE HERE, AFTER ALL.

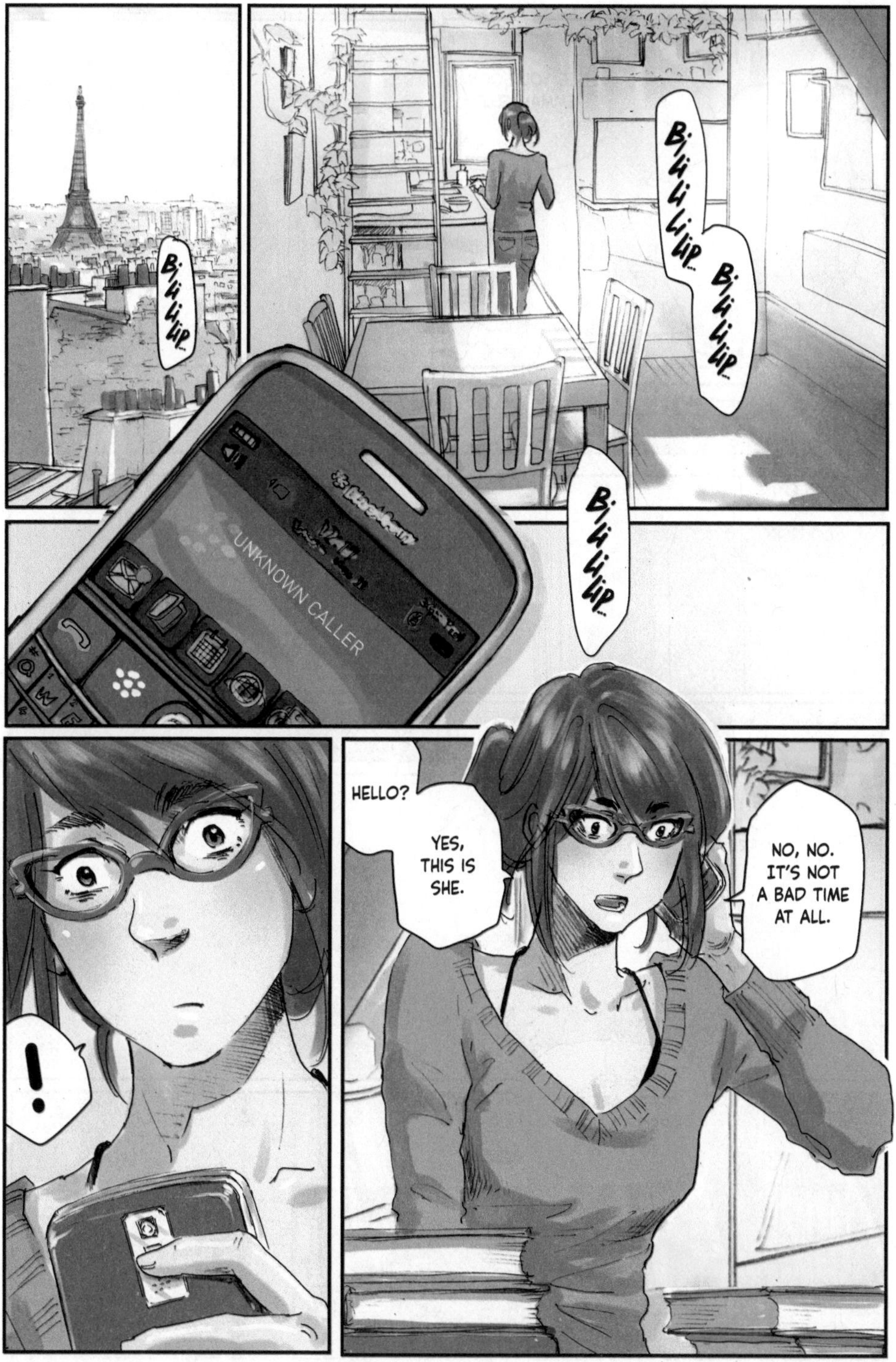
Bilililip...
Bilililip...
Bilililip...
UNKNOWN CALLER
Bilililip...
!
HELLO?
YES, THIS IS SHE.
NO, NO. IT'S NOT A BAD TIME AT ALL.

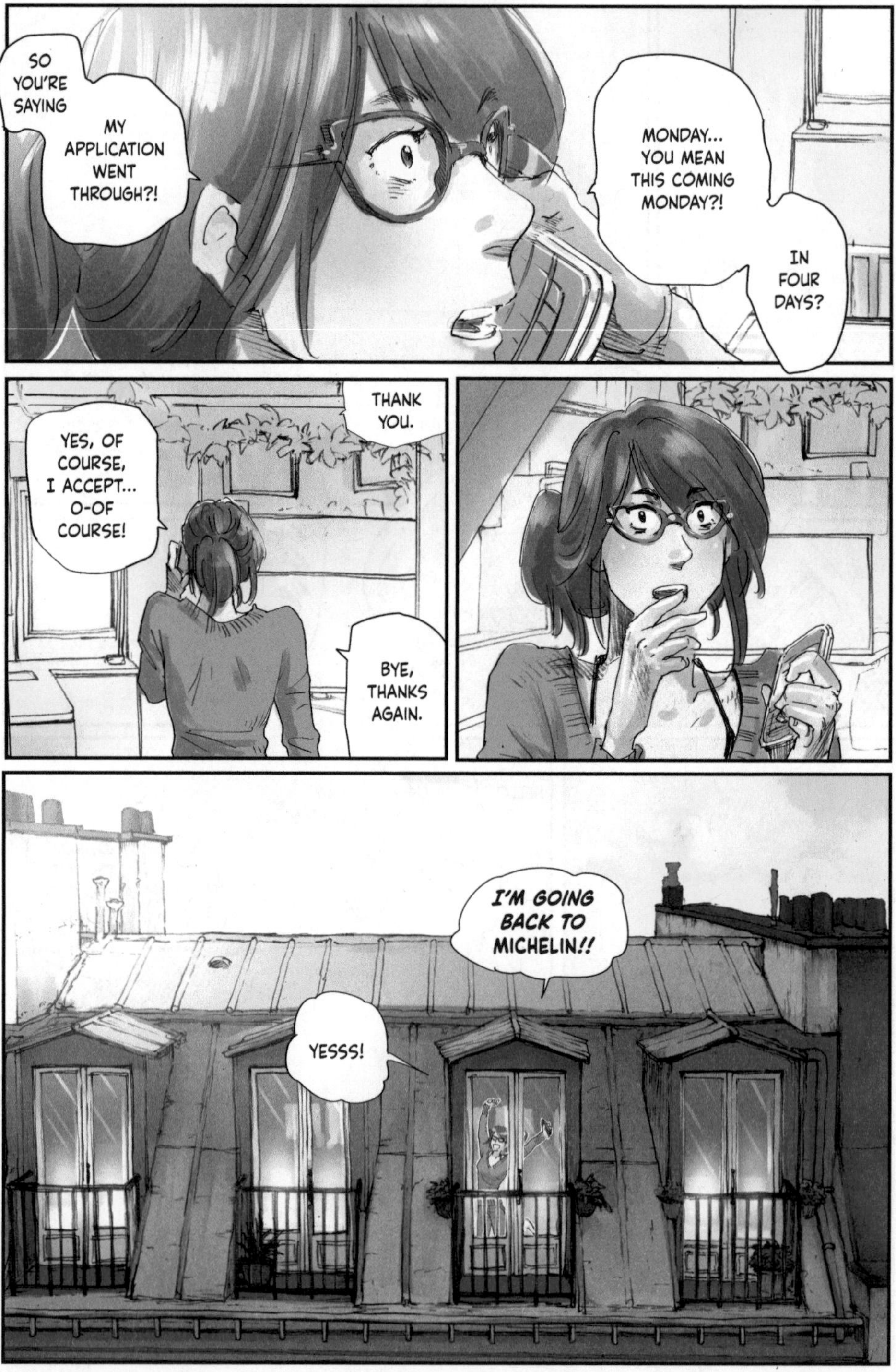
SO YOU'RE SAYING MY APPLICATION WENT THROUGH?!
MONDAY... YOU MEAN THIS COMING MONDAY?!
IN FOUR DAYS?
YES, OF COURSE, I ACCEPT... O-OF COURSE!
THANK YOU.
BYE, THANKS AGAIN.
I'M GOING BACK TO MICHELIN!!
YESSS!

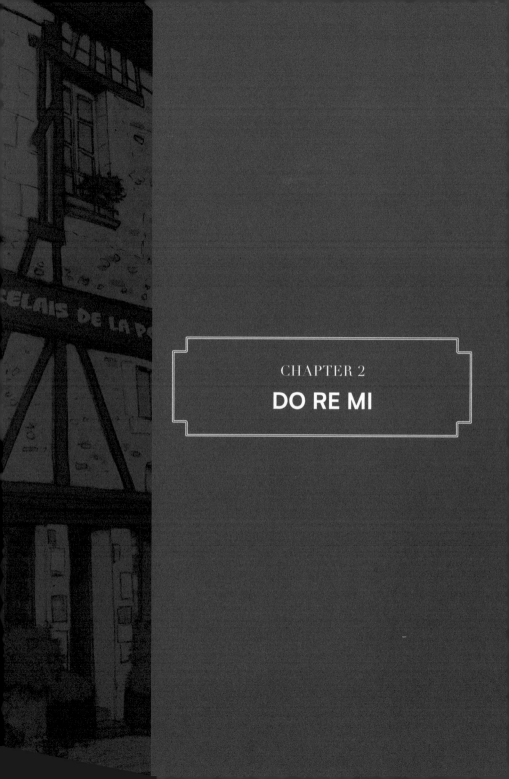

CHAPTER 2
DO RE MI

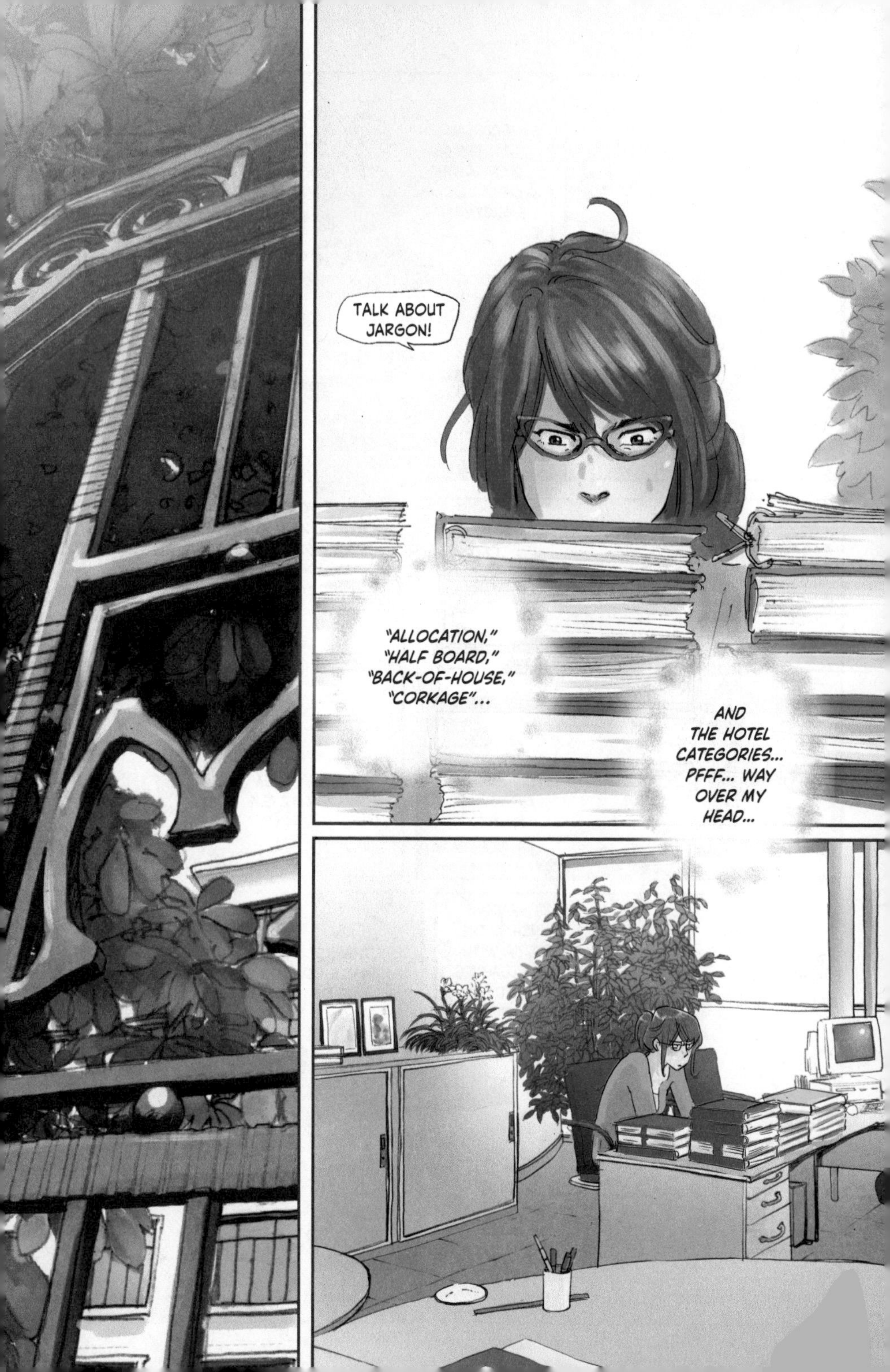
TALK ABOUT JARGON!
"ALLOCATION," "HALF BOARD," "BACK-OF-HOUSE," "CORKAGE"...
AND THE HOTEL CATEGORIES... PFFF... WAY OVER MY HEAD...

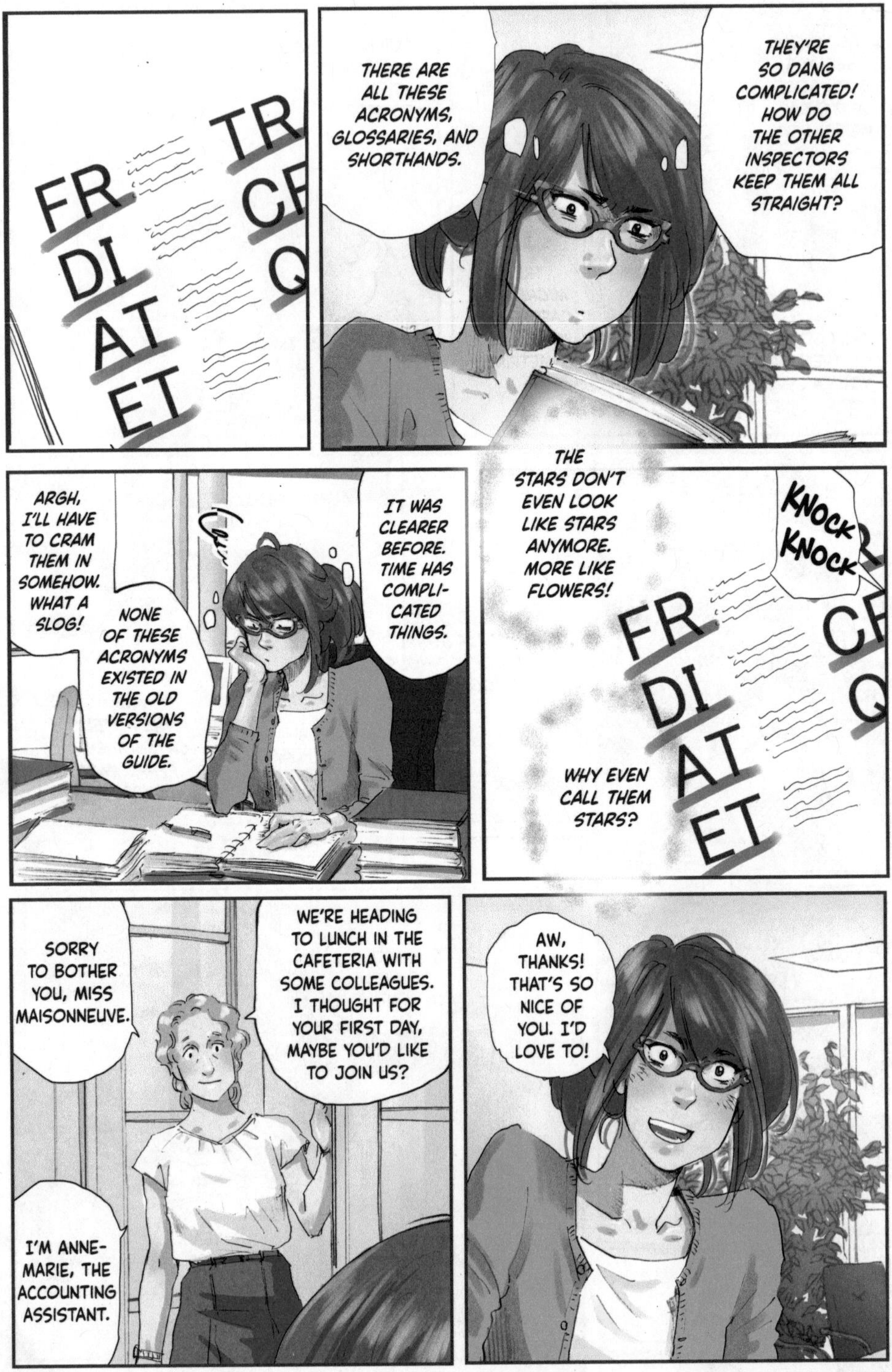

TR
FR
DI
AT
ET
Q
THERE ARE ALL THESE ACRONYMS, GLOSSARIES, AND SHORTHANDS.
THEY'RE SO DANG COMPLICATED! HOW DO THE OTHER INSPECTORS KEEP THEM ALL STRAIGHT?
ARGH, I'LL HAVE TO CRAM THEM IN SOMEHOW. WHAT A SLOG!
NONE OF THESE ACRONYMS EXISTED IN THE OLD VERSIONS OF THE GUIDE.
IT WAS CLEARER BEFORE. TIME HAS COMPLICATED THINGS.
THE STARS DON'T EVEN LOOK LIKE STARS ANYMORE. MORE LIKE FLOWERS!
FR
DI
AT
ET
Q
WHY EVEN CALL THEM STARS?
KNOCK KNOCK
SORRY TO BOTHER YOU, MISS MAISONNEUVE.
I'M ANNE-MARIE, THE ACCOUNTING ASSISTANT.
WE'RE HEADING TO LUNCH IN THE CAFETERIA WITH SOME COLLEAGUES. I THOUGHT FOR YOUR FIRST DAY, MAYBE YOU'D LIKE TO JOIN US?
AW, THANKS! THAT'S SO NICE OF YOU. I'D LOVE TO!

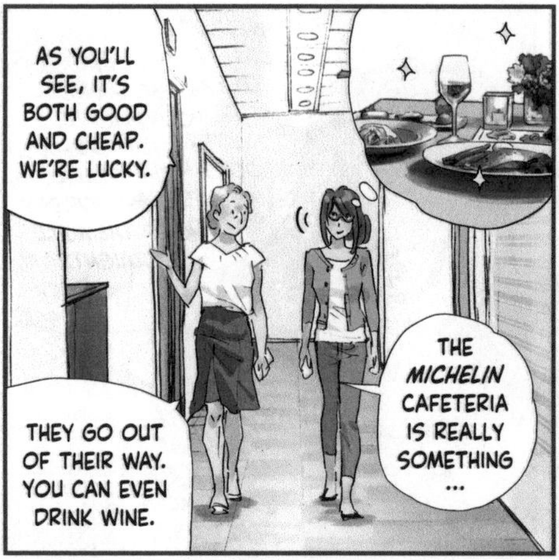
AS YOU'LL SEE, IT'S BOTH GOOD AND CHEAP. WE'RE LUCKY.
THE *MICHELIN* CAFETERIA IS REALLY SOMETHING ...
THEY GO OUT OF THEIR WAY. YOU CAN EVEN DRINK WINE.
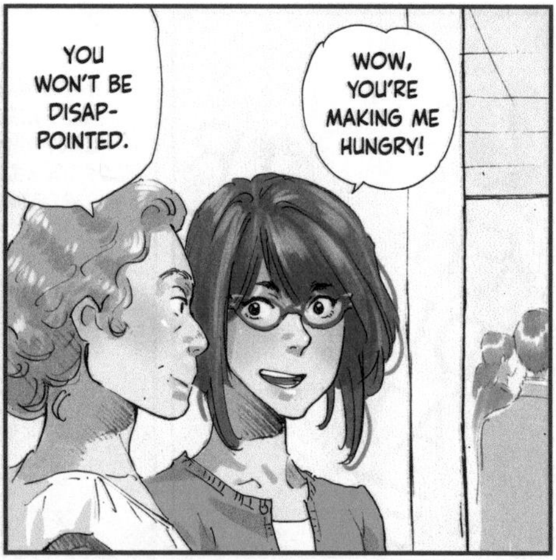
YOU WON'T BE DISAP-POINTED.
WOW, YOU'RE MAKING ME HUNGRY!
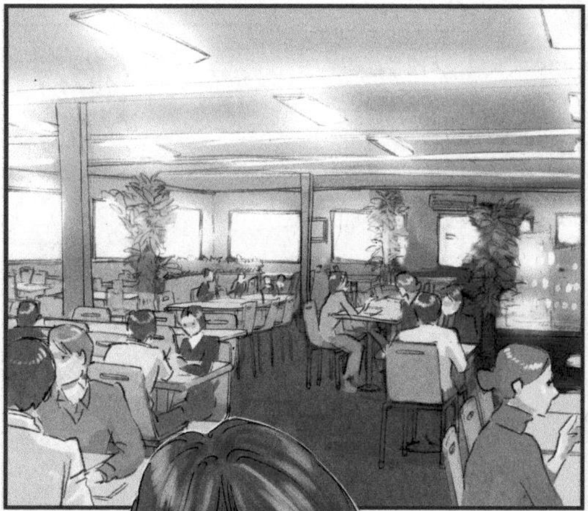
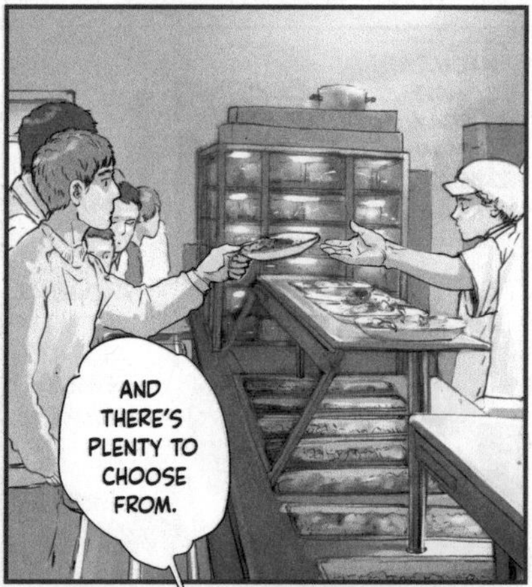
AND THERE'S PLENTY TO CHOOSE FROM.
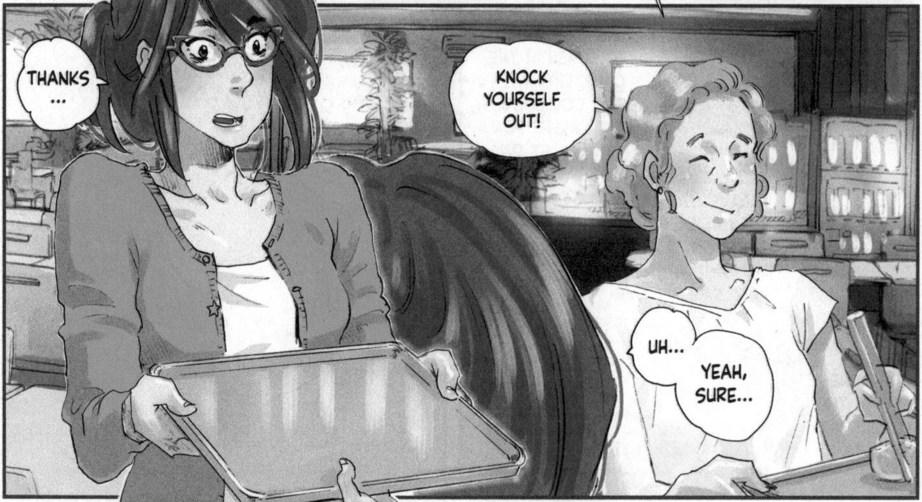
THANKS ...
KNOCK YOURSELF OUT!
UH...
YEAH, SURE...

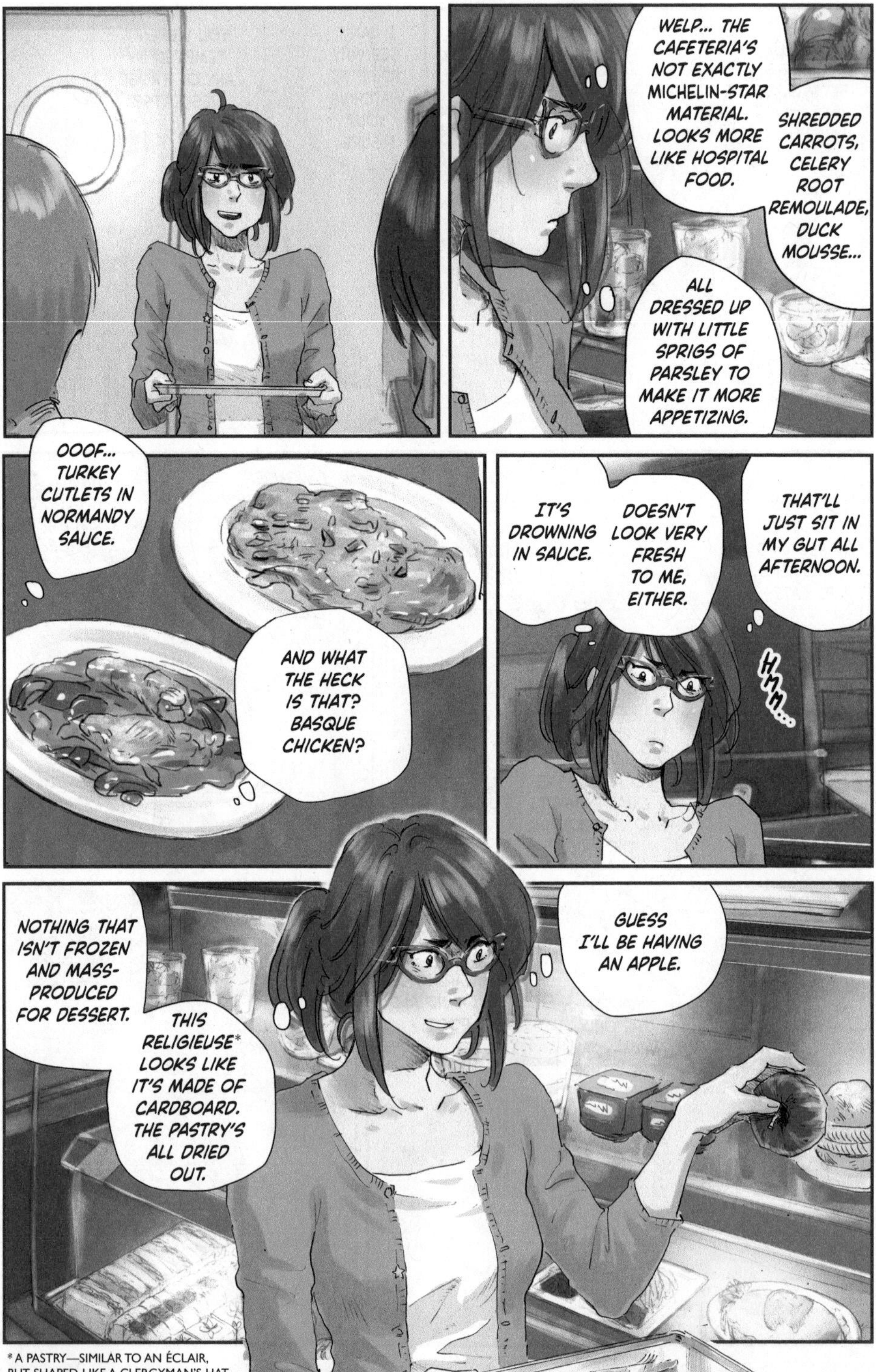
WELP... THE CAFETERIA'S NOT EXACTLY MICHELIN-STAR MATERIAL. LOOKS MORE LIKE HOSPITAL FOOD.
SHREDDED CARROTS, CELERY ROOT REMOULADE, DUCK MOUSSE...
ALL DRESSED UP WITH LITTLE SPRIGS OF PARSLEY TO MAKE IT MORE APPETIZING.
OOOF... TURKEY CUTLETS IN NORMANDY SAUCE.
AND WHAT THE HECK IS THAT? BASQUE CHICKEN?
IT'S DROWNING IN SAUCE.
DOESN'T LOOK VERY FRESH TO ME, EITHER.
THAT'LL JUST SIT IN MY GUT ALL AFTERNOON.
HMM...
NOTHING THAT ISN'T FROZEN AND MASS-PRODUCED FOR DESSERT.
THIS RELIGIEUSE* LOOKS LIKE IT'S MADE OF CARDBOARD. THE PASTRY'S ALL DRIED OUT.
GUESS I'LL BE HAVING AN APPLE.

* A PASTRY—SIMILAR TO AN ÉCLAIR, BUT SHAPED LIKE A CLERGYMAN'S HAT.

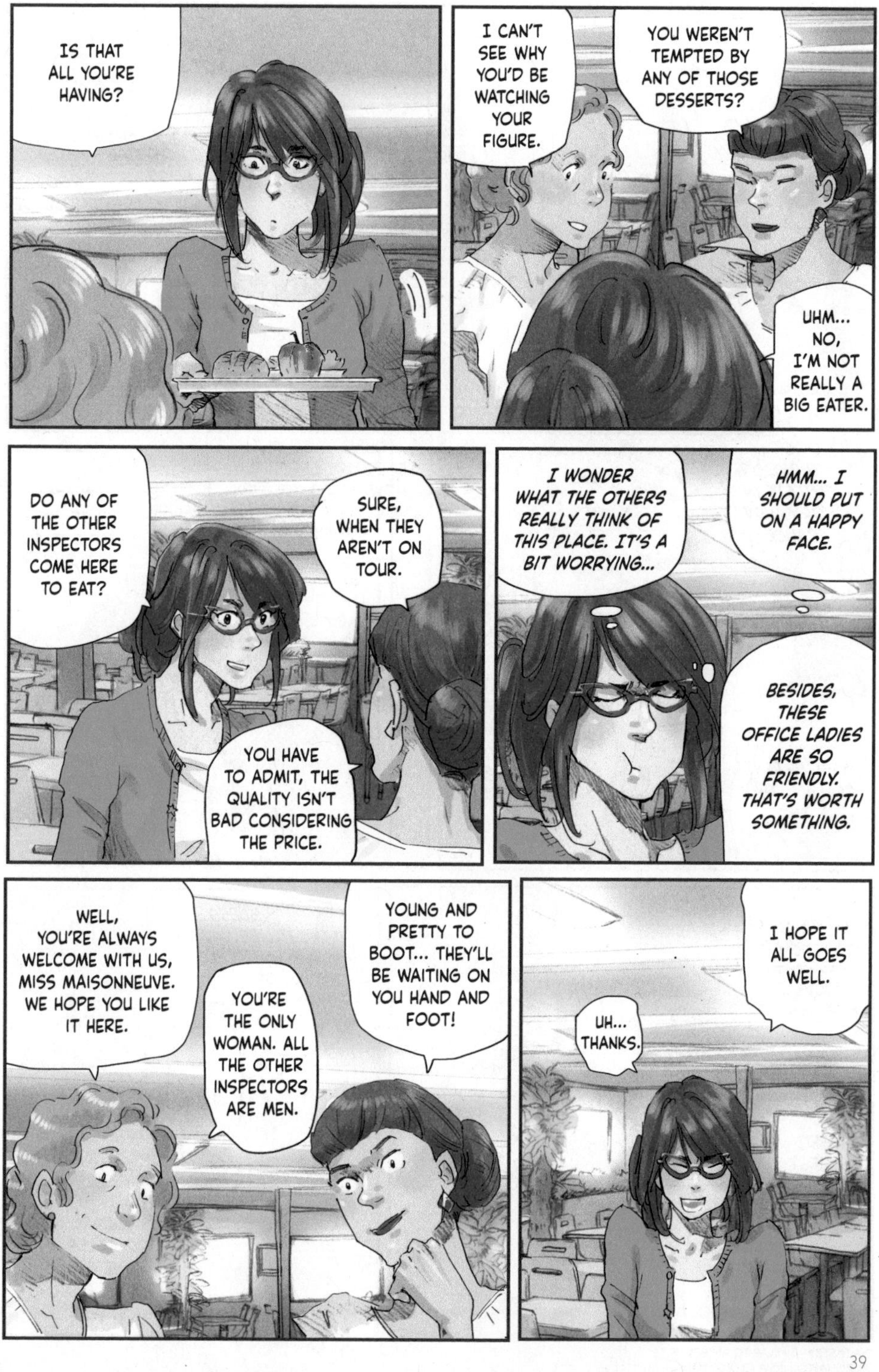
IS THAT ALL YOU'RE HAVING?
I CAN'T SEE WHY YOU'D BE WATCHING YOUR FIGURE.
YOU WEREN'T TEMPTED BY ANY OF THOSE DESSERTS?
UHM... NO, I'M NOT REALLY A BIG EATER.
DO ANY OF THE OTHER INSPECTORS COME HERE TO EAT?
SURE, WHEN THEY AREN'T ON TOUR.
YOU HAVE TO ADMIT, THE QUALITY ISN'T BAD CONSIDERING THE PRICE.
I WONDER WHAT THE OTHERS REALLY THINK OF THIS PLACE. IT'S A BIT WORRYING...
HMM... I SHOULD PUT ON A HAPPY FACE.
BESIDES, THESE OFFICE LADIES ARE SO FRIENDLY. THAT'S WORTH SOMETHING.
WELL, YOU'RE ALWAYS WELCOME WITH US, MISS MAISONNEUVE. WE HOPE YOU LIKE IT HERE.
YOU'RE THE ONLY WOMAN. ALL THE OTHER INSPECTORS ARE MEN.
YOUNG AND PRETTY TO BOOT... THEY'LL BE WAITING ON YOU HAND AND FOOT!
I HOPE IT ALL GOES WELL.
UH... THANKS.

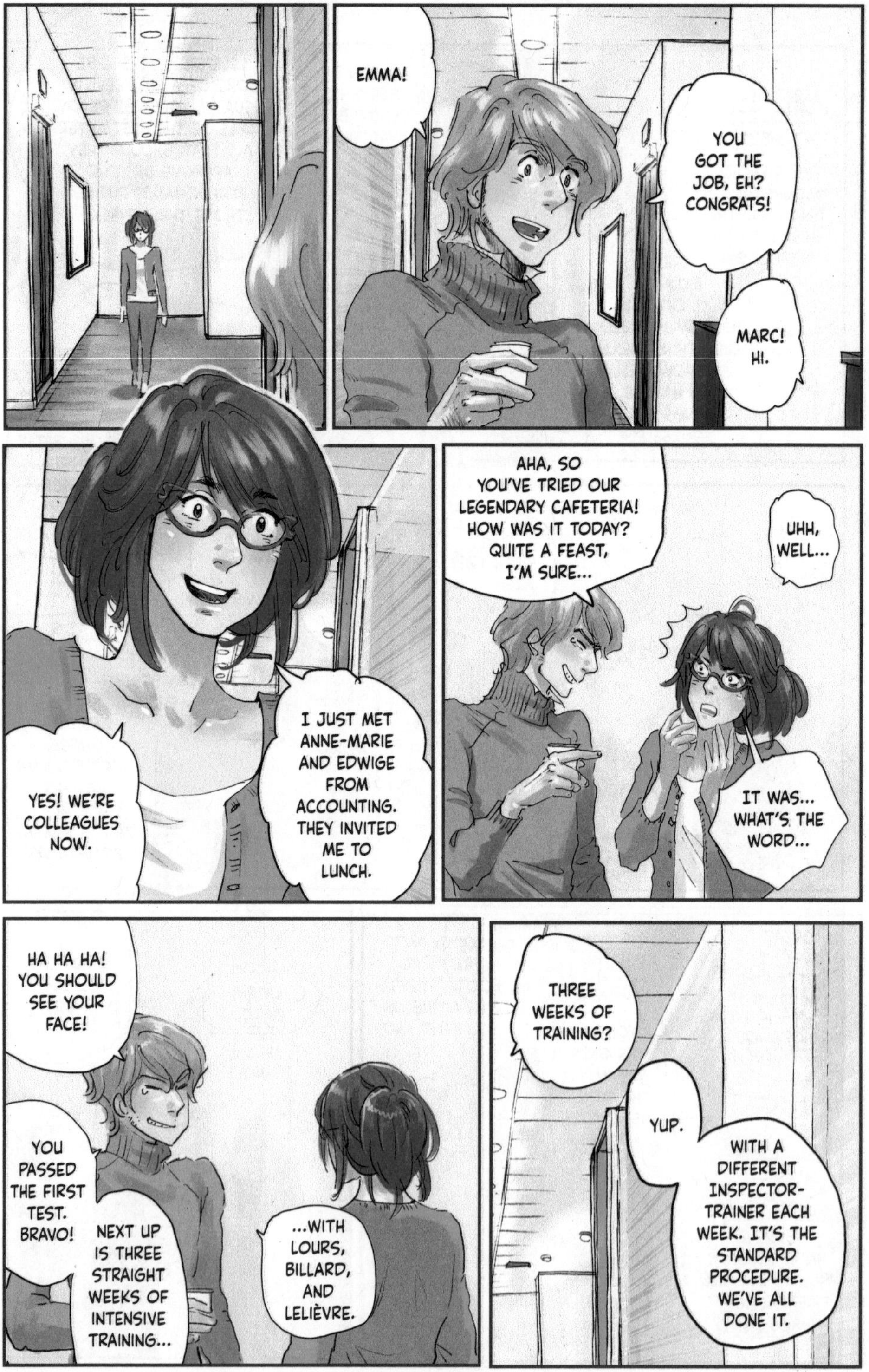
EMMA!
YOU GOT THE JOB, EH? CONGRATS!
MARC! HI.
YES! WE'RE COLLEAGUES NOW.
I JUST MET ANNE-MARIE AND EDWIGE FROM ACCOUNTING. THEY INVITED ME TO LUNCH.
AHA, SO YOU'VE TRIED OUR LEGENDARY CAFETERIA! HOW WAS IT TODAY? QUITE A FEAST, I'M SURE...
UHH, WELL...
IT WAS... WHAT'S THE WORD...
HA HA HA! YOU SHOULD SEE YOUR FACE!
YOU PASSED THE FIRST TEST. BRAVO!
NEXT UP IS THREE STRAIGHT WEEKS OF INTENSIVE TRAINING...
...WITH LOURS, BILLARD, AND LELIÈVRE.
THREE WEEKS OF TRAINING?
YUP.
WITH A DIFFERENT INSPECTOR-TRAINER EACH WEEK. IT'S THE STANDARD PROCEDURE. WE'VE ALL DONE IT.

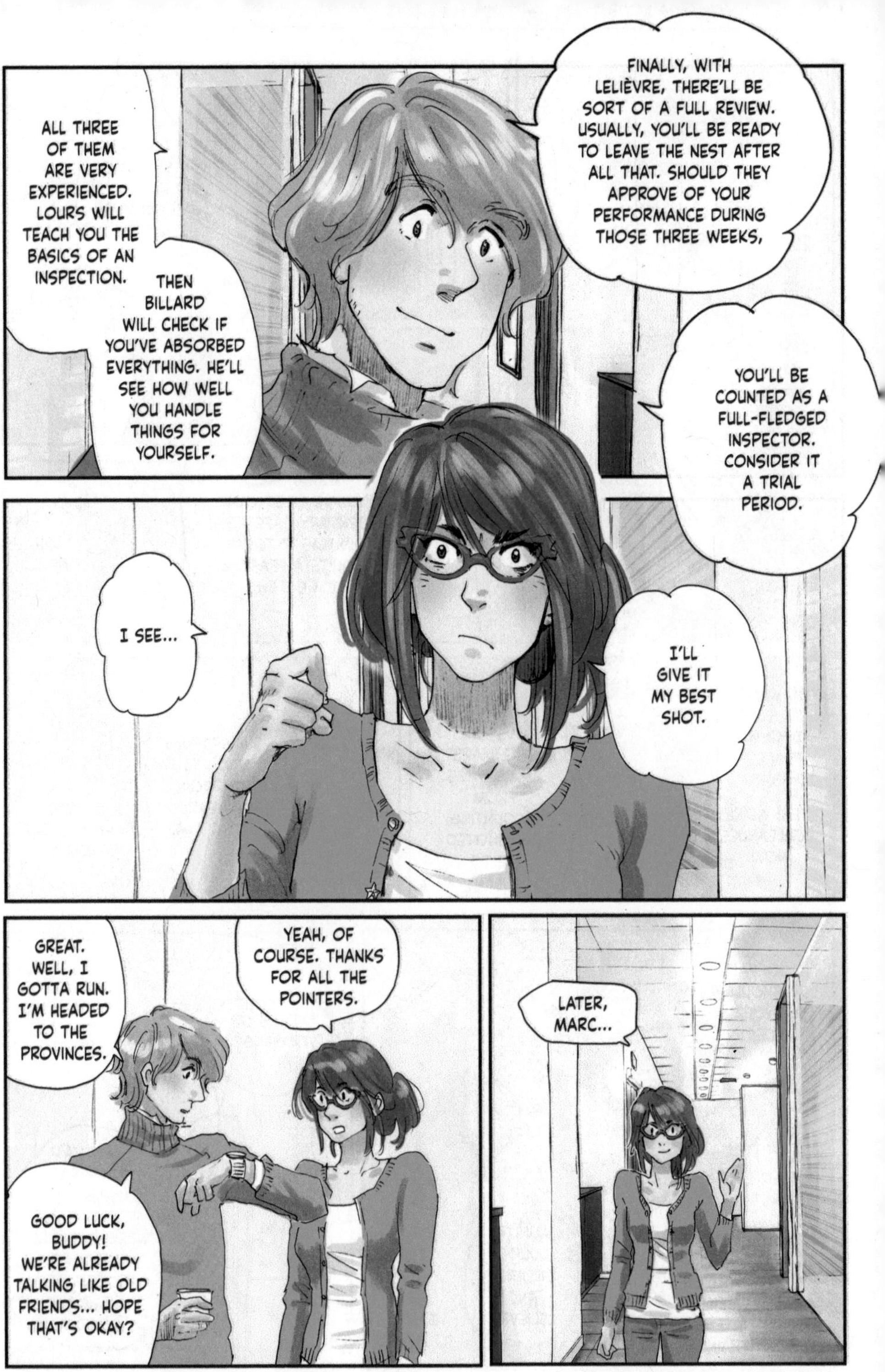
ALL THREE OF THEM ARE VERY EXPERIENCED. LOURS WILL TEACH YOU THE BASICS OF AN INSPECTION.
THEN BILLARD WILL CHECK IF YOU'VE ABSORBED EVERYTHING. HE'LL SEE HOW WELL YOU HANDLE THINGS FOR YOURSELF.
FINALLY, WITH LELIÈVRE, THERE'LL BE SORT OF A FULL REVIEW. USUALLY, YOU'LL BE READY TO LEAVE THE NEST AFTER ALL THAT. SHOULD THEY APPROVE OF YOUR PERFORMANCE DURING THOSE THREE WEEKS,
YOU'LL BE COUNTED AS A FULL-FLEDGED INSPECTOR. CONSIDER IT A TRIAL PERIOD.
I SEE...
I'LL GIVE IT MY BEST SHOT.
GREAT. WELL, I GOTTA RUN. I'M HEADED TO THE PROVINCES.
YEAH, OF COURSE. THANKS FOR ALL THE POINTERS.
GOOD LUCK, BUDDY! WE'RE ALREADY TALKING LIKE OLD FRIENDS... HOPE THAT'S OKAY?
LATER, MARC...

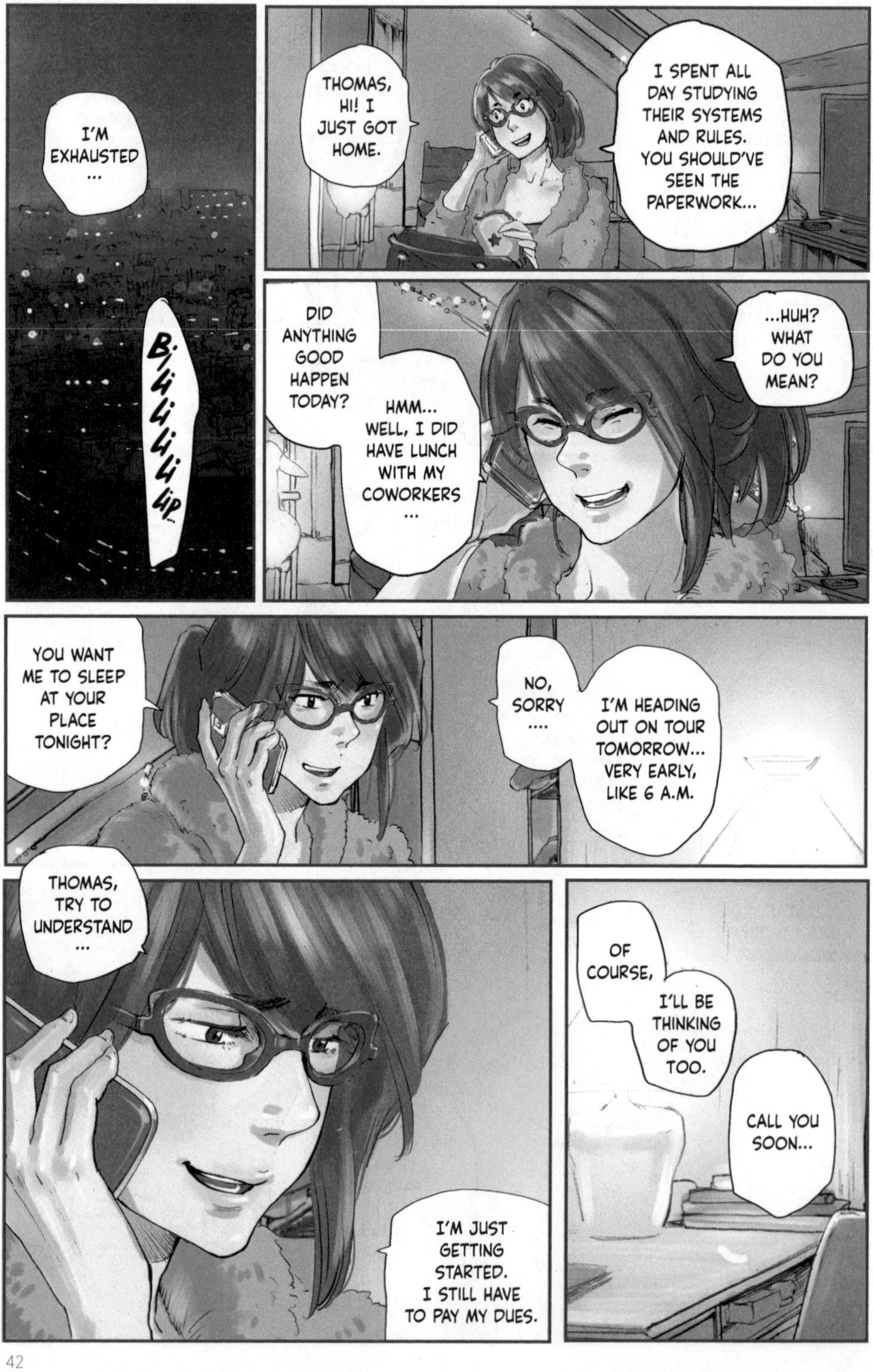
I'M EXHAUSTED ...
Biiiiiiip...
THOMAS, HI! I JUST GOT HOME.
I SPENT ALL DAY STUDYING THEIR SYSTEMS AND RULES. YOU SHOULD'VE SEEN THE PAPERWORK...
DID ANYTHING GOOD HAPPEN TODAY?
HMM... WELL, I DID HAVE LUNCH WITH MY COWORKERS ...
...HUH? WHAT DO YOU MEAN?
YOU WANT ME TO SLEEP AT YOUR PLACE TONIGHT?
NO, SORRY ....
I'M HEADING OUT ON TOUR TOMORROW... VERY EARLY, LIKE 6 A.M.
THOMAS, TRY TO UNDERSTAND ...
I'M JUST GETTING STARTED. I STILL HAVE TO PAY MY DUES.
OF COURSE,
I'LL BE THINKING OF YOU TOO.
CALL YOU SOON...

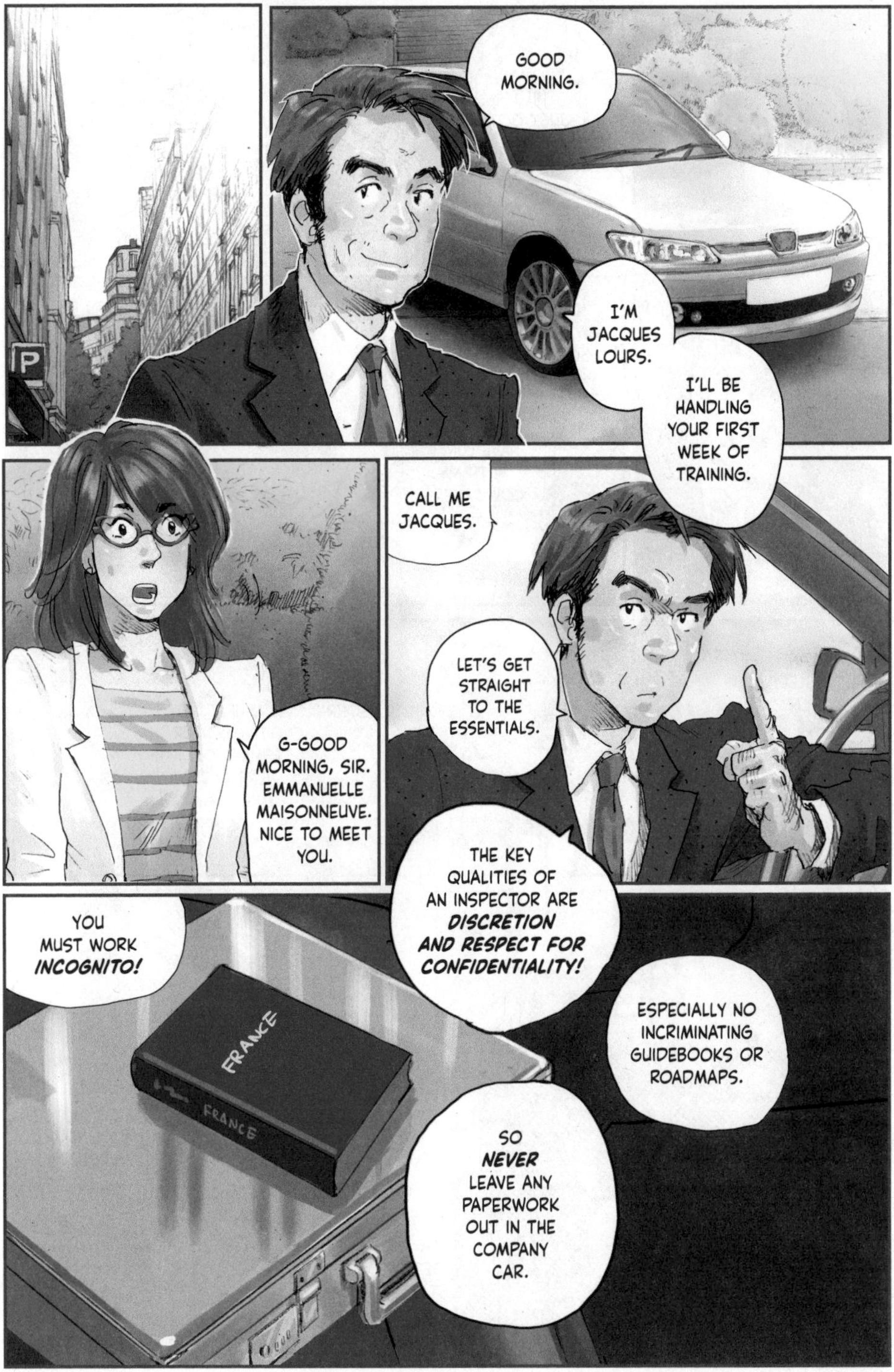
GOOD MORNING.
I'M JACQUES LOURS.
I'LL BE HANDLING YOUR FIRST WEEK OF TRAINING.
G-GOOD MORNING, SIR. EMMANUELLE MAISONNEUVE. NICE TO MEET YOU.
CALL ME JACQUES.
LET'S GET STRAIGHT TO THE ESSENTIALS.
THE KEY QUALITIES OF AN INSPECTOR ARE ***DISCRETION AND RESPECT FOR CONFIDENTIALITY!***
YOU MUST WORK ***INCOGNITO!***
FRANCE
FRANCE
ESPECIALLY NO INCRIMINATING GUIDEBOOKS OR ROADMAPS.
SO ***NEVER*** LEAVE ANY PAPERWORK OUT IN THE COMPANY CAR.

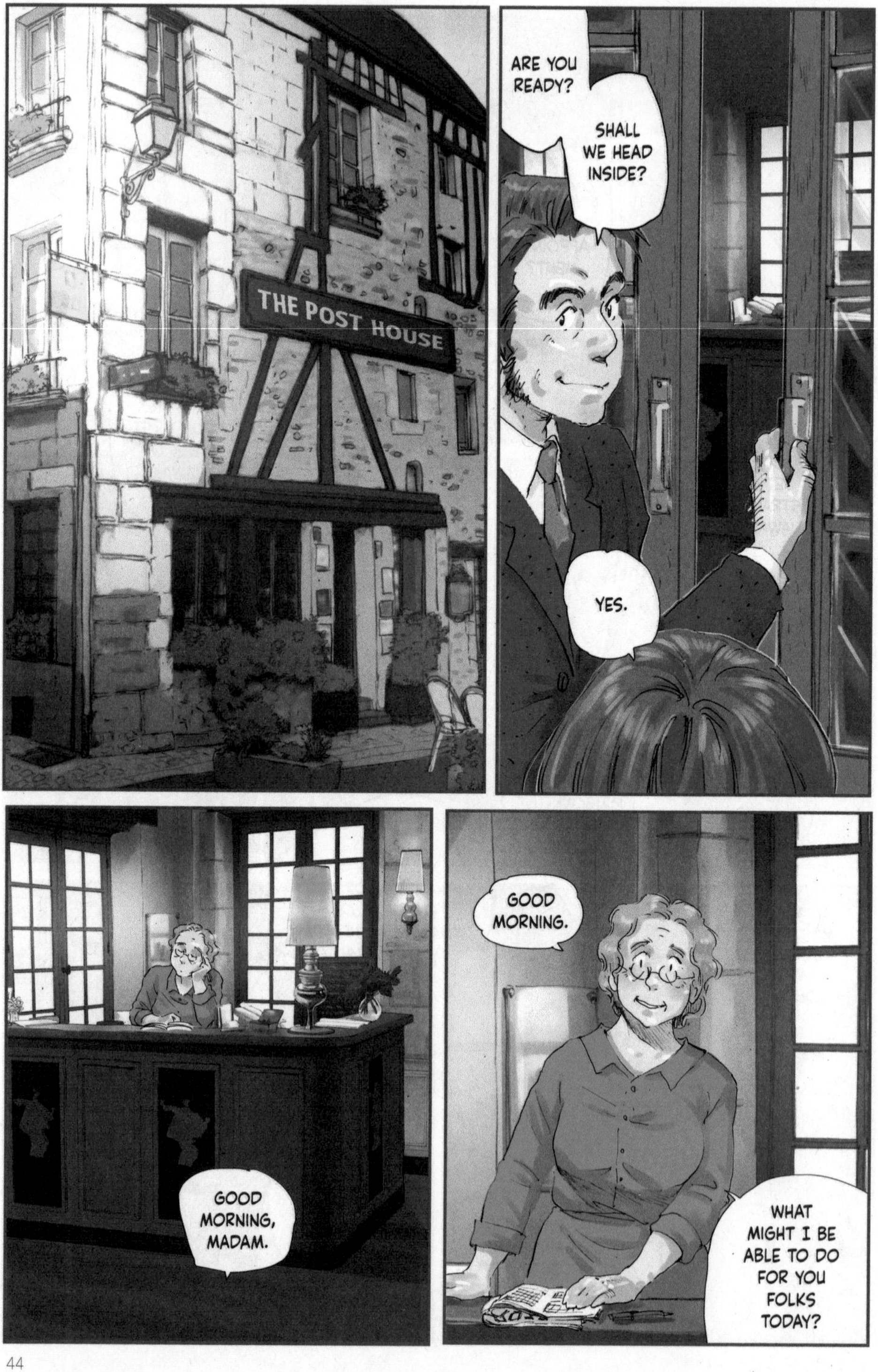
THE POST HOUSE
ARE YOU READY?
SHALL WE HEAD INSIDE?
YES.
GOOD MORNING, MADAM.
GOOD MORNING.
WHAT MIGHT I BE ABLE TO DO FOR YOU FOLKS TODAY?

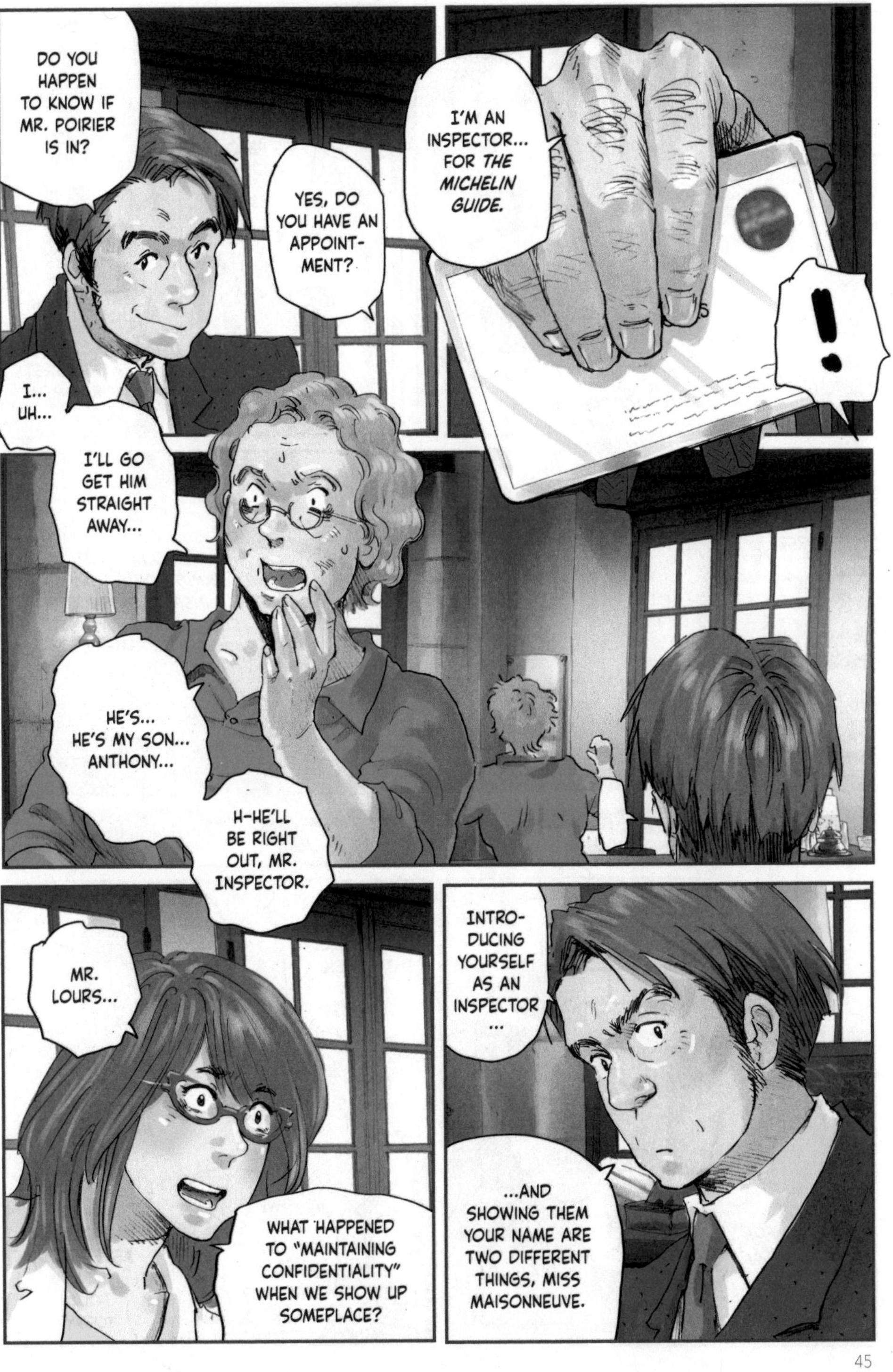
DO YOU HAPPEN TO KNOW IF MR. POIRIER IS IN?
YES, DO YOU HAVE AN APPOINT-MENT?
I'M AN INSPECTOR... FOR *THE MICHELIN GUIDE.*
!
I... UH...
I'LL GO GET HIM STRAIGHT AWAY...
HE'S... HE'S MY SON... ANTHONY...
H-HE'LL BE RIGHT OUT, MR. INSPECTOR.
MR. LOURS...
WHAT HAPPENED TO "MAINTAINING CONFIDENTIALITY" WHEN WE SHOW UP SOMEPLACE?
INTRO-DUCING YOURSELF AS AN INSPECTOR ...
...AND SHOWING THEM YOUR NAME ARE TWO DIFFERENT THINGS, MISS MAISONNEUVE.

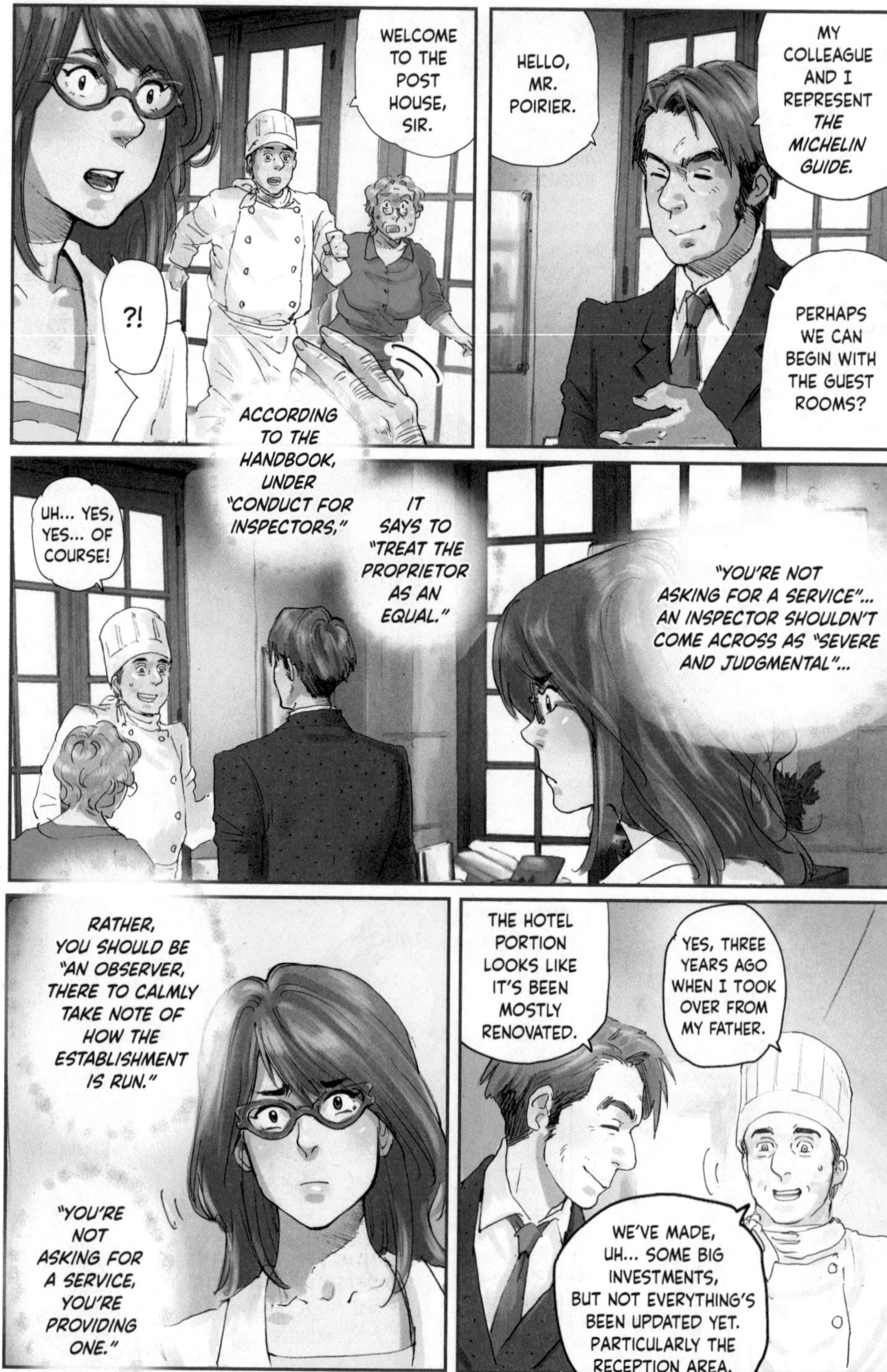
WELCOME TO THE POST HOUSE, SIR.
?!
HELLO, MR. POIRIER.
MY COLLEAGUE AND I REPRESENT *THE MICHELIN GUIDE.*
PERHAPS WE CAN BEGIN WITH THE GUEST ROOMS?
UH... YES, YES... OF COURSE!
ACCORDING TO THE HANDBOOK, UNDER "CONDUCT FOR INSPECTORS,"
IT SAYS TO "TREAT THE PROPRIETOR AS AN EQUAL."
"YOU'RE NOT ASKING FOR A SERVICE"... AN INSPECTOR SHOULDN'T COME ACROSS AS "SEVERE AND JUDGMENTAL"...
RATHER, YOU SHOULD BE "AN OBSERVER, THERE TO CALMLY TAKE NOTE OF HOW THE ESTABLISHMENT IS RUN."
"YOU'RE NOT ASKING FOR A SERVICE, YOU'RE PROVIDING ONE."
THE HOTEL PORTION LOOKS LIKE IT'S BEEN MOSTLY RENOVATED.
YES, THREE YEARS AGO WHEN I TOOK OVER FROM MY FATHER.
WE'VE MADE, UH... SOME BIG INVESTMENTS, BUT NOT EVERYTHING'S BEEN UPDATED YET. PARTICULARLY THE RECEPTION AREA.

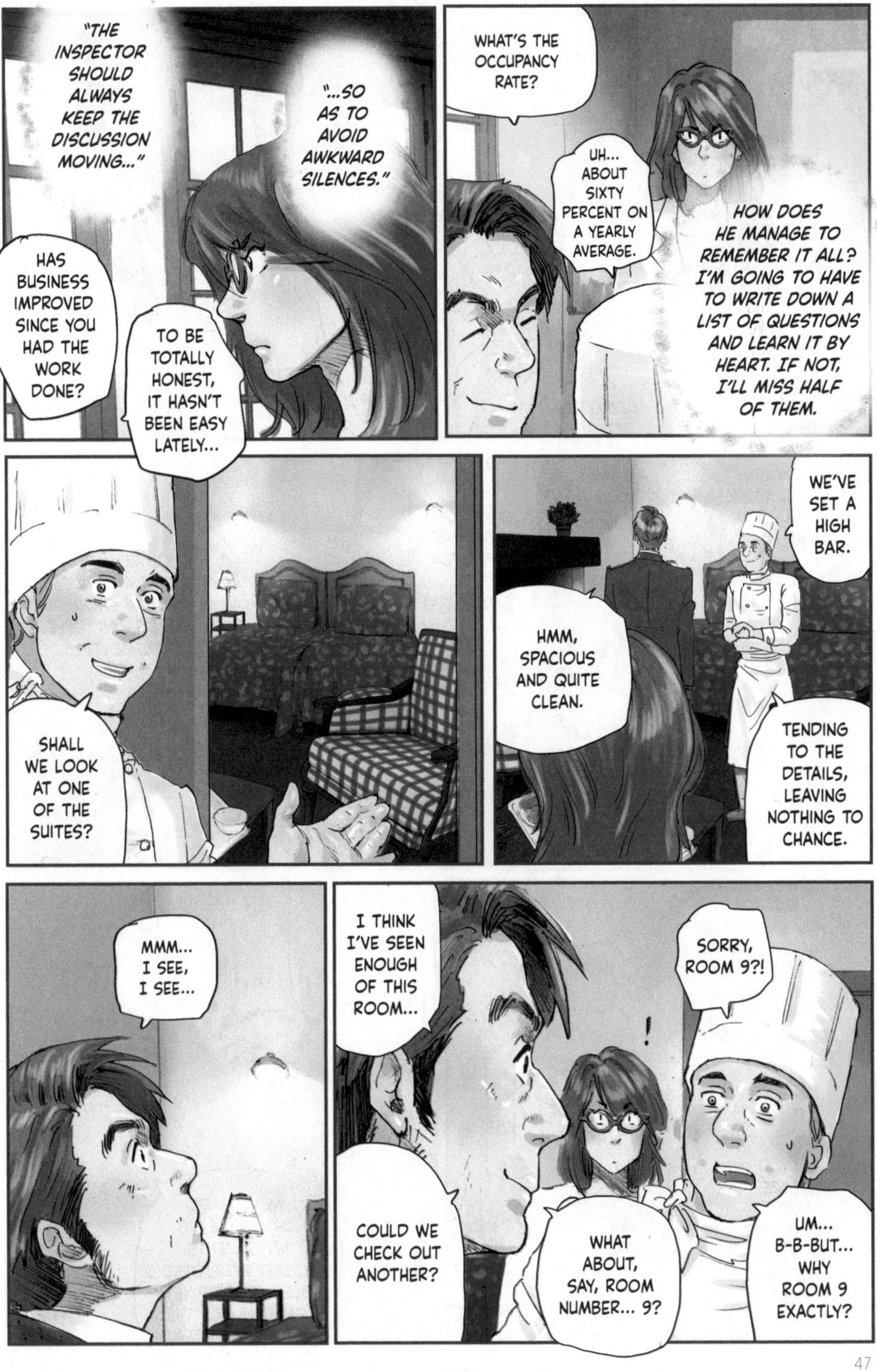
"THE INSPECTOR SHOULD ALWAYS KEEP THE DISCUSSION MOVING..."
"...SO AS TO AVOID AWKWARD SILENCES."
HAS BUSINESS IMPROVED SINCE YOU HAD THE WORK DONE?
TO BE TOTALLY HONEST, IT HASN'T BEEN EASY LATELY...
WHAT'S THE OCCUPANCY RATE?
UH... ABOUT SIXTY PERCENT ON A YEARLY AVERAGE.
HOW DOES HE MANAGE TO REMEMBER IT ALL? I'M GOING TO HAVE TO WRITE DOWN A LIST OF QUESTIONS AND LEARN IT BY HEART. IF NOT, I'LL MISS HALF OF THEM.
SHALL WE LOOK AT ONE OF THE SUITES?
WE'VE SET A HIGH BAR.
HMM, SPACIOUS AND QUITE CLEAN.
TENDING TO THE DETAILS, LEAVING NOTHING TO CHANCE.
MMM... I SEE, I SEE...
I THINK I'VE SEEN ENOUGH OF THIS ROOM...
COULD WE CHECK OUT ANOTHER?
WHAT ABOUT, SAY, ROOM NUMBER... 9?
!
SORRY, ROOM 9?!
UM... B-B-BUT... WHY ROOM 9 EXACTLY?

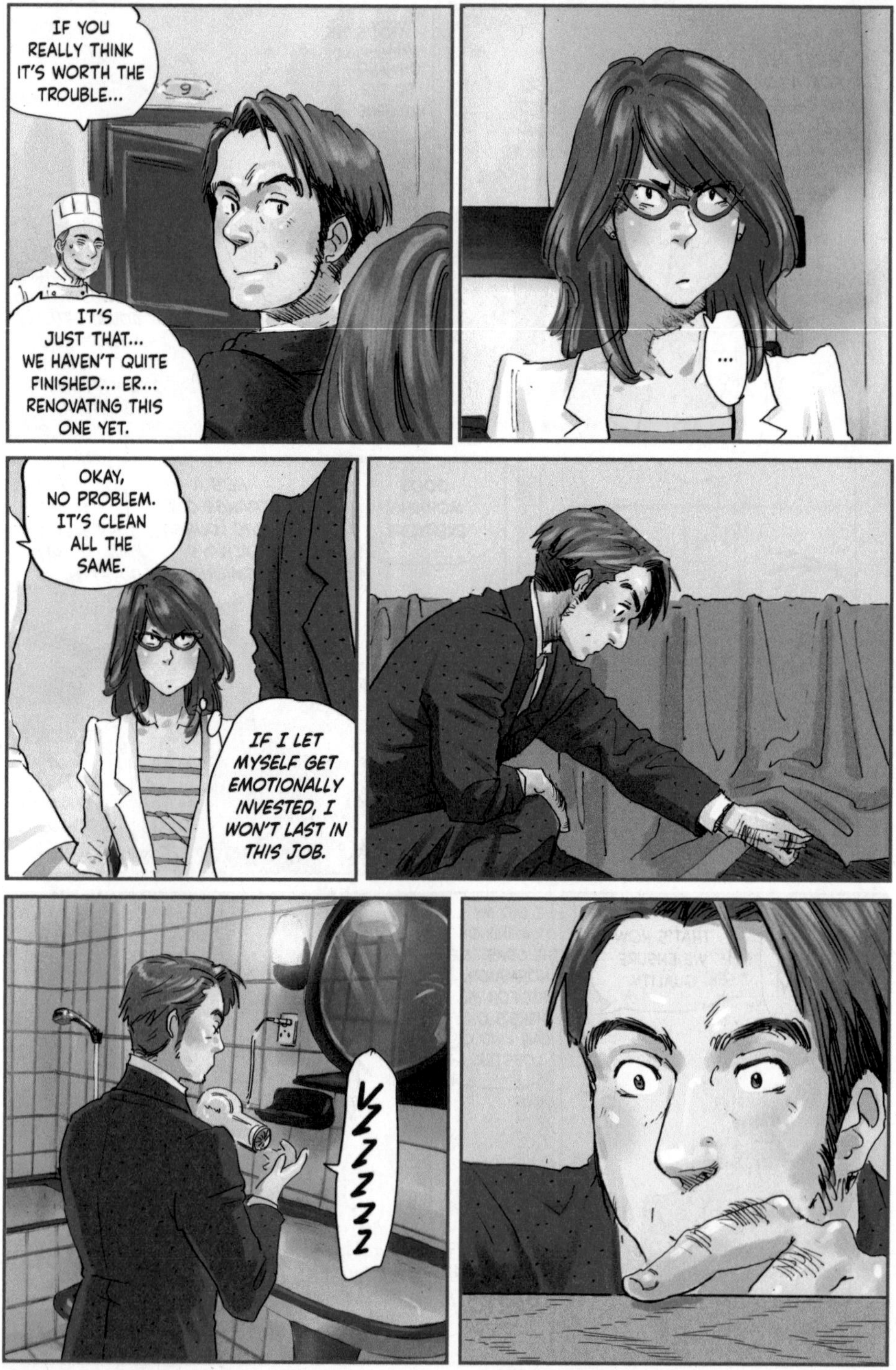

IF YOU REALLY THINK IT'S WORTH THE TROUBLE...
IT'S JUST THAT... WE HAVEN'T QUITE FINISHED... ER... RENOVATING THIS ONE YET.
...
OKAY, NO PROBLEM. IT'S CLEAN ALL THE SAME.
IF I LET MYSELF GET EMOTIONALLY INVESTED, I WON'T LAST IN THIS JOB.
VZZZZZ

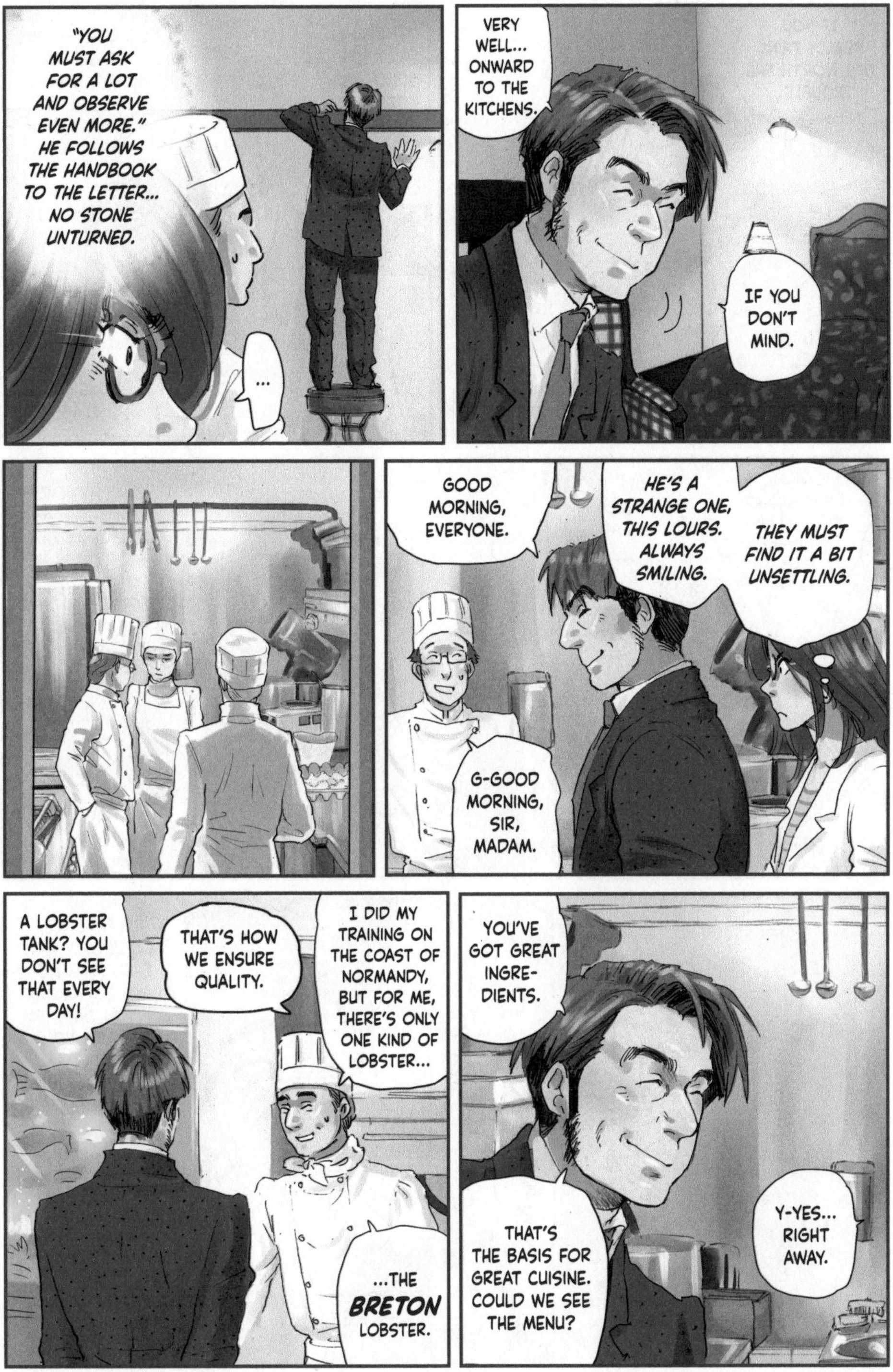
"YOU MUST ASK FOR A LOT AND OBSERVE EVEN MORE." HE FOLLOWS THE HANDBOOK TO THE LETTER... NO STONE UNTURNED.
...
VERY WELL... ONWARD TO THE KITCHENS.
IF YOU DON'T MIND.
GOOD MORNING, EVERYONE.
HE'S A STRANGE ONE, THIS LOURS. ALWAYS SMILING.
THEY MUST FIND IT A BIT UNSETTLING.
G-GOOD MORNING, SIR, MADAM.
A LOBSTER TANK? YOU DON'T SEE THAT EVERY DAY!
THAT'S HOW WE ENSURE QUALITY.
I DID MY TRAINING ON THE COAST OF NORMANDY, BUT FOR ME, THERE'S ONLY ONE KIND OF LOBSTER...
...THE ***BRETON*** LOBSTER.
YOU'VE GOT GREAT INGRE-DIENTS.
THAT'S THE BASIS FOR GREAT CUISINE. COULD WE SEE THE MENU?
Y-YES... RIGHT AWAY.

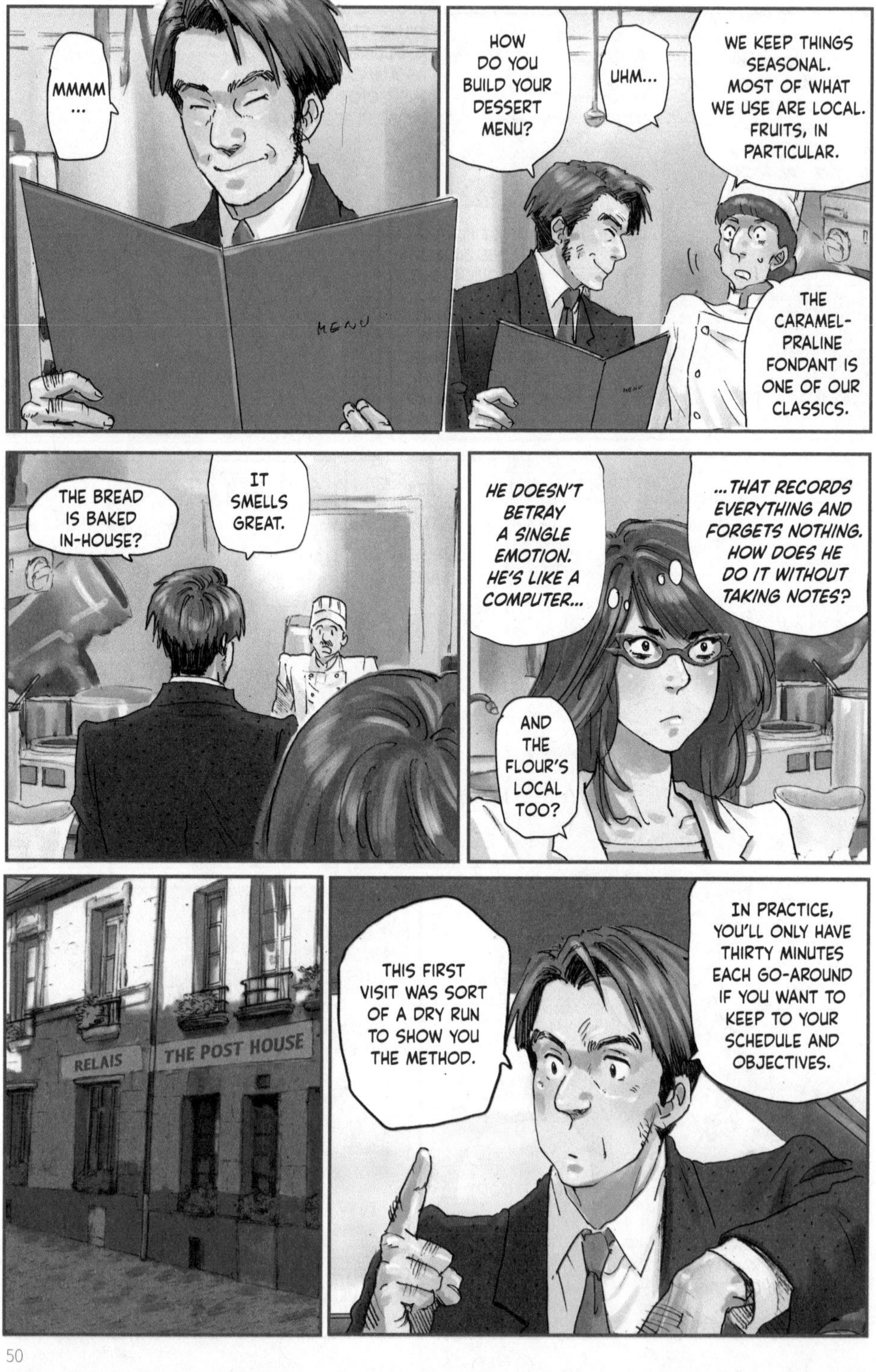
MMMM ...
MENU
HOW DO YOU BUILD YOUR DESSERT MENU?
UHM...
WE KEEP THINGS SEASONAL. MOST OF WHAT WE USE ARE LOCAL. FRUITS, IN PARTICULAR.
MENU
THE CARAMEL-PRALINE FONDANT IS ONE OF OUR CLASSICS.
THE BREAD IS BAKED IN-HOUSE?
IT SMELLS GREAT.
HE DOESN'T BETRAY A SINGLE EMOTION. HE'S LIKE A COMPUTER...
...THAT RECORDS EVERYTHING AND FORGETS NOTHING. HOW DOES HE DO IT WITHOUT TAKING NOTES?
AND THE FLOUR'S LOCAL TOO?
RELAIS
THE POST HOUSE
THIS FIRST VISIT WAS SORT OF A DRY RUN TO SHOW YOU THE METHOD.
IN PRACTICE, YOU'LL ONLY HAVE THIRTY MINUTES EACH GO-AROUND IF YOU WANT TO KEEP TO YOUR SCHEDULE AND OBJECTIVES.

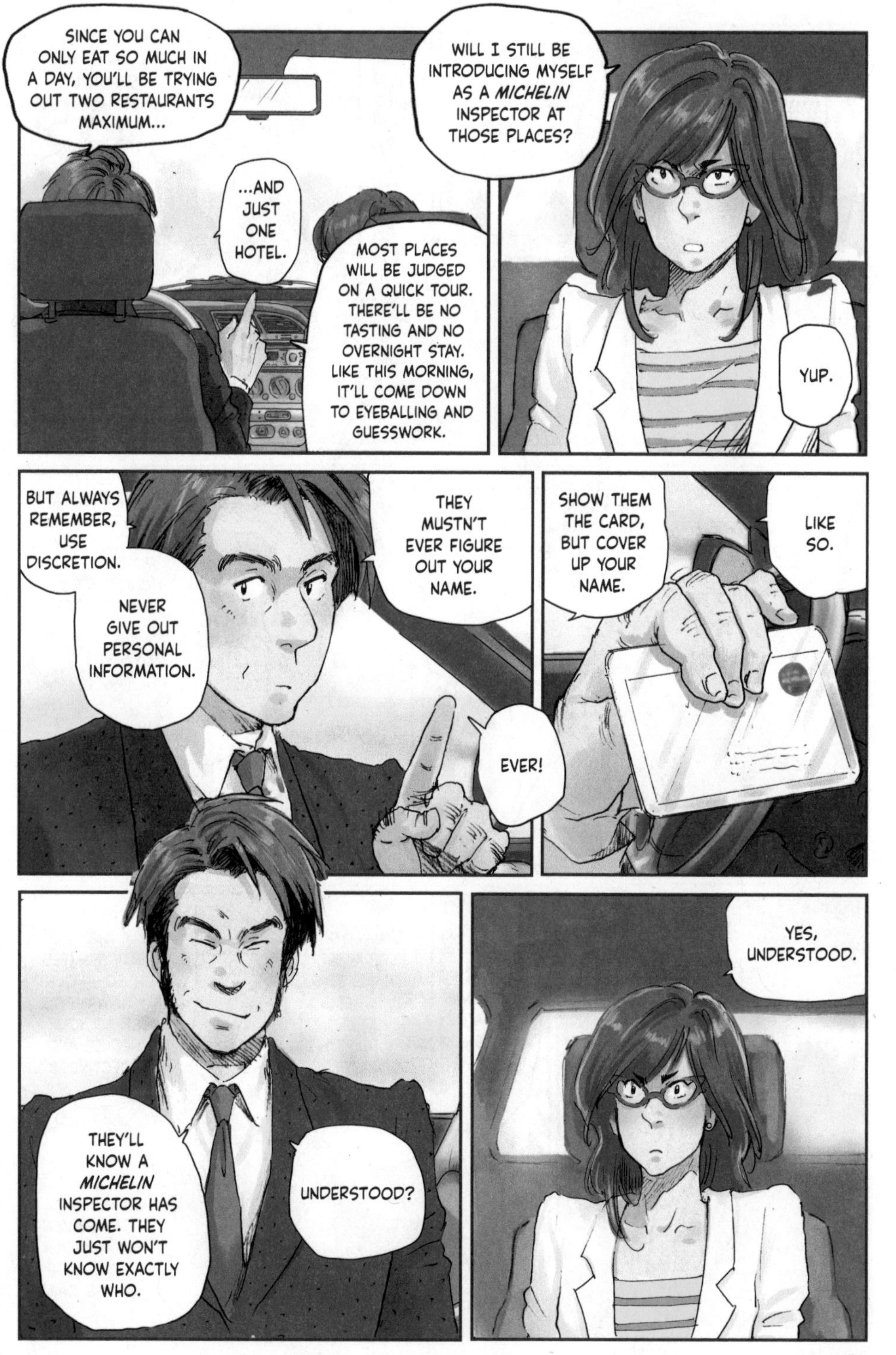
SINCE YOU CAN ONLY EAT SO MUCH IN A DAY, YOU'LL BE TRYING OUT TWO RESTAURANTS MAXIMUM...
...AND JUST ONE HOTEL.
MOST PLACES WILL BE JUDGED ON A QUICK TOUR. THERE'LL BE NO TASTING AND NO OVERNIGHT STAY. LIKE THIS MORNING, IT'LL COME DOWN TO EYEBALLING AND GUESSWORK.
WILL I STILL BE INTRODUCING MYSELF AS A *MICHELIN* INSPECTOR AT THOSE PLACES?
YUP.
BUT ALWAYS REMEMBER, USE DISCRETION.
NEVER GIVE OUT PERSONAL INFORMATION.
THEY MUSTN'T EVER FIGURE OUT YOUR NAME.
EVER!
SHOW THEM THE CARD, BUT COVER UP YOUR NAME.
LIKE SO.
THEY'LL KNOW A *MICHELIN* INSPECTOR HAS COME. THEY JUST WON'T KNOW EXACTLY WHO.
UNDERSTOOD?
YES, UNDERSTOOD.

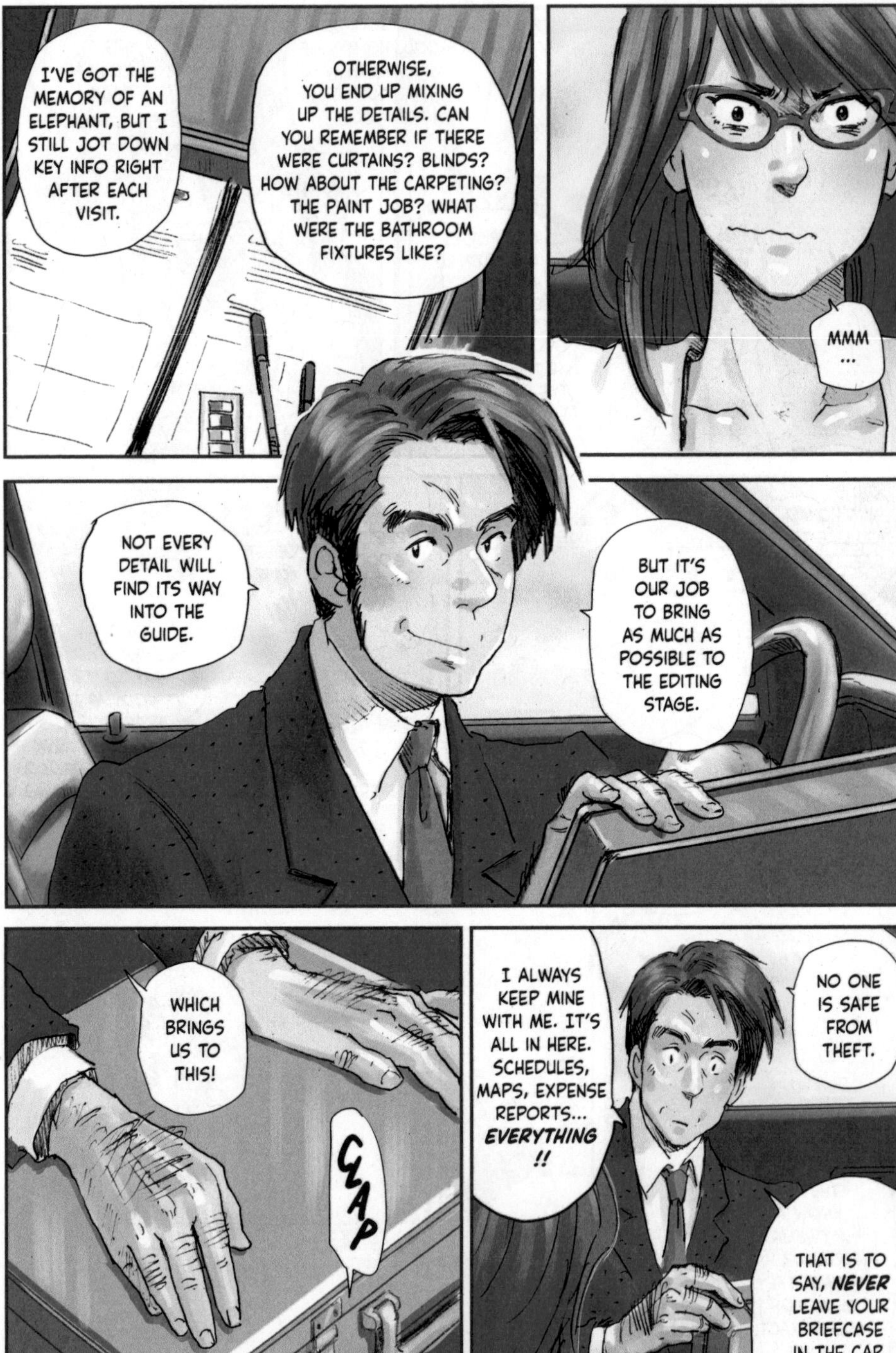
I'VE GOT THE MEMORY OF AN ELEPHANT, BUT I STILL JOT DOWN KEY INFO RIGHT AFTER EACH VISIT.
OTHERWISE, YOU END UP MIXING UP THE DETAILS. CAN YOU REMEMBER IF THERE WERE CURTAINS? BLINDS? HOW ABOUT THE CARPETING? THE PAINT JOB? WHAT WERE THE BATHROOM FIXTURES LIKE?
MMM ...
NOT EVERY DETAIL WILL FIND ITS WAY INTO THE GUIDE.
BUT IT'S OUR JOB TO BRING AS MUCH AS POSSIBLE TO THE EDITING STAGE.
WHICH BRINGS US TO THIS!
CLAP
I ALWAYS KEEP MINE WITH ME. IT'S ALL IN HERE. SCHEDULES, MAPS, EXPENSE REPORTS... ***EVERYTHING*** !!
NO ONE IS SAFE FROM THEFT.
THAT IS TO SAY, ***NEVER*** LEAVE YOUR BRIEFCASE IN THE CAR.

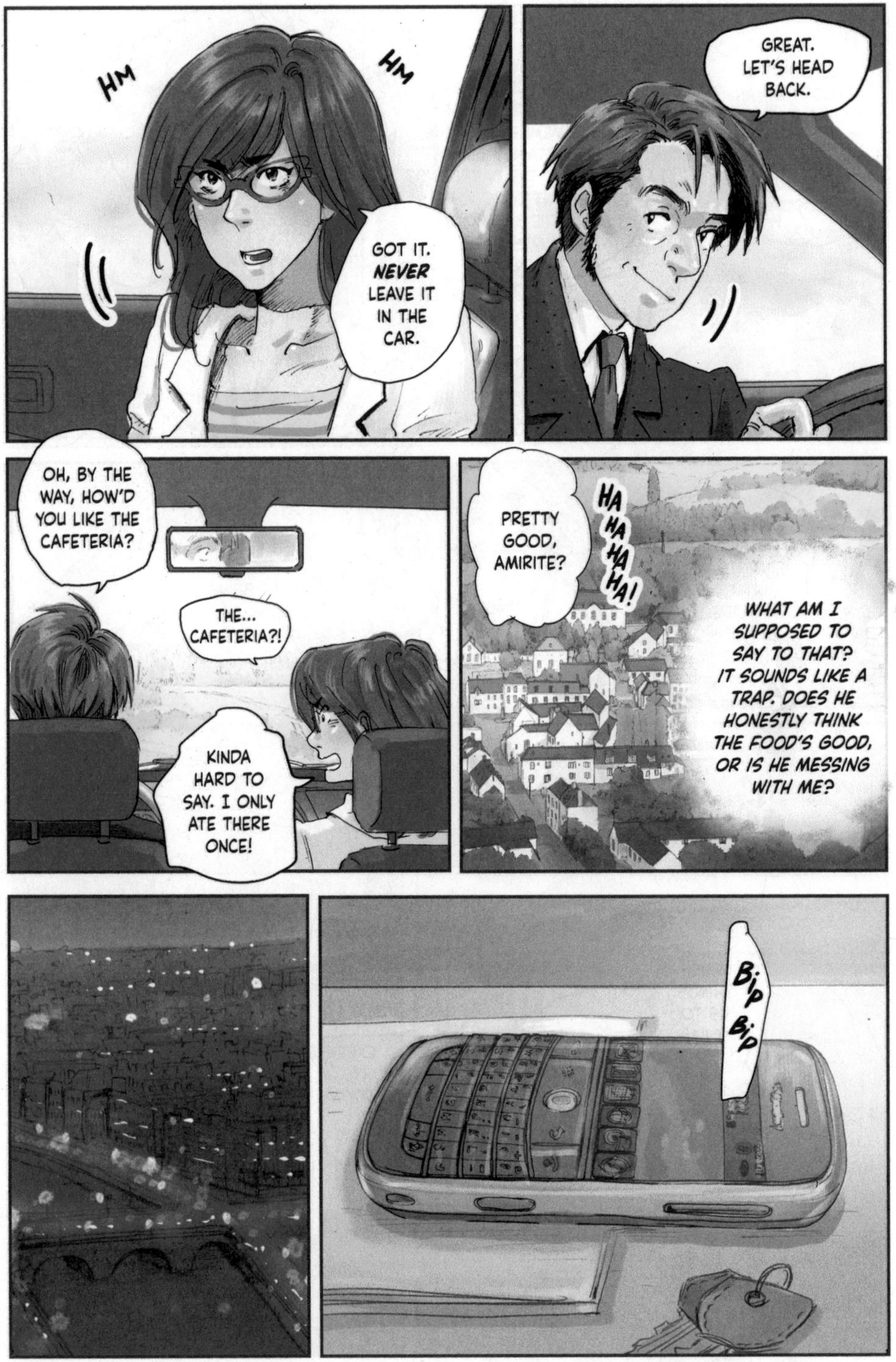
HM
HM
GOT IT. NEVER LEAVE IT IN THE CAR.
GREAT. LET'S HEAD BACK.
OH, BY THE WAY, HOW'D YOU LIKE THE CAFETERIA?
THE... CAFETERIA?!
KINDA HARD TO SAY. I ONLY ATE THERE ONCE!
PRETTY GOOD, AMIRITE?
HA HA HA HA HA!
WHAT AM I SUPPOSED TO SAY TO THAT? IT SOUNDS LIKE A TRAP. DOES HE HONESTLY THINK THE FOOD'S GOOD, OR IS HE MESSING WITH ME?
Bip Bip

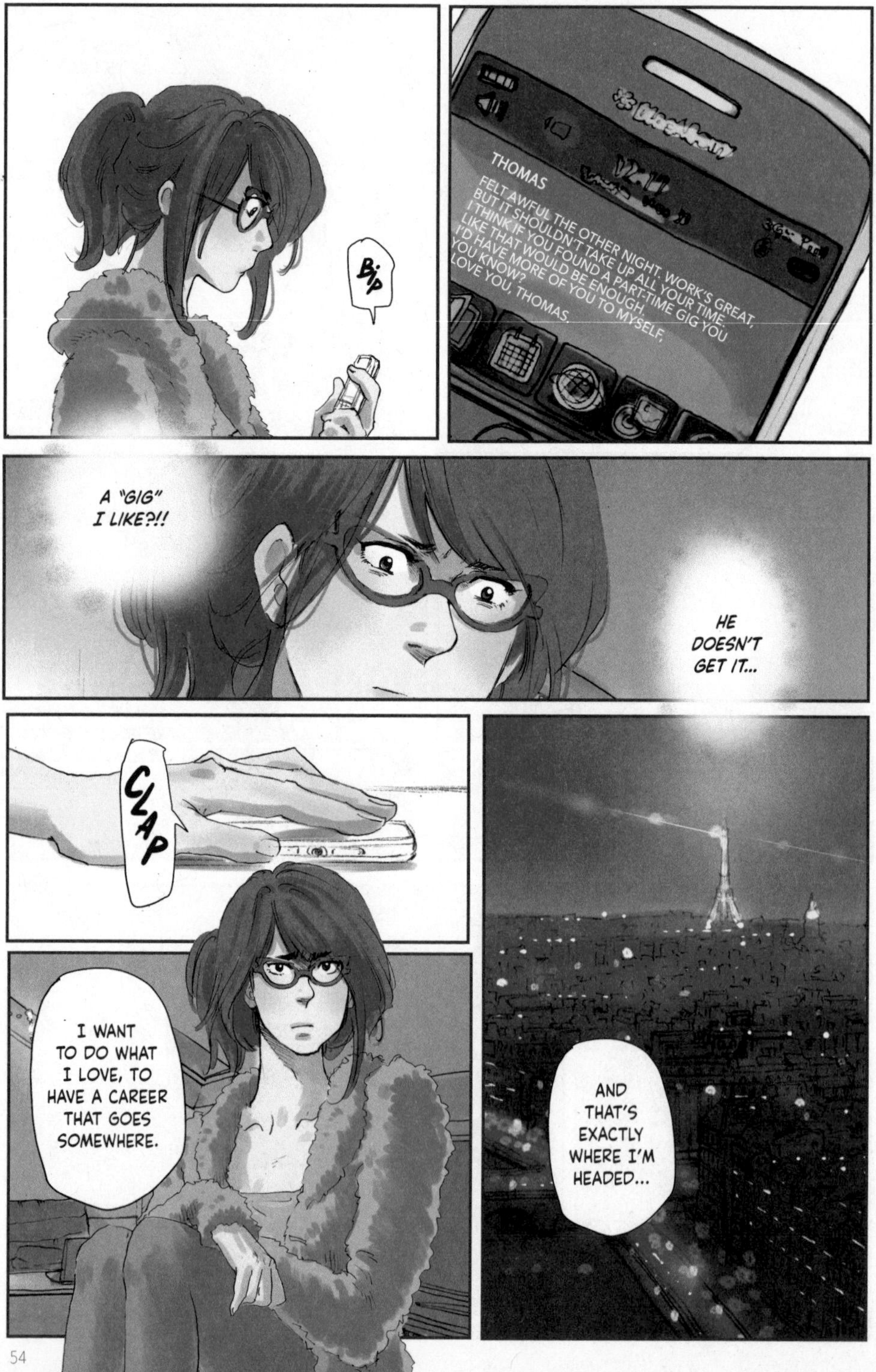
BIP
THOMAS
FELT AWFUL THE OTHER NIGHT. WORK'S GREAT, BUT IT SHOULDN'T TAKE UP ALL YOUR TIME. I THINK IF YOU FOUND A PART-TIME GIG YOU LIKE THAT WOULD BE ENOUGH. I'D HAVE MORE OF YOU TO MYSELF, YOU KNOW?
LOVE YOU, THOMAS.
A "GIG" I LIKE?!!
HE DOESN'T GET IT...
CLAP
I WANT TO DO WHAT I LOVE, TO HAVE A CAREER THAT GOES SOMEWHERE.
AND THAT'S EXACTLY WHERE I'M HEADED...

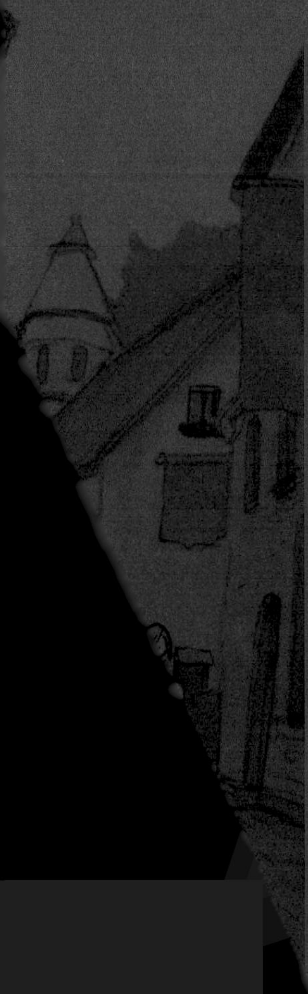

CHAPTER 3

SCALES AND ARPEGGIOS

GOOD MORNING, YOU MUST BE MR. BILLARD?

AH, THERE YOU ARE.

I WASN'T EXPECTING SOMEONE SO YOUTHFUL.

I'M EMMANUELLE MAISONNEUVE. IT'S A PLEASURE TO MEET YOU.

OUR FIRST STOP FOR THE DAY IS A STANDALONE RESTAURANT, WHICH MEANS THERE ARE

NO GUEST ROOMS TO INSPECT. THAT SHOULD MAKE FOR AN EASY START.

YOU'VE GOT THE PROCEDURE DOWN, I TAKE IT?

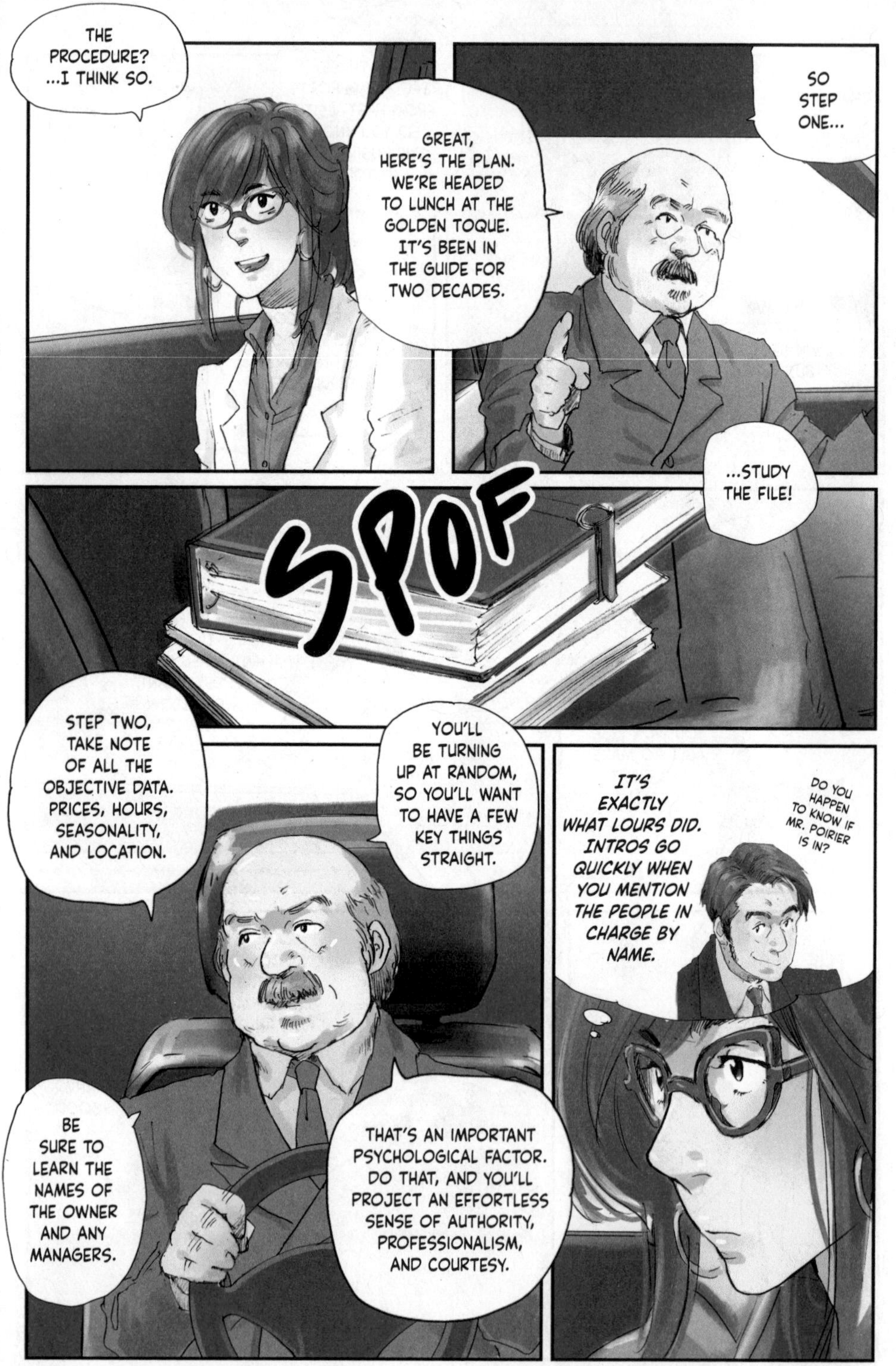
THE PROCEDURE? ...I THINK SO.
GREAT, HERE'S THE PLAN. WE'RE HEADED TO LUNCH AT THE GOLDEN TOQUE. IT'S BEEN IN THE GUIDE FOR TWO DECADES.
SO STEP ONE...
...STUDY THE FILE!
SPOF
STEP TWO, TAKE NOTE OF ALL THE OBJECTIVE DATA. PRICES, HOURS, SEASONALITY, AND LOCATION.
YOU'LL BE TURNING UP AT RANDOM, SO YOU'LL WANT TO HAVE A FEW KEY THINGS STRAIGHT.
BE SURE TO LEARN THE NAMES OF THE OWNER AND ANY MANAGERS.
THAT'S AN IMPORTANT PSYCHOLOGICAL FACTOR. DO THAT, AND YOU'LL PROJECT AN EFFORTLESS SENSE OF AUTHORITY, PROFESSIONALISM, AND COURTESY.
IT'S EXACTLY WHAT LOURS DID. INTROS GO QUICKLY WHEN YOU MENTION THE PEOPLE IN CHARGE BY NAME.
DO YOU HAPPEN TO KNOW IF MR. POIRIER IS IN?

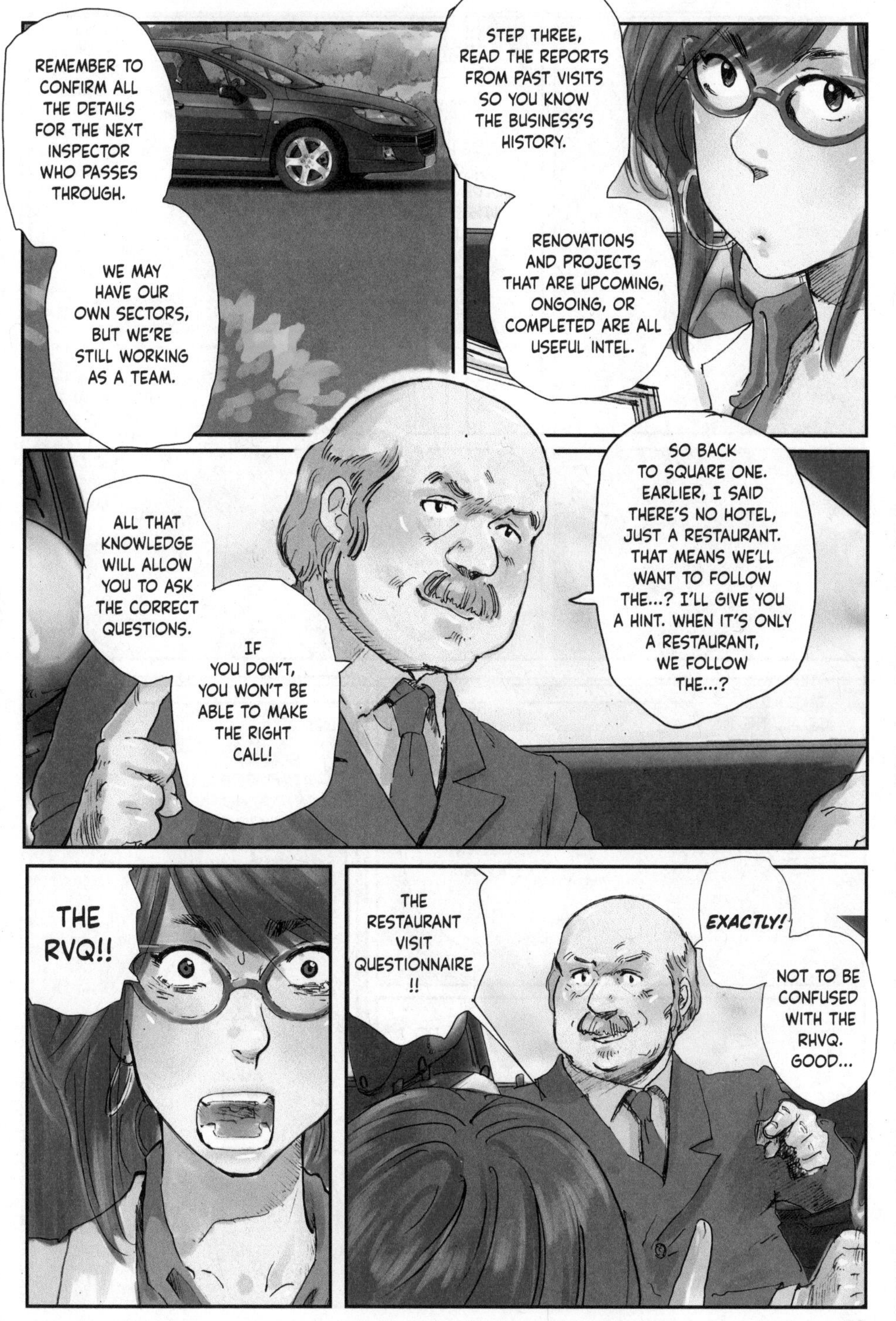
REMEMBER TO CONFIRM ALL THE DETAILS FOR THE NEXT INSPECTOR WHO PASSES THROUGH.
WE MAY HAVE OUR OWN SECTORS, BUT WE'RE STILL WORKING AS A TEAM.
STEP THREE, READ THE REPORTS FROM PAST VISITS SO YOU KNOW THE BUSINESS'S HISTORY.
RENOVATIONS AND PROJECTS THAT ARE UPCOMING, ONGOING, OR COMPLETED ARE ALL USEFUL INTEL.
ALL THAT KNOWLEDGE WILL ALLOW YOU TO ASK THE CORRECT QUESTIONS.
IF YOU DON'T, YOU WON'T BE ABLE TO MAKE THE RIGHT CALL!
SO BACK TO SQUARE ONE. EARLIER, I SAID THERE'S NO HOTEL, JUST A RESTAURANT. THAT MEANS WE'LL WANT TO FOLLOW THE...? I'LL GIVE YOU A HINT. WHEN IT'S ONLY A RESTAURANT, WE FOLLOW THE...?
THE RVQ!!
THE RESTAURANT VISIT QUESTIONNAIRE !!
EXACTLY!
NOT TO BE CONFUSED WITH THE RHVQ. GOOD...

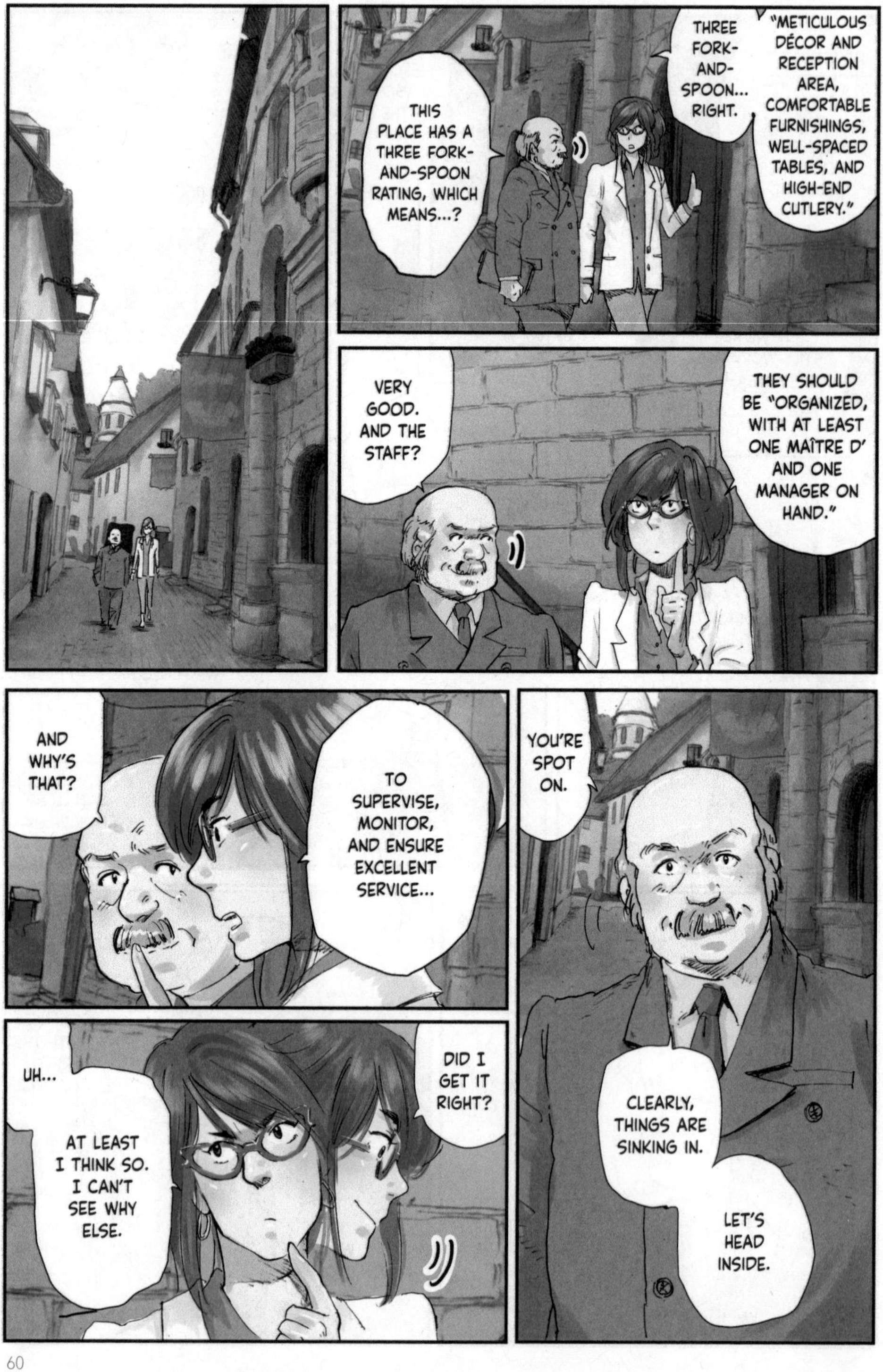

THIS PLACE HAS A THREE FORK-AND-SPOON RATING, WHICH MEANS...?
THREE FORK-AND-SPOON... RIGHT.
"METICULOUS DÉCOR AND RECEPTION AREA, COMFORTABLE FURNISHINGS, WELL-SPACED TABLES, AND HIGH-END CUTLERY."
VERY GOOD. AND THE STAFF?
THEY SHOULD BE "ORGANIZED, WITH AT LEAST ONE MAÎTRE D' AND ONE MANAGER ON HAND."
AND WHY'S THAT?
TO SUPERVISE, MONITOR, AND ENSURE EXCELLENT SERVICE...
YOU'RE SPOT ON.
CLEARLY, THINGS ARE SINKING IN.
LET'S HEAD INSIDE.
UH...
AT LEAST I THINK SO. I CAN'T SEE WHY ELSE.
DID I GET IT RIGHT?

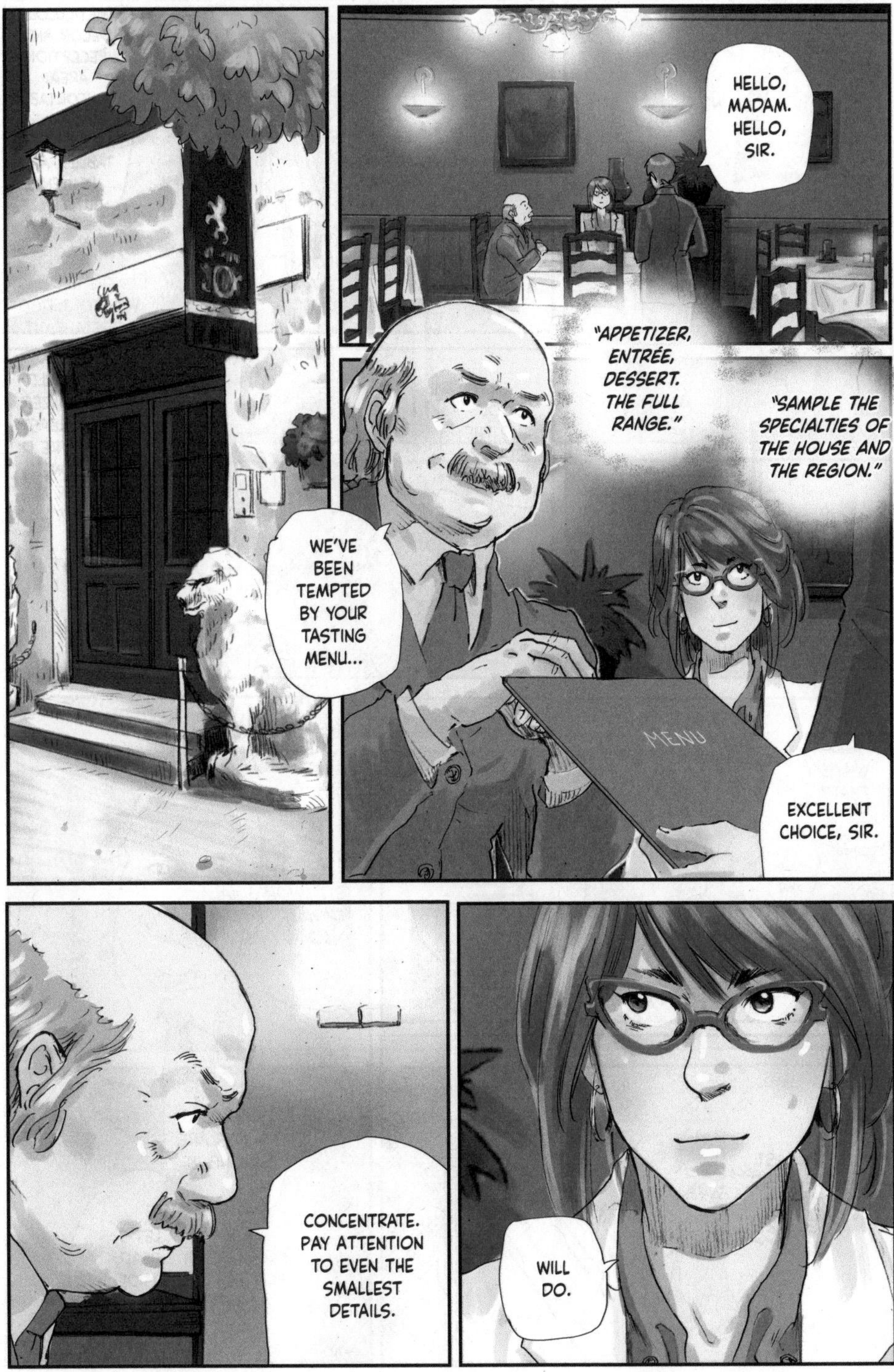
HELLO, MADAM. HELLO, SIR.
WE'VE BEEN TEMPTED BY YOUR TASTING MENU...
"APPETIZER, ENTRÉE, DESSERT. THE FULL RANGE."
"SAMPLE THE SPECIALTIES OF THE HOUSE AND THE REGION."
MENU
EXCELLENT CHOICE, SIR.
CONCENTRATE. PAY ATTENTION TO EVEN THE SMALLEST DETAILS.
WILL DO.

IT'S LESS INTERESTING IF WE ORDER THE SAME THINGS.

BUT SINCE YOU'RE IN TRAINING, WE'LL WANT TO COMPARE NOTES.

WE'RE ALSO ON A TIGHTER BUDGET. THIS WAY, WE CAN AVOID ORDERING À LA CARTE.

YOU CAN'T GO WRONG WITH A TASTING MENU.

Menu
Veal and foie gras paté
jar of oyster mushrooms with citrus
Red Label Limousin* beef tenderloin,
potato madeleine
caramelized shallot and Corrèze wine
Artisan cheese boar
Fourme d'Ambert** co
e salad with balsamic
f caramelized Limous
with
wild honey
Meadowsweet
with
caramel sauce

IT'S OFTEN THE BEST WAY TO JUDGE A RESTAURANT. THE GREATEST CHEFS ARE TO BE JUDGED BY THEIR SMALLEST PLATES.

NEXT, WE HAVE...

THE LIMOUSIN BEEF TENDERLOIN, POTATO MADELEINE, AND A SHALLOT WITH CORRÈZE WINE REDUCTION.

AFTER THAT NEVER-ENDING FOIE GRAS...

THIS FEELS A BIT UNORIGINAL. THOUGH IT DOES LOOK GREAT.

MADELEINE'S A BIT DENSE. SAUCE IS TOO ACIDIC.

BETTER LEAVE SOME ROOM FOR WHAT'S COMING NEXT.

62 * LIMOUSIN IS A RURAL AREA IN CENTRAL FRANCE, FAMOUS FOR ITS CHESTNUT-RED BEEF CATTLE.
** FOURME D'AMBERT IS A SEMI-HARD COW'S MILK BLUE CHEESE MADE IN AUVERGNE.

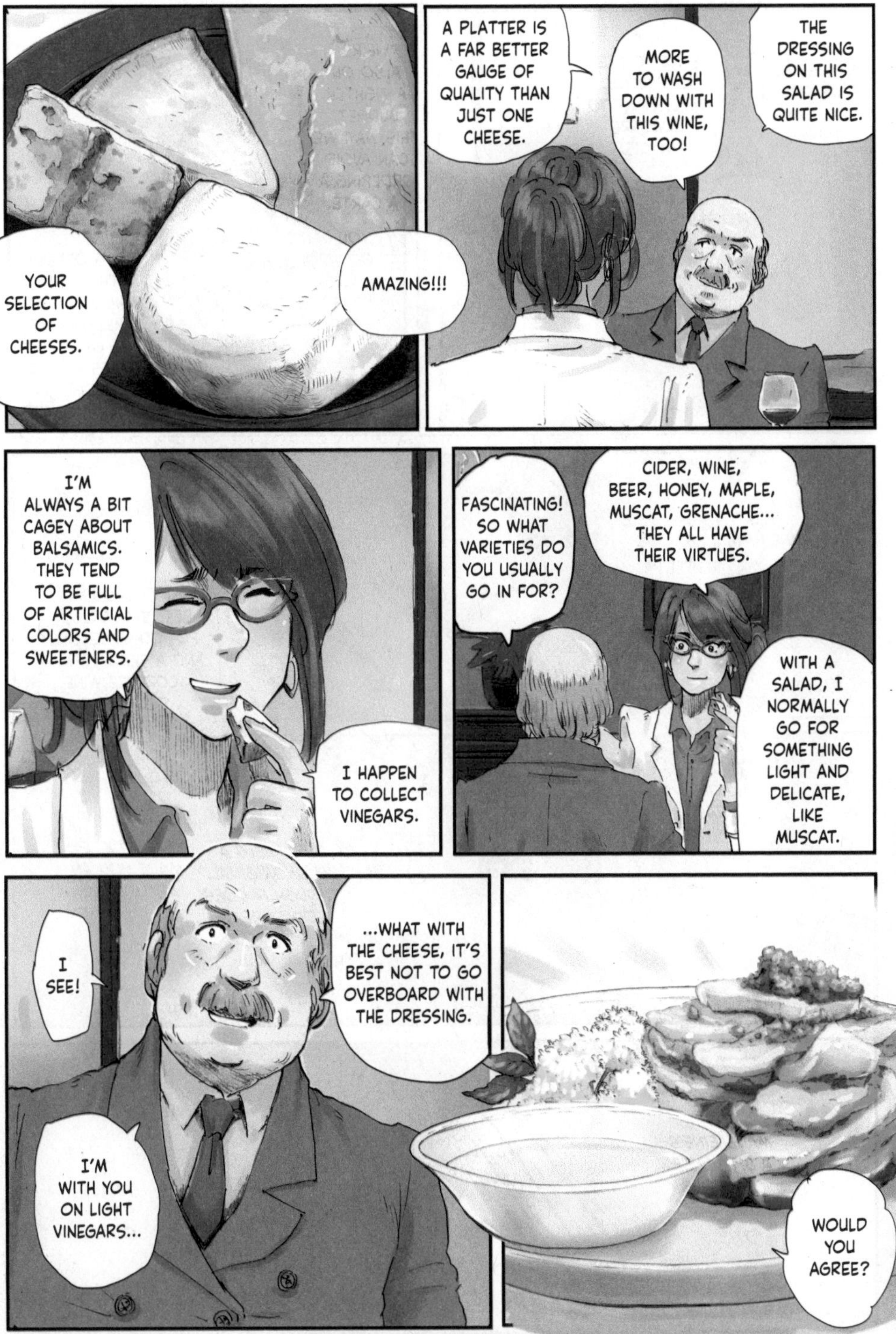
YOUR SELECTION OF CHEESES.
AMAZING!!!
A PLATTER IS A FAR BETTER GAUGE OF QUALITY THAN JUST ONE CHEESE.
MORE TO WASH DOWN WITH THIS WINE, TOO!
THE DRESSING ON THIS SALAD IS QUITE NICE.
I'M ALWAYS A BIT CAGEY ABOUT BALSAMICS. THEY TEND TO BE FULL OF ARTIFICIAL COLORS AND SWEETENERS.
I HAPPEN TO COLLECT VINEGARS.
FASCINATING! SO WHAT VARIETIES DO YOU USUALLY GO IN FOR?
CIDER, WINE, BEER, HONEY, MAPLE, MUSCAT, GRENACHE... THEY ALL HAVE THEIR VIRTUES.
WITH A SALAD, I NORMALLY GO FOR SOMETHING LIGHT AND DELICATE, LIKE MUSCAT.
I SEE!
I'M WITH YOU ON LIGHT VINEGARS...
...WHAT WITH THE CHEESE, IT'S BEST NOT TO GO OVERBOARD WITH THE DRESSING.
WOULD YOU AGREE?

I JUST LOVE APPLES.

ESPECIALLY REINETTES* ...

...SWEET, YET SLIGHTLY SOUR...

...FIRM, BUT MELTS LIKE CANDY!

DO YOU COLLECT APPLES AS WELL?

* REINETTE, MEANING "LITTLE QUEEN," IS A TERM THAT COVERS A LARGE FAMILY OF HERITAGE APPLE CULTIVARS.

HM? NO, BUT THERE'S A SPICE IN HERE ...

...IT'S SUBTLE, BUT IT CHANGES EVERY-THING...

SWEETIE, I MADE YOU AN APPLE CAKE.

MMM! GRANNY!

IT SMELLS SO GOOD!

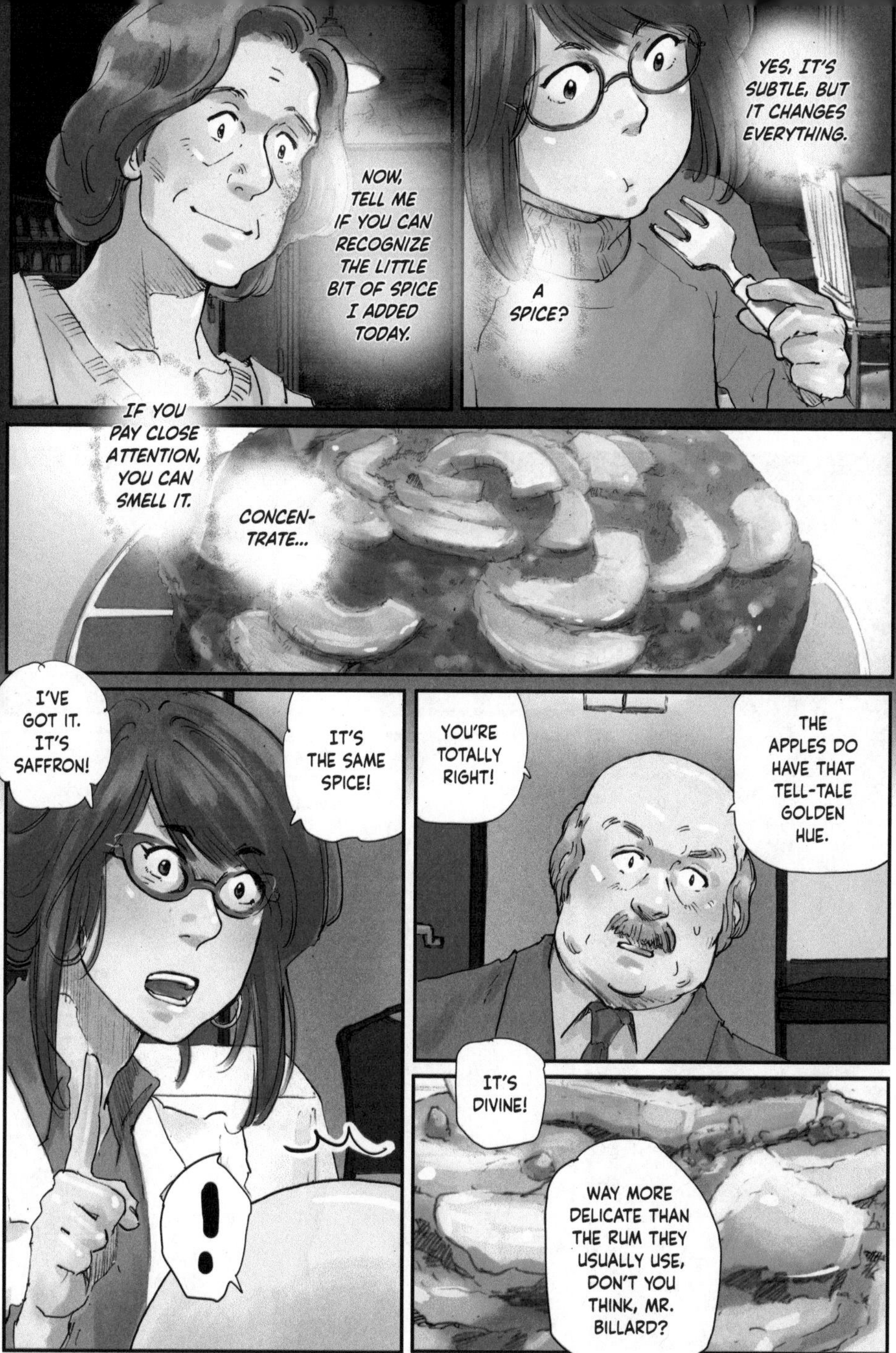
NOW, TELL ME IF YOU CAN RECOGNIZE THE LITTLE BIT OF SPICE I ADDED TODAY.
A SPICE?
YES, IT'S SUBTLE, BUT IT CHANGES EVERYTHING.
IF YOU PAY CLOSE ATTENTION, YOU CAN SMELL IT.
CONCEN-TRATE...
I'VE GOT IT. IT'S SAFFRON!
IT'S THE SAME SPICE!
!
YOU'RE TOTALLY RIGHT!
THE APPLES DO HAVE THAT TELL-TALE GOLDEN HUE.
IT'S DIVINE!
WAY MORE DELICATE THAN THE RUM THEY USUALLY USE, DON'T YOU THINK, MR. BILLARD?

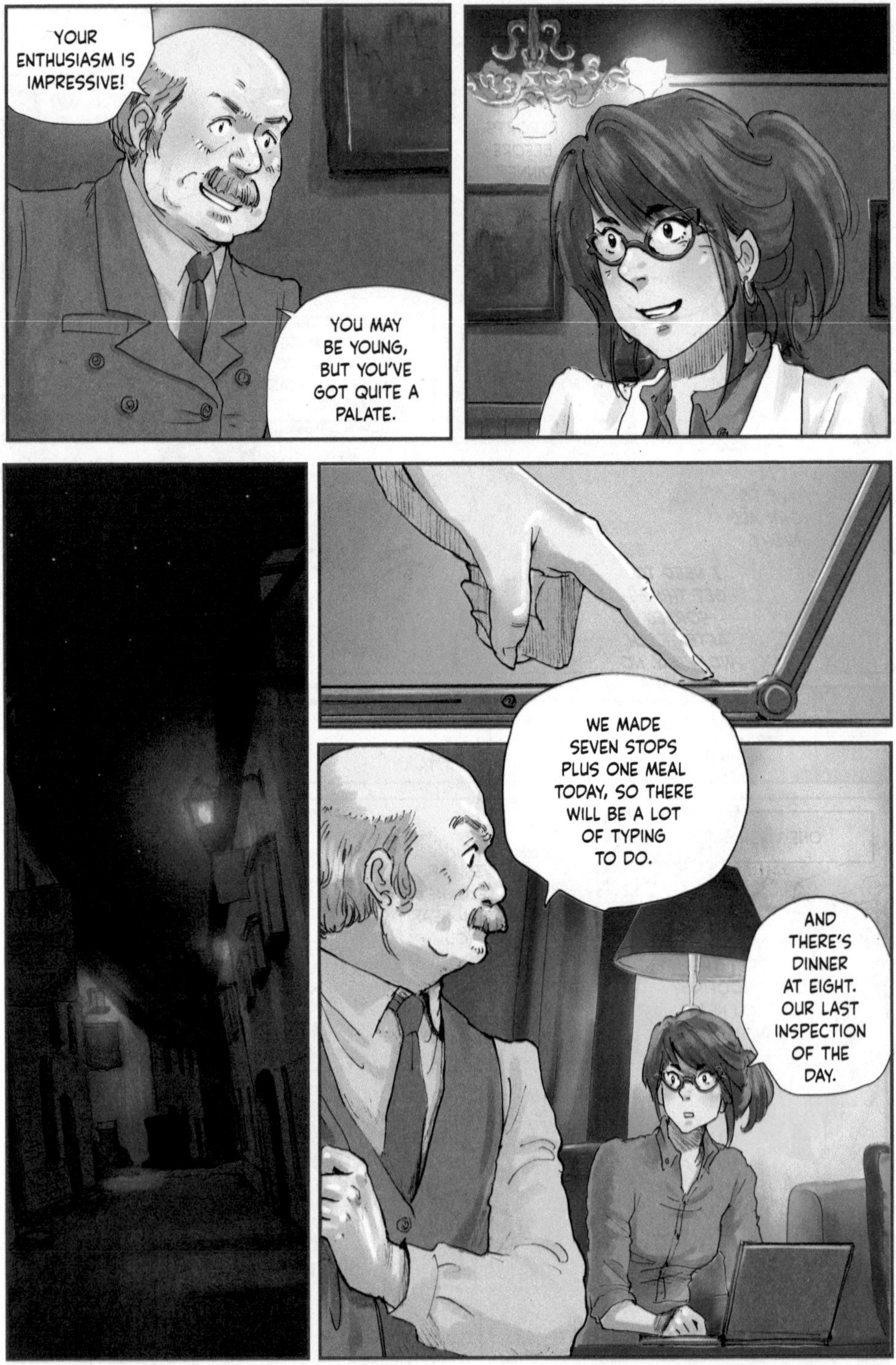
YOUR ENTHUSIASM IS IMPRESSIVE!
YOU MAY BE YOUNG, BUT YOU'VE GOT QUITE A PALATE.
WE MADE SEVEN STOPS PLUS ONE MEAL TODAY, SO THERE WILL BE A LOT OF TYPING TO DO.
AND THERE'S DINNER AT EIGHT. OUR LAST INSPECTION OF THE DAY.

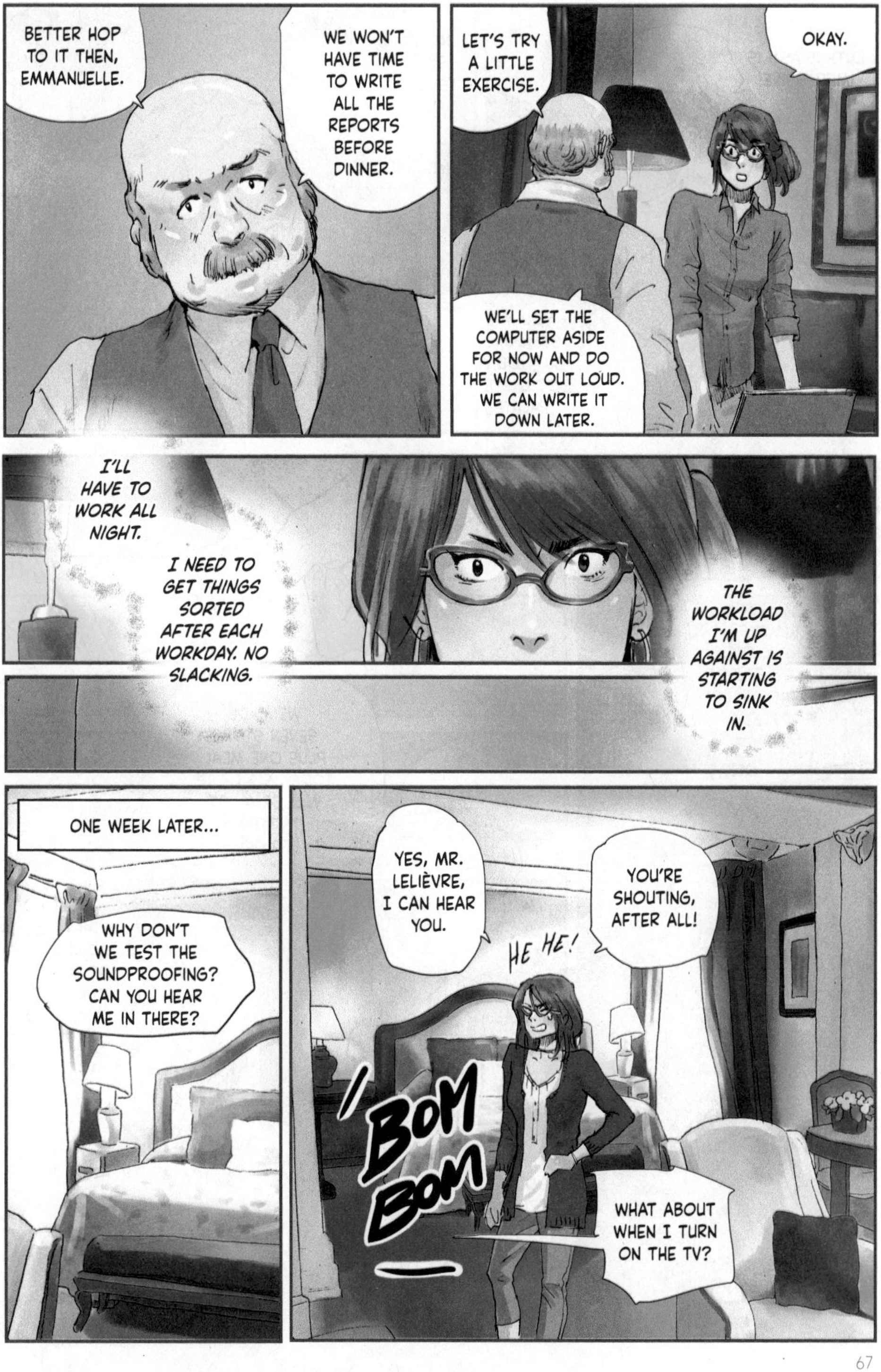
BETTER HOP TO IT THEN, EMMANUELLE.
WE WON'T HAVE TIME TO WRITE ALL THE REPORTS BEFORE DINNER.
LET'S TRY A LITTLE EXERCISE.
OKAY.
WE'LL SET THE COMPUTER ASIDE FOR NOW AND DO THE WORK OUT LOUD. WE CAN WRITE IT DOWN LATER.
I'LL HAVE TO WORK ALL NIGHT.
I NEED TO GET THINGS SORTED AFTER EACH WORKDAY. NO SLACKING.
THE WORKLOAD I'M UP AGAINST IS STARTING TO SINK IN.
ONE WEEK LATER...
WHY DON'T WE TEST THE SOUNDPROOFING? CAN YOU HEAR ME IN THERE?
YES, MR. LELIÈVRE, I CAN HEAR YOU.
YOU'RE SHOUTING, AFTER ALL!
HE HE!
BOM BOM
WHAT ABOUT WHEN I TURN ON THE TV?

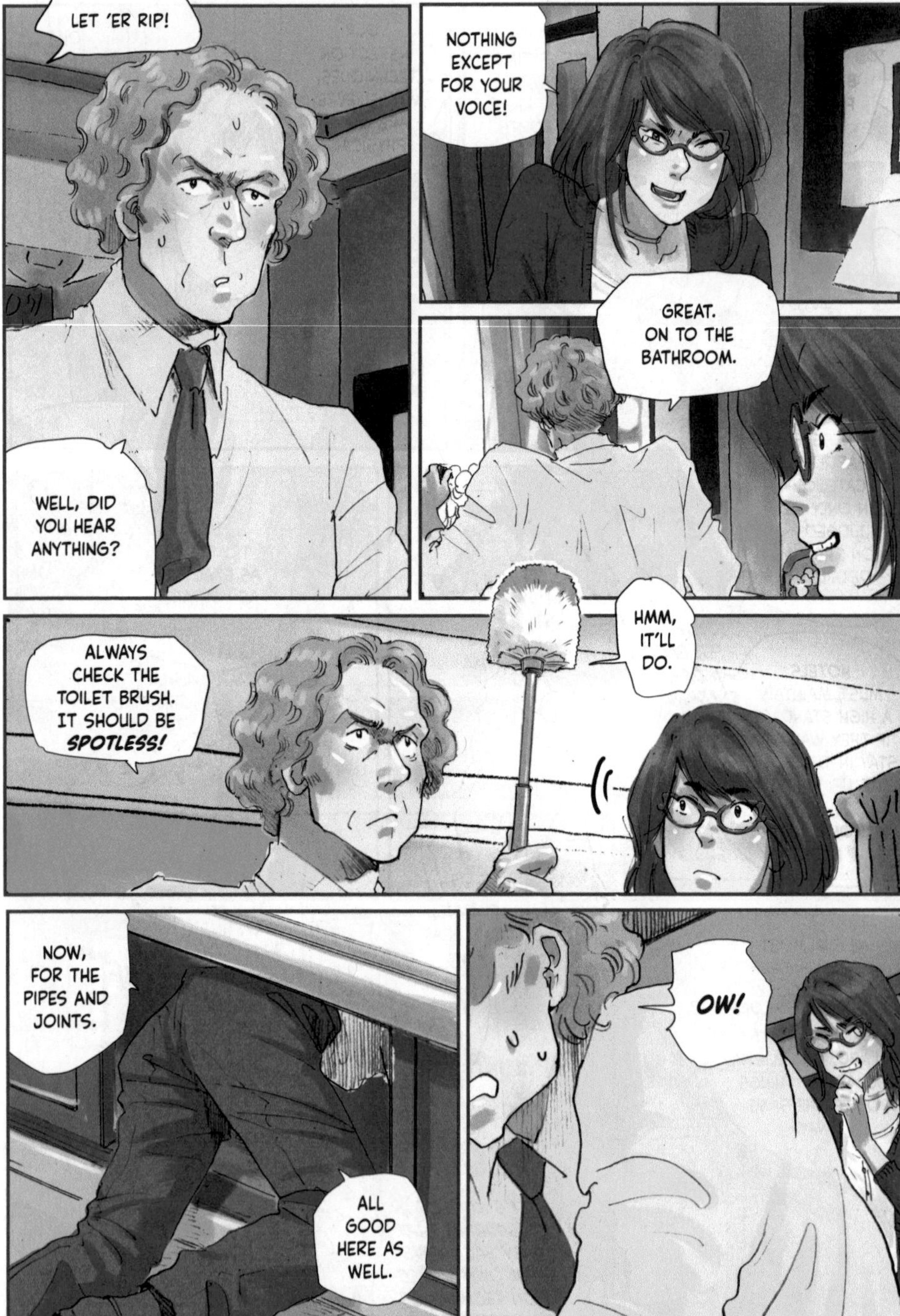

LET 'ER RIP!
WELL, DID YOU HEAR ANYTHING?
NOTHING EXCEPT FOR YOUR VOICE!
GREAT. ON TO THE BATHROOM.
ALWAYS CHECK THE TOILET BRUSH. IT SHOULD BE *SPOTLESS!*
HMM, IT'LL DO.
NOW, FOR THE PIPES AND JOINTS.
ALL GOOD HERE AS WELL.
OW!

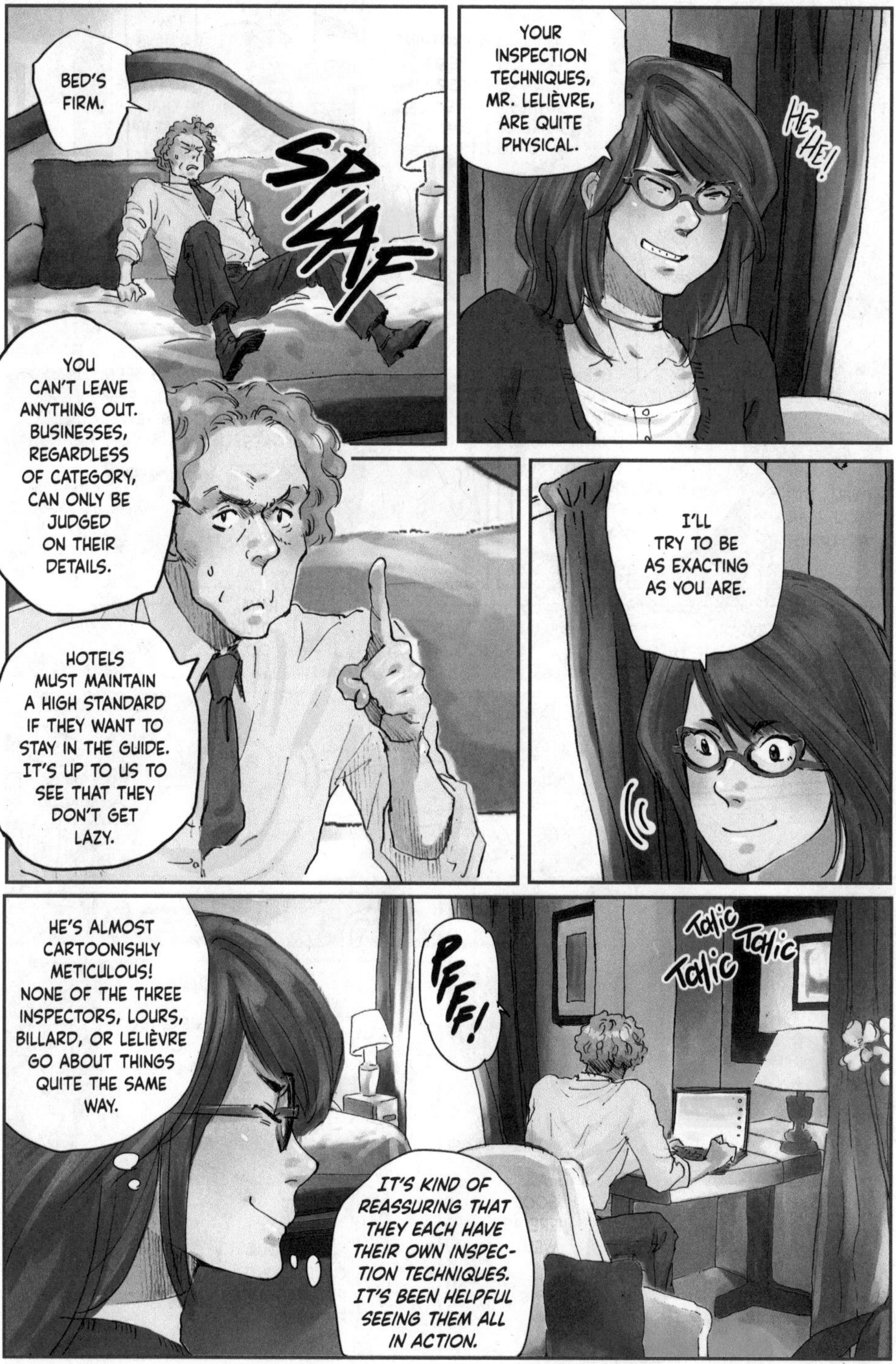
BED'S FIRM.
SPLAF
YOUR INSPECTION TECHNIQUES, MR. LELIÈVRE, ARE QUITE PHYSICAL.
HE HE!
YOU CAN'T LEAVE ANYTHING OUT. BUSINESSES, REGARDLESS OF CATEGORY, CAN ONLY BE JUDGED ON THEIR DETAILS.
HOTELS MUST MAINTAIN A HIGH STANDARD IF THEY WANT TO STAY IN THE GUIDE. IT'S UP TO US TO SEE THAT THEY DON'T GET LAZY.
I'LL TRY TO BE AS EXACTING AS YOU ARE.
HE'S ALMOST CARTOONISHLY METICULOUS! NONE OF THE THREE INSPECTORS, LOURS, BILLARD, OR LELIÈVRE GO ABOUT THINGS QUITE THE SAME WAY.
PFFF!
Tclic Tclic Tclic
IT'S KIND OF REASSURING THAT THEY EACH HAVE THEIR OWN INSPECTION TECHNIQUES. IT'S BEEN HELPFUL SEEING THEM ALL IN ACTION.

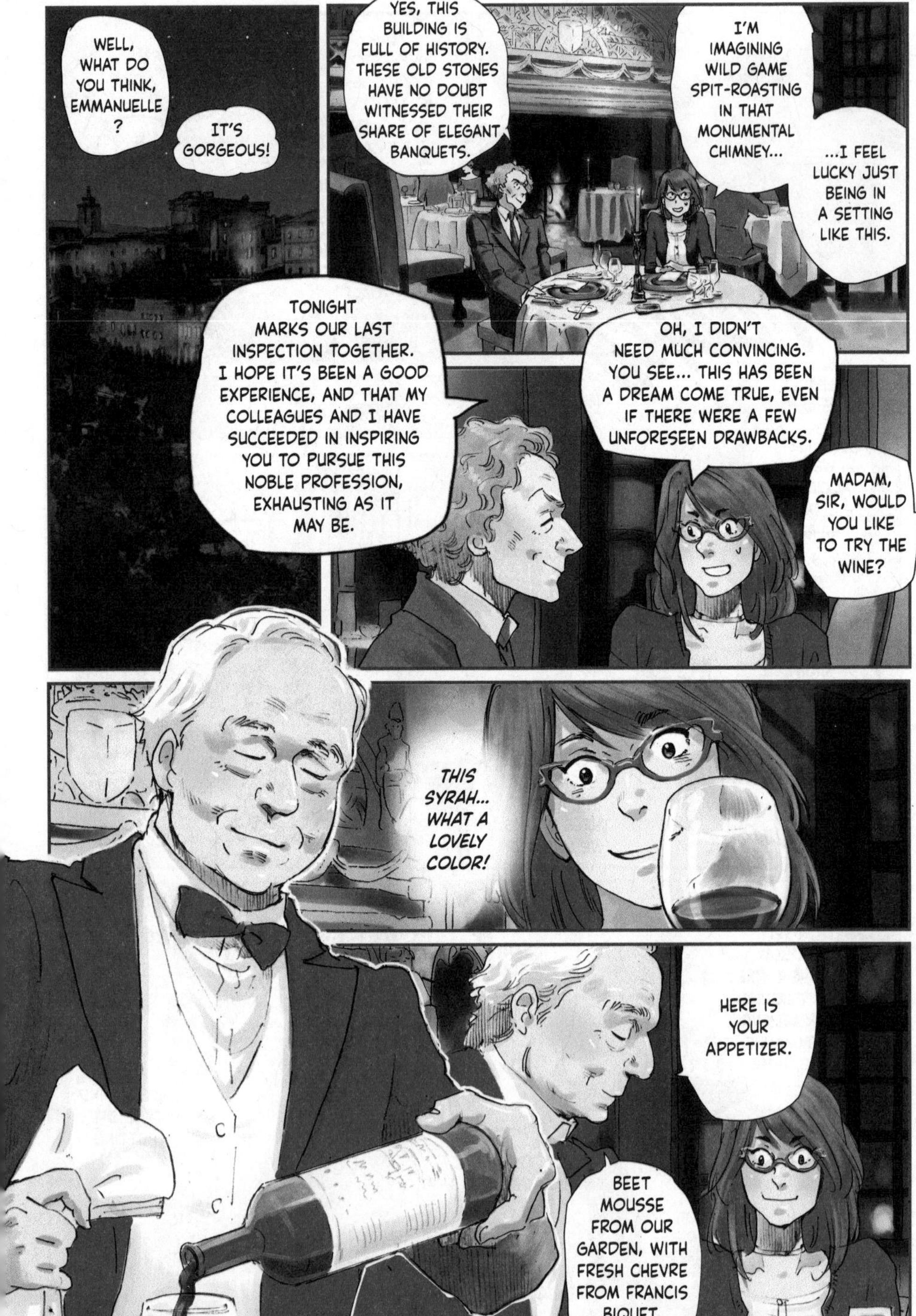
WELL, WHAT DO YOU THINK, EMMANUELLE?
IT'S GORGEOUS!
YES, THIS BUILDING IS FULL OF HISTORY. THESE OLD STONES HAVE NO DOUBT WITNESSED THEIR SHARE OF ELEGANT BANQUETS.
I'M IMAGINING WILD GAME SPIT-ROASTING IN THAT MONUMENTAL CHIMNEY...
...I FEEL LUCKY JUST BEING IN A SETTING LIKE THIS.
TONIGHT MARKS OUR LAST INSPECTION TOGETHER. I HOPE IT'S BEEN A GOOD EXPERIENCE, AND THAT MY COLLEAGUES AND I HAVE SUCCEEDED IN INSPIRING YOU TO PURSUE THIS NOBLE PROFESSION, EXHAUSTING AS IT MAY BE.
OH, I DIDN'T NEED MUCH CONVINCING. YOU SEE... THIS HAS BEEN A DREAM COME TRUE, EVEN IF THERE WERE A FEW UNFORESEEN DRAWBACKS.
MADAM, SIR, WOULD YOU LIKE TO TRY THE WINE?
THIS SYRAH... WHAT A LOVELY COLOR!
HERE IS YOUR APPETIZER.
BEET MOUSSE FROM OUR GARDEN, WITH FRESH CHEVRE FROM FRANCIS BIQUET.

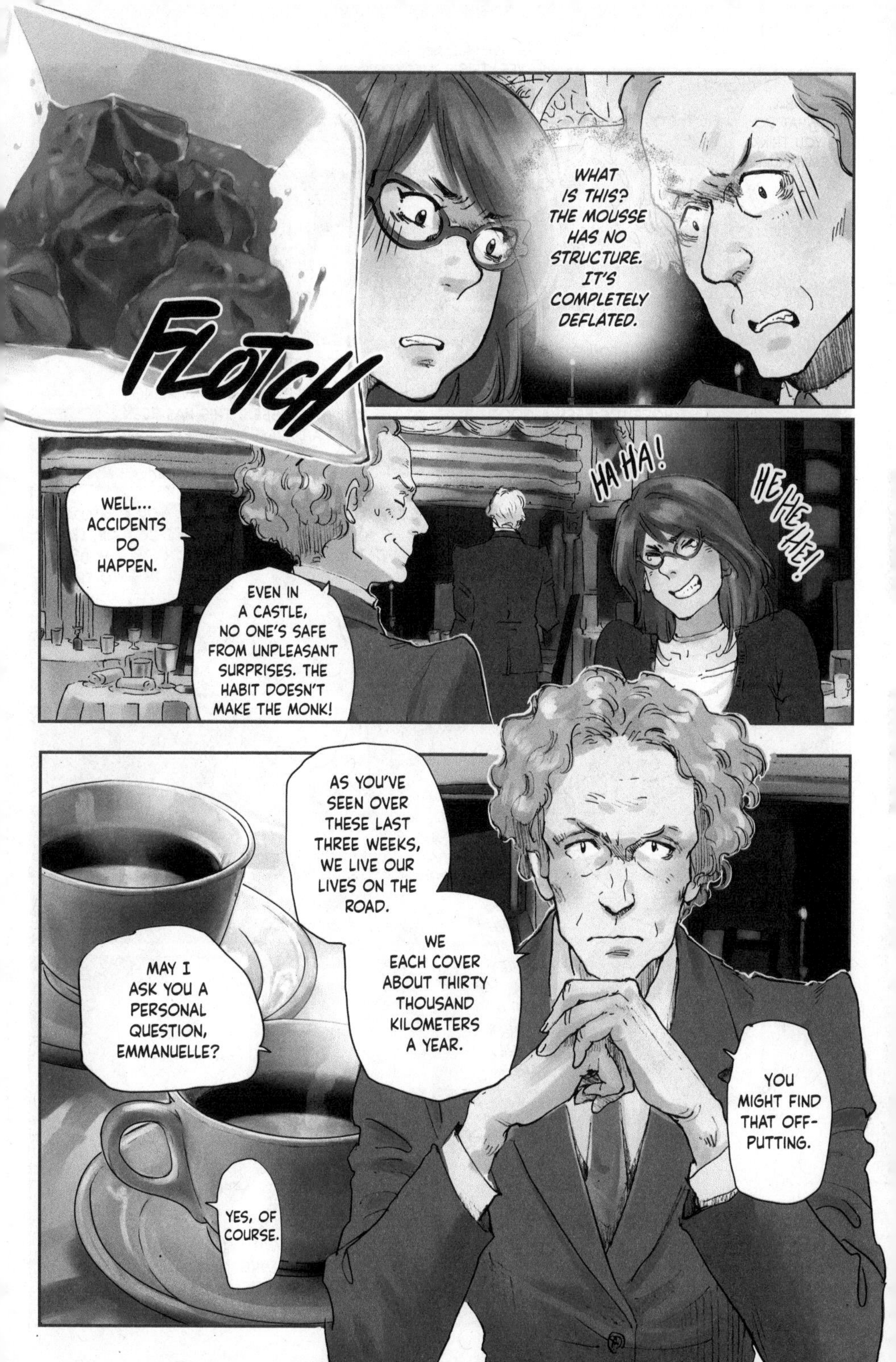
FLOTCH
WHAT IS THIS? THE MOUSSE HAS NO STRUCTURE. IT'S COMPLETELY DEFLATED.
HA HA!
HE HE HE!
WELL... ACCIDENTS DO HAPPEN.
EVEN IN A CASTLE, NO ONE'S SAFE FROM UNPLEASANT SURPRISES. THE HABIT DOESN'T MAKE THE MONK!
AS YOU'VE SEEN OVER THESE LAST THREE WEEKS, WE LIVE OUR LIVES ON THE ROAD.
WE EACH COVER ABOUT THIRTY THOUSAND KILOMETERS A YEAR.
YOU MIGHT FIND THAT OFF-PUTTING.
MAY I ASK YOU A PERSONAL QUESTION, EMMANUELLE?
YES, OF COURSE.

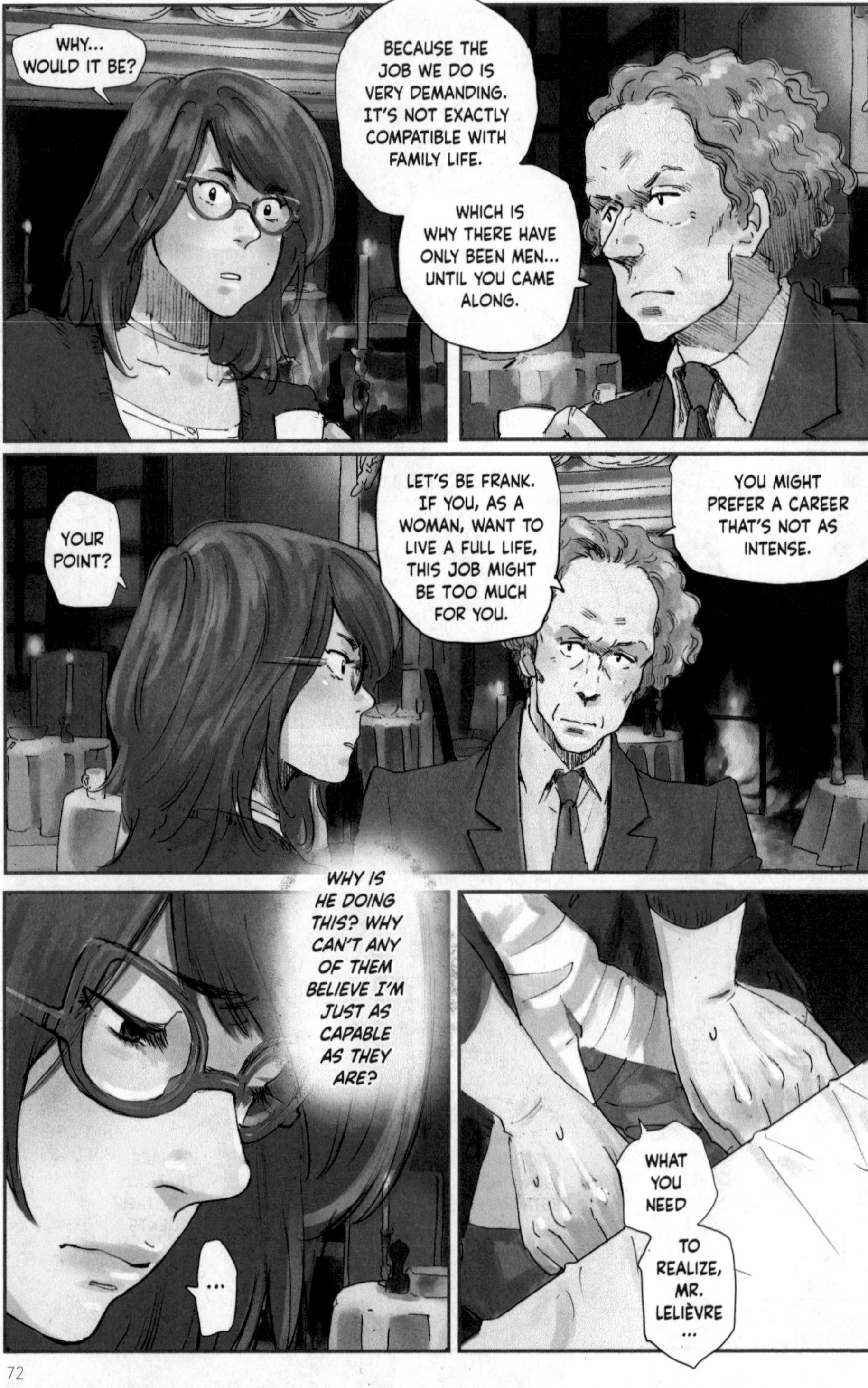
WHY... WOULD IT BE?
BECAUSE THE JOB WE DO IS VERY DEMANDING. IT'S NOT EXACTLY COMPATIBLE WITH FAMILY LIFE.
WHICH IS WHY THERE HAVE ONLY BEEN MEN... UNTIL YOU CAME ALONG.
YOUR POINT?
LET'S BE FRANK. IF YOU, AS A WOMAN, WANT TO LIVE A FULL LIFE, THIS JOB MIGHT BE TOO MUCH FOR YOU.
YOU MIGHT PREFER A CAREER THAT'S NOT AS INTENSE.
WHY IS HE DOING THIS? WHY CAN'T ANY OF THEM BELIEVE I'M JUST AS CAPABLE AS THEY ARE?
...
WHAT YOU NEED
TO REALIZE, MR. LELIÈVRE ...

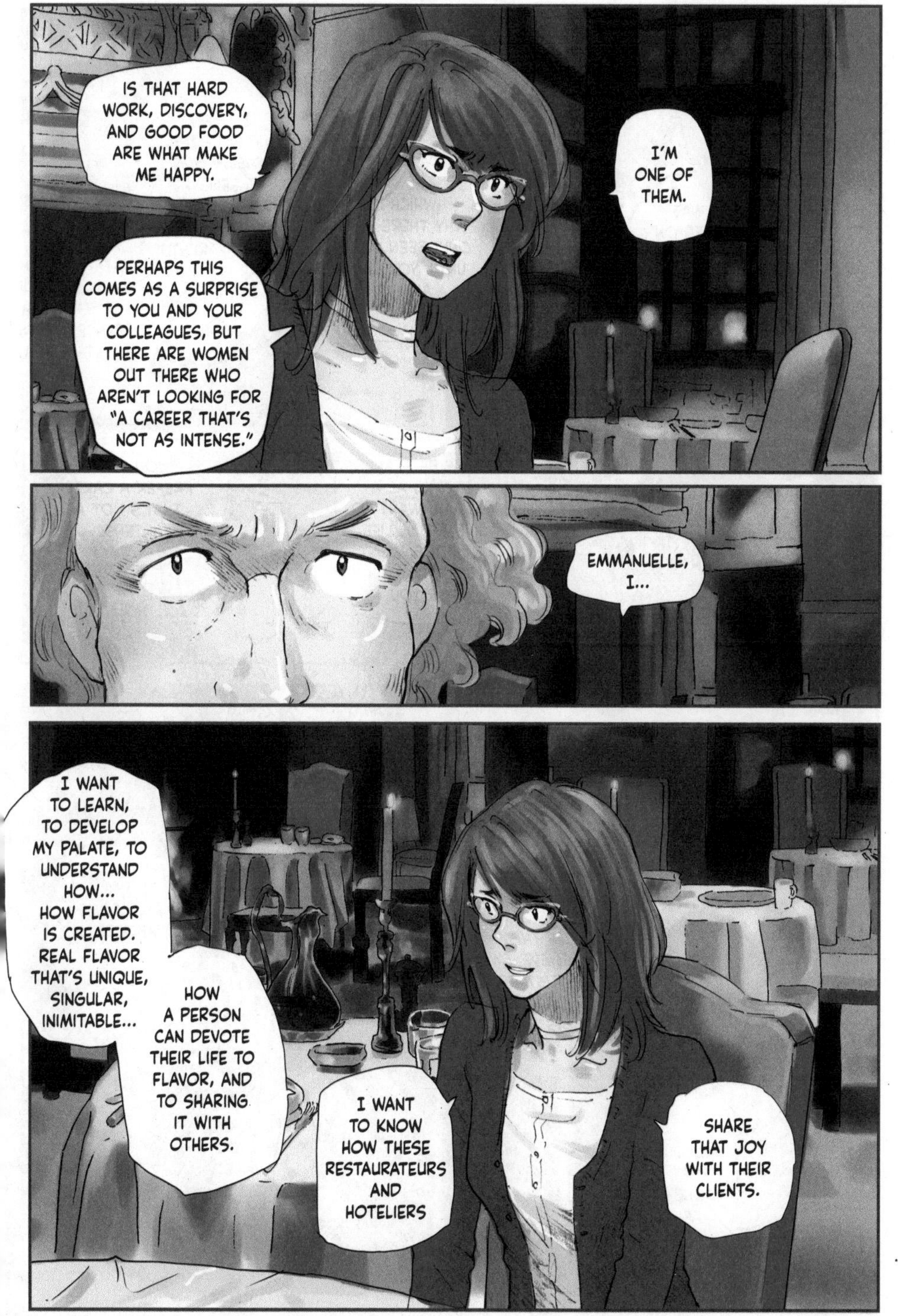
IS THAT HARD WORK, DISCOVERY, AND GOOD FOOD ARE WHAT MAKE ME HAPPY.
I'M ONE OF THEM.
PERHAPS THIS COMES AS A SURPRISE TO YOU AND YOUR COLLEAGUES, BUT THERE ARE WOMEN OUT THERE WHO AREN'T LOOKING FOR "A CAREER THAT'S NOT AS INTENSE."
EMMANUELLE, I...
I WANT TO LEARN, TO DEVELOP MY PALATE, TO UNDERSTAND HOW... HOW FLAVOR IS CREATED. REAL FLAVOR THAT'S UNIQUE, SINGULAR, INIMITABLE...
HOW A PERSON CAN DEVOTE THEIR LIFE TO FLAVOR, AND TO SHARING IT WITH OTHERS.
I WANT TO KNOW HOW THESE RESTAURATEURS AND HOTELIERS
SHARE THAT JOY WITH THEIR CLIENTS.

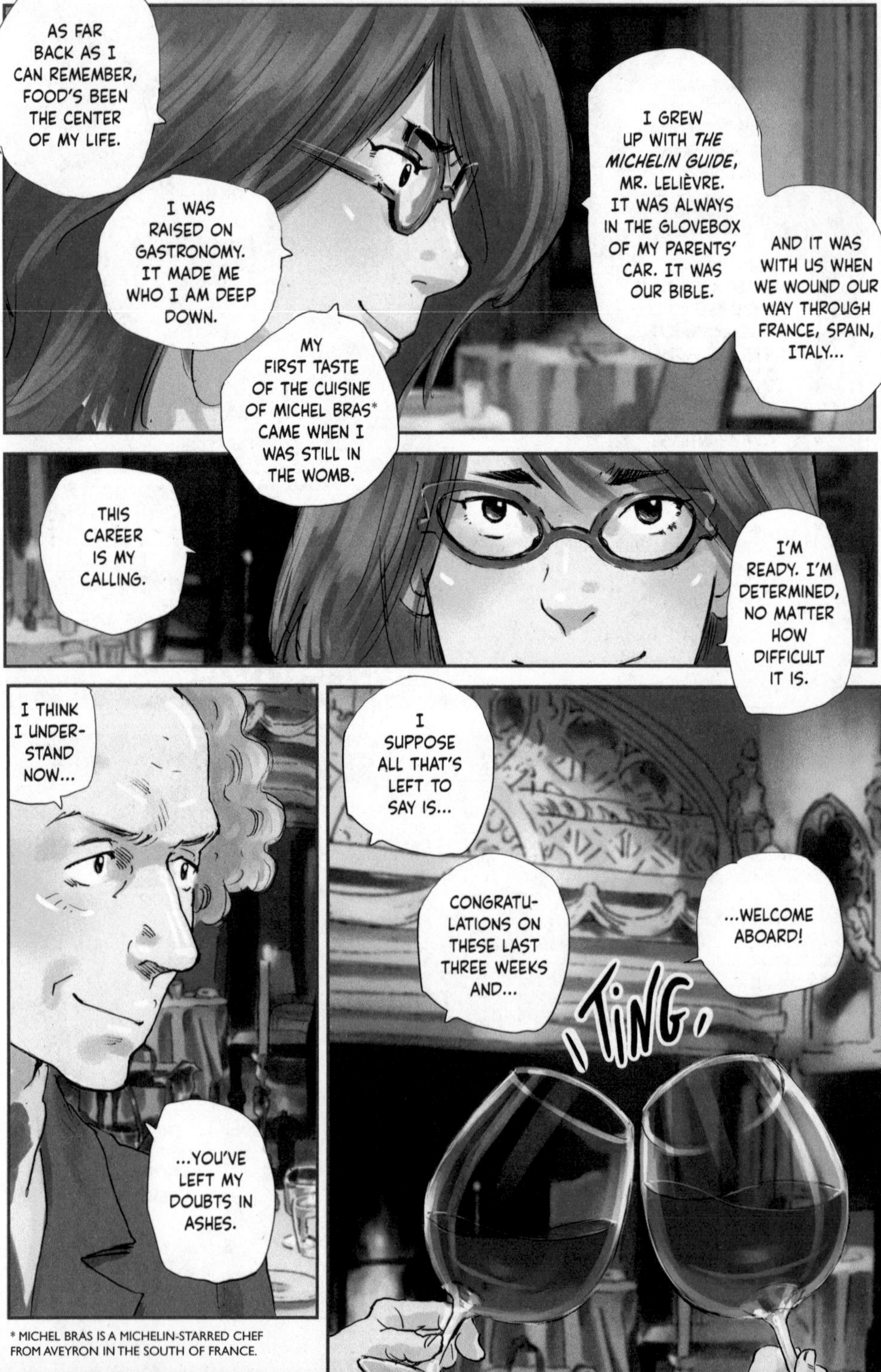
AS FAR BACK AS I CAN REMEMBER, FOOD'S BEEN THE CENTER OF MY LIFE.
I WAS RAISED ON GASTRONOMY. IT MADE ME WHO I AM DEEP DOWN.
MY FIRST TASTE OF THE CUISINE OF MICHEL BRAS* CAME WHEN I WAS STILL IN THE WOMB.
I GREW UP WITH *THE MICHELIN GUIDE*, MR. LELIÈVRE. IT WAS ALWAYS IN THE GLOVEBOX OF MY PARENTS' CAR. IT WAS OUR BIBLE.
AND IT WAS WITH US WHEN WE WOUND OUR WAY THROUGH FRANCE, SPAIN, ITALY...
THIS CAREER IS MY CALLING.
I'M READY. I'M DETERMINED, NO MATTER HOW DIFFICULT IT IS.
I THINK I UNDER-STAND NOW...
...YOU'VE LEFT MY DOUBTS IN ASHES.
I SUPPOSE ALL THAT'S LEFT TO SAY IS...
CONGRATU-LATIONS ON THESE LAST THREE WEEKS AND...
...WELCOME ABOARD!
TING

* MICHEL BRAS IS A MICHELIN-STARRED CHEF FROM AVEYRON IN THE SOUTH OF FRANCE.

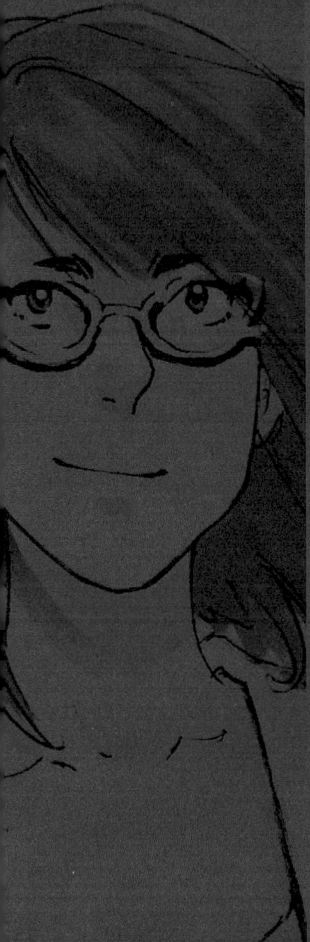

CHAPTER 4

INITIATION

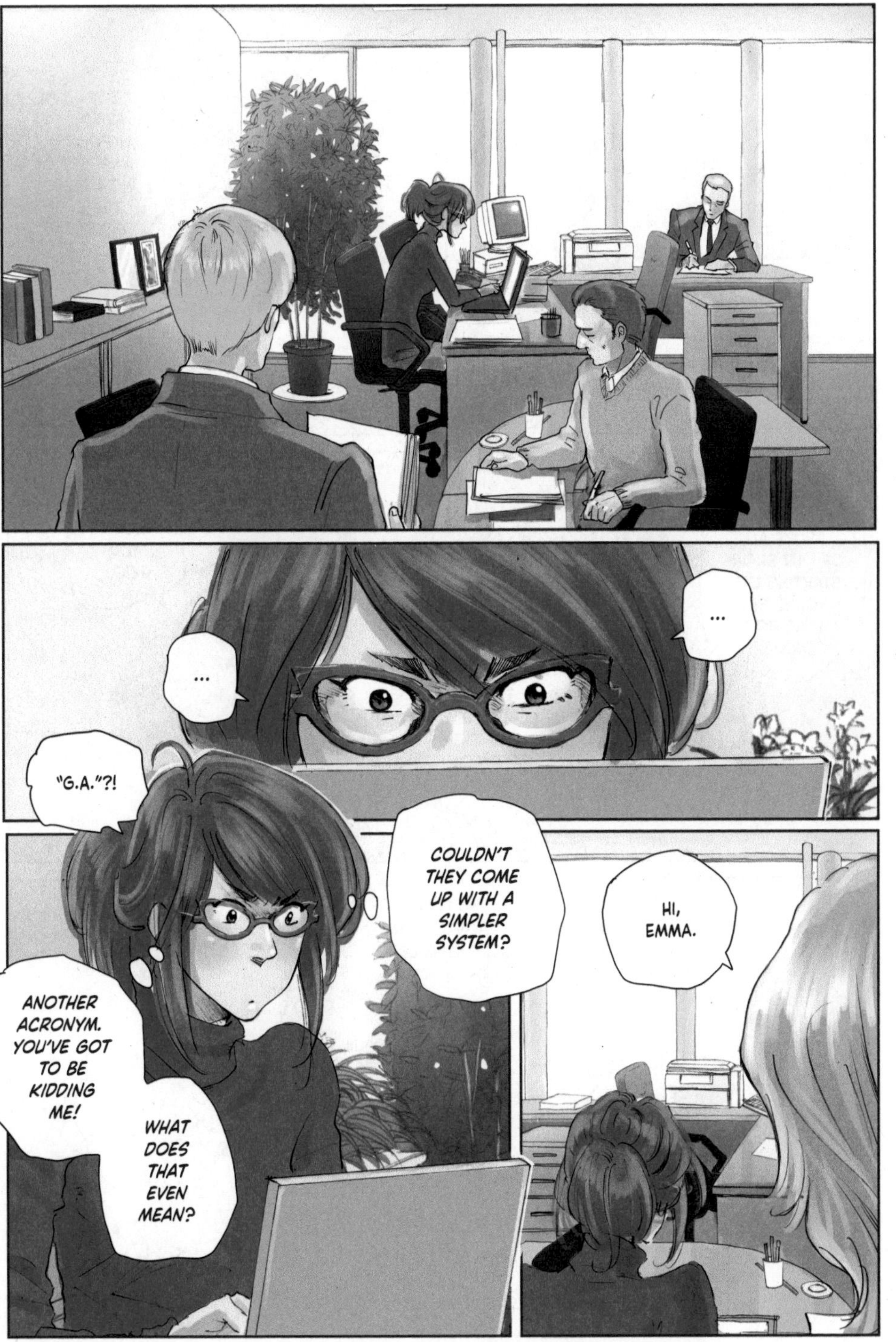
...
...
"G.A."?!
ANOTHER ACRONYM. YOU'VE GOT TO BE KIDDING ME!
WHAT DOES THAT EVEN MEAN?
COULDN'T THEY COME UP WITH A SIMPLER SYSTEM?
HI, EMMA.

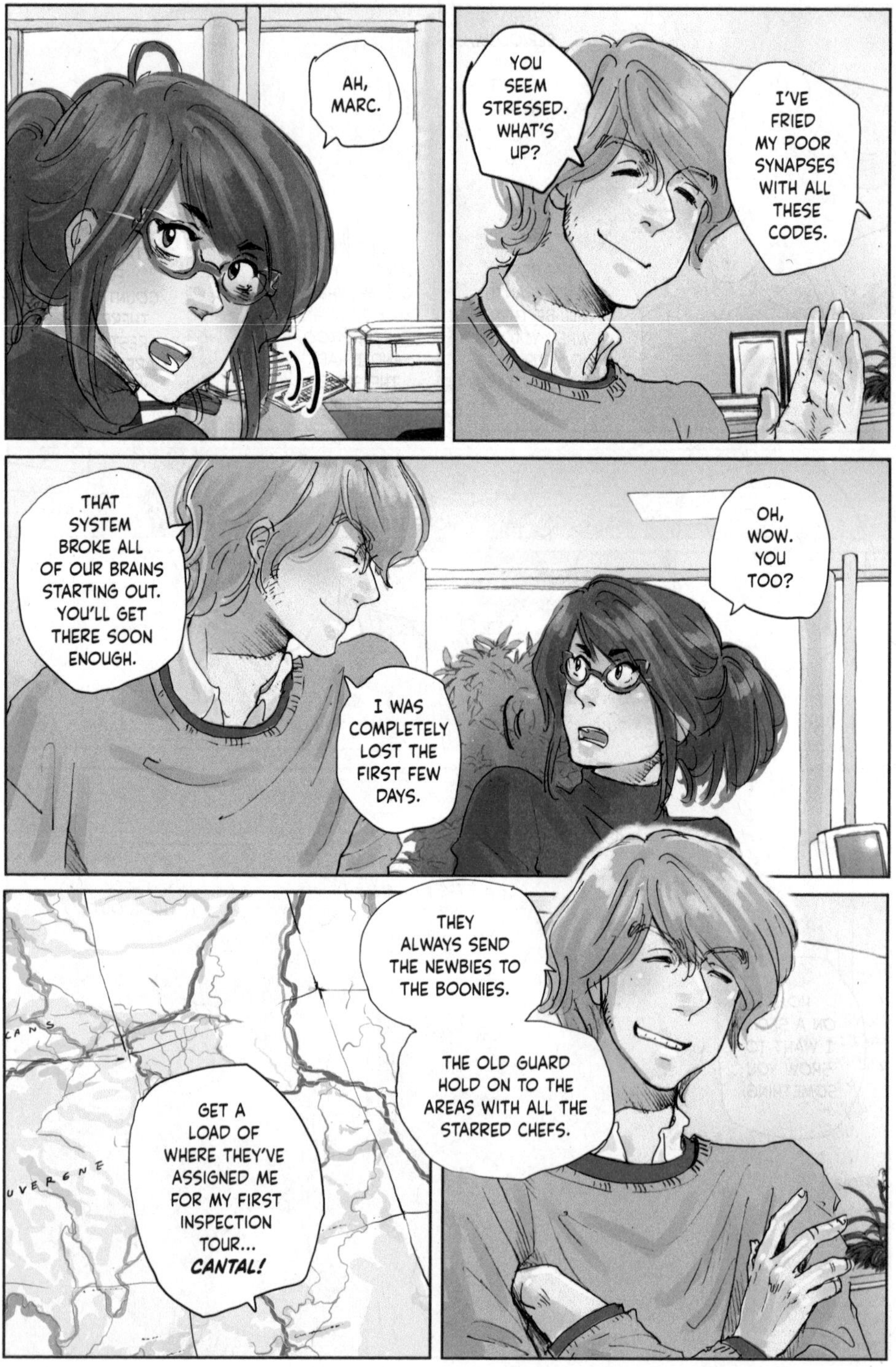
AH, MARC.
YOU SEEM STRESSED. WHAT'S UP?
I'VE FRIED MY POOR SYNAPSES WITH ALL THESE CODES.
THAT SYSTEM BROKE ALL OF OUR BRAINS STARTING OUT. YOU'LL GET THERE SOON ENOUGH.
OH, WOW. YOU TOO?
I WAS COMPLETELY LOST THE FIRST FEW DAYS.
GET A LOAD OF WHERE THEY'VE ASSIGNED ME FOR MY FIRST INSPECTION TOUR... ***CANTAL!***
THEY ALWAYS SEND THE NEWBIES TO THE BOONIES.
THE OLD GUARD HOLD ON TO THE AREAS WITH ALL THE STARRED CHEFS.

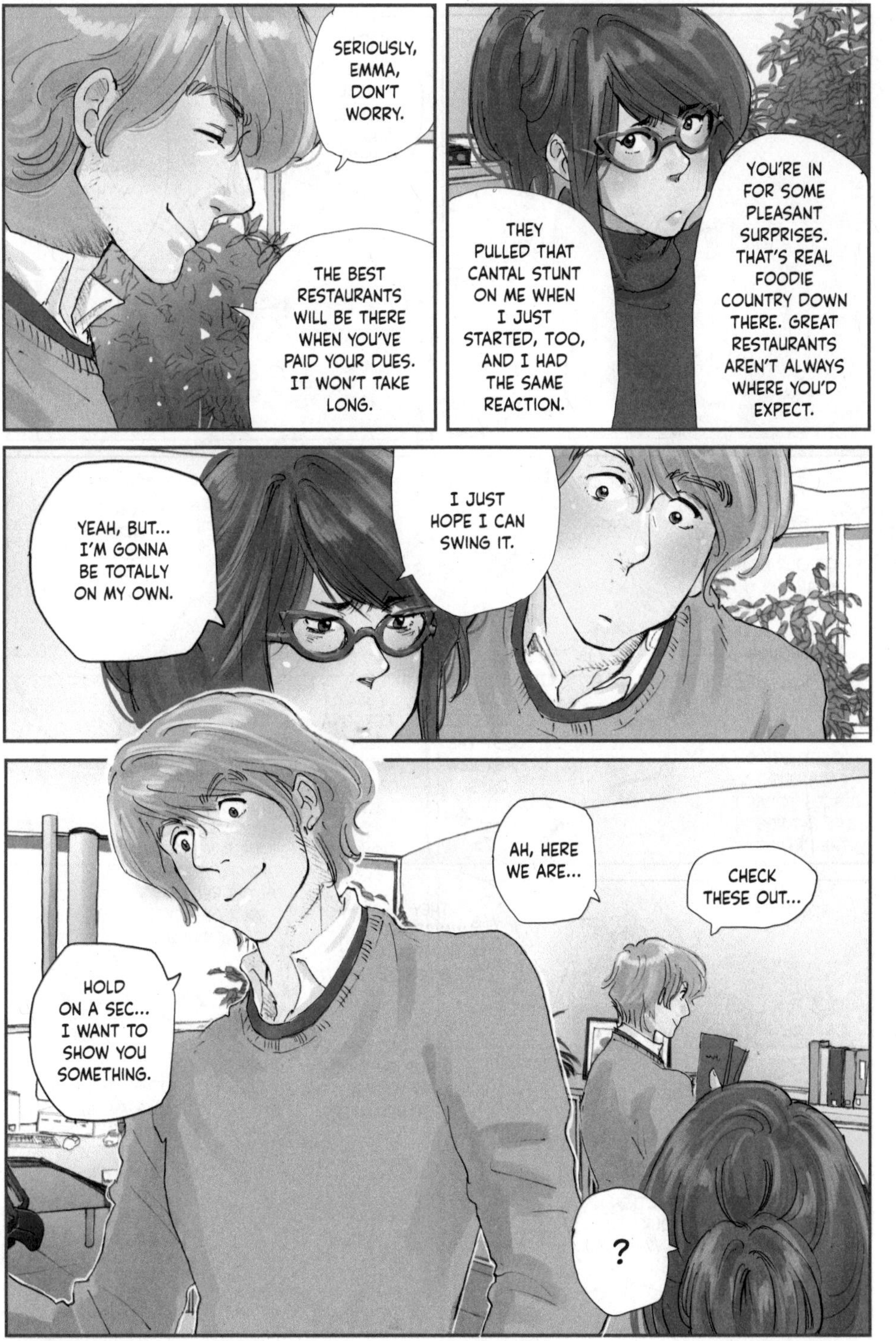
SERIOUSLY, EMMA, DON'T WORRY.
THE BEST RESTAURANTS WILL BE THERE WHEN YOU'VE PAID YOUR DUES. IT WON'T TAKE LONG.
THEY PULLED THAT CANTAL STUNT ON ME WHEN I JUST STARTED, TOO, AND I HAD THE SAME REACTION.
YOU'RE IN FOR SOME PLEASANT SURPRISES. THAT'S REAL FOODIE COUNTRY DOWN THERE. GREAT RESTAURANTS AREN'T ALWAYS WHERE YOU'D EXPECT.
YEAH, BUT... I'M GONNA BE TOTALLY ON MY OWN.
I JUST HOPE I CAN SWING IT.
HOLD ON A SEC... I WANT TO SHOW YOU SOMETHING.
AH, HERE WE ARE...
CHECK THESE OUT...
?

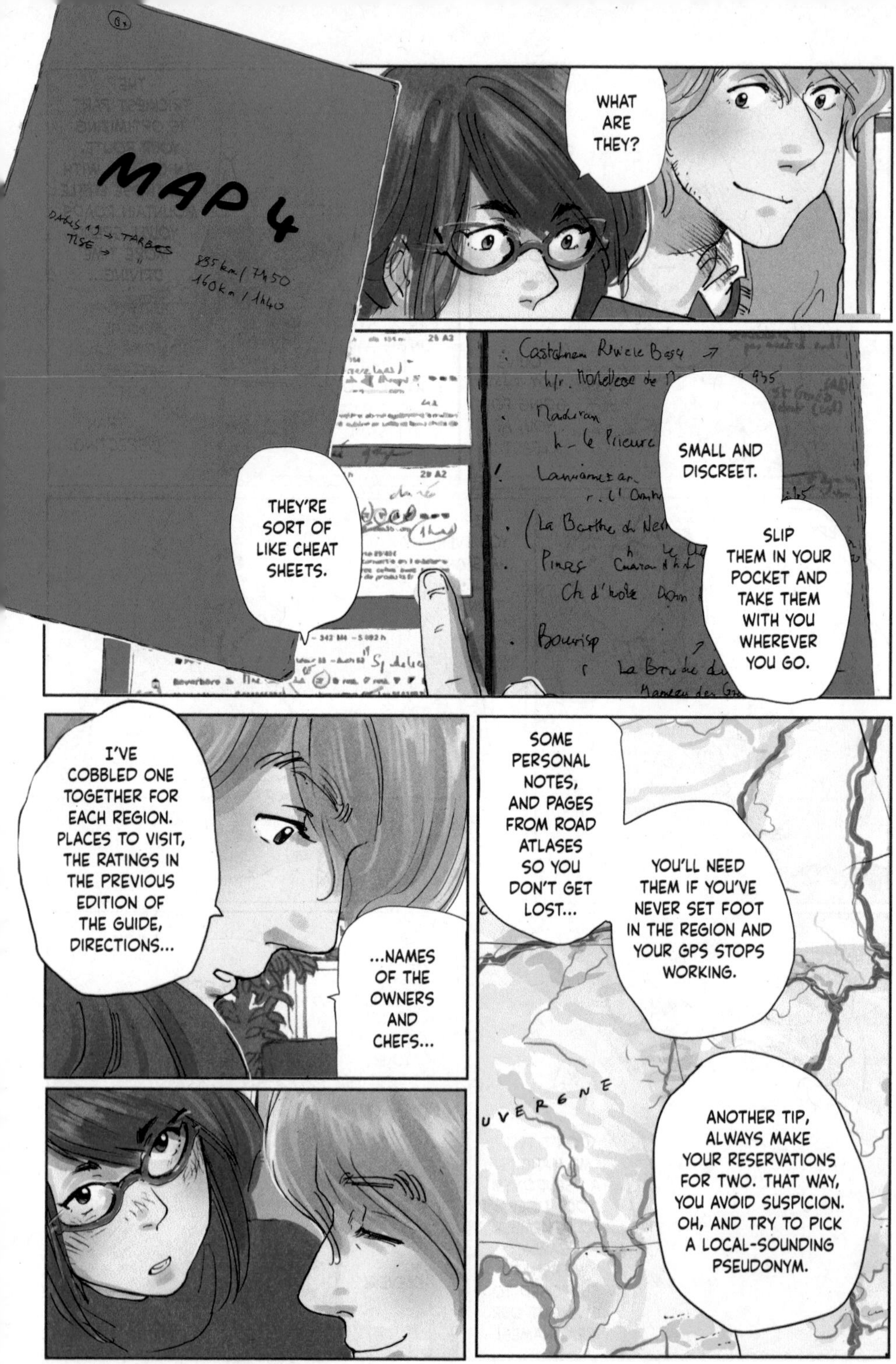
MAP 4
WHAT ARE THEY?
THEY'RE SORT OF LIKE CHEAT SHEETS.
SMALL AND DISCREET.
SLIP THEM IN YOUR POCKET AND TAKE THEM WITH YOU WHEREVER YOU GO.
I'VE COBBLED ONE TOGETHER FOR EACH REGION. PLACES TO VISIT, THE RATINGS IN THE PREVIOUS EDITION OF THE GUIDE, DIRECTIONS...
...NAMES OF THE OWNERS AND CHEFS...
SOME PERSONAL NOTES, AND PAGES FROM ROAD ATLASES SO YOU DON'T GET LOST...
YOU'LL NEED THEM IF YOU'VE NEVER SET FOOT IN THE REGION AND YOUR GPS STOPS WORKING.
ANOTHER TIP, ALWAYS MAKE YOUR RESERVATIONS FOR TWO. THAT WAY, YOU AVOID SUSPICION. OH, AND TRY TO PICK A LOCAL-SOUNDING PSEUDONYM.

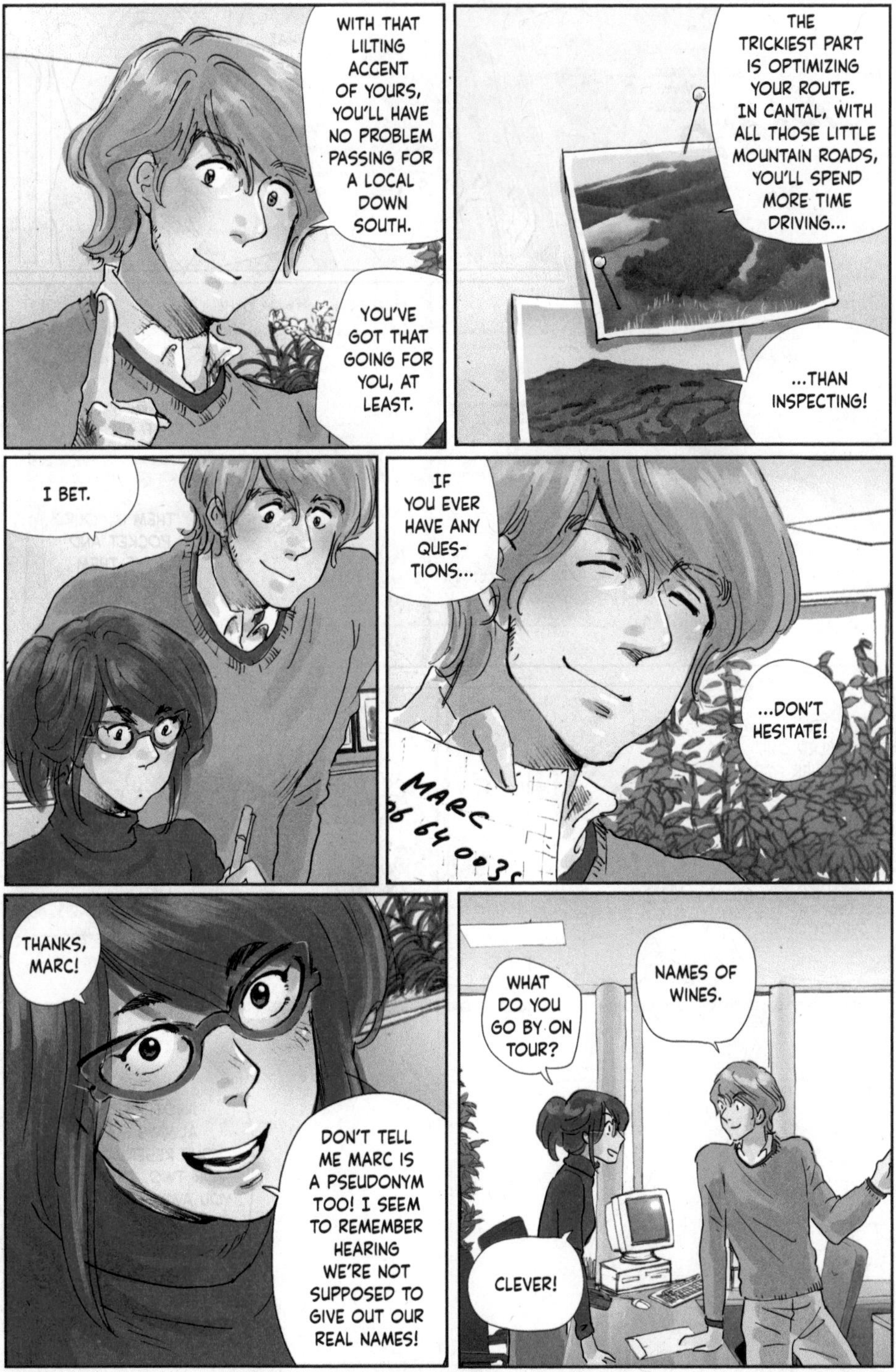
WITH THAT LILTING ACCENT OF YOURS, YOU'LL HAVE NO PROBLEM PASSING FOR A LOCAL DOWN SOUTH.
YOU'VE GOT THAT GOING FOR YOU, AT LEAST.
THE TRICKIEST PART IS OPTIMIZING YOUR ROUTE. IN CANTAL, WITH ALL THOSE LITTLE MOUNTAIN ROADS, YOU'LL SPEND MORE TIME DRIVING...
...THAN INSPECTING!
I BET.
IF YOU EVER HAVE ANY QUES-TIONS...
...DON'T HESITATE!
MARC
THANKS, MARC!
DON'T TELL ME MARC IS A PSEUDONYM TOO! I SEEM TO REMEMBER HEARING WE'RE NOT SUPPOSED TO GIVE OUT OUR REAL NAMES!
WHAT DO YOU GO BY ON TOUR?
NAMES OF WINES.
CLEVER!

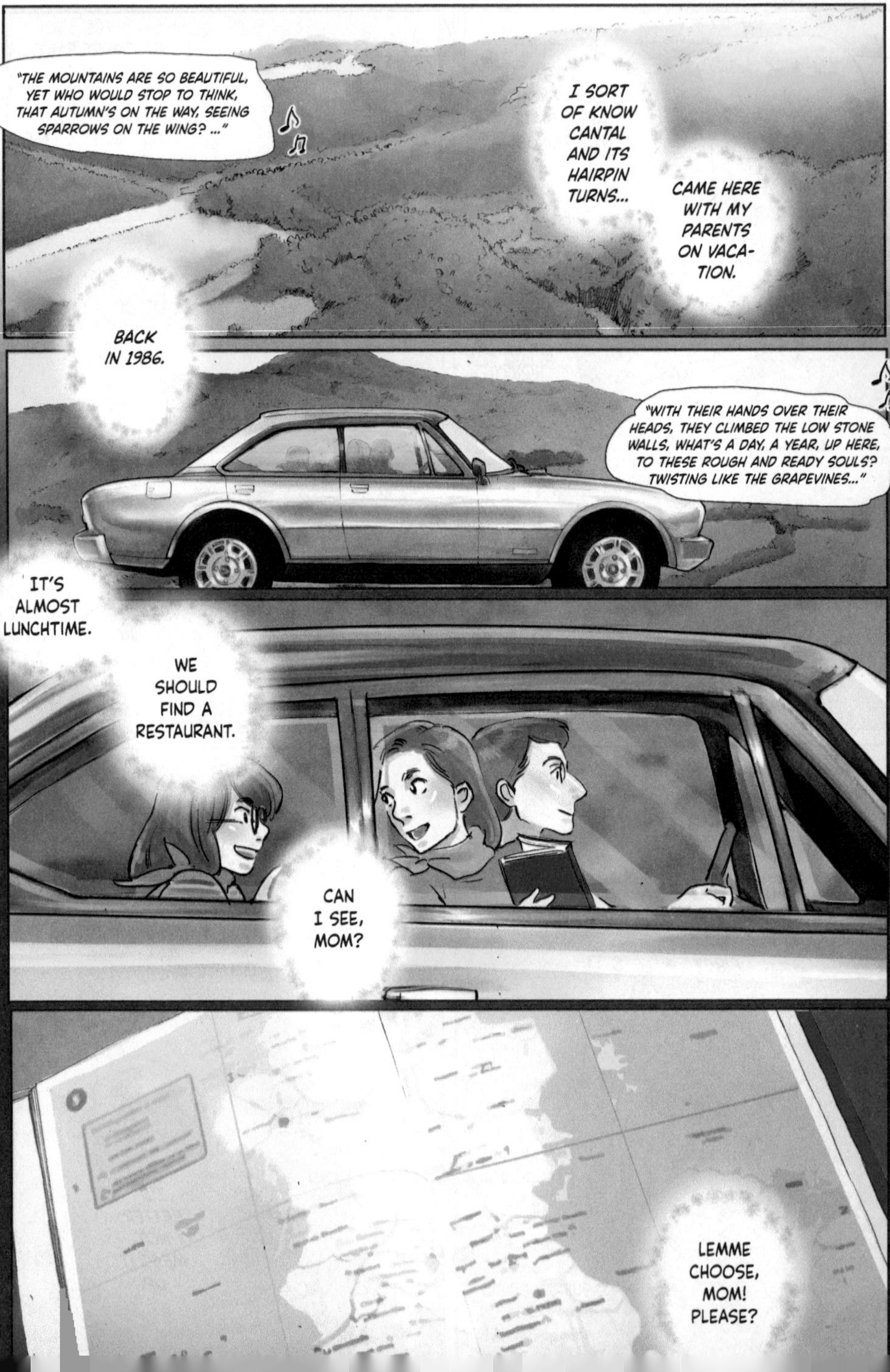
"THE MOUNTAINS ARE SO BEAUTIFUL, YET WHO WOULD STOP TO THINK, THAT AUTUMN'S ON THE WAY, SEEING SPARROWS ON THE WING? ..."
I SORT OF KNOW CANTAL AND ITS HAIRPIN TURNS...
CAME HERE WITH MY PARENTS ON VACA-TION.
BACK IN 1986.
"WITH THEIR HANDS OVER THEIR HEADS, THEY CLIMBED THE LOW STONE WALLS, WHAT'S A DAY, A YEAR, UP HERE, TO THESE ROUGH AND READY SOULS? TWISTING LIKE THE GRAPEVINES..."
IT'S ALMOST LUNCHTIME.
WE SHOULD FIND A RESTAURANT.
CAN I SEE, MOM?
LEMME CHOOSE, MOM! PLEASE?

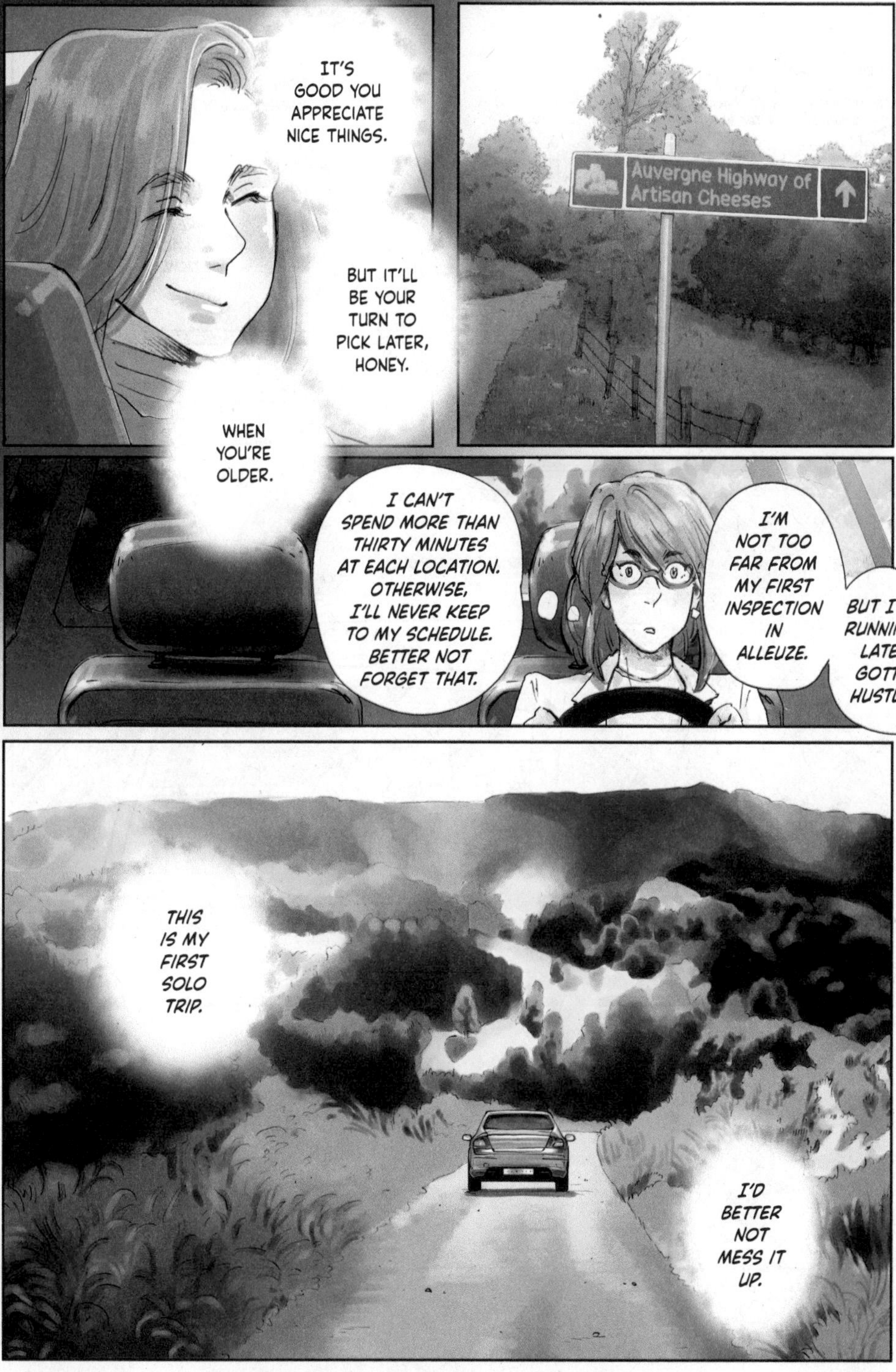
IT'S GOOD YOU APPRECIATE NICE THINGS.
BUT IT'LL BE YOUR TURN TO PICK LATER, HONEY.
WHEN YOU'RE OLDER.
Auvergne Highway of Artisan Cheeses
I CAN'T SPEND MORE THAN THIRTY MINUTES AT EACH LOCATION. OTHERWISE, I'LL NEVER KEEP TO MY SCHEDULE. BETTER NOT FORGET THAT.
I'M NOT TOO FAR FROM MY FIRST INSPECTION IN ALLEUZE.
BUT I'M RUNNING LATE. GOTTA HUSTLE.
THIS IS MY FIRST SOLO TRIP.
I'D BETTER NOT MESS IT UP.

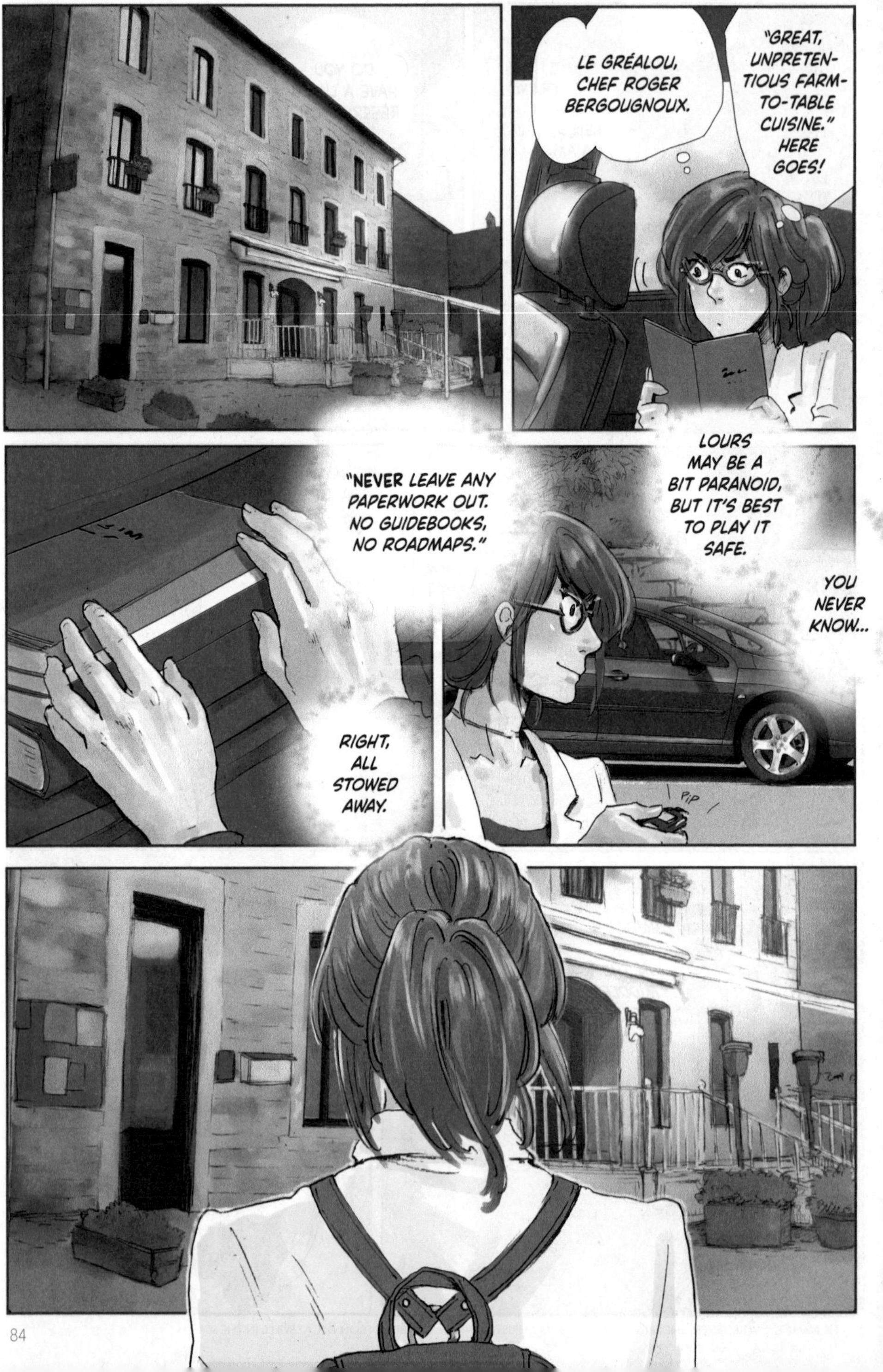
LE GRÉALOU, CHEF ROGER BERGOUGNOUX.
"GREAT, UNPRETEN-TIOUS FARM-TO-TABLE CUISINE." HERE GOES!
"NEVER LEAVE ANY PAPERWORK OUT. NO GUIDEBOOKS, NO ROADMAPS."
RIGHT, ALL STOWED AWAY.
LOURS MAY BE A BIT PARANOID, BUT IT'S BEST TO PLAY IT SAFE.
YOU NEVER KNOW...
PIP

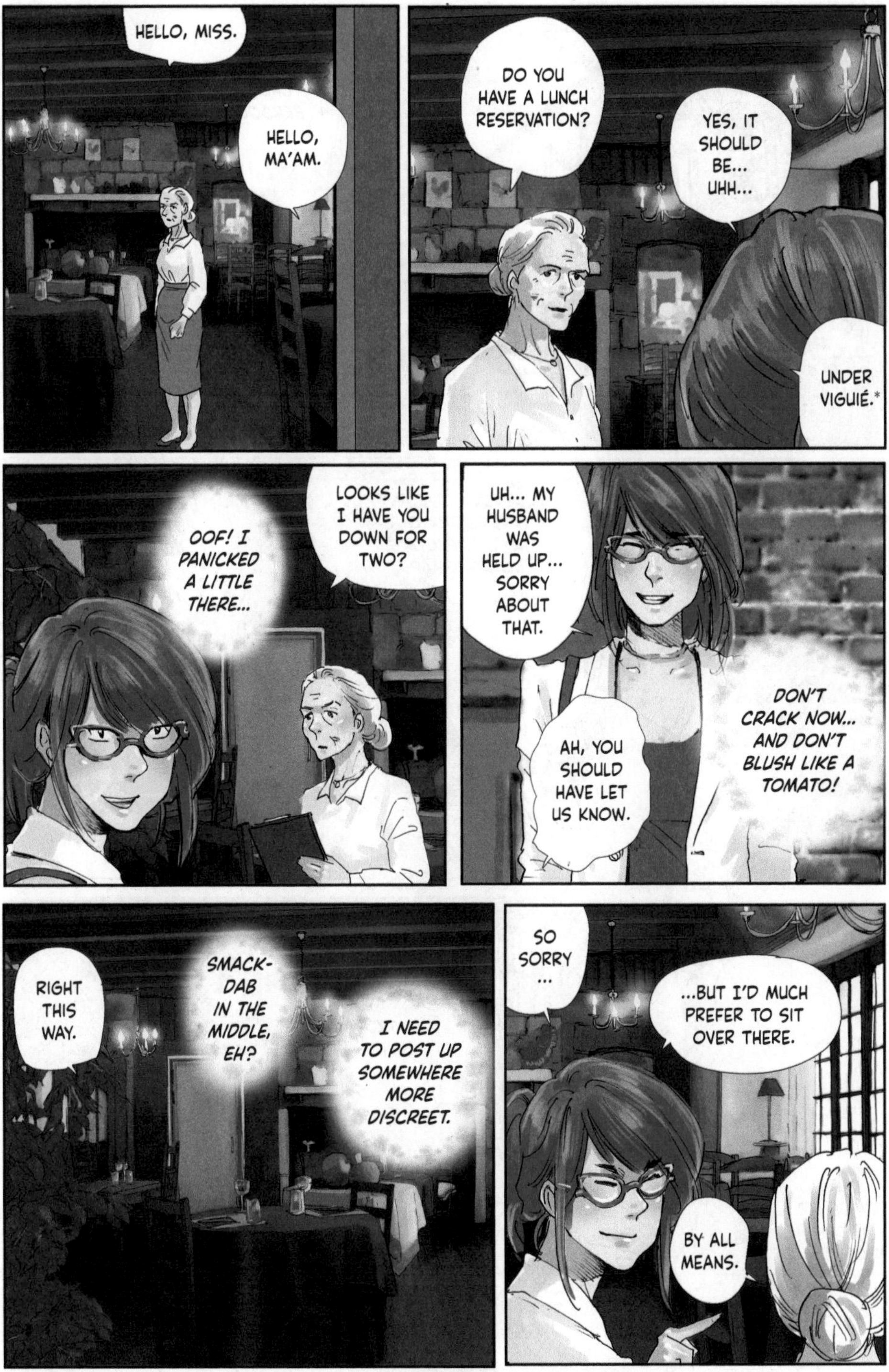
HELLO, MISS.
HELLO, MA'AM.
DO YOU HAVE A LUNCH RESERVATION?
YES, IT SHOULD BE... UHH...
UNDER VIGUIÉ.*
OOF! I PANICKED A LITTLE THERE...
LOOKS LIKE I HAVE YOU DOWN FOR TWO?
UH... MY HUSBAND WAS HELD UP... SORRY ABOUT THAT.
DON'T CRACK NOW... AND DON'T BLUSH LIKE A TOMATO!
AH, YOU SHOULD HAVE LET US KNOW.
RIGHT THIS WAY.
SMACK-DAB IN THE MIDDLE, EH?
I NEED TO POST UP SOMEWHERE MORE DISCREET.
SO SORRY ...
...BUT I'D MUCH PREFER TO SIT OVER THERE.
BY ALL MEANS.

* THE NAME EMMA RESERVED UNDER IS A REFERENCE TO CHRISTIAN VIGUIÉ, A WRITER FROM DECAZEVILLE IN THE SOUTH OF FRANCE.

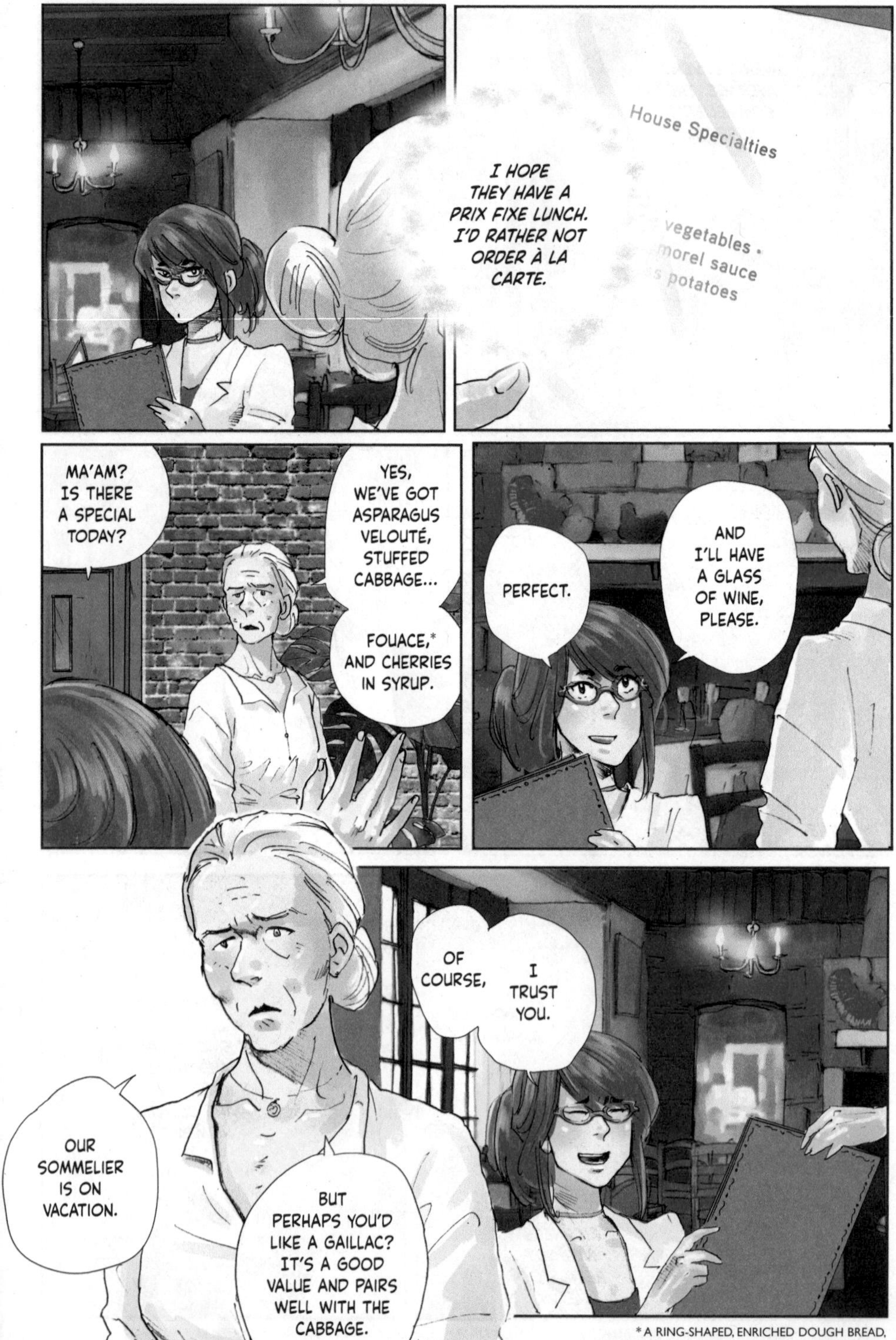
I HOPE THEY HAVE A PRIX FIXE LUNCH. I'D RATHER NOT ORDER À LA CARTE.
House Specialties
vegetables ·
morel sauce
potatoes
MA'AM? IS THERE A SPECIAL TODAY?
YES, WE'VE GOT ASPARAGUS VELOUTÉ, STUFFED CABBAGE...
FOUACE,* AND CHERRIES IN SYRUP.
PERFECT.
AND I'LL HAVE A GLASS OF WINE, PLEASE.
OUR SOMMELIER IS ON VACATION.
BUT PERHAPS YOU'D LIKE A GAILLAC? IT'S A GOOD VALUE AND PAIRS WELL WITH THE CABBAGE.
OF COURSE,
I TRUST YOU.

* A RING-SHAPED, ENRICHED DOUGH BREAD, OFTEN FLAVORED WITH ORANGE BLOSSOM WATER.

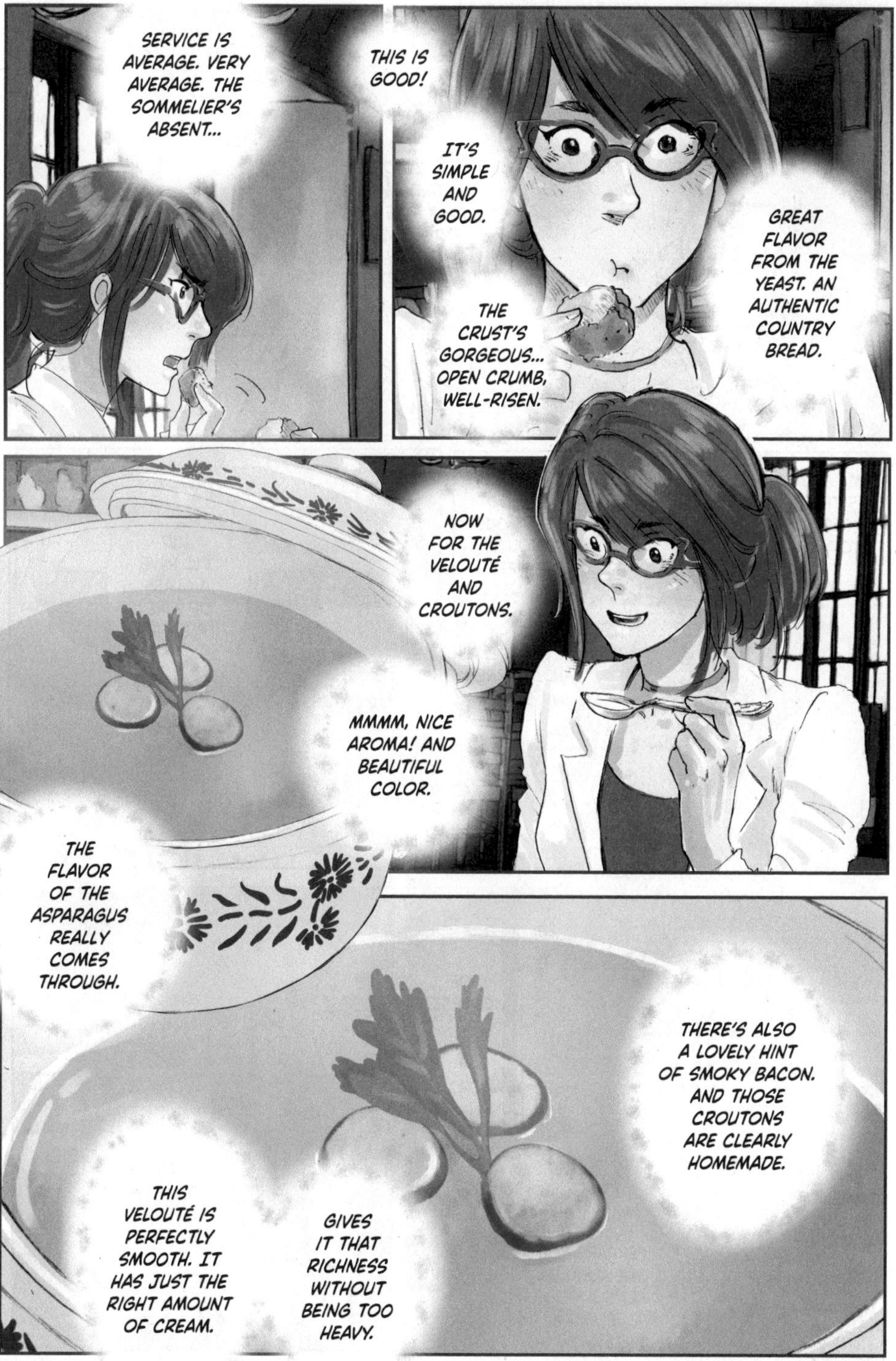
SERVICE IS AVERAGE. VERY AVERAGE. THE SOMMELIER'S ABSENT...
THIS IS GOOD!
IT'S SIMPLE AND GOOD.
THE CRUST'S GORGEOUS... OPEN CRUMB, WELL-RISEN.
GREAT FLAVOR FROM THE YEAST. AN AUTHENTIC COUNTRY BREAD.
NOW FOR THE VELOUTÉ AND CROUTONS.
MMMM, NICE AROMA! AND BEAUTIFUL COLOR.
THE FLAVOR OF THE ASPARAGUS REALLY COMES THROUGH.
THIS VELOUTÉ IS PERFECTLY SMOOTH. IT HAS JUST THE RIGHT AMOUNT OF CREAM.
GIVES IT THAT RICHNESS WITHOUT BEING TOO HEAVY.
THERE'S ALSO A LOVELY HINT OF SMOKY BACON. AND THOSE CROUTONS ARE CLEARLY HOMEMADE.

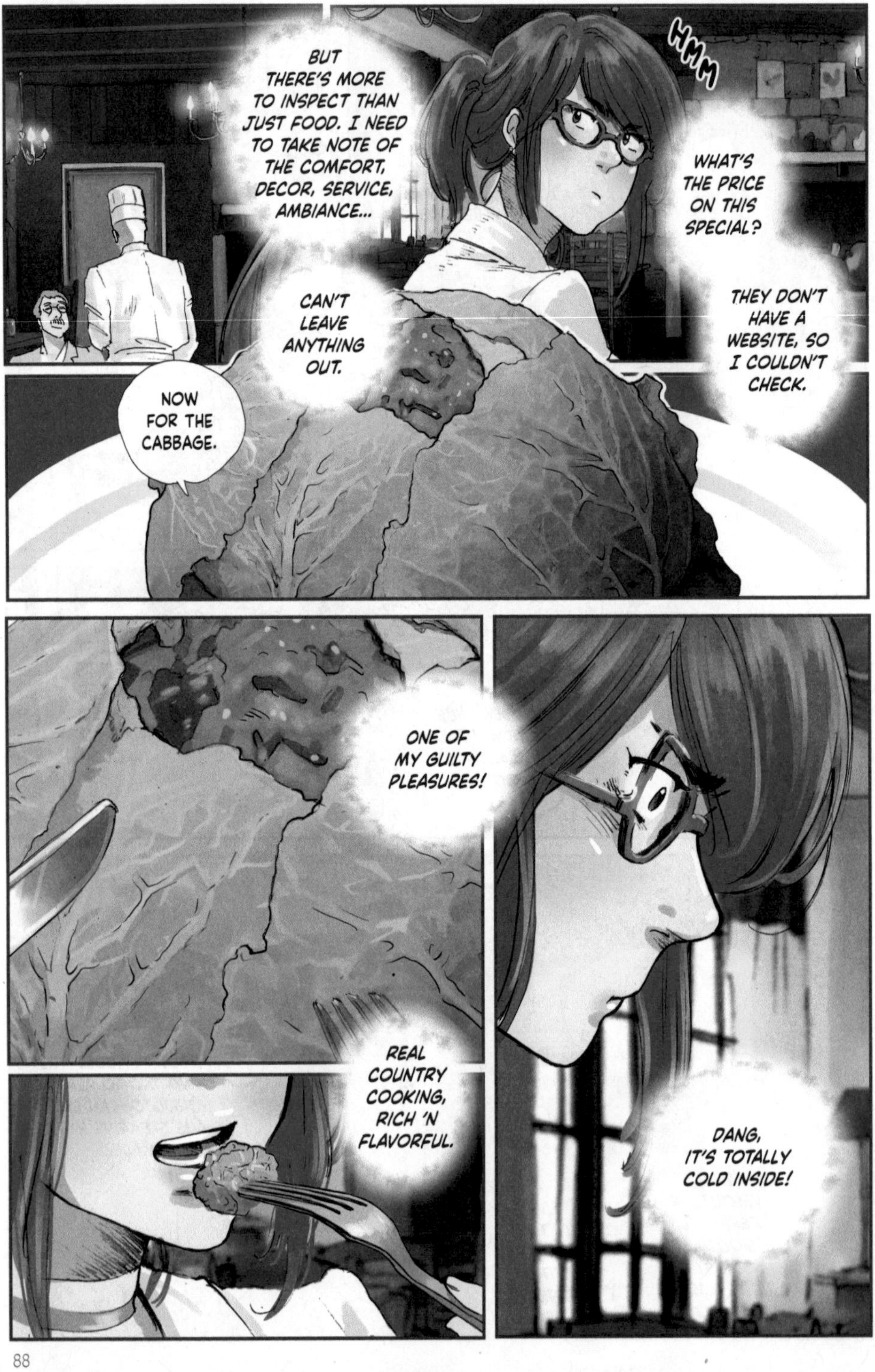
BUT THERE'S MORE TO INSPECT THAN JUST FOOD. I NEED TO TAKE NOTE OF THE COMFORT, DECOR, SERVICE, AMBIANCE...
HMM
WHAT'S THE PRICE ON THIS SPECIAL?
CAN'T LEAVE ANYTHING OUT.
THEY DON'T HAVE A WEBSITE, SO I COULDN'T CHECK.
NOW FOR THE CABBAGE.
ONE OF MY GUILTY PLEASURES!
REAL COUNTRY COOKING, RICH 'N FLAVORFUL.
DANG, IT'S TOTALLY COLD INSIDE!

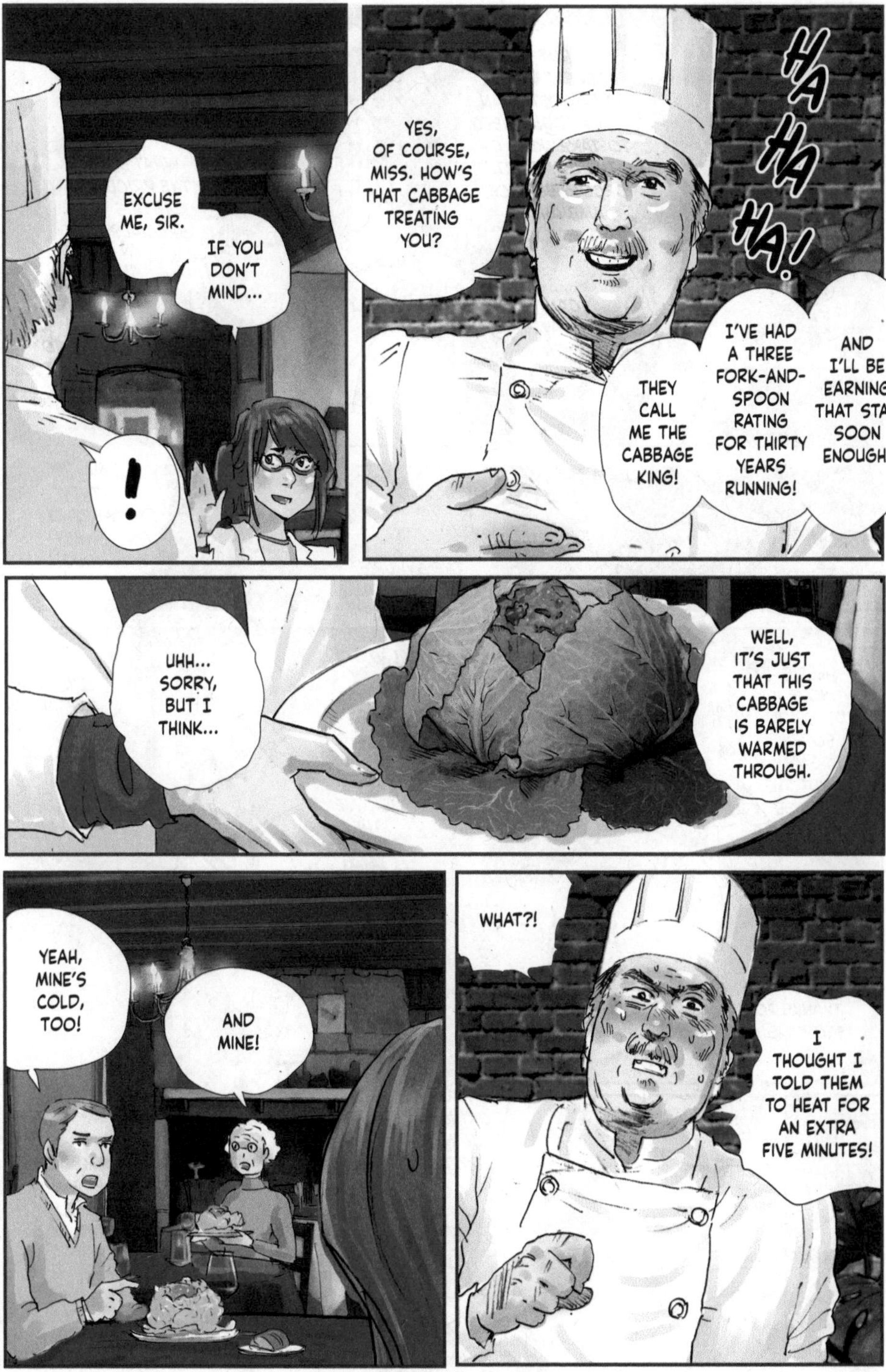
EXCUSE ME, SIR.
IF YOU DON'T MIND...
!
YES, OF COURSE, MISS. HOW'S THAT CABBAGE TREATING YOU?
HA HA HA HA!
THEY CALL ME THE CABBAGE KING!
I'VE HAD A THREE FORK-AND-SPOON RATING FOR THIRTY YEARS RUNNING!
AND I'LL BE EARNING THAT STAR SOON ENOUGH.
UHH... SORRY, BUT I THINK...
WELL, IT'S JUST THAT THIS CABBAGE IS BARELY WARMED THROUGH.
YEAH, MINE'S COLD, TOO!
AND MINE!
WHAT?!
I THOUGHT I TOLD THEM TO HEAT FOR AN EXTRA FIVE MINUTES!

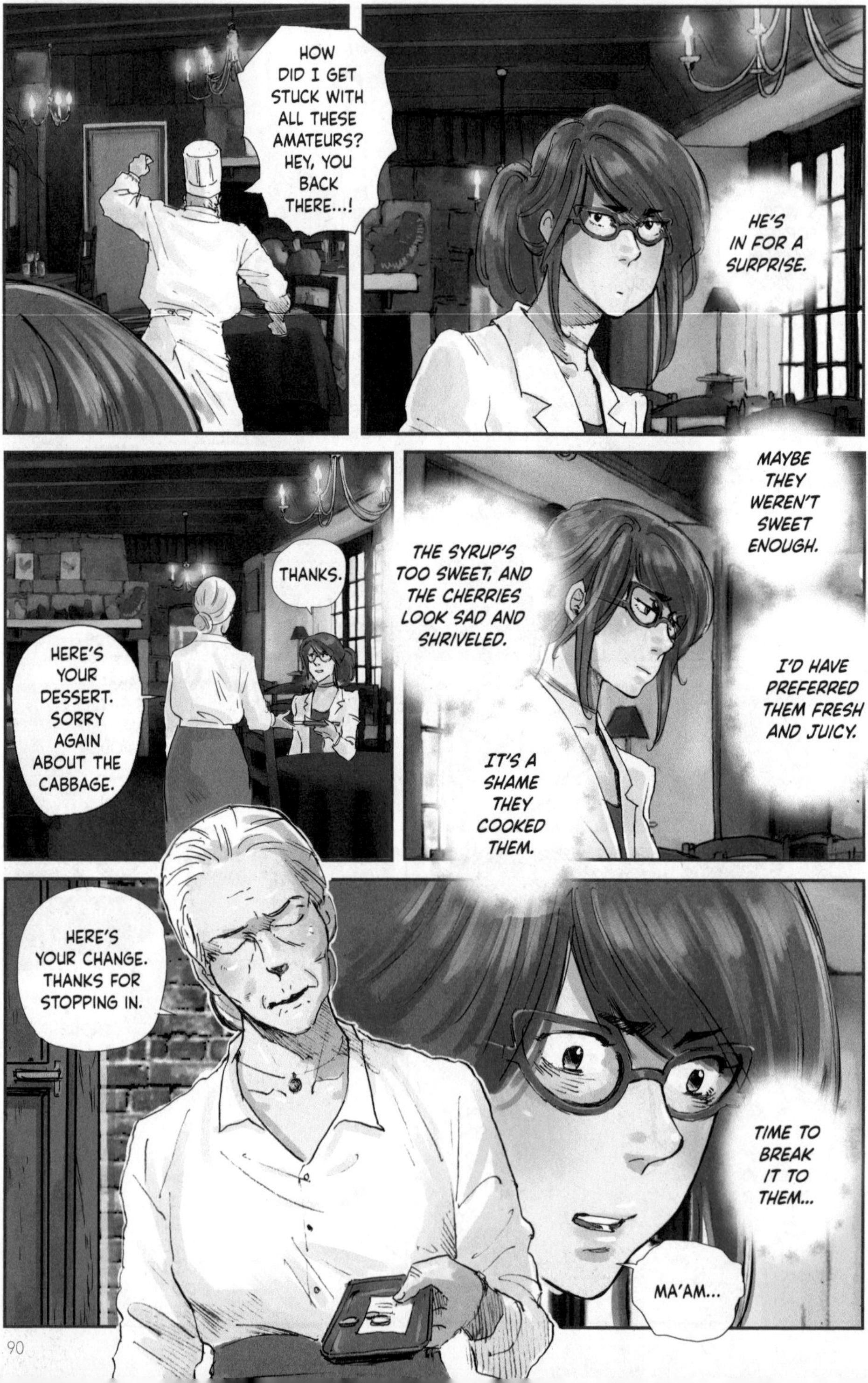

HOW DID I GET STUCK WITH ALL THESE AMATEURS? HEY, YOU BACK THERE...!
HE'S IN FOR A SURPRISE.
THANKS.
HERE'S YOUR DESSERT. SORRY AGAIN ABOUT THE CABBAGE.
THE SYRUP'S TOO SWEET, AND THE CHERRIES LOOK SAD AND SHRIVELED.
MAYBE THEY WEREN'T SWEET ENOUGH.
I'D HAVE PREFERRED THEM FRESH AND JUICY.
IT'S A SHAME THEY COOKED THEM.
HERE'S YOUR CHANGE. THANKS FOR STOPPING IN.
TIME TO BREAK IT TO THEM...
MA'AM...

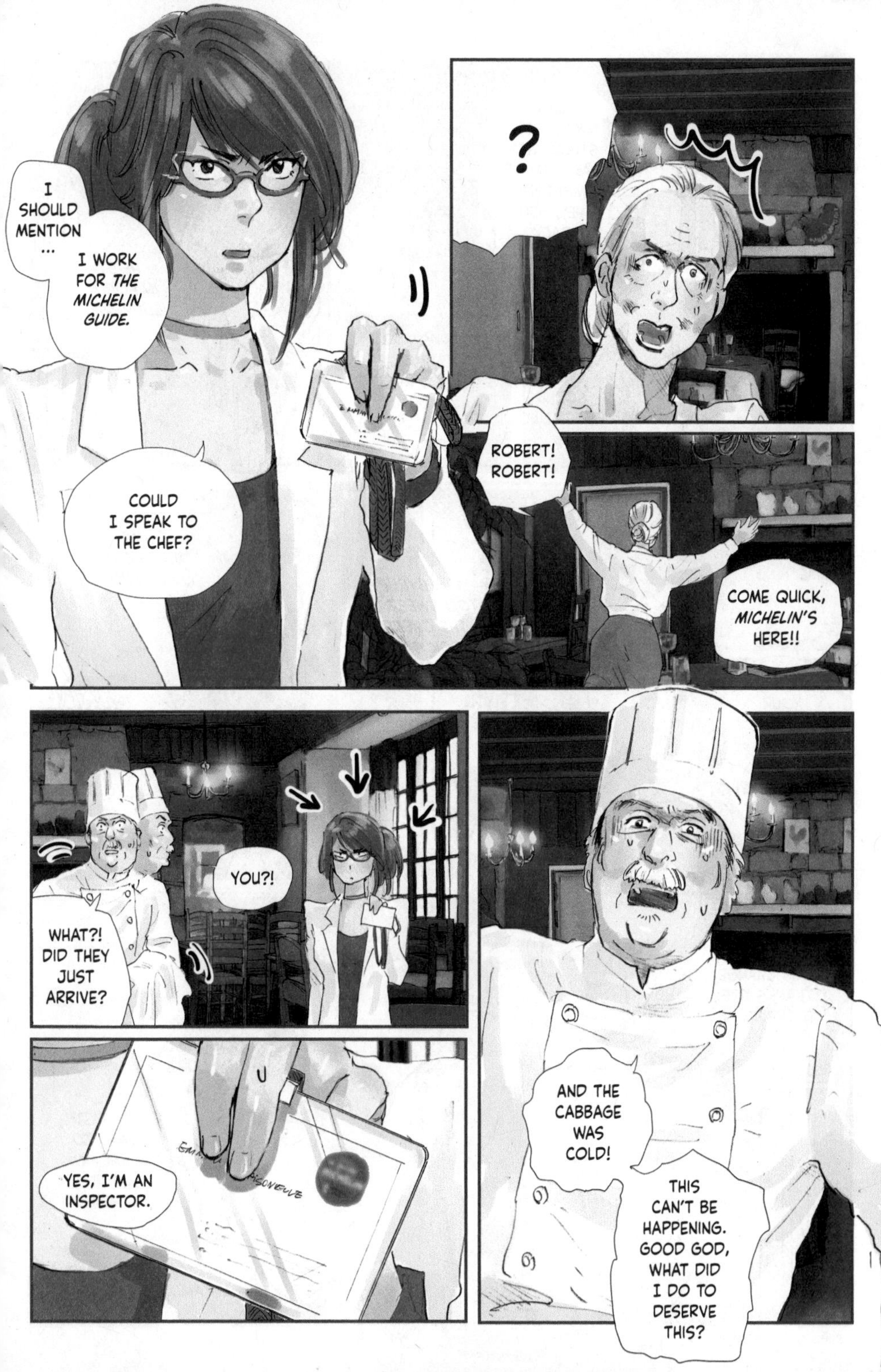
I SHOULD MENTION ...
I WORK FOR *THE MICHELIN GUIDE.*
COULD I SPEAK TO THE CHEF?
?
ROBERT! ROBERT!
COME QUICK, *MICHELIN'S* HERE!!
WHAT?! DID THEY JUST ARRIVE?
YOU?!
YES, I'M AN INSPECTOR.
AND THE CABBAGE WAS COLD!
THIS CAN'T BE HAPPENING. GOOD GOD, WHAT DID I DO TO DESERVE THIS?

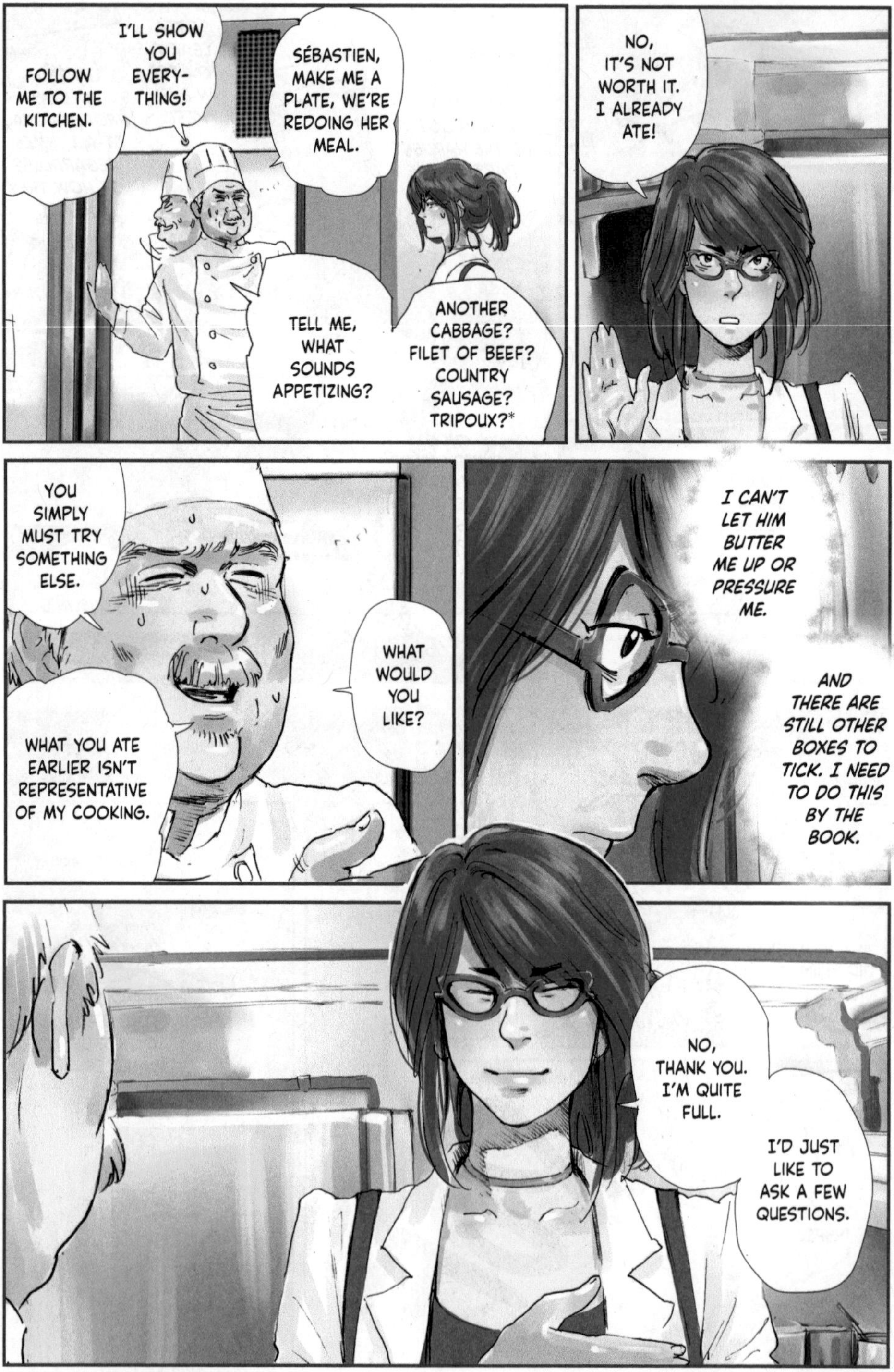
FOLLOW ME TO THE KITCHEN.
I'LL SHOW YOU EVERY-THING!
SÉBASTIEN, MAKE ME A PLATE, WE'RE REDOING HER MEAL.
TELL ME, WHAT SOUNDS APPETIZING?
ANOTHER CABBAGE? FILET OF BEEF? COUNTRY SAUSAGE? TRIPOUX?*
NO, IT'S NOT WORTH IT. I ALREADY ATE!
YOU SIMPLY MUST TRY SOMETHING ELSE.
WHAT WOULD YOU LIKE?
WHAT YOU ATE EARLIER ISN'T REPRESENTATIVE OF MY COOKING.
I CAN'T LET HIM BUTTER ME UP OR PRESSURE ME.
AND THERE ARE STILL OTHER BOXES TO TICK. I NEED TO DO THIS BY THE BOOK.
NO, THANK YOU. I'M QUITE FULL.
I'D JUST LIKE TO ASK A FEW QUESTIONS.

* BRAISED, STUFFED SHEEP TRIPE.

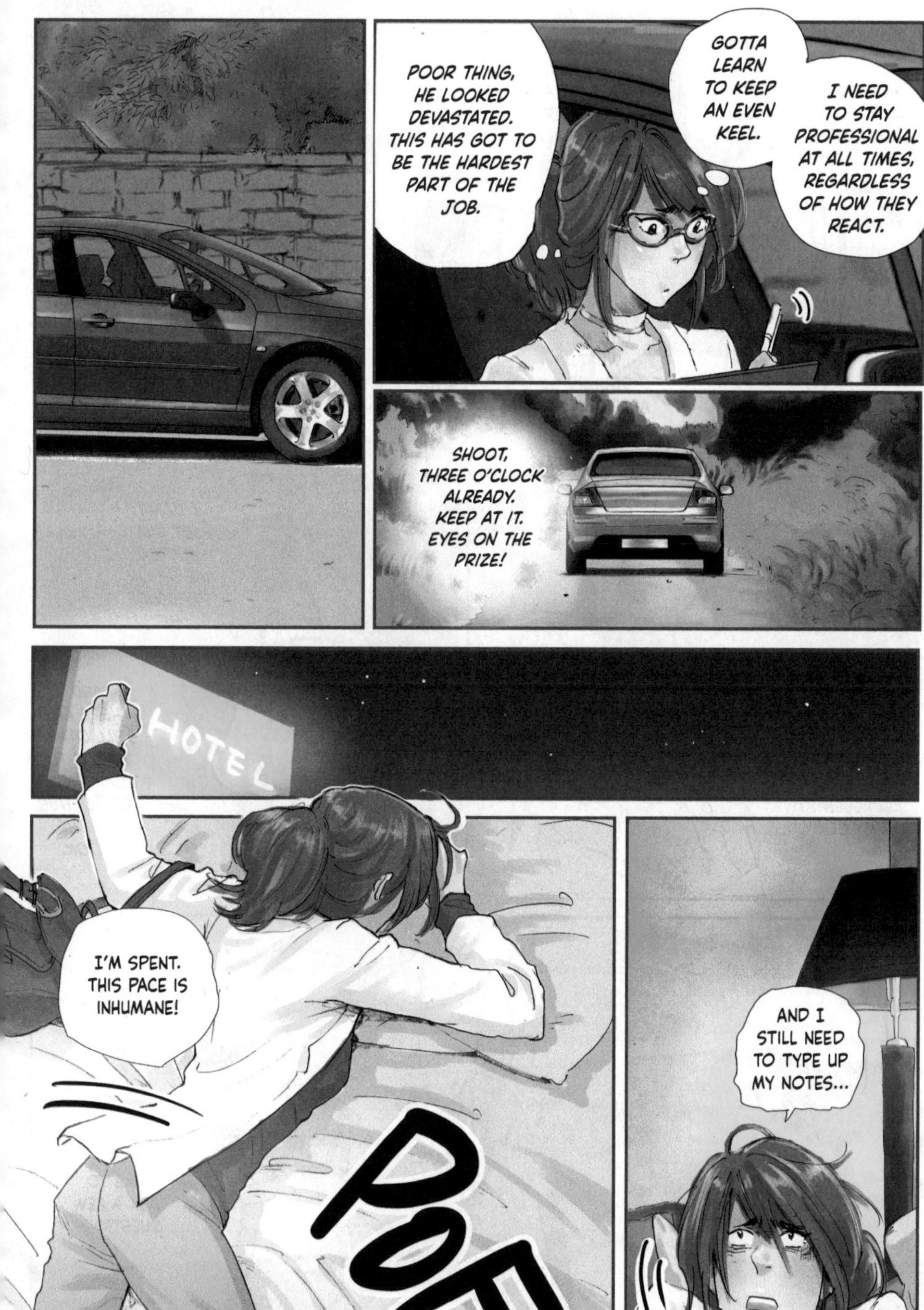
POOR THING, HE LOOKED DEVASTATED. THIS HAS GOT TO BE THE HARDEST PART OF THE JOB.
GOTTA LEARN TO KEEP AN EVEN KEEL.
I NEED TO STAY PROFESSIONAL AT ALL TIMES, REGARDLESS OF HOW THEY REACT.
SHOOT, THREE O'CLOCK ALREADY. KEEP AT IT. EYES ON THE PRIZE!
HOTEL
I'M SPENT. THIS PACE IS INHUMANE!
POF
AND I STILL NEED TO TYPE UP MY NOTES...

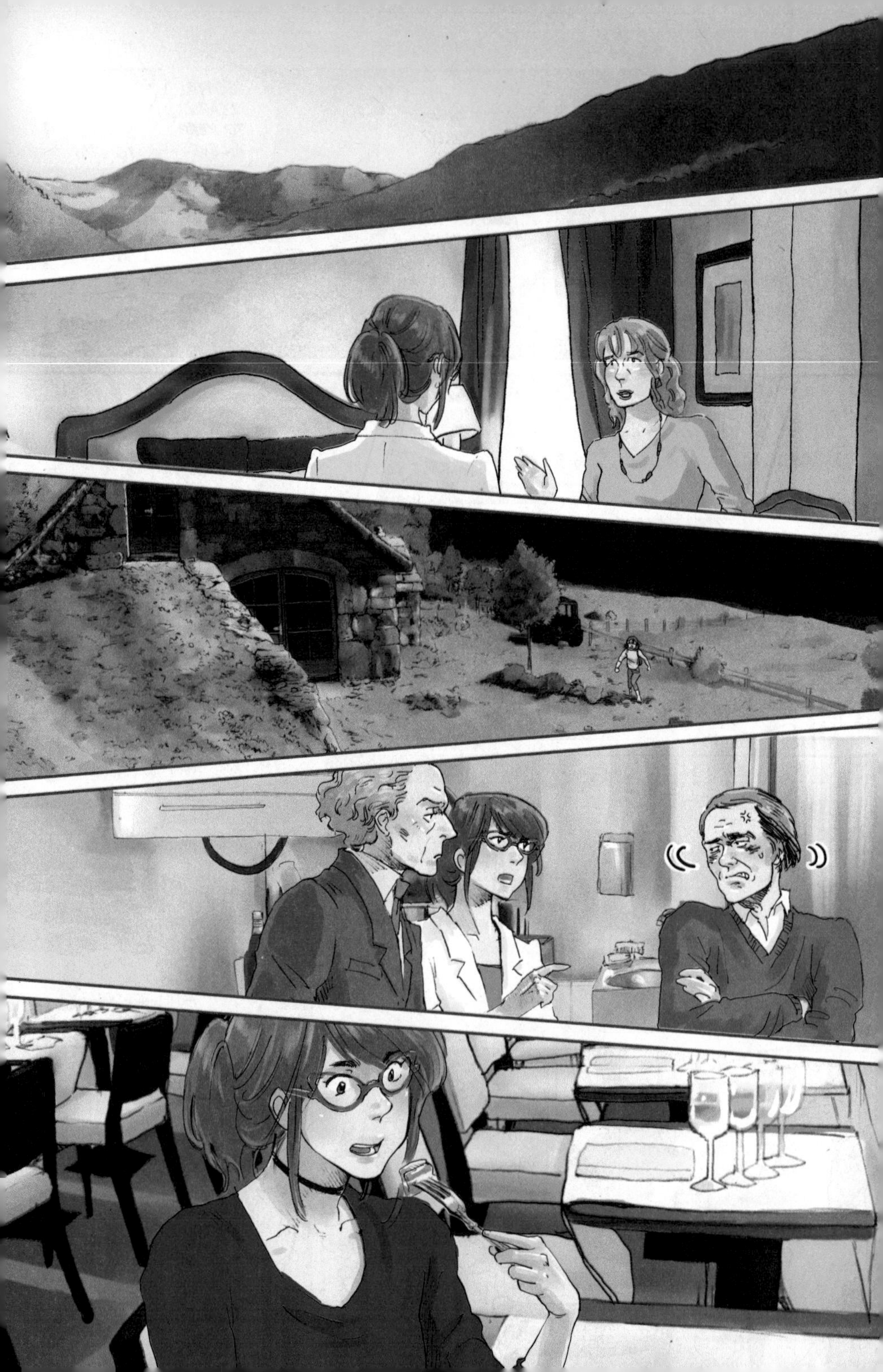

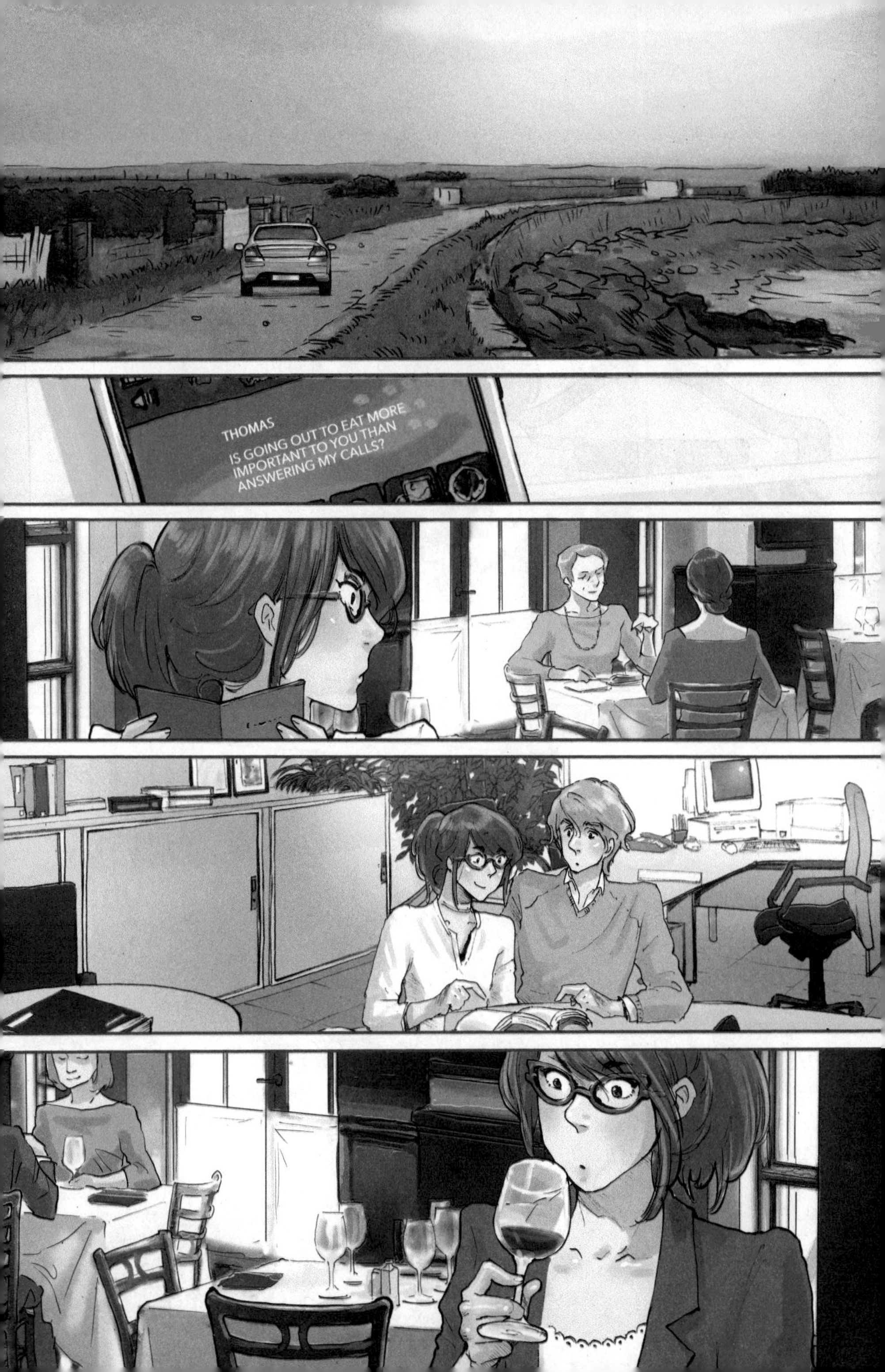
THOMAS
IS GOING OUT TO EAT MORE IMPORTANT TO YOU THAN ANSWERING MY CALLS?

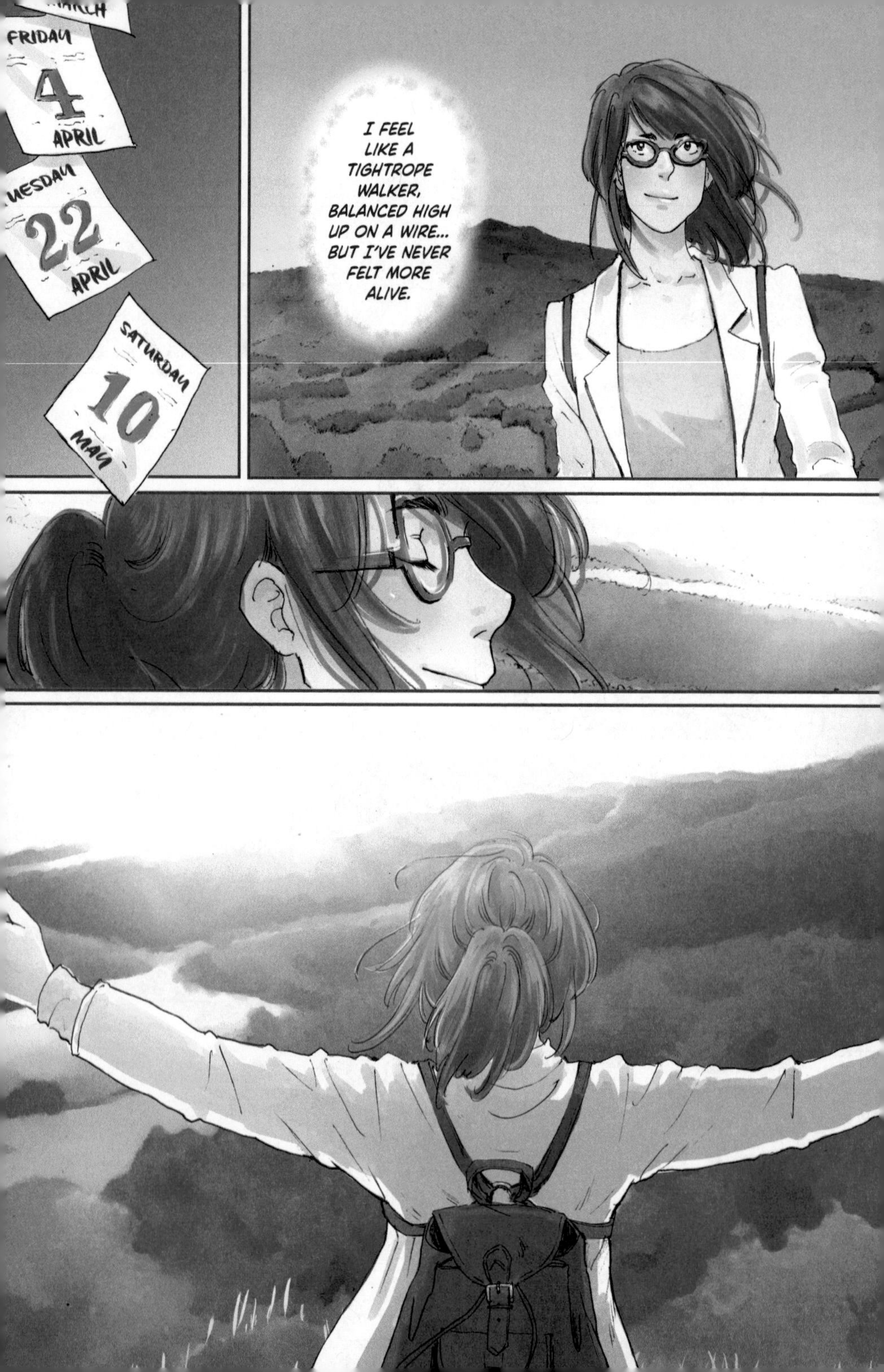
FRIDAY
4
APRIL
22
APRIL
SATURDAY
10
MAY
I FEEL LIKE A TIGHTROPE WALKER, BALANCED HIGH UP ON A WIRE... BUT I'VE NEVER FELT MORE ALIVE.

CHAPTER 5

AT LE PÈRE CLAUDE

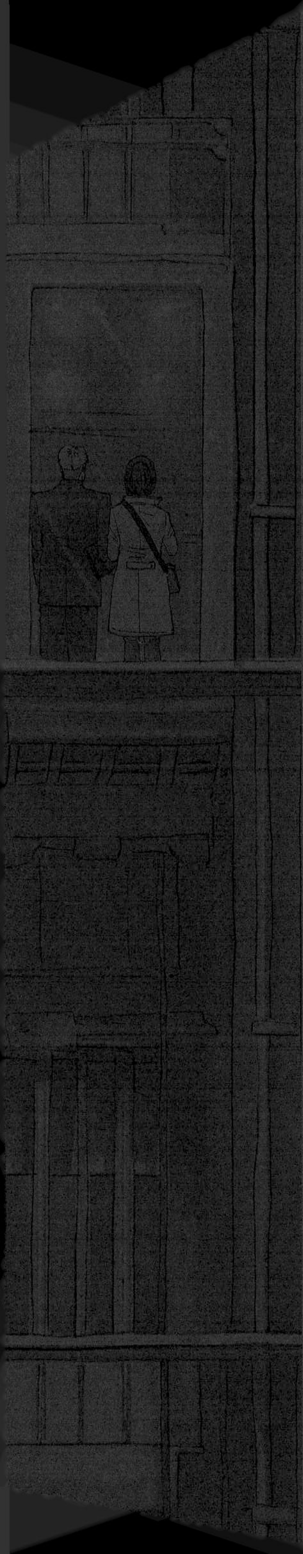

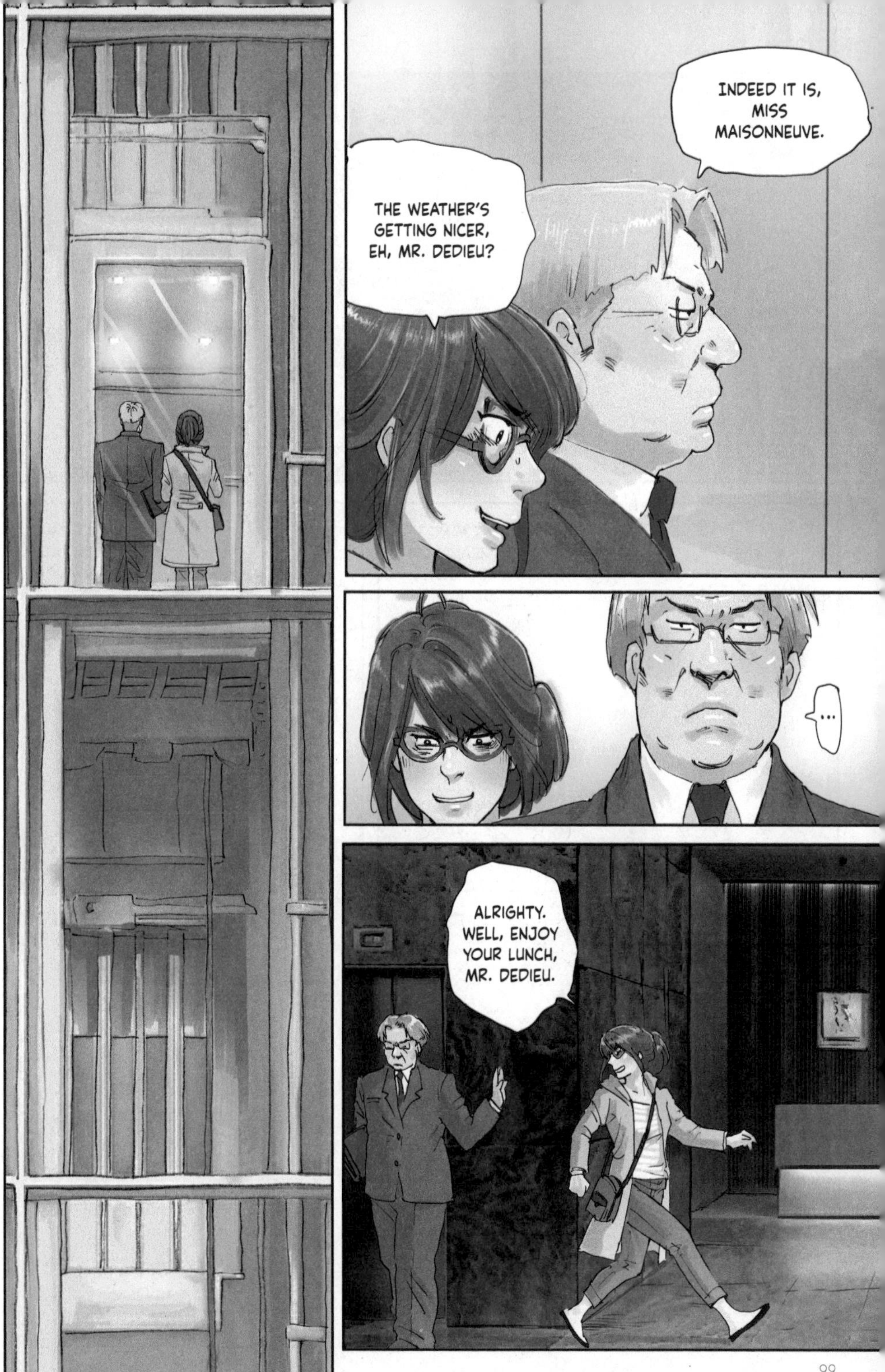
THE WEATHER'S GETTING NICER, EH, MR. DEDIEU?
INDEED IT IS, MISS MAISONNEUVE.
...
ALRIGHTY. WELL, ENJOY YOUR LUNCH, MR. DEDIEU.

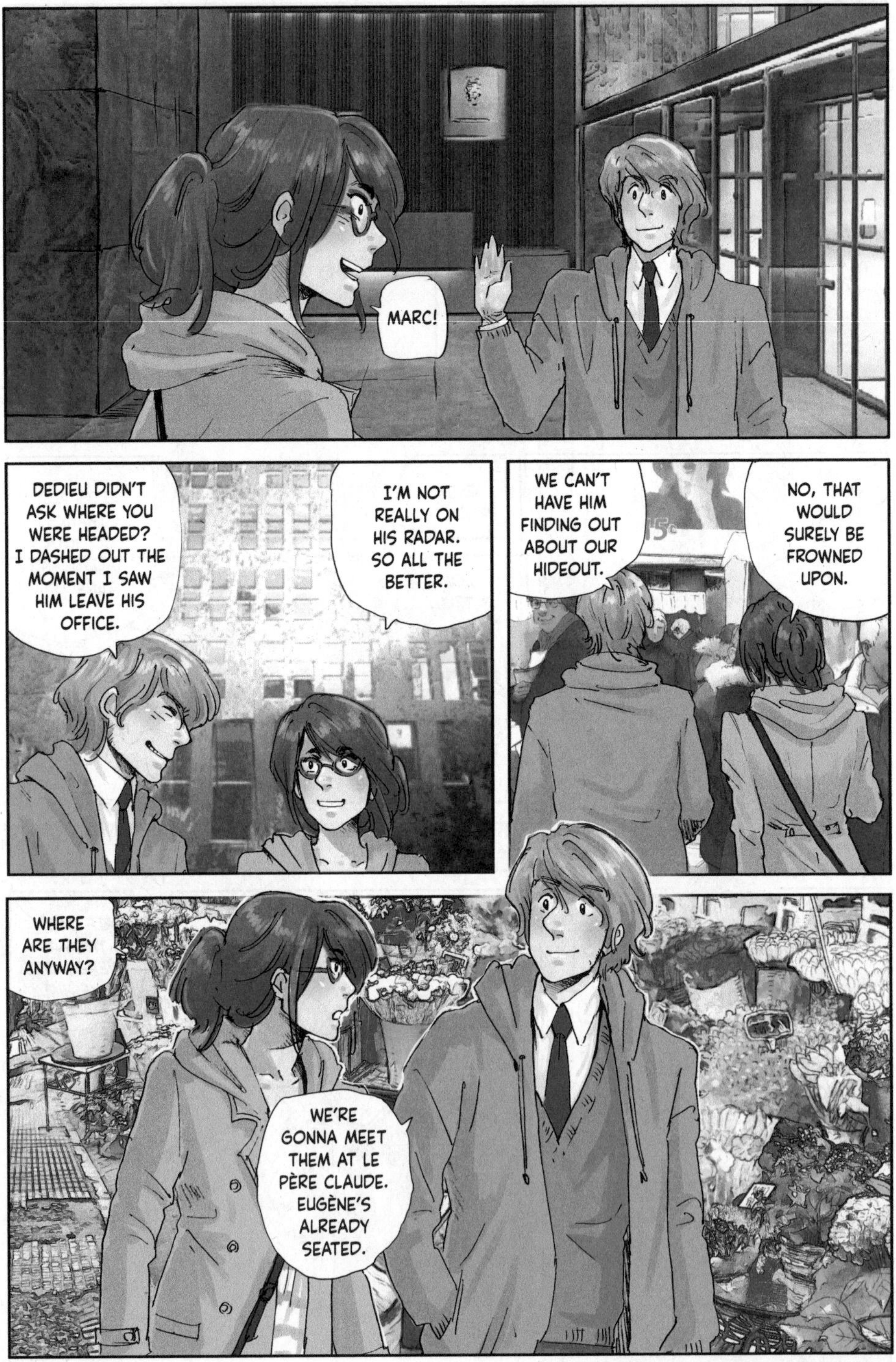
MARC!
DEDIEU DIDN'T ASK WHERE YOU WERE HEADED? I DASHED OUT THE MOMENT I SAW HIM LEAVE HIS OFFICE.
I'M NOT REALLY ON HIS RADAR. SO ALL THE BETTER.
WE CAN'T HAVE HIM FINDING OUT ABOUT OUR HIDEOUT.
NO, THAT WOULD SURELY BE FROWNED UPON.
WHERE ARE THEY ANYWAY?
WE'RE GONNA MEET THEM AT LE PÈRE CLAUDE. EUGÈNE'S ALREADY SEATED.

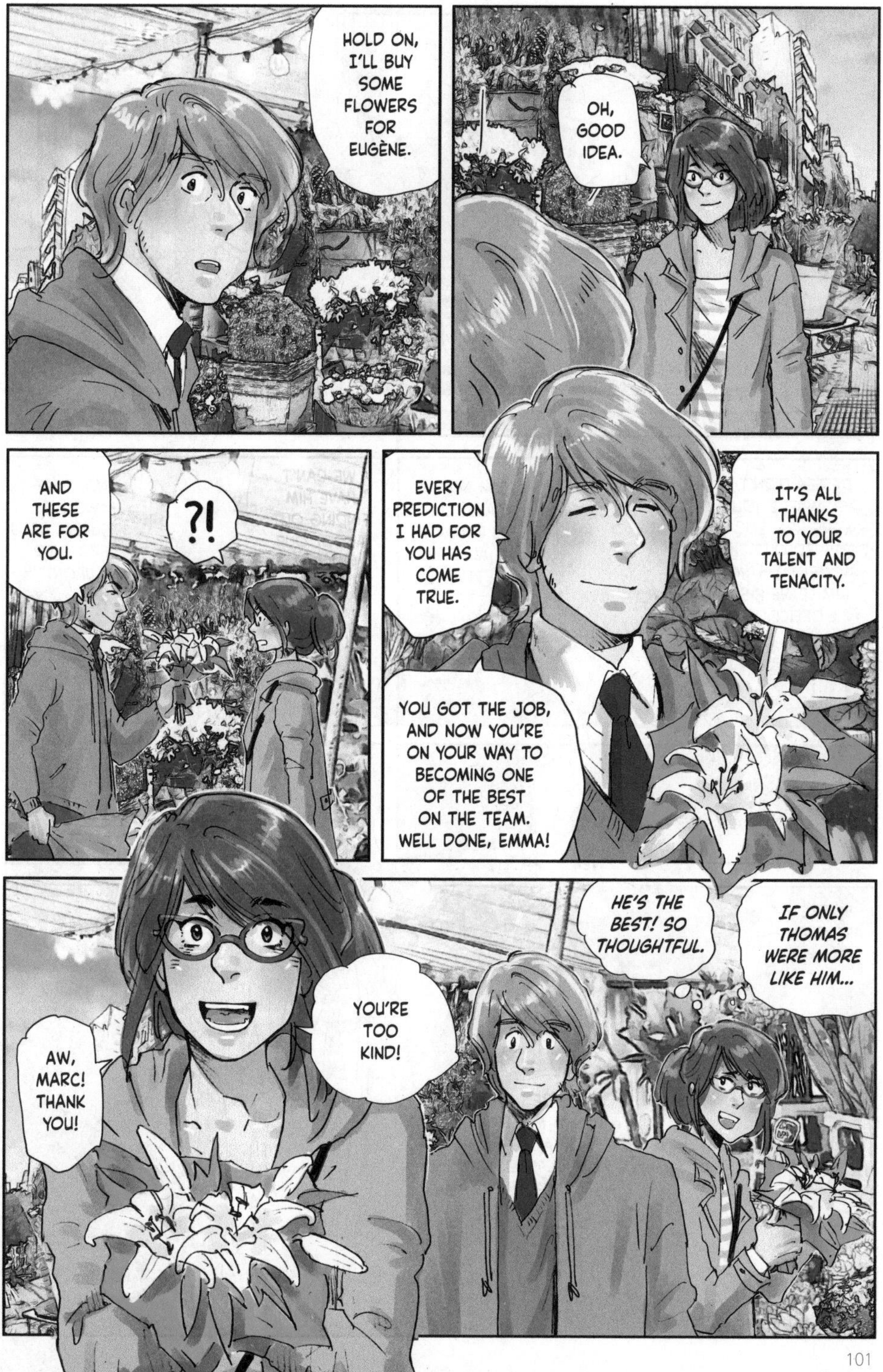
HOLD ON, I'LL BUY SOME FLOWERS FOR EUGÈNE.
OH, GOOD IDEA.
AND THESE ARE FOR YOU.
?!
EVERY PREDICTION I HAD FOR YOU HAS COME TRUE.
IT'S ALL THANKS TO YOUR TALENT AND TENACITY.
YOU GOT THE JOB, AND NOW YOU'RE ON YOUR WAY TO BECOMING ONE OF THE BEST ON THE TEAM. WELL DONE, EMMA!
AW, MARC! THANK YOU!
YOU'RE TOO KIND!
HE'S THE BEST! SO THOUGHTFUL.
IF ONLY THOMAS WERE MORE LIKE HIM...

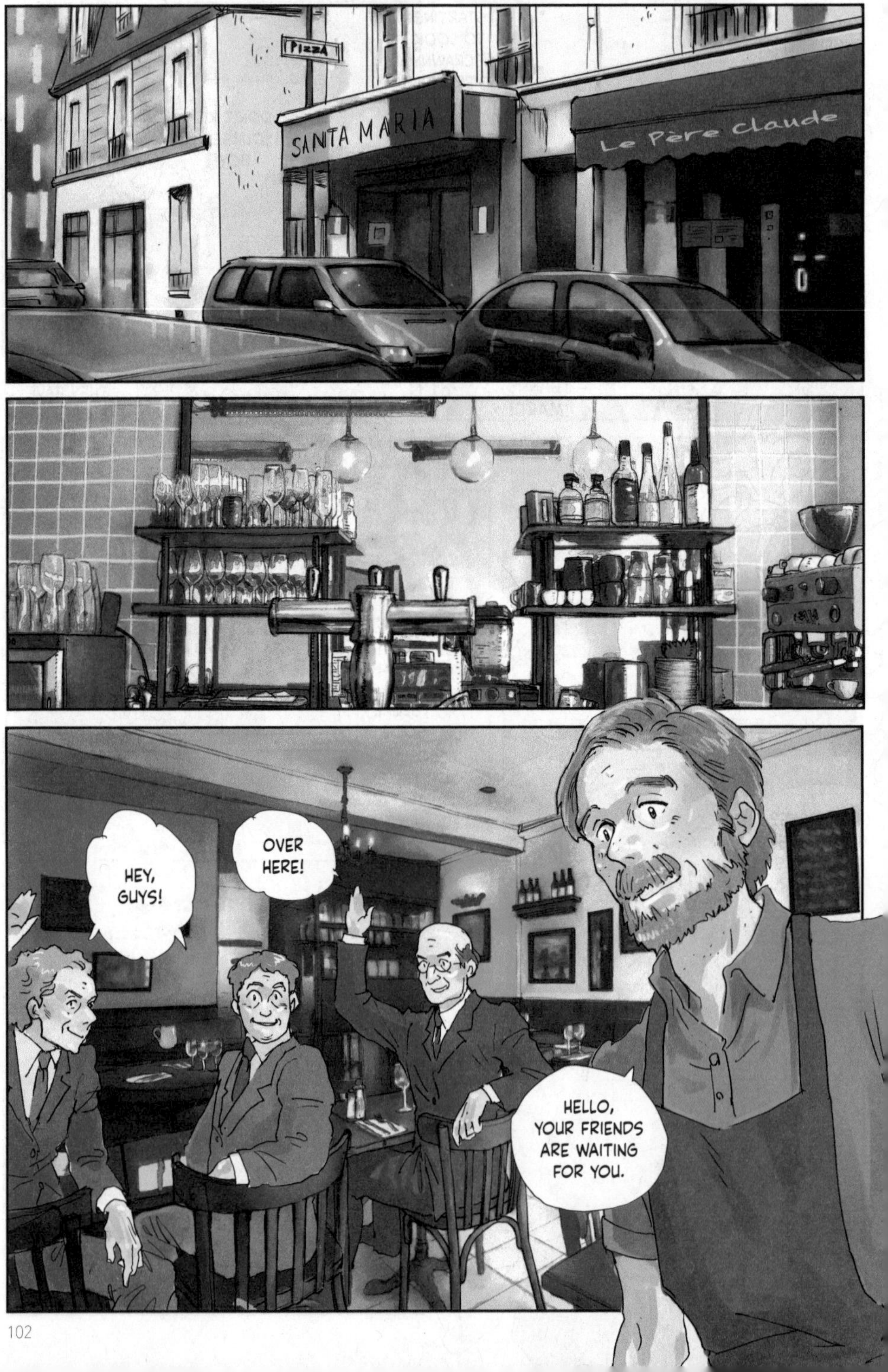
PIZZA
SANTA MARIA
Le Père claude
HEY, GUYS!
OVER HERE!
HELLO, YOUR FRIENDS ARE WAITING FOR YOU.

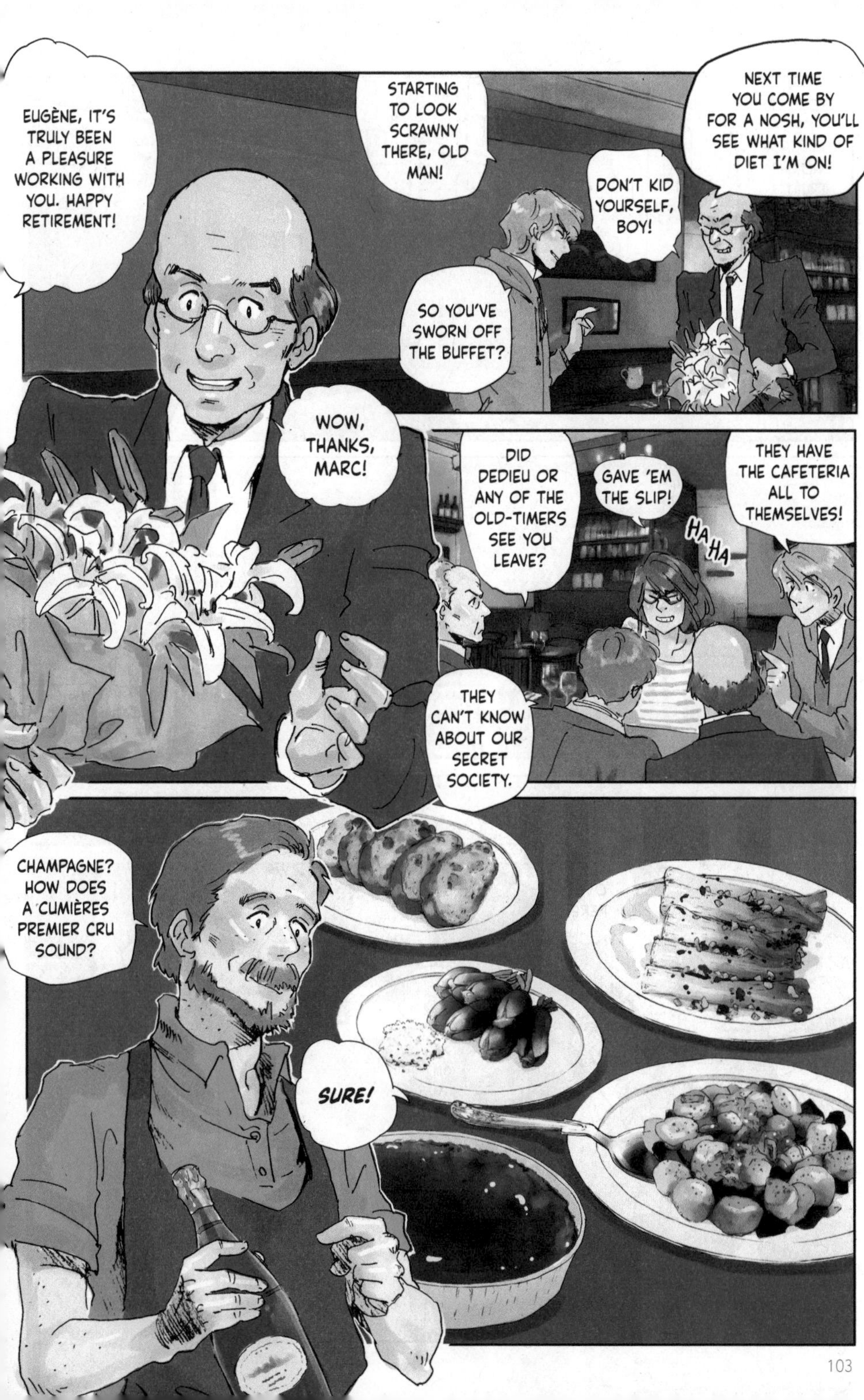
EUGÈNE, IT'S TRULY BEEN A PLEASURE WORKING WITH YOU. HAPPY RETIREMENT!
STARTING TO LOOK SCRAWNY THERE, OLD MAN!
DON'T KID YOURSELF, BOY!
SO YOU'VE SWORN OFF THE BUFFET?
NEXT TIME YOU COME BY FOR A NOSH, YOU'LL SEE WHAT KIND OF DIET I'M ON!
WOW, THANKS, MARC!
DID DEDIEU OR ANY OF THE OLD-TIMERS SEE YOU LEAVE?
GAVE 'EM THE SLIP!
HA HA
THEY HAVE THE CAFETERIA ALL TO THEMSELVES!
THEY CAN'T KNOW ABOUT OUR SECRET SOCIETY.
CHAMPAGNE? HOW DOES A CUMIÈRES PREMIER CRU SOUND?
SURE!

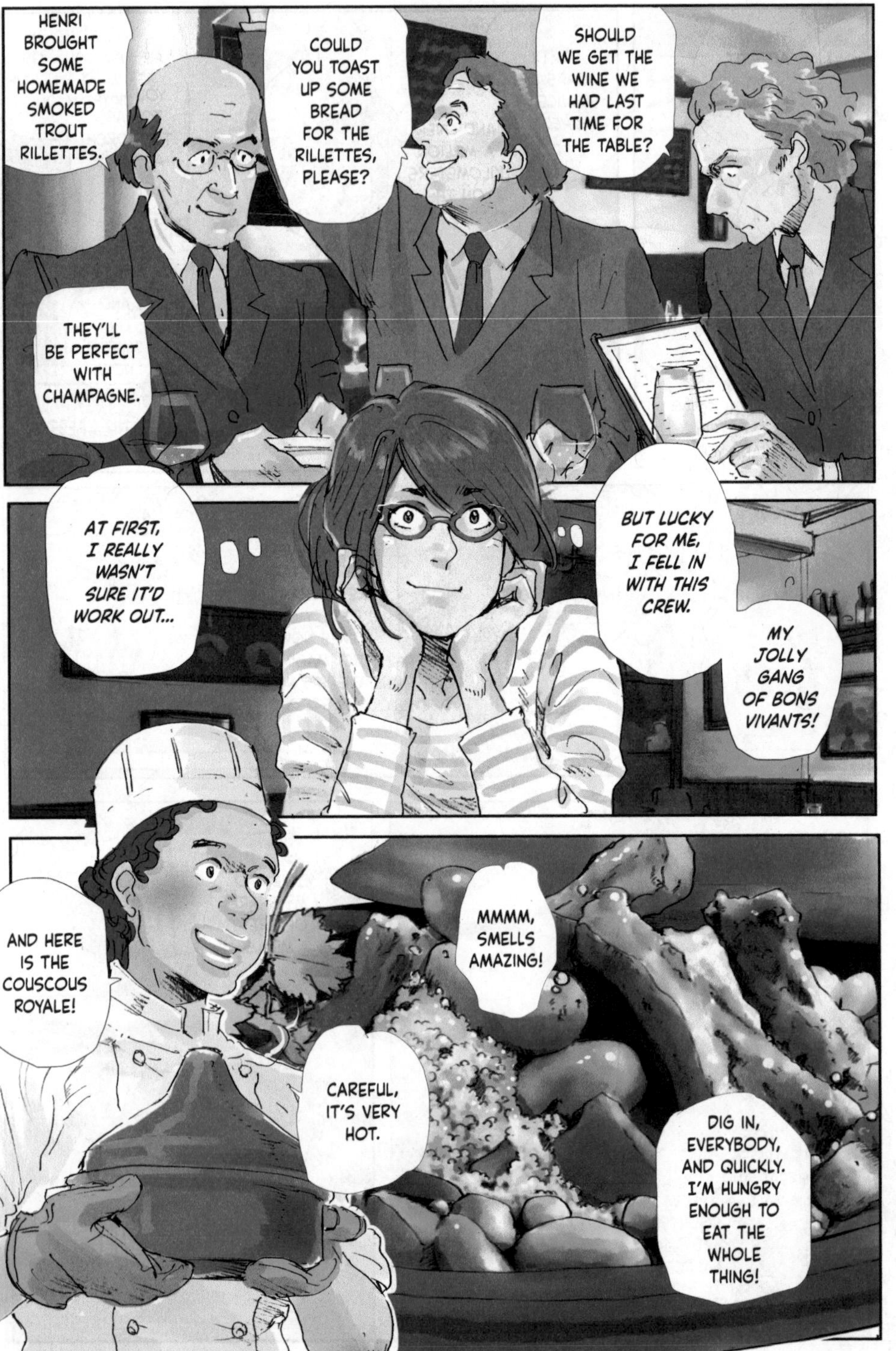
HENRI BROUGHT SOME HOMEMADE SMOKED TROUT RILLETTES.
COULD YOU TOAST UP SOME BREAD FOR THE RILLETTES, PLEASE?
SHOULD WE GET THE WINE WE HAD LAST TIME FOR THE TABLE?
THEY'LL BE PERFECT WITH CHAMPAGNE.
AT FIRST, I REALLY WASN'T SURE IT'D WORK OUT...
BUT LUCKY FOR ME, I FELL IN WITH THIS CREW.
MY JOLLY GANG OF BONS VIVANTS!
AND HERE IS THE COUSCOUS ROYALE!
MMMM, SMELLS AMAZING!
CAREFUL, IT'S VERY HOT.
DIG IN, EVERYBODY, AND QUICKLY. I'M HUNGRY ENOUGH TO EAT THE WHOLE THING!

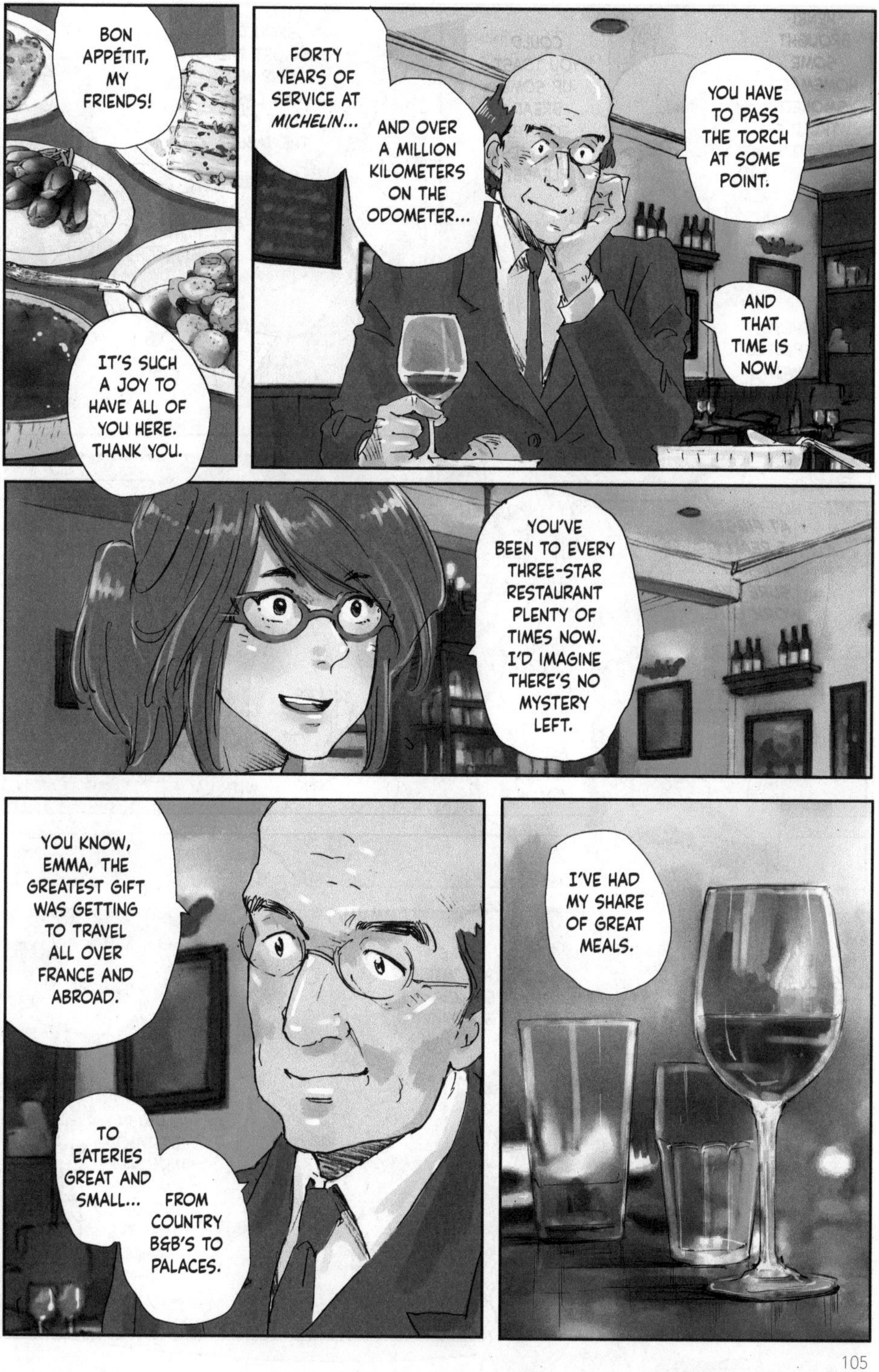
BON APPÉTIT, MY FRIENDS!
IT'S SUCH A JOY TO HAVE ALL OF YOU HERE. THANK YOU.
FORTY YEARS OF SERVICE AT *MICHELIN*...
AND OVER A MILLION KILOMETERS ON THE ODOMETER...
YOU HAVE TO PASS THE TORCH AT SOME POINT.
AND THAT TIME IS NOW.
YOU'VE BEEN TO EVERY THREE-STAR RESTAURANT PLENTY OF TIMES NOW. I'D IMAGINE THERE'S NO MYSTERY LEFT.
YOU KNOW, EMMA, THE GREATEST GIFT WAS GETTING TO TRAVEL ALL OVER FRANCE AND ABROAD.
TO EATERIES GREAT AND SMALL...
FROM COUNTRY B&B'S TO PALACES.
I'VE HAD MY SHARE OF GREAT MEALS.

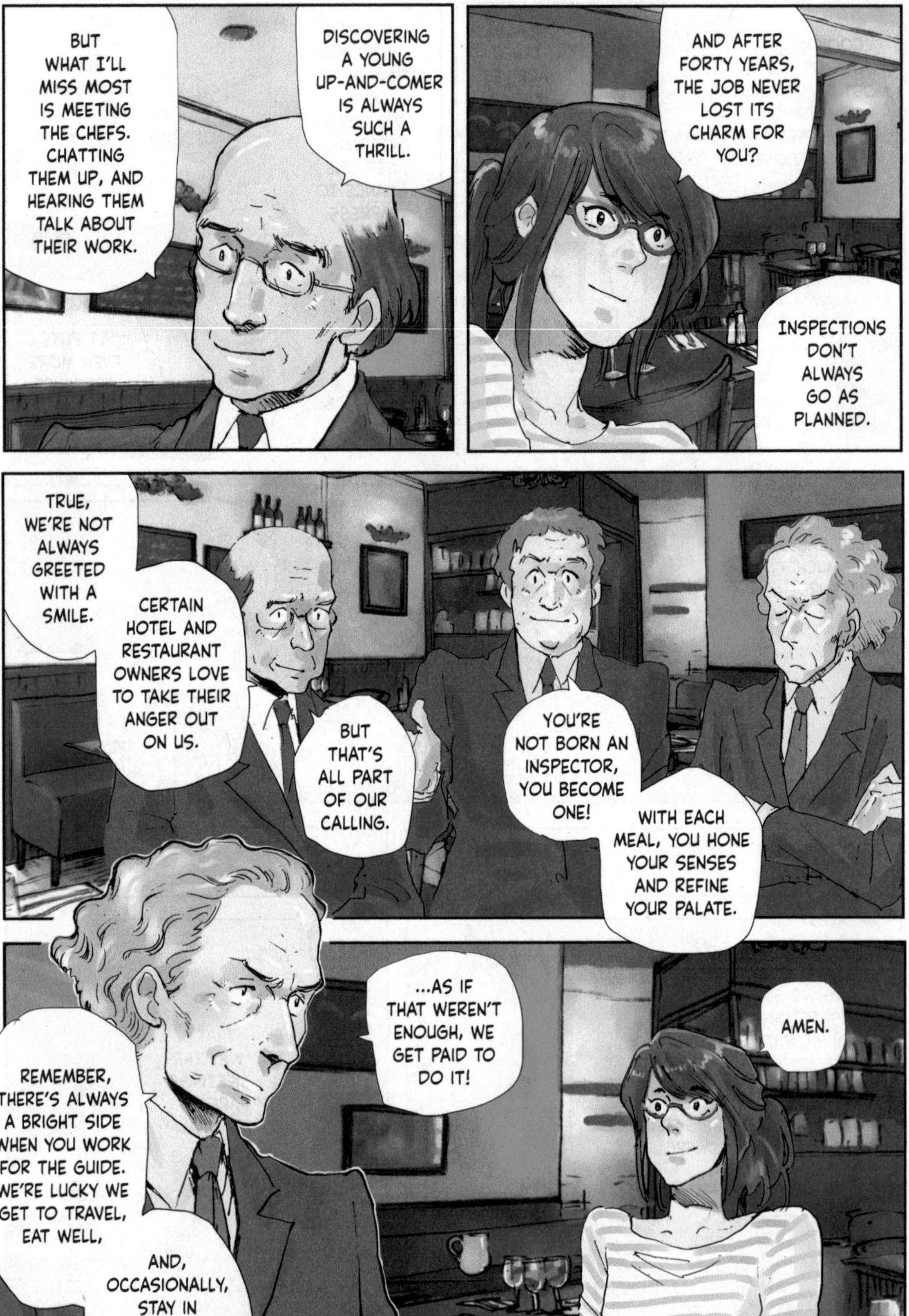
BUT WHAT I'LL MISS MOST IS MEETING THE CHEFS. CHATTING THEM UP, AND HEARING THEM TALK ABOUT THEIR WORK.
DISCOVERING A YOUNG UP-AND-COMER IS ALWAYS SUCH A THRILL.
AND AFTER FORTY YEARS, THE JOB NEVER LOST ITS CHARM FOR YOU?
INSPECTIONS DON'T ALWAYS GO AS PLANNED.
TRUE, WE'RE NOT ALWAYS GREETED WITH A SMILE.
CERTAIN HOTEL AND RESTAURANT OWNERS LOVE TO TAKE THEIR ANGER OUT ON US.
BUT THAT'S ALL PART OF OUR CALLING.
YOU'RE NOT BORN AN INSPECTOR, YOU BECOME ONE!
WITH EACH MEAL, YOU HONE YOUR SENSES AND REFINE YOUR PALATE.
REMEMBER, THERE'S ALWAYS A BRIGHT SIDE WHEN YOU WORK FOR THE GUIDE. WE'RE LUCKY WE GET TO TRAVEL, EAT WELL,
AND, OCCASIONALLY, STAY IN EXTRAVAGANT HOTELS...
...AS IF THAT WEREN'T ENOUGH, WE GET PAID TO DO IT!
AMEN.

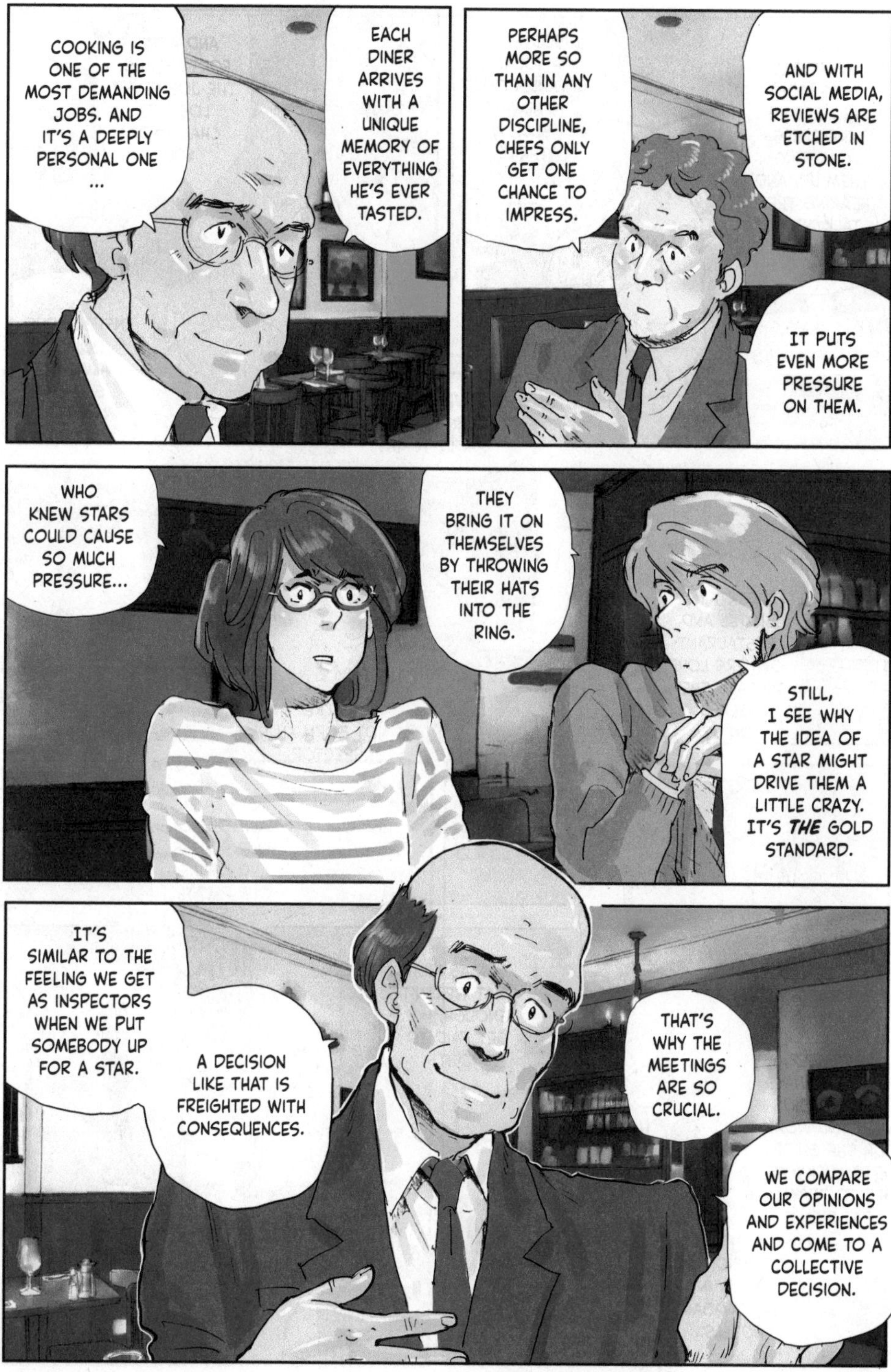
COOKING IS ONE OF THE MOST DEMANDING JOBS. AND IT'S A DEEPLY PERSONAL ONE ...
EACH DINER ARRIVES WITH A UNIQUE MEMORY OF EVERYTHING HE'S EVER TASTED.
PERHAPS MORE SO THAN IN ANY OTHER DISCIPLINE, CHEFS ONLY GET ONE CHANCE TO IMPRESS.
AND WITH SOCIAL MEDIA, REVIEWS ARE ETCHED IN STONE.
IT PUTS EVEN MORE PRESSURE ON THEM.
WHO KNEW STARS COULD CAUSE SO MUCH PRESSURE...
THEY BRING IT ON THEMSELVES BY THROWING THEIR HATS INTO THE RING.
STILL, I SEE WHY THE IDEA OF A STAR MIGHT DRIVE THEM A LITTLE CRAZY. IT'S ***THE*** GOLD STANDARD.
IT'S SIMILAR TO THE FEELING WE GET AS INSPECTORS WHEN WE PUT SOMEBODY UP FOR A STAR.
A DECISION LIKE THAT IS FREIGHTED WITH CONSEQUENCES.
THAT'S WHY THE MEETINGS ARE SO CRUCIAL.
WE COMPARE OUR OPINIONS AND EXPERIENCES AND COME TO A COLLECTIVE DECISION.

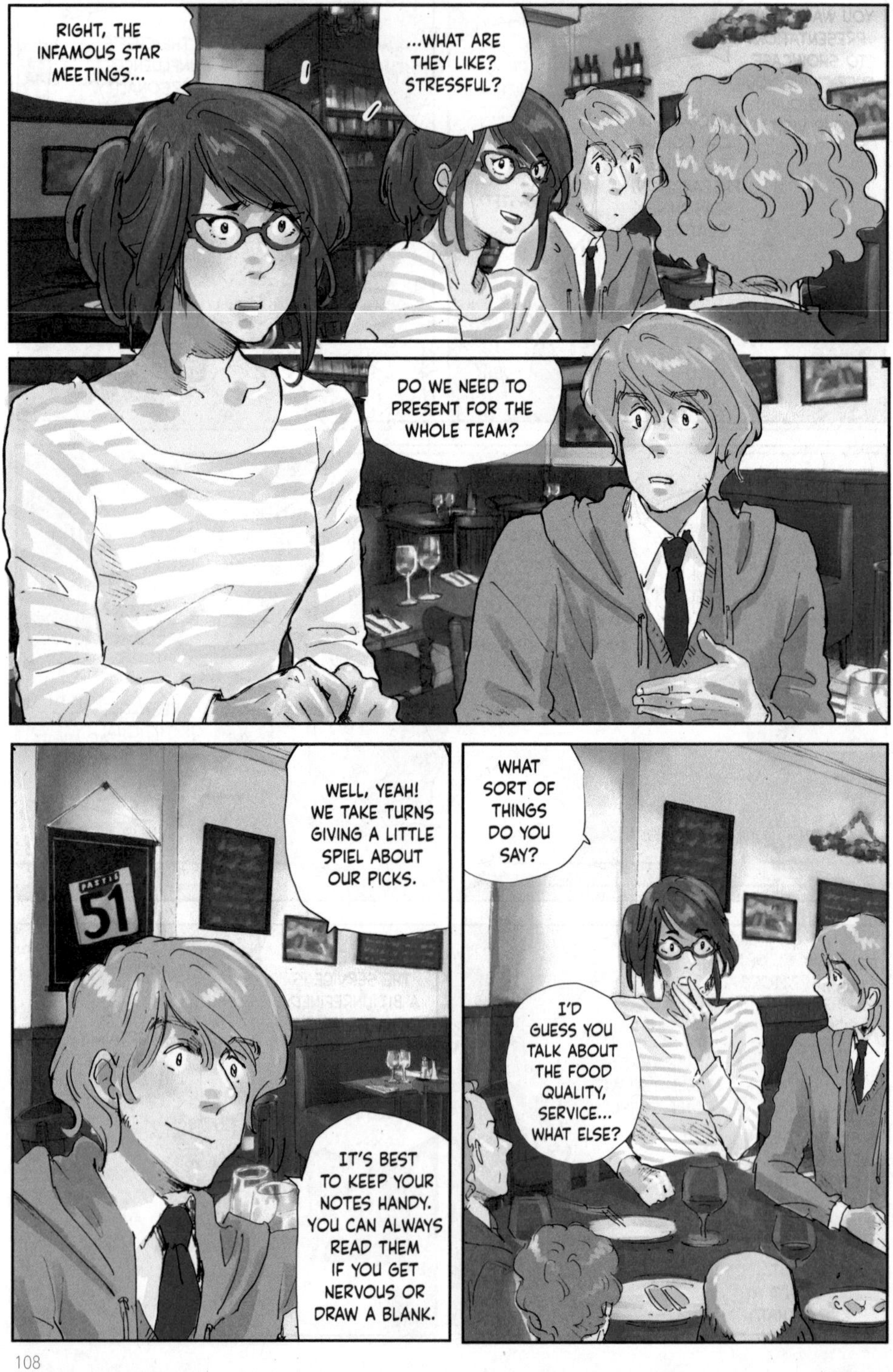
RIGHT, THE INFAMOUS STAR MEETINGS...
...WHAT ARE THEY LIKE? STRESSFUL?
DO WE NEED TO PRESENT FOR THE WHOLE TEAM?
WELL, YEAH! WE TAKE TURNS GIVING A LITTLE SPIEL ABOUT OUR PICKS.
IT'S BEST TO KEEP YOUR NOTES HANDY. YOU CAN ALWAYS READ THEM IF YOU GET NERVOUS OR DRAW A BLANK.
WHAT SORT OF THINGS DO YOU SAY?
I'D GUESS YOU TALK ABOUT THE FOOD QUALITY, SERVICE... WHAT ELSE?

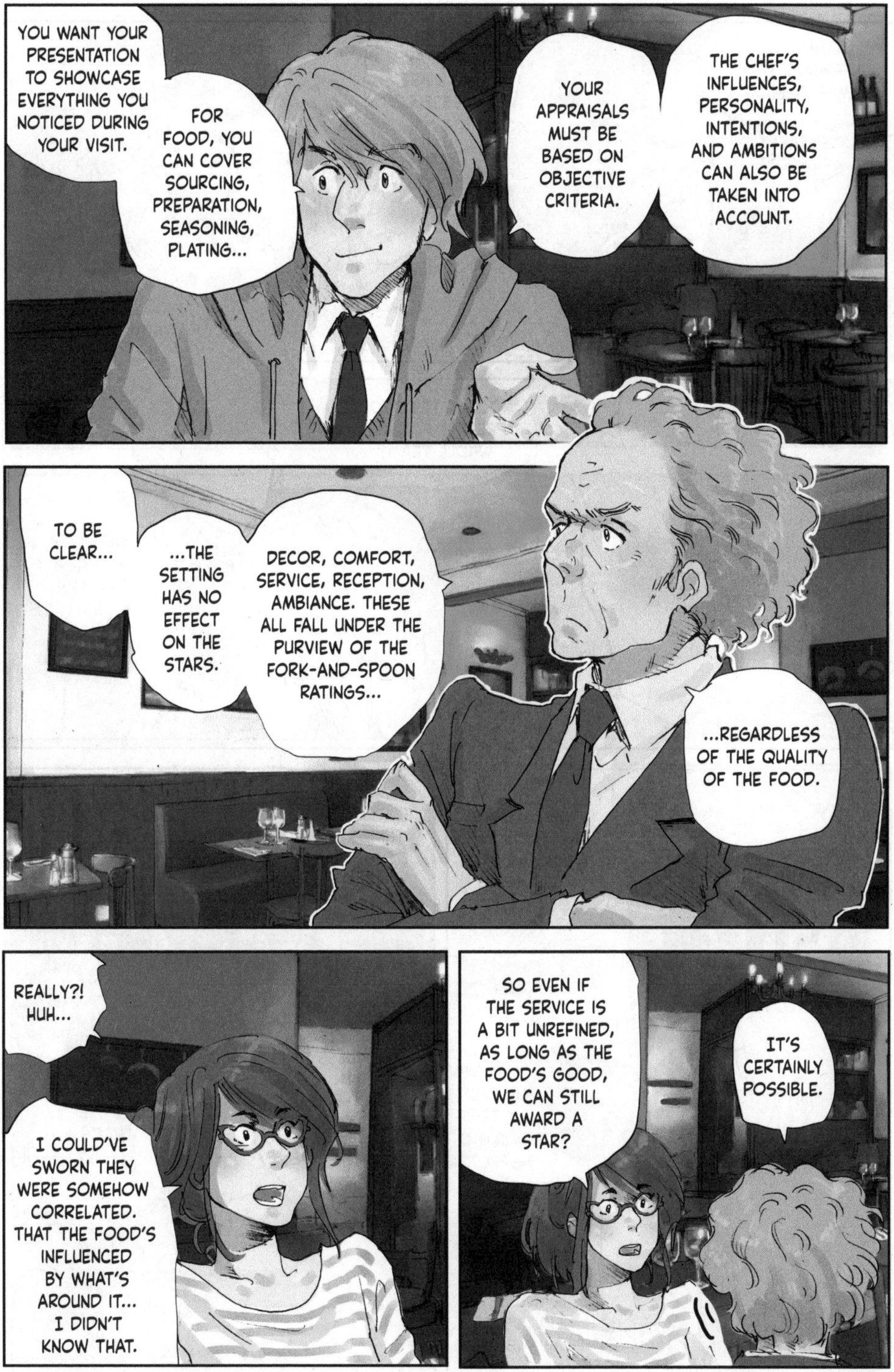
YOU WANT YOUR PRESENTATION TO SHOWCASE EVERYTHING YOU NOTICED DURING YOUR VISIT.
FOR FOOD, YOU CAN COVER SOURCING, PREPARATION, SEASONING, PLATING...
YOUR APPRAISALS MUST BE BASED ON OBJECTIVE CRITERIA.
THE CHEF'S INFLUENCES, PERSONALITY, INTENTIONS, AND AMBITIONS CAN ALSO BE TAKEN INTO ACCOUNT.
TO BE CLEAR...
...THE SETTING HAS NO EFFECT ON THE STARS.
DECOR, COMFORT, SERVICE, RECEPTION, AMBIANCE. THESE ALL FALL UNDER THE PURVIEW OF THE FORK-AND-SPOON RATINGS...
...REGARDLESS OF THE QUALITY OF THE FOOD.
REALLY?! HUH...
I COULD'VE SWORN THEY WERE SOMEHOW CORRELATED. THAT THE FOOD'S INFLUENCED BY WHAT'S AROUND IT... I DIDN'T KNOW THAT.
SO EVEN IF THE SERVICE IS A BIT UNREFINED, AS LONG AS THE FOOD'S GOOD, WE CAN STILL AWARD A STAR?
IT'S CERTAINLY POSSIBLE.

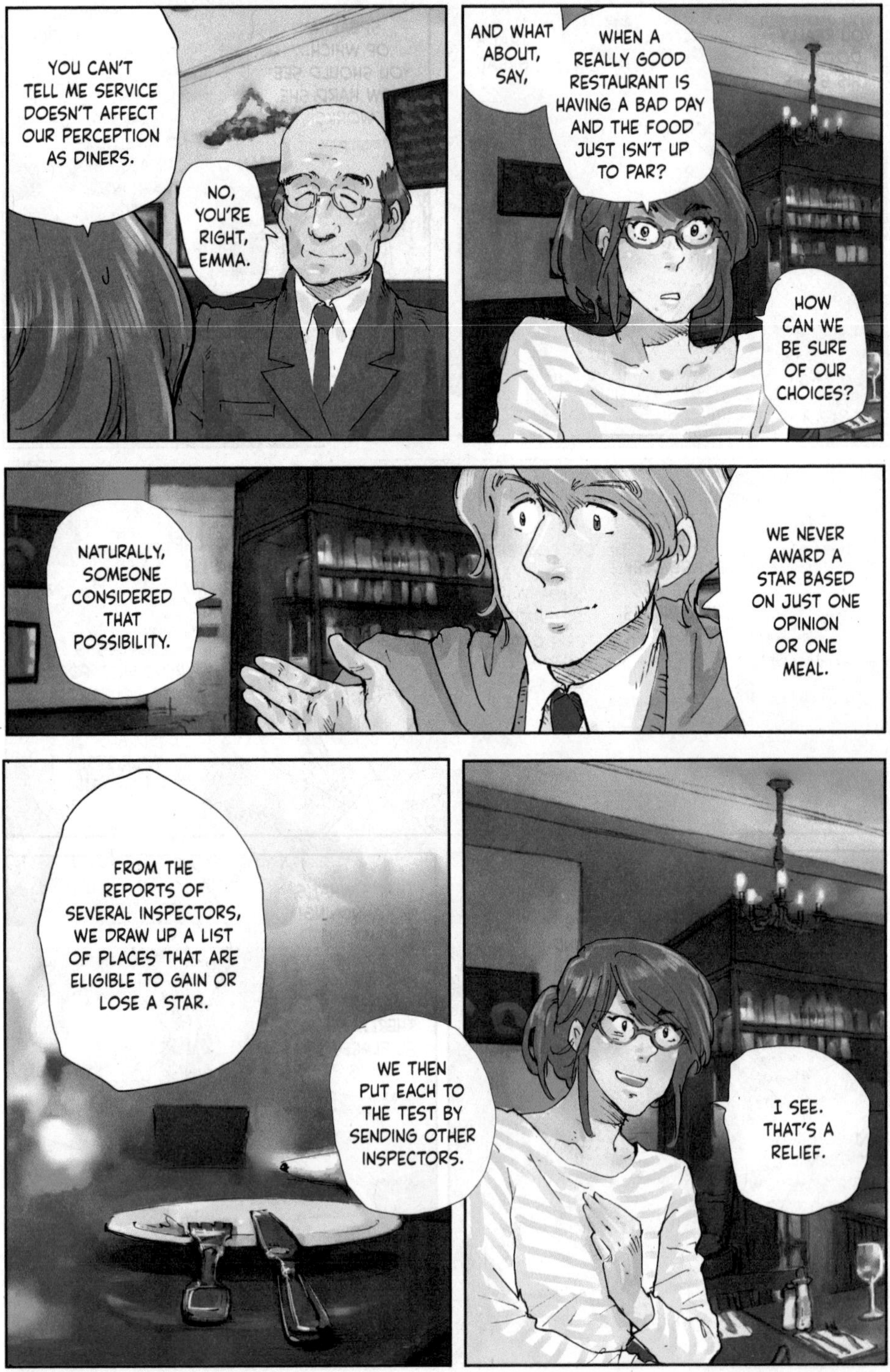
YOU CAN'T TELL ME SERVICE DOESN'T AFFECT OUR PERCEPTION AS DINERS.
NO, YOU'RE RIGHT, EMMA.
AND WHAT ABOUT, SAY,
WHEN A REALLY GOOD RESTAURANT IS HAVING A BAD DAY AND THE FOOD JUST ISN'T UP TO PAR?
HOW CAN WE BE SURE OF OUR CHOICES?
NATURALLY, SOMEONE CONSIDERED THAT POSSIBILITY.
WE NEVER AWARD A STAR BASED ON JUST ONE OPINION OR ONE MEAL.
FROM THE REPORTS OF SEVERAL INSPECTORS, WE DRAW UP A LIST OF PLACES THAT ARE ELIGIBLE TO GAIN OR LOSE A STAR.
WE THEN PUT EACH TO THE TEST BY SENDING OTHER INSPECTORS.
I SEE. THAT'S A RELIEF.

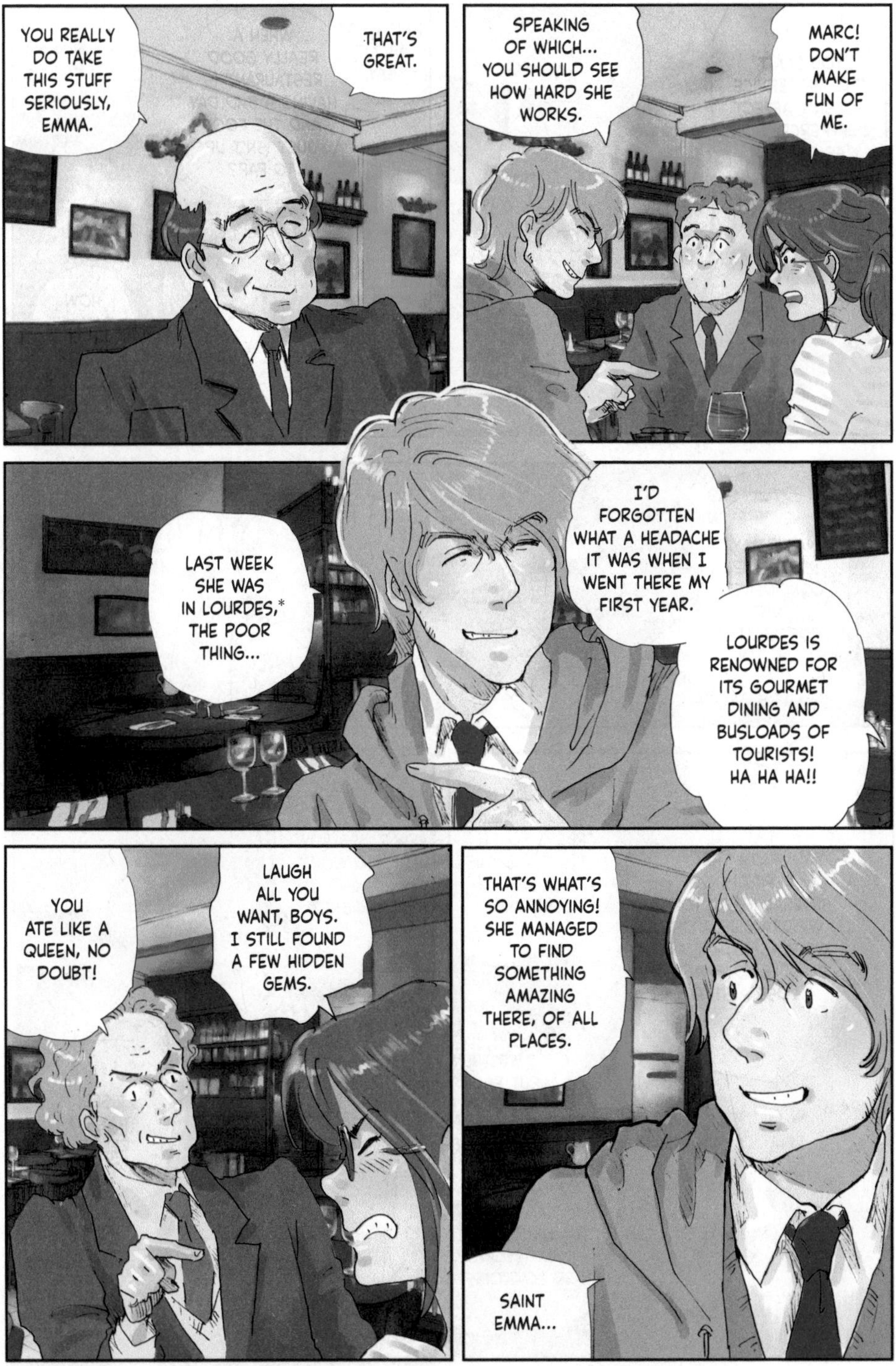
YOU REALLY DO TAKE THIS STUFF SERIOUSLY, EMMA.
THAT'S GREAT.
SPEAKING OF WHICH... YOU SHOULD SEE HOW HARD SHE WORKS.
MARC! DON'T MAKE FUN OF ME.
LAST WEEK SHE WAS IN LOURDES,* THE POOR THING...
I'D FORGOTTEN WHAT A HEADACHE IT WAS WHEN I WENT THERE MY FIRST YEAR.
LOURDES IS RENOWNED FOR ITS GOURMET DINING AND BUSLOADS OF TOURISTS! HA HA HA!!
YOU ATE LIKE A QUEEN, NO DOUBT!
LAUGH ALL YOU WANT, BOYS. I STILL FOUND A FEW HIDDEN GEMS.
THAT'S WHAT'S SO ANNOYING! SHE MANAGED TO FIND SOMETHING AMAZING THERE, OF ALL PLACES.
SAINT EMMA...

* LOURDES, NESTLED IN THE FOOTHILLS OF THE PYRENEES, IS A MAJOR DESTINATION FOR RELIGIOUS TOURISM. IT'S KNOWN FOR ITS SPRING-FED HOLY WATERS, WHICH ARE BOTTLED AND SOLD.

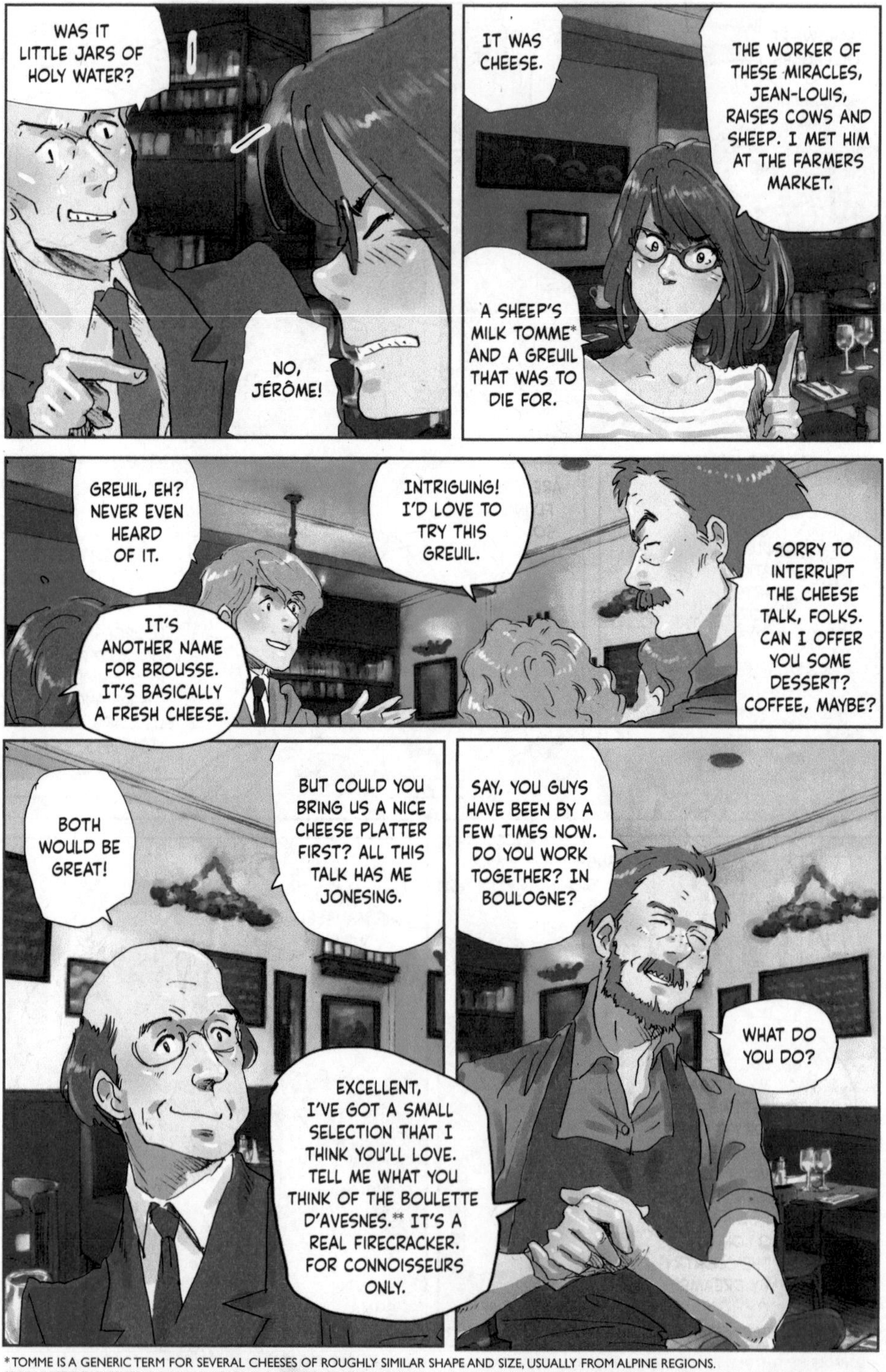
WAS IT LITTLE JARS OF HOLY WATER?
NO, JÉRÔME!
IT WAS CHEESE.
THE WORKER OF THESE MIRACLES, JEAN-LOUIS, RAISES COWS AND SHEEP. I MET HIM AT THE FARMERS MARKET.
A SHEEP'S MILK TOMME* AND A GREUIL THAT WAS TO DIE FOR.
GREUIL, EH? NEVER EVEN HEARD OF IT.
IT'S ANOTHER NAME FOR BROUSSE. IT'S BASICALLY A FRESH CHEESE.
INTRIGUING! I'D LOVE TO TRY THIS GREUIL.
SORRY TO INTERRUPT THE CHEESE TALK, FOLKS. CAN I OFFER YOU SOME DESSERT? COFFEE, MAYBE?
BOTH WOULD BE GREAT!
BUT COULD YOU BRING US A NICE CHEESE PLATTER FIRST? ALL THIS TALK HAS ME JONESING.
EXCELLENT, I'VE GOT A SMALL SELECTION THAT I THINK YOU'LL LOVE. TELL ME WHAT YOU THINK OF THE BOULETTE D'AVESNES.** IT'S A REAL FIRECRACKER. FOR CONNOISSEURS ONLY.
SAY, YOU GUYS HAVE BEEN BY A FEW TIMES NOW. DO YOU WORK TOGETHER? IN BOULOGNE?
WHAT DO YOU DO?

* TOMME IS A GENERIC TERM FOR SEVERAL CHEESES OF ROUGHLY SIMILAR SHAPE AND SIZE, USUALLY FROM ALPINE REGIONS.

** BOULETTE D'AVESNES IS A SMALL, STRONG-SMELLING CONICAL CHEESE PACKED WITH HERBS. IT'S PRODUCED NEAR THE BELGIAN BORDER.

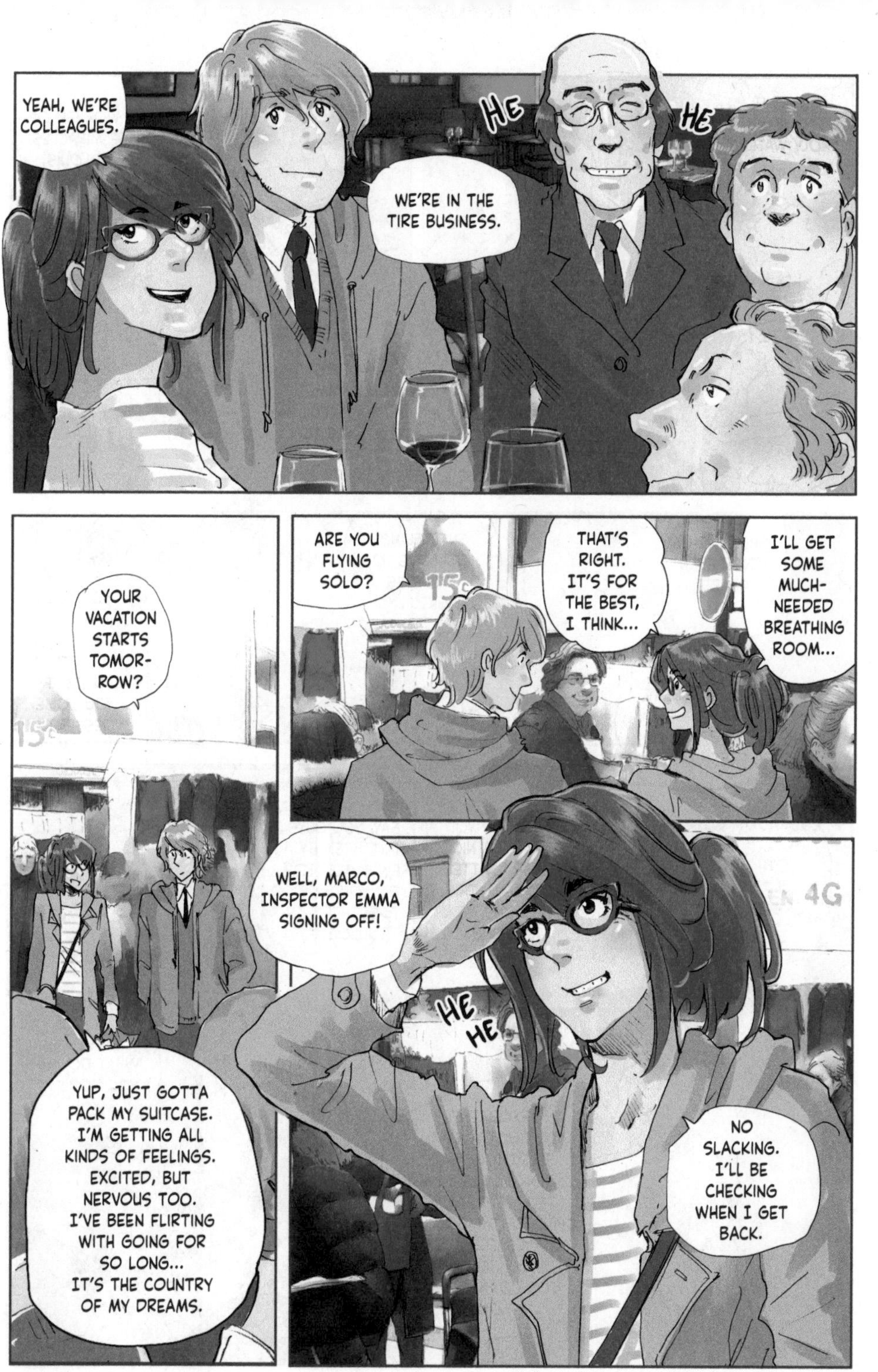
YEAH, WE'RE COLLEAGUES.
HE
HE
WE'RE IN THE TIRE BUSINESS.
YOUR VACATION STARTS TOMOR-ROW?
YUP, JUST GOTTA PACK MY SUITCASE. I'M GETTING ALL KINDS OF FEELINGS. EXCITED, BUT NERVOUS TOO. I'VE BEEN FLIRTING WITH GOING FOR SO LONG... IT'S THE COUNTRY OF MY DREAMS.
ARE YOU FLYING SOLO?
THAT'S RIGHT. IT'S FOR THE BEST, I THINK...
I'LL GET SOME MUCH-NEEDED BREATHING ROOM...
WELL, MARCO, INSPECTOR EMMA SIGNING OFF!
HE
HE
NO SLACKING. I'LL BE CHECKING WHEN I GET BACK.

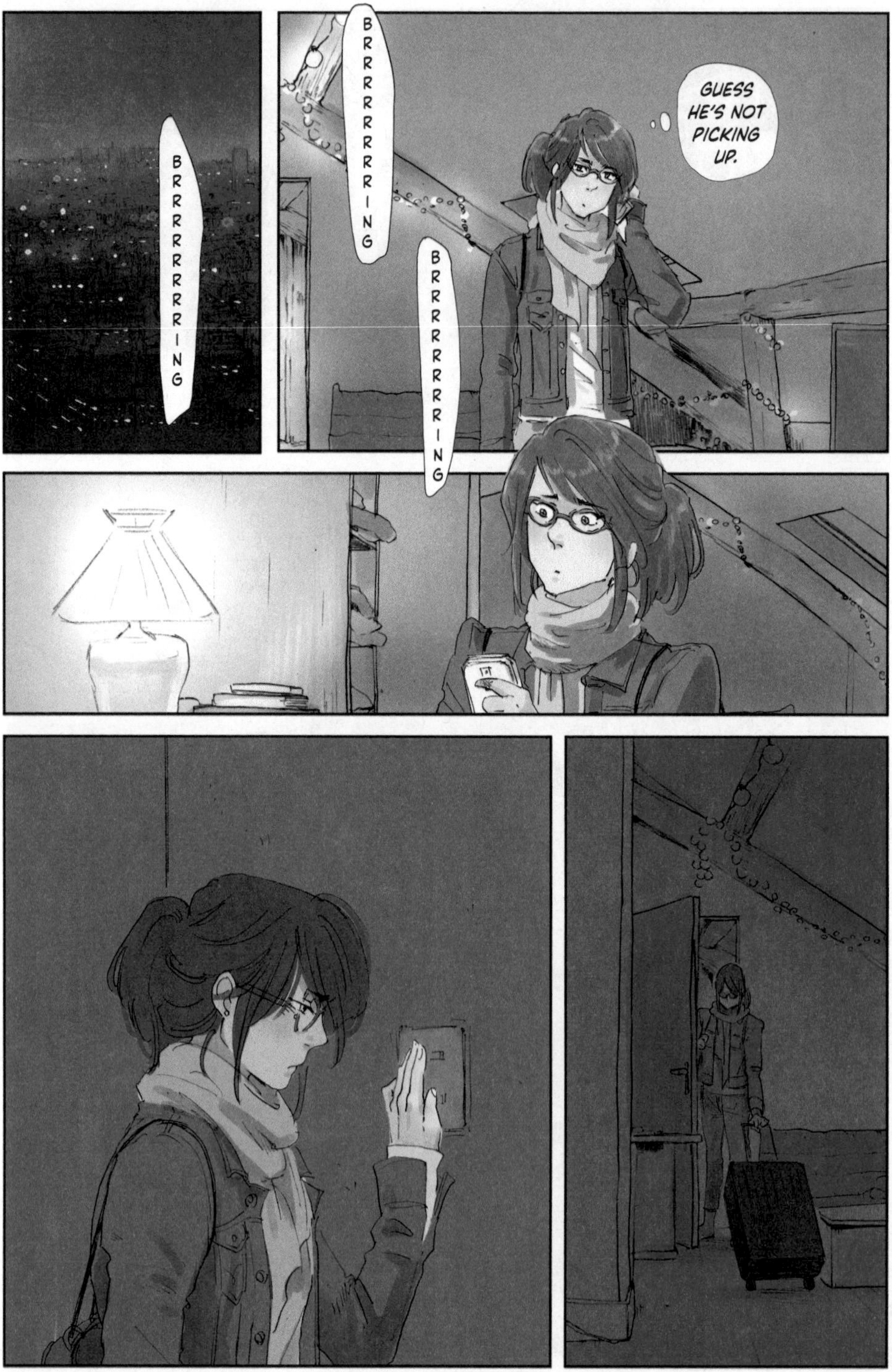
BRRRRRRRRING
BRRRRRRRRING
BRRRRRRRRING
GUESS HE'S NOT PICKING UP.

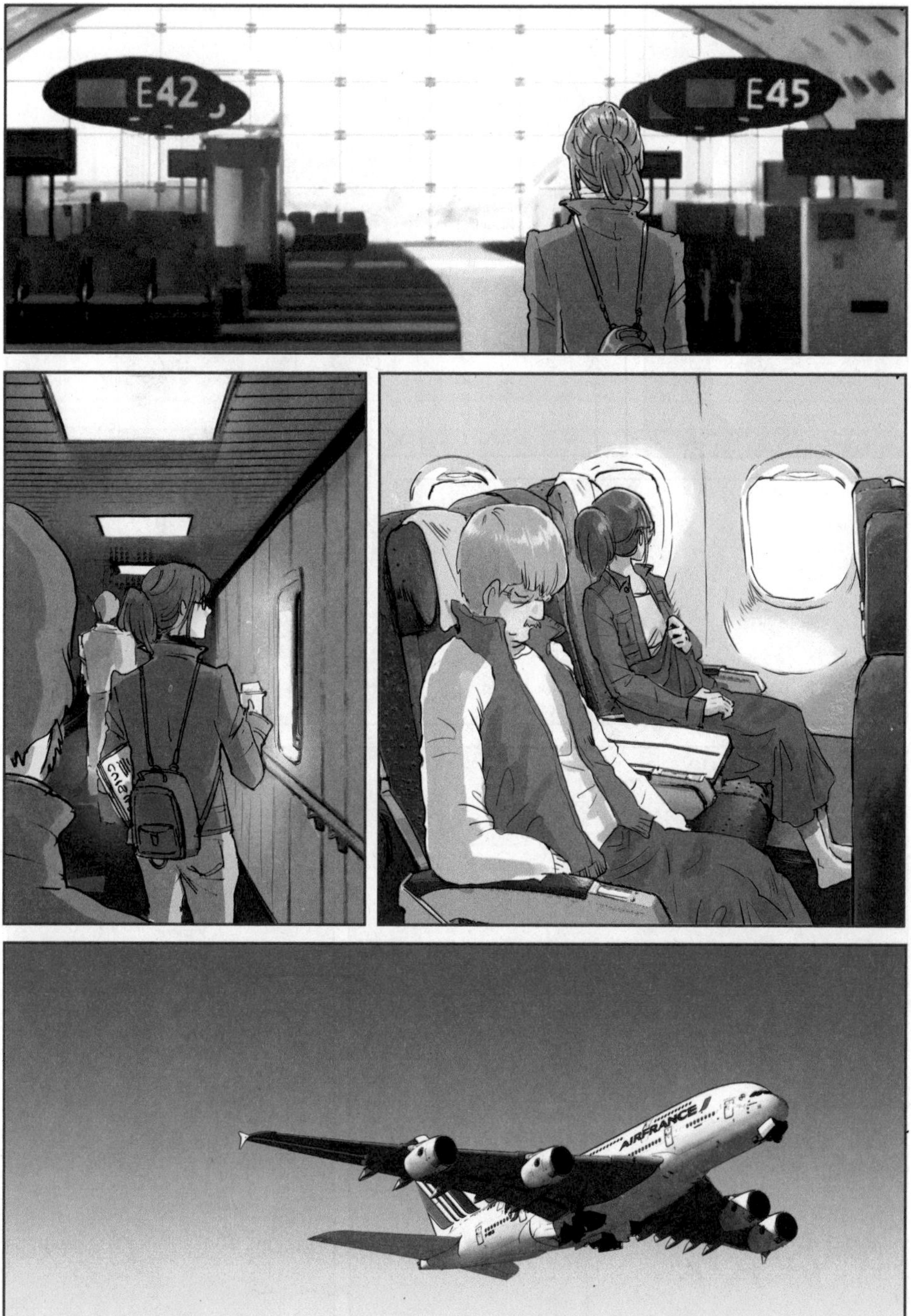
E42
E45
AIRFRANCE

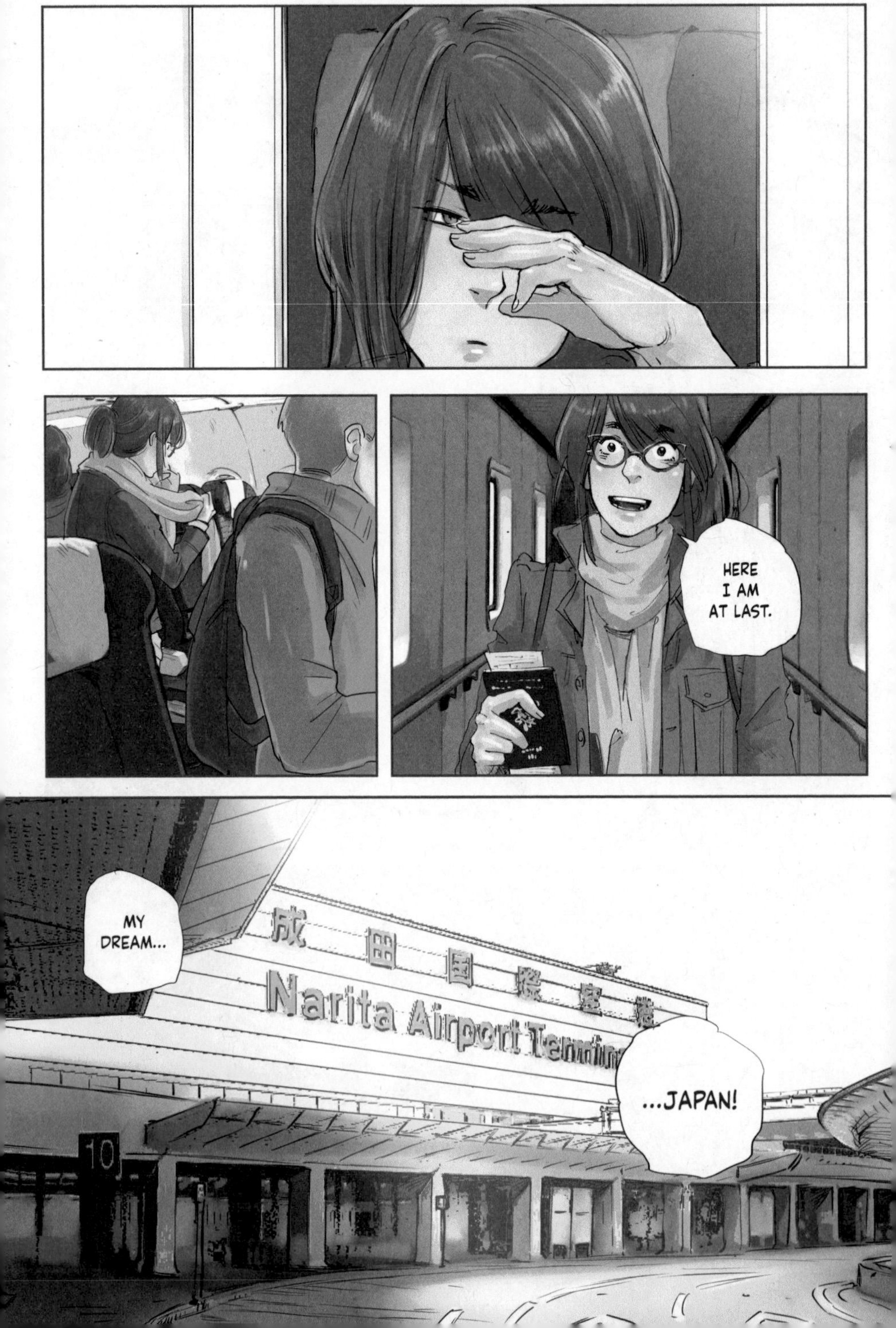
HERE I AM AT LAST.
MY DREAM...
Narita Airport
...JAPAN!

CHAPTER 6

IN JAPAN

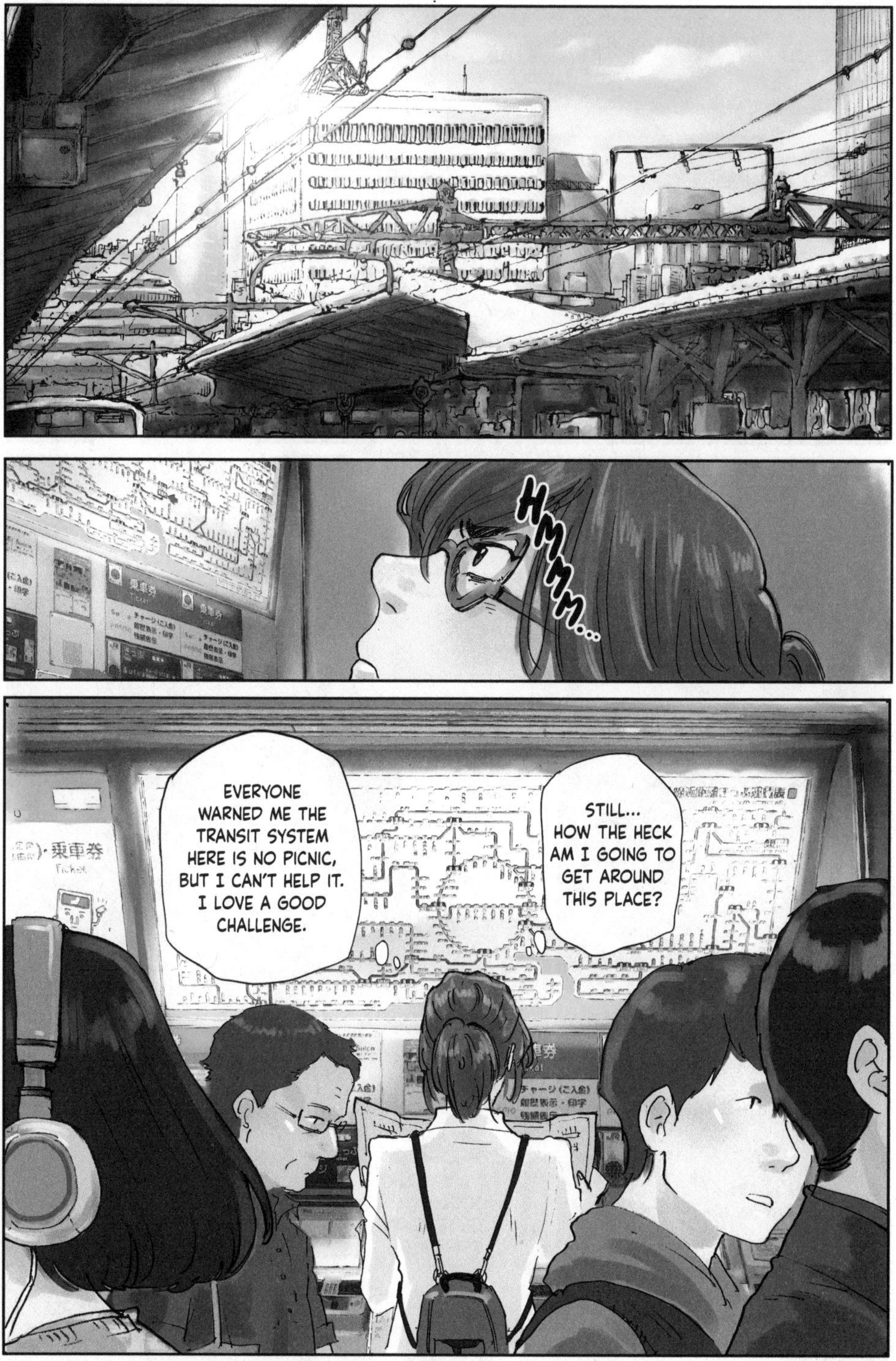
HMMM...
EVERYONE WARNED ME THE TRANSIT SYSTEM HERE IS NO PICNIC, BUT I CAN'T HELP IT. I LOVE A GOOD CHALLENGE.
STILL... HOW THE HECK AM I GOING TO GET AROUND THIS PLACE?

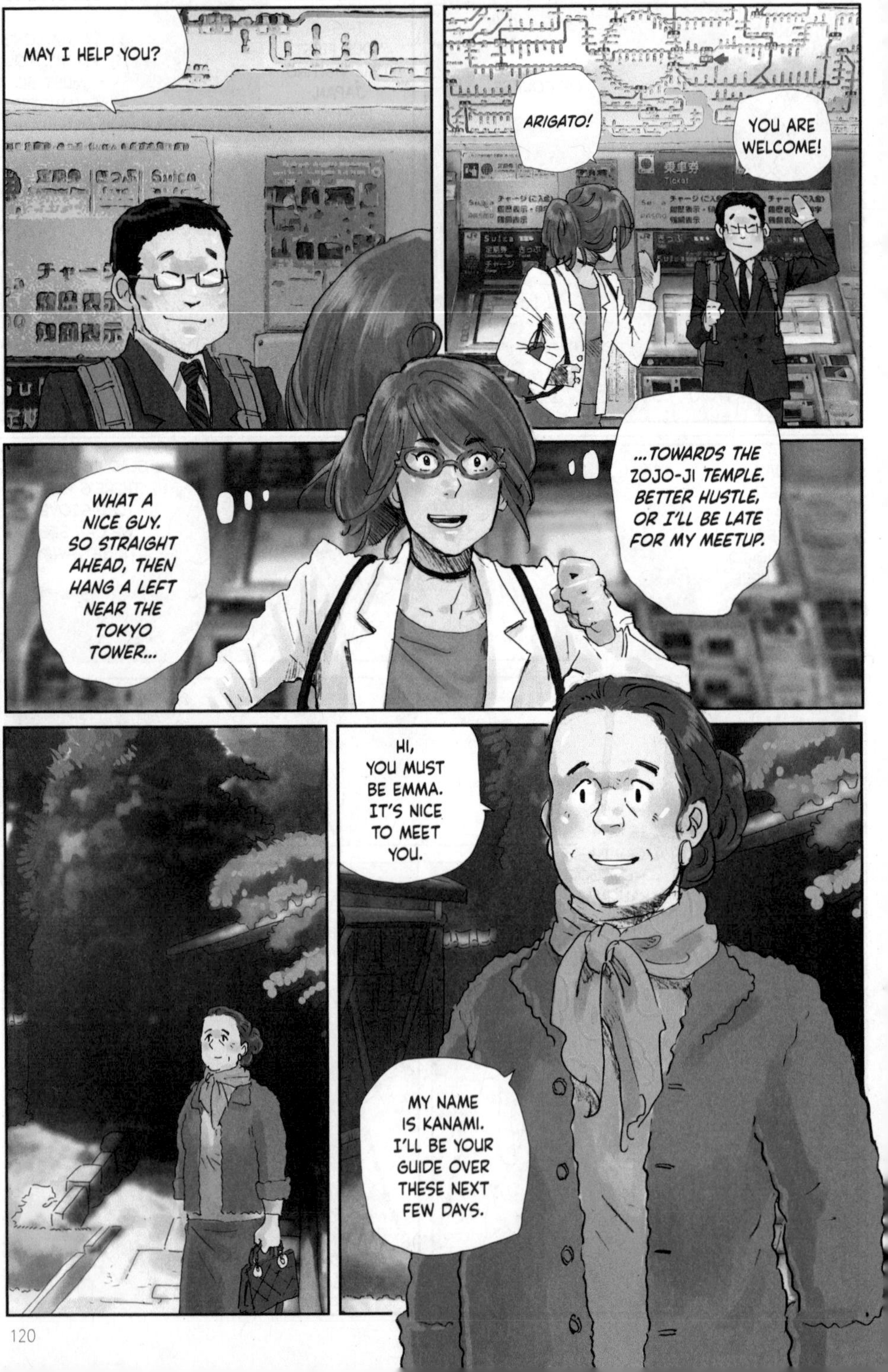
MAY I HELP YOU?
ARIGATO!
YOU ARE WELCOME!
WHAT A NICE GUY. SO STRAIGHT AHEAD, THEN HANG A LEFT NEAR THE TOKYO TOWER...
...TOWARDS THE ZOJO-JI TEMPLE. BETTER HUSTLE, OR I'LL BE LATE FOR MY MEETUP.
HI, YOU MUST BE EMMA. IT'S NICE TO MEET YOU.
MY NAME IS KANAMI. I'LL BE YOUR GUIDE OVER THESE NEXT FEW DAYS.

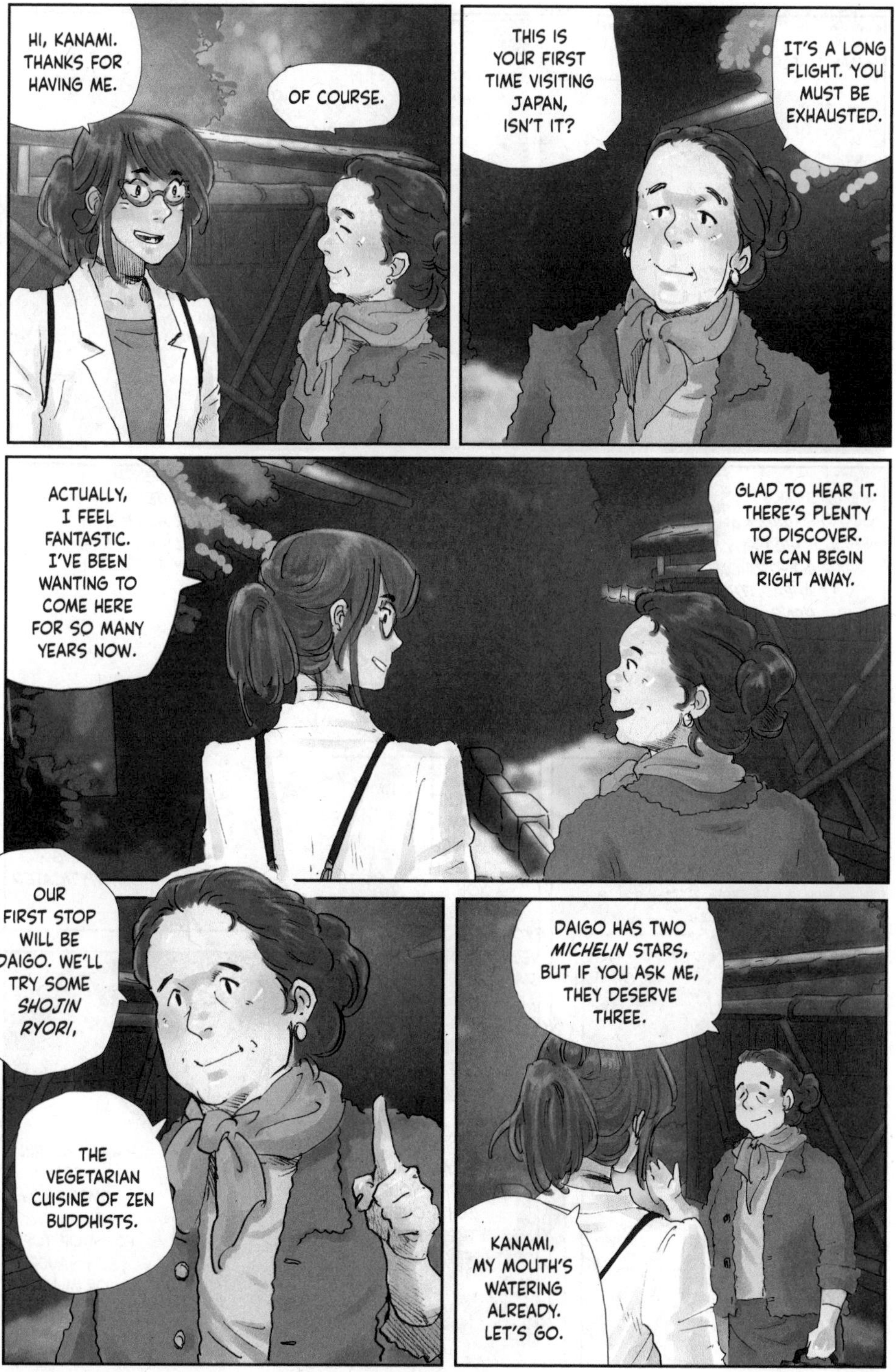
HI, KANAMI. THANKS FOR HAVING ME.
OF COURSE.
THIS IS YOUR FIRST TIME VISITING JAPAN, ISN'T IT?
IT'S A LONG FLIGHT. YOU MUST BE EXHAUSTED.
ACTUALLY, I FEEL FANTASTIC. I'VE BEEN WANTING TO COME HERE FOR SO MANY YEARS NOW.
GLAD TO HEAR IT. THERE'S PLENTY TO DISCOVER. WE CAN BEGIN RIGHT AWAY.
OUR FIRST STOP WILL BE DAIGO. WE'LL TRY SOME *SHOJIN RYORI*,
THE VEGETARIAN CUISINE OF ZEN BUDDHISTS.
DAIGO HAS TWO *MICHELIN* STARS, BUT IF YOU ASK ME, THEY DESERVE THREE.
KANAMI, MY MOUTH'S WATERING ALREADY. LET'S GO.

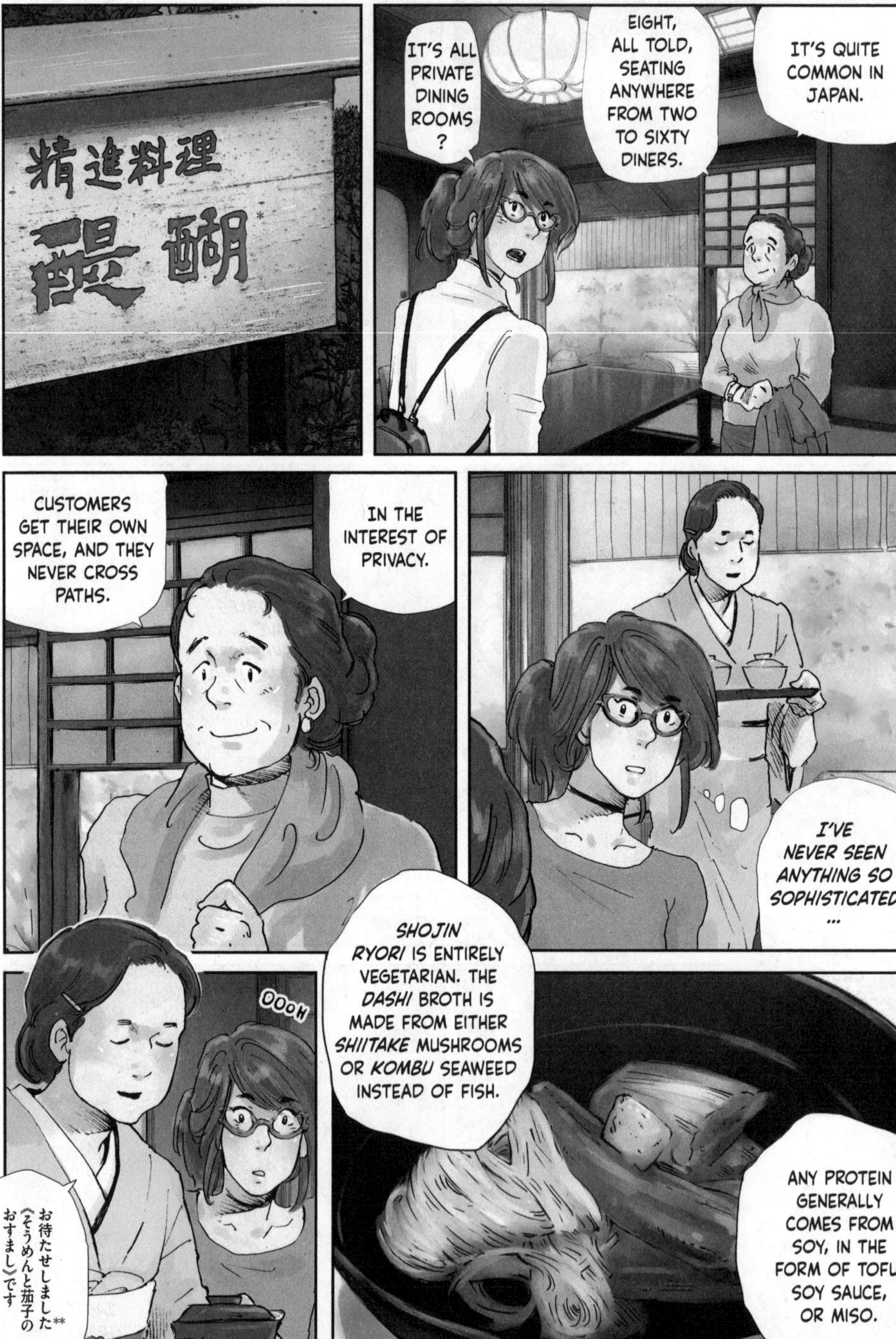

精進料理
醍醐*
IT'S ALL PRIVATE DINING ROOMS?
EIGHT, ALL TOLD, SEATING ANYWHERE FROM TWO TO SIXTY DINERS.
IT'S QUITE COMMON IN JAPAN.
CUSTOMERS GET THEIR OWN SPACE, AND THEY NEVER CROSS PATHS.
IN THE INTEREST OF PRIVACY.
I'VE NEVER SEEN ANYTHING SO SOPHISTICATED...
OOOH
お待たせしました《そうめんと茄子のおすまし》です**
SHOJIN RYORI IS ENTIRELY VEGETARIAN. THE *DASHI* BROTH IS MADE FROM EITHER *SHIITAKE* MUSHROOMS OR *KOMBU* SEAWEED INSTEAD OF FISH.
ANY PROTEIN GENERALLY COMES FROM SOY, IN THE FORM OF TOFU, SOY SAUCE, OR MISO.

* DAIGO.

** HERE IS YOUR CLEAR SOUP WITH EGGPLANT AND SOMEN NOODLES.

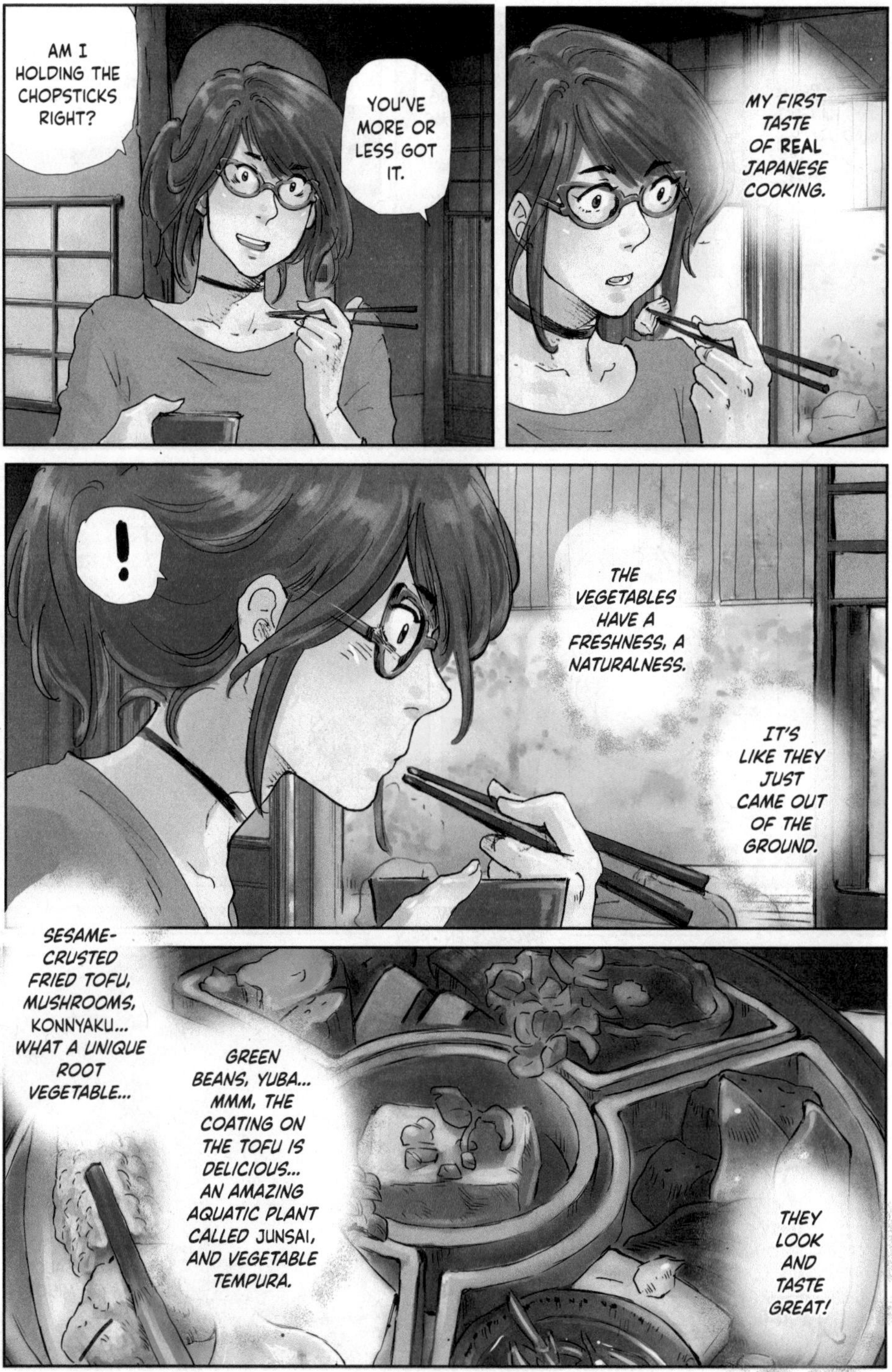
AM I HOLDING THE CHOPSTICKS RIGHT?
YOU'VE MORE OR LESS GOT IT.
MY FIRST TASTE OF REAL JAPANESE COOKING.
!
THE VEGETABLES HAVE A FRESHNESS, A NATURALNESS.
IT'S LIKE THEY JUST CAME OUT OF THE GROUND.
SESAME-CRUSTED FRIED TOFU, MUSHROOMS, KONNYAKU... WHAT A UNIQUE ROOT VEGETABLE...
GREEN BEANS, YUBA... MMM, THE COATING ON THE TOFU IS DELICIOUS... AN AMAZING AQUATIC PLANT CALLED JUNSAI, AND VEGETABLE TEMPURA.
THEY LOOK AND TASTE GREAT!

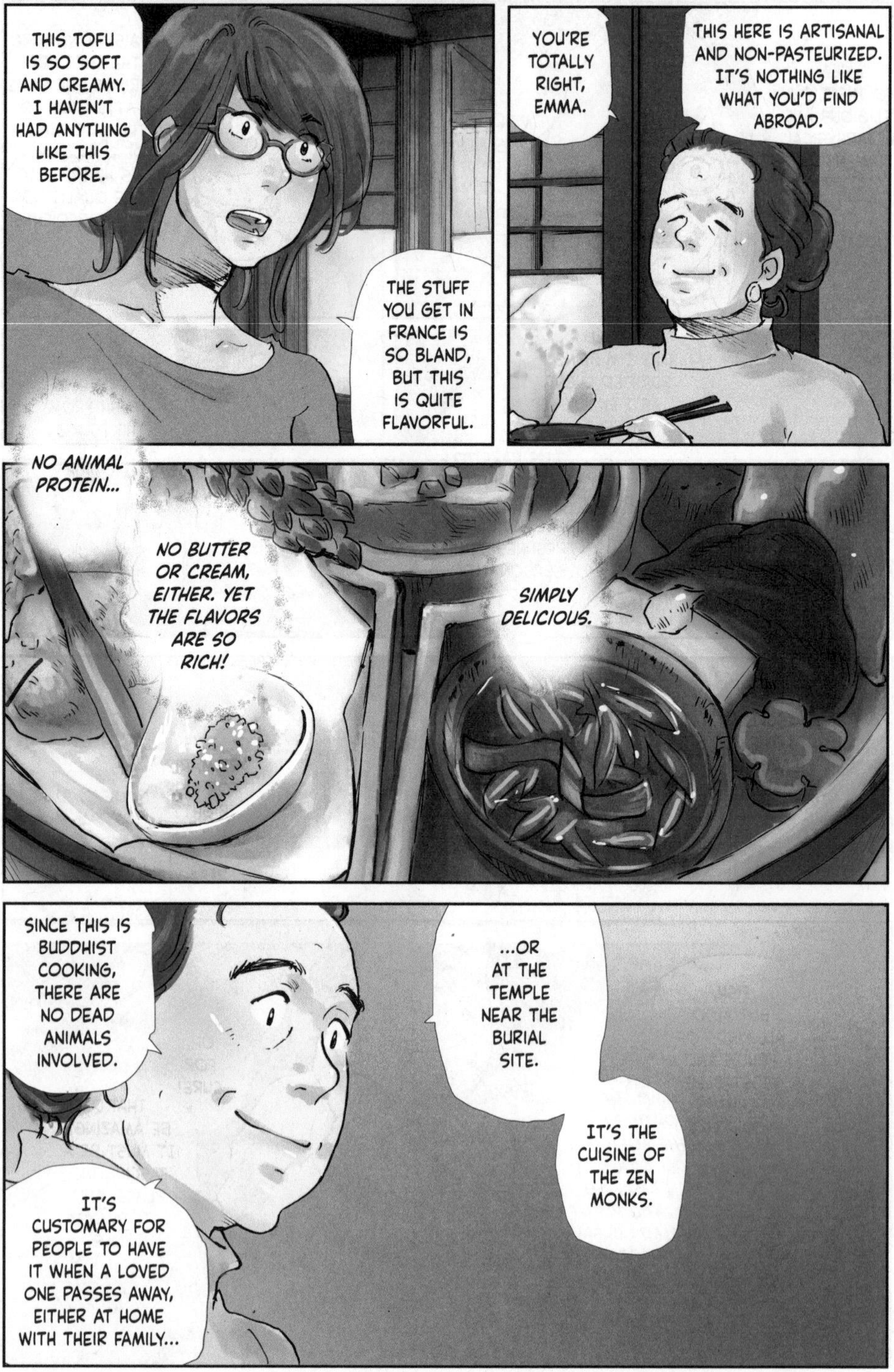
THIS TOFU IS SO SOFT AND CREAMY. I HAVEN'T HAD ANYTHING LIKE THIS BEFORE.
THE STUFF YOU GET IN FRANCE IS SO BLAND, BUT THIS IS QUITE FLAVORFUL.
YOU'RE TOTALLY RIGHT, EMMA.
THIS HERE IS ARTISANAL AND NON-PASTEURIZED. IT'S NOTHING LIKE WHAT YOU'D FIND ABROAD.
NO ANIMAL PROTEIN...
NO BUTTER OR CREAM, EITHER. YET THE FLAVORS ARE SO RICH!
SIMPLY DELICIOUS.
SINCE THIS IS BUDDHIST COOKING, THERE ARE NO DEAD ANIMALS INVOLVED.
IT'S CUSTOMARY FOR PEOPLE TO HAVE IT WHEN A LOVED ONE PASSES AWAY, EITHER AT HOME WITH THEIR FAMILY...
...OR AT THE TEMPLE NEAR THE BURIAL SITE.
IT'S THE CUISINE OF THE ZEN MONKS.

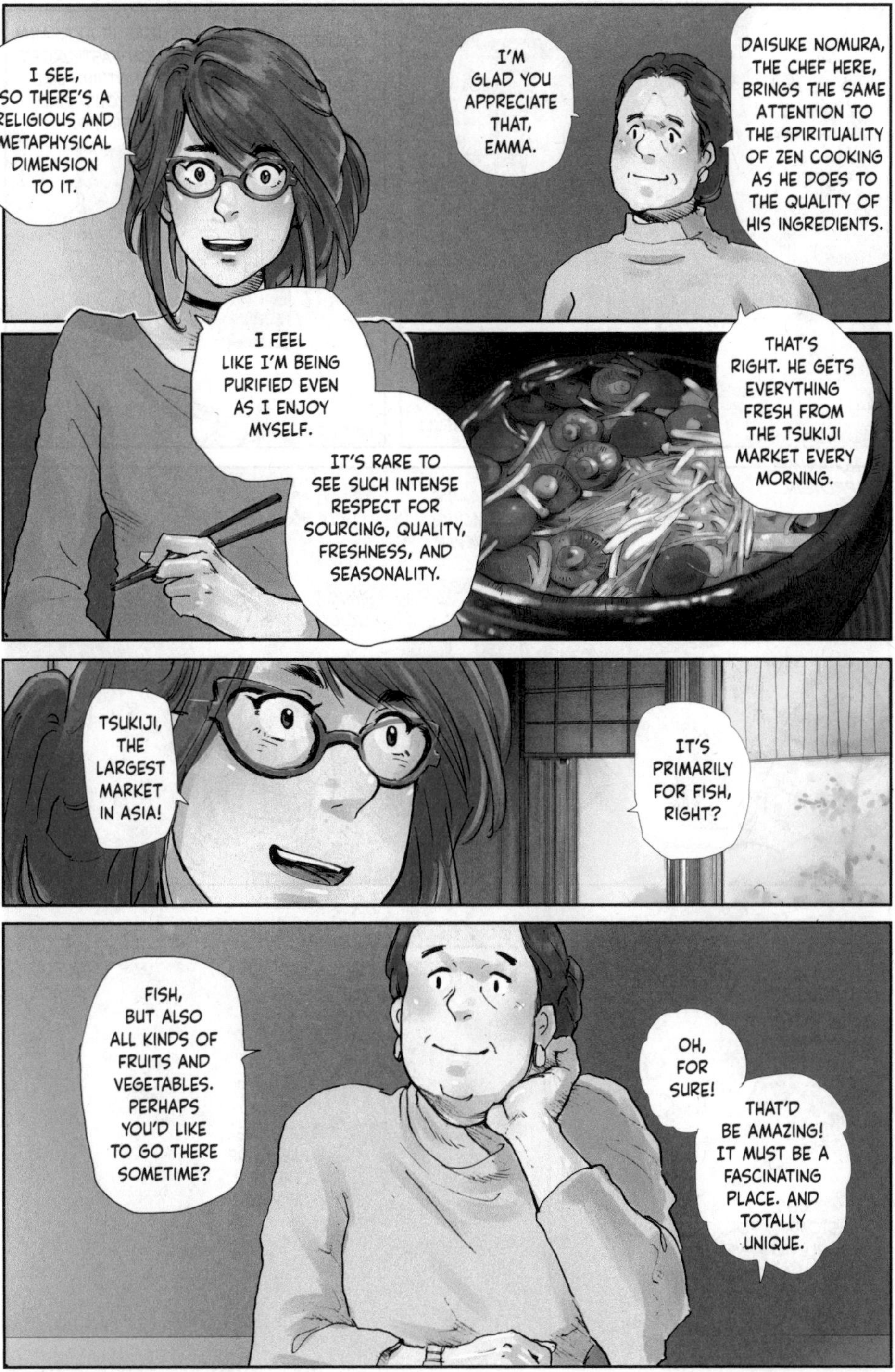

I SEE, SO THERE'S A RELIGIOUS AND METAPHYSICAL DIMENSION TO IT.
I'M GLAD YOU APPRECIATE THAT, EMMA.
DAISUKE NOMURA, THE CHEF HERE, BRINGS THE SAME ATTENTION TO THE SPIRITUALITY OF ZEN COOKING AS HE DOES TO THE QUALITY OF HIS INGREDIENTS.
I FEEL LIKE I'M BEING PURIFIED EVEN AS I ENJOY MYSELF.
IT'S RARE TO SEE SUCH INTENSE RESPECT FOR SOURCING, QUALITY, FRESHNESS, AND SEASONALITY.
THAT'S RIGHT. HE GETS EVERYTHING FRESH FROM THE TSUKIJI MARKET EVERY MORNING.
TSUKIJI, THE LARGEST MARKET IN ASIA!
IT'S PRIMARILY FOR FISH, RIGHT?
FISH, BUT ALSO ALL KINDS OF FRUITS AND VEGETABLES. PERHAPS YOU'D LIKE TO GO THERE SOMETIME?
OH, FOR SURE!
THAT'D BE AMAZING! IT MUST BE A FASCINATING PLACE. AND TOTALLY UNIQUE.

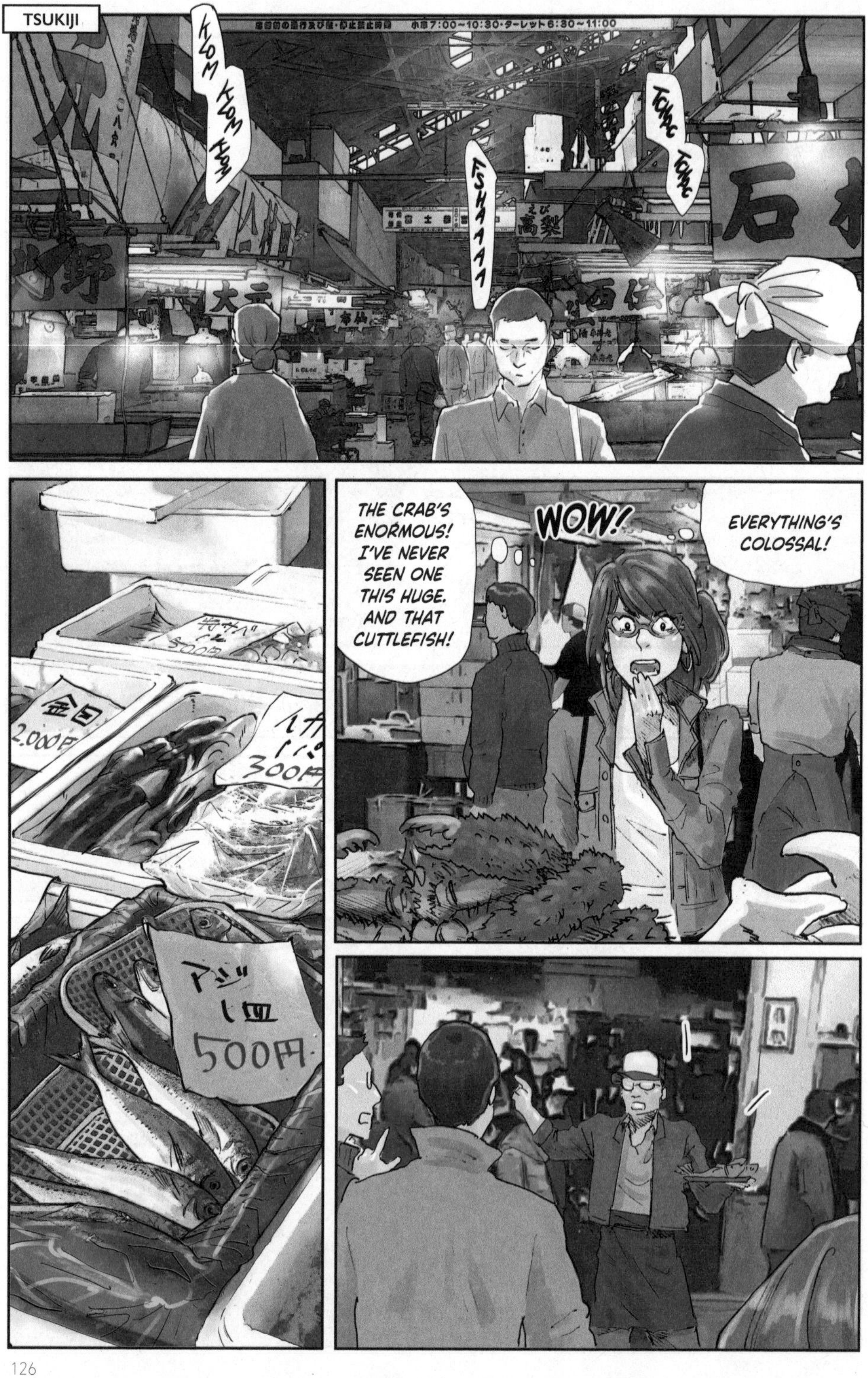
TSUKIJI
KLOM KLOM KLOM
FSHAAAAAA
TCHAC TCHAC
金目
2,000円
300円
アジ
1皿
500円
THE CRAB'S ENORMOUS! I'VE NEVER SEEN ONE THIS HUGE. AND THAT CUTTLEFISH!
WOW!
EVERYTHING'S COLOSSAL!

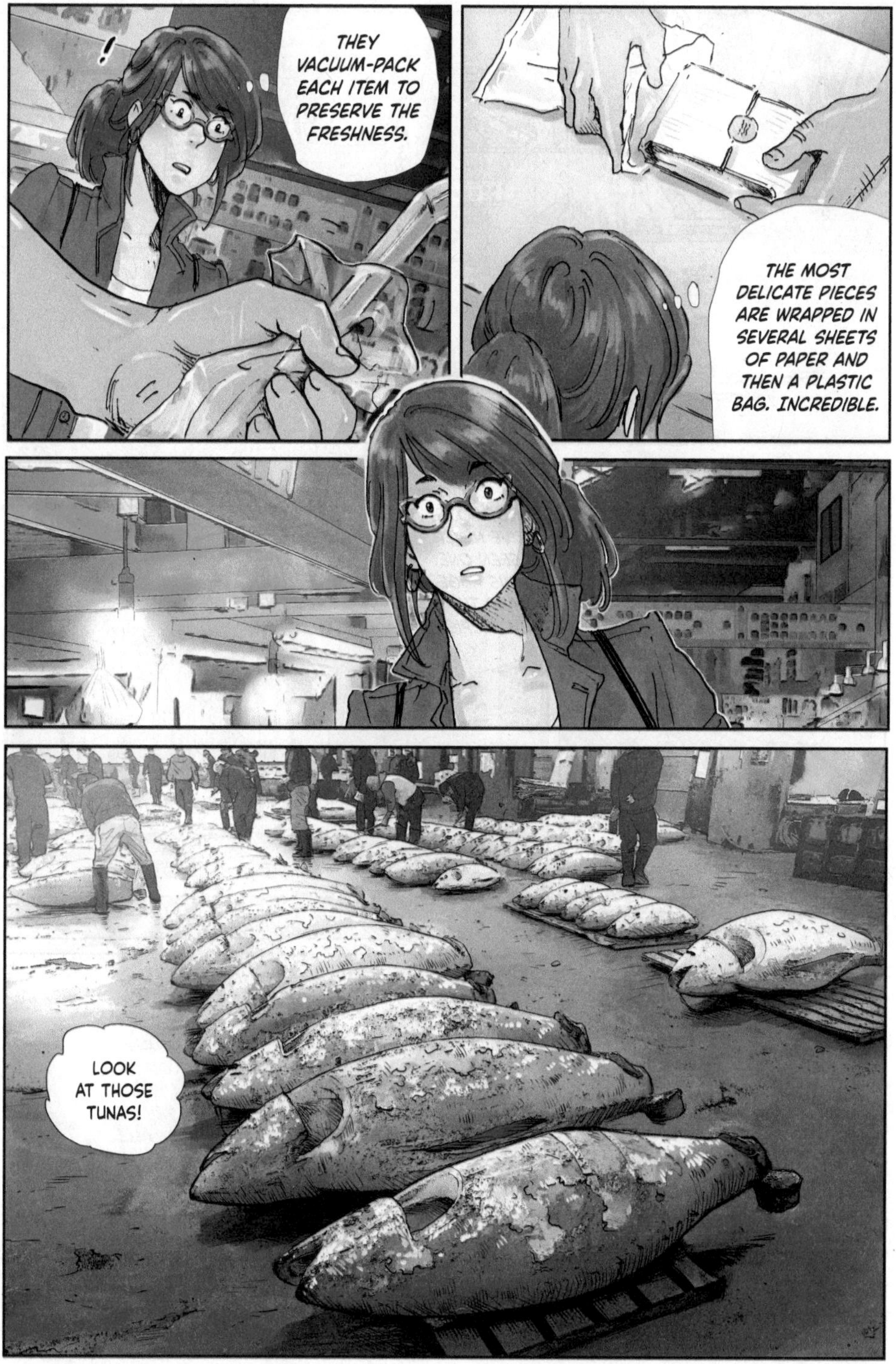
!
THEY VACUUM-PACK EACH ITEM TO PRESERVE THE FRESHNESS.
THE MOST DELICATE PIECES ARE WRAPPED IN SEVERAL SHEETS OF PAPER AND THEN A PLASTIC BAG. INCREDIBLE.
LOOK AT THOSE TUNAS!

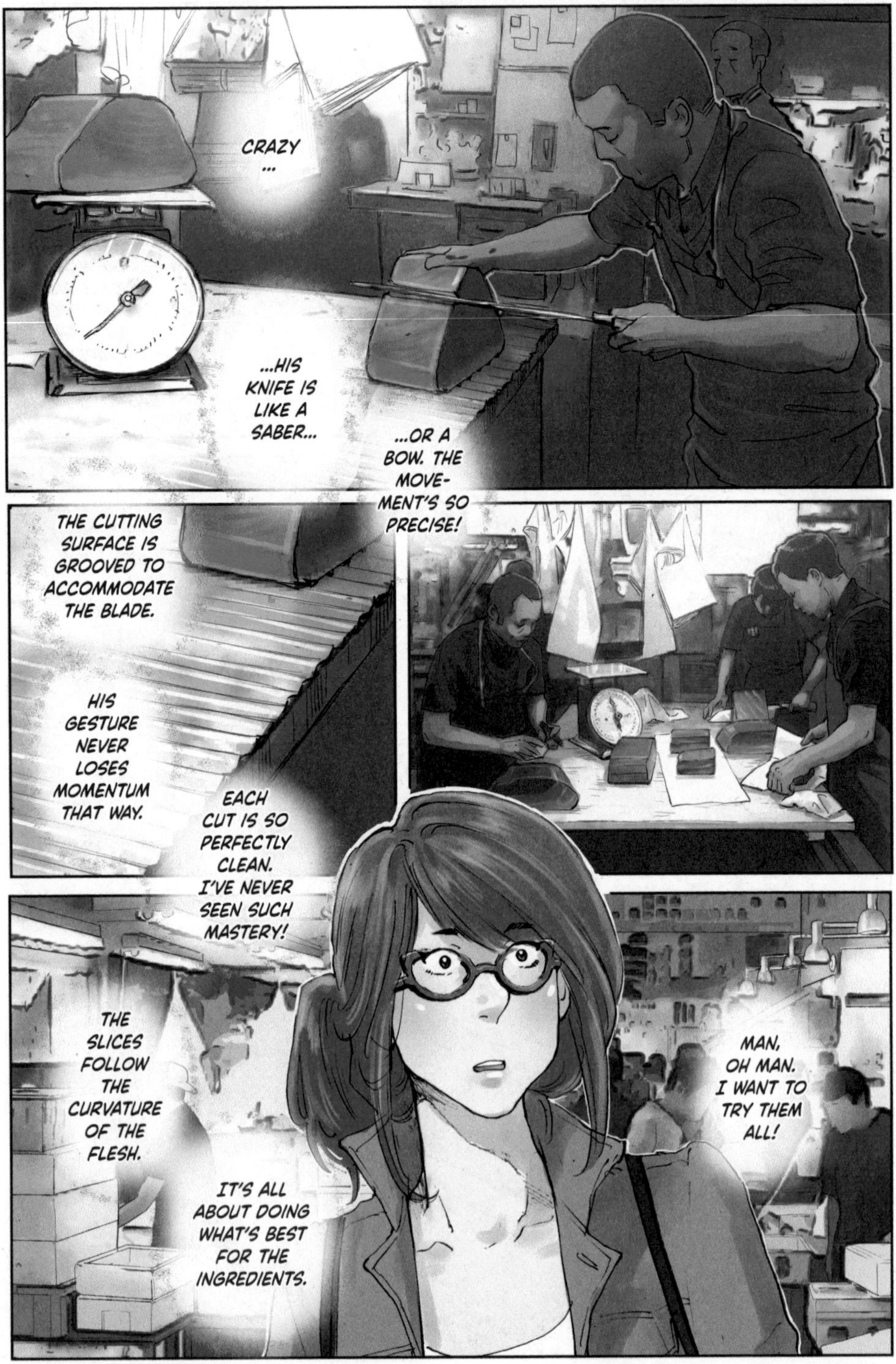
CRAZY ...
...HIS KNIFE IS LIKE A SABER...
...OR A BOW. THE MOVEMENT'S SO PRECISE!
THE CUTTING SURFACE IS GROOVED TO ACCOMMODATE THE BLADE.
HIS GESTURE NEVER LOSES MOMENTUM THAT WAY.
EACH CUT IS SO PERFECTLY CLEAN. I'VE NEVER SEEN SUCH MASTERY!
THE SLICES FOLLOW THE CURVATURE OF THE FLESH.
IT'S ALL ABOUT DOING WHAT'S BEST FOR THE INGREDIENTS.
MAN, OH MAN. I WANT TO TRY THEM ALL!

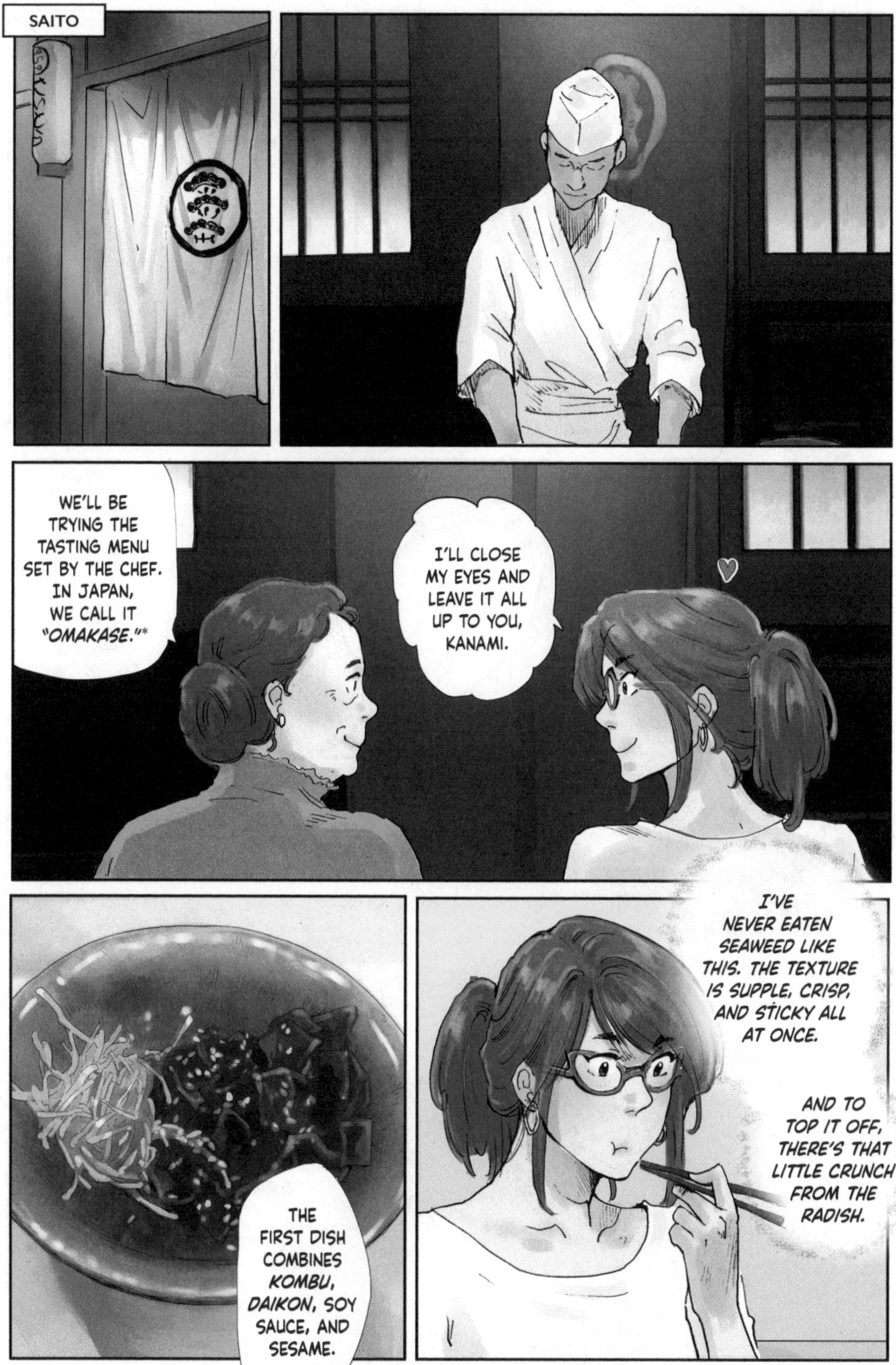
SAITO
WE'LL BE TRYING THE TASTING MENU SET BY THE CHEF. IN JAPAN, WE CALL IT "OMAKASE."*
I'LL CLOSE MY EYES AND LEAVE IT ALL UP TO YOU, KANAMI.
THE FIRST DISH COMBINES KOMBU, DAIKON, SOY SAUCE, AND SESAME.
I'VE NEVER EATEN SEAWEED LIKE THIS. THE TEXTURE IS SUPPLE, CRISP, AND STICKY ALL AT ONCE.
AND TO TOP IT OFF, THERE'S THAT LITTLE CRUNCH FROM THE RADISH.

* LITERALLY TRANSLATES TO "I'LL LEAVE IT UP TO YOU."

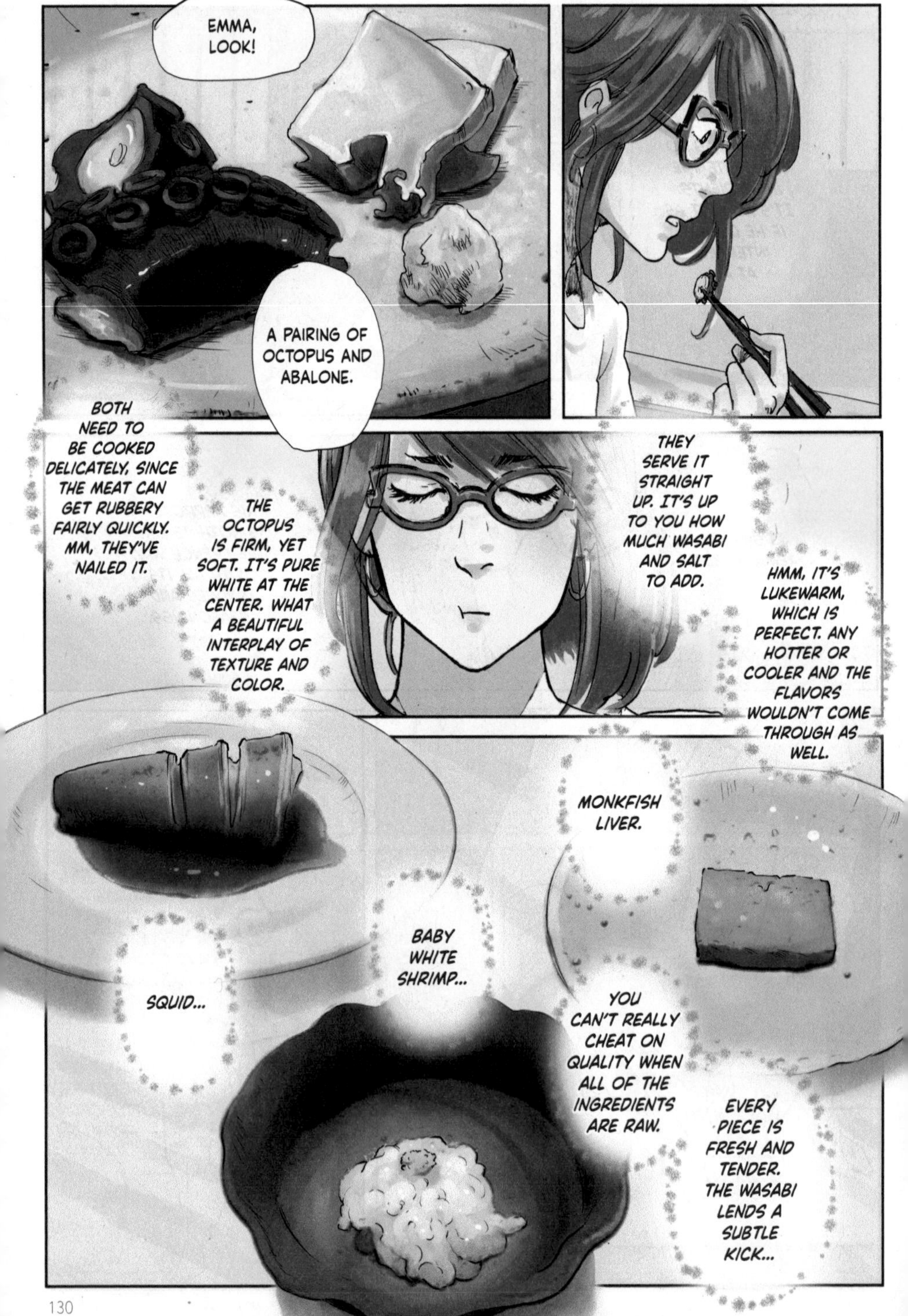

EMMA, LOOK!
A PAIRING OF OCTOPUS AND ABALONE.
BOTH NEED TO BE COOKED DELICATELY, SINCE THE MEAT CAN GET RUBBERY FAIRLY QUICKLY. MM, THEY'VE NAILED IT.
THE OCTOPUS IS FIRM, YET SOFT. IT'S PURE WHITE AT THE CENTER. WHAT A BEAUTIFUL INTERPLAY OF TEXTURE AND COLOR.
THEY SERVE IT STRAIGHT UP. IT'S UP TO YOU HOW MUCH WASABI AND SALT TO ADD.
HMM, IT'S LUKEWARM, WHICH IS PERFECT. ANY HOTTER OR COOLER AND THE FLAVORS WOULDN'T COME THROUGH AS WELL.
SQUID...
BABY WHITE SHRIMP...
MONKFISH LIVER.
YOU CAN'T REALLY CHEAT ON QUALITY WHEN ALL OF THE INGREDIENTS ARE RAW.
EVERY PIECE IS FRESH AND TENDER. THE WASABI LENDS A SUBTLE KICK...

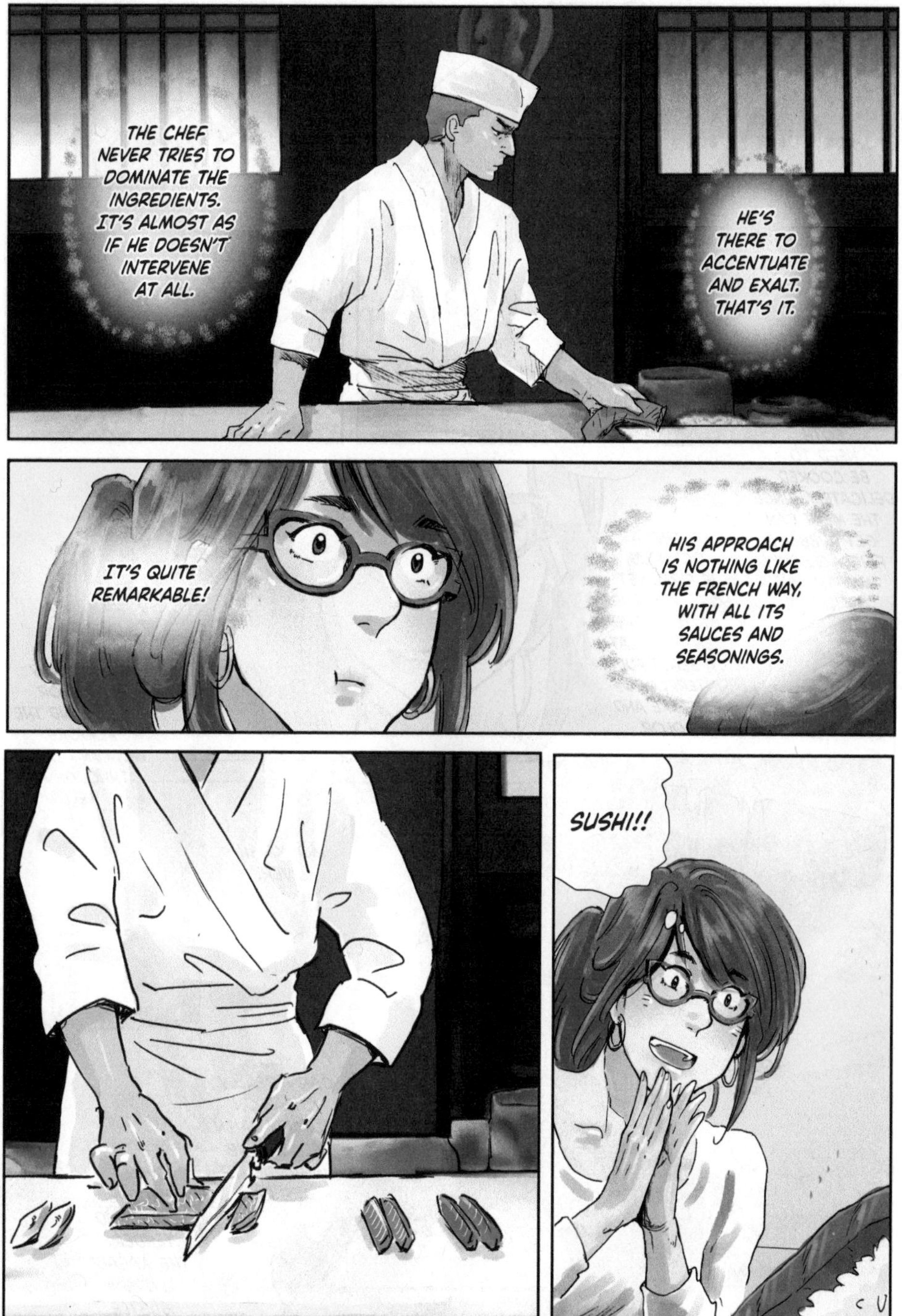
THE CHEF NEVER TRIES TO DOMINATE THE INGREDIENTS. IT'S ALMOST AS IF HE DOESN'T INTERVENE AT ALL.
HE'S THERE TO ACCENTUATE AND EXALT. THAT'S IT.
IT'S QUITE REMARKABLE!
HIS APPROACH IS NOTHING LIKE THE FRENCH WAY, WITH ALL ITS SAUCES AND SEASONINGS.
SUSHI!!

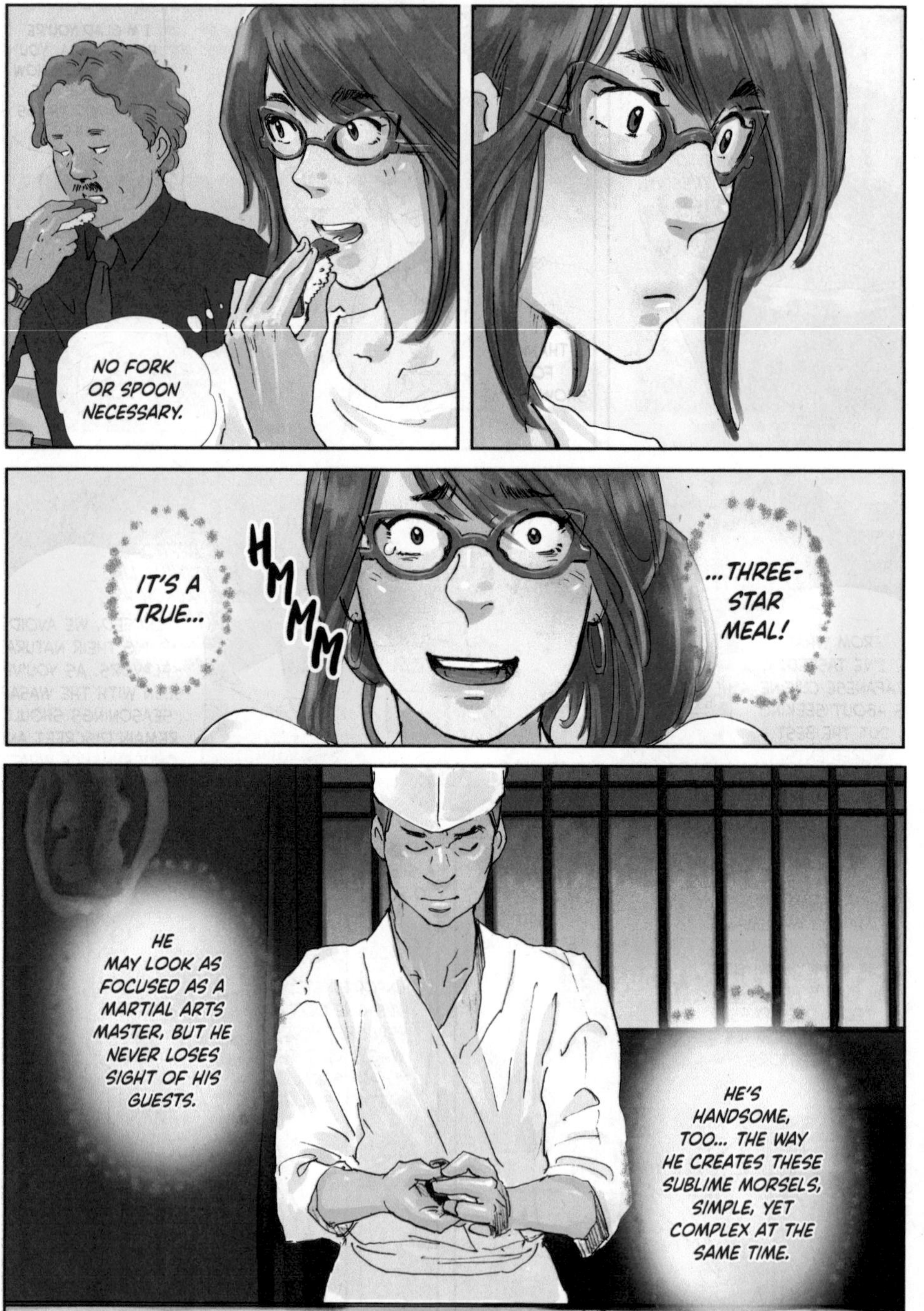
NO FORK OR SPOON NECESSARY.
IT'S A TRUE...
HMMM
...THREE-STAR MEAL!
HE MAY LOOK AS FOCUSED AS A MARTIAL ARTS MASTER, BUT HE NEVER LOSES SIGHT OF HIS GUESTS.
HE'S HANDSOME, TOO... THE WAY HE CREATES THESE SUBLIME MORSELS, SIMPLE, YET COMPLEX AT THE SAME TIME.

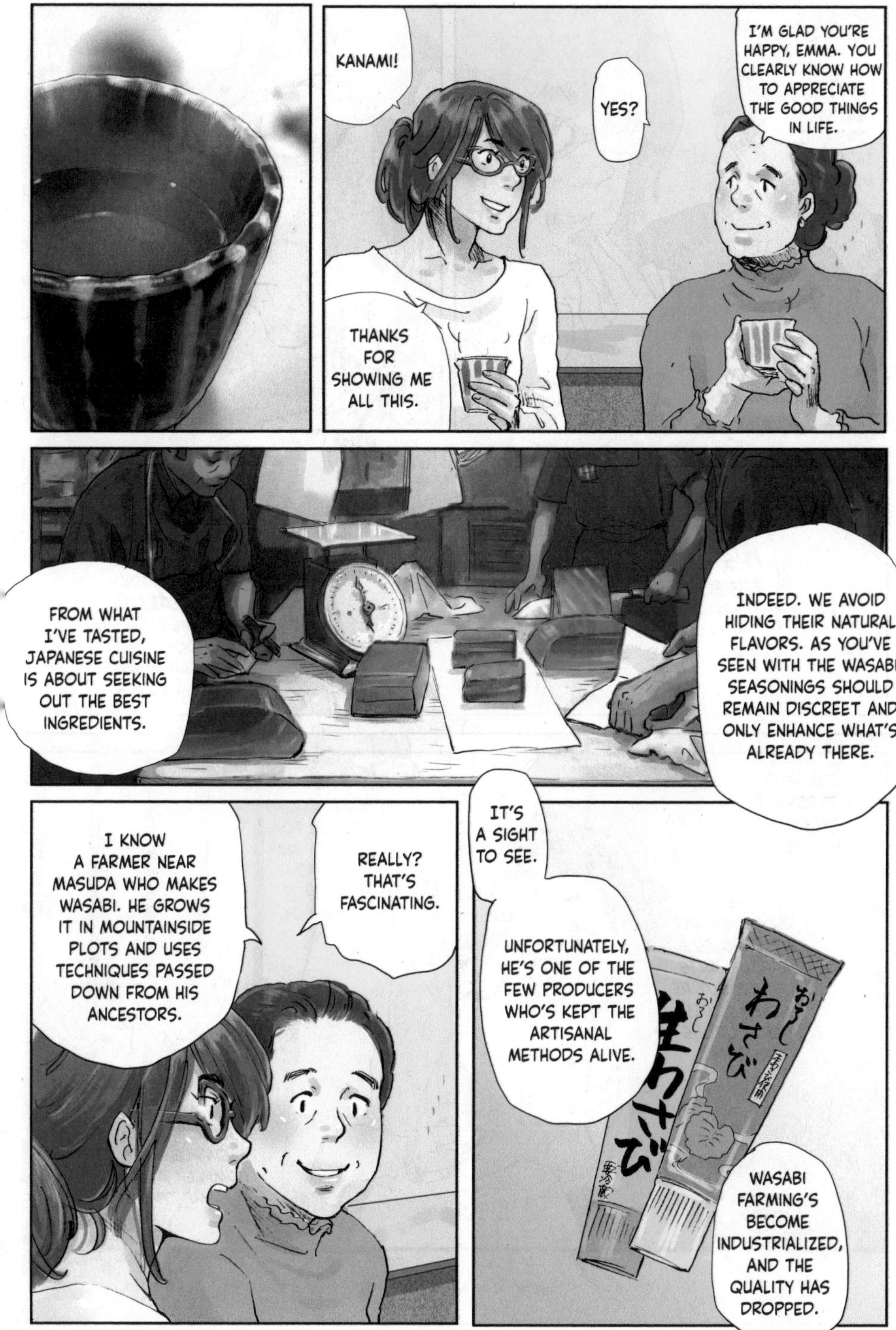
KANAMI!
YES?
THANKS FOR SHOWING ME ALL THIS.
I'M GLAD YOU'RE HAPPY, EMMA. YOU CLEARLY KNOW HOW TO APPRECIATE THE GOOD THINGS IN LIFE.
FROM WHAT I'VE TASTED, JAPANESE CUISINE IS ABOUT SEEKING OUT THE BEST INGREDIENTS.
INDEED. WE AVOID HIDING THEIR NATURAL FLAVORS. AS YOU'VE SEEN WITH THE WASABI, SEASONINGS SHOULD REMAIN DISCREET AND ONLY ENHANCE WHAT'S ALREADY THERE.
I KNOW A FARMER NEAR MASUDA WHO MAKES WASABI. HE GROWS IT IN MOUNTAINSIDE PLOTS AND USES TECHNIQUES PASSED DOWN FROM HIS ANCESTORS.
REALLY? THAT'S FASCINATING.
IT'S A SIGHT TO SEE.
UNFORTUNATELY, HE'S ONE OF THE FEW PRODUCERS WHO'S KEPT THE ARTISANAL METHODS ALIVE.
WASABI FARMING'S BECOME INDUSTRIALIZED, AND THE QUALITY HAS DROPPED.

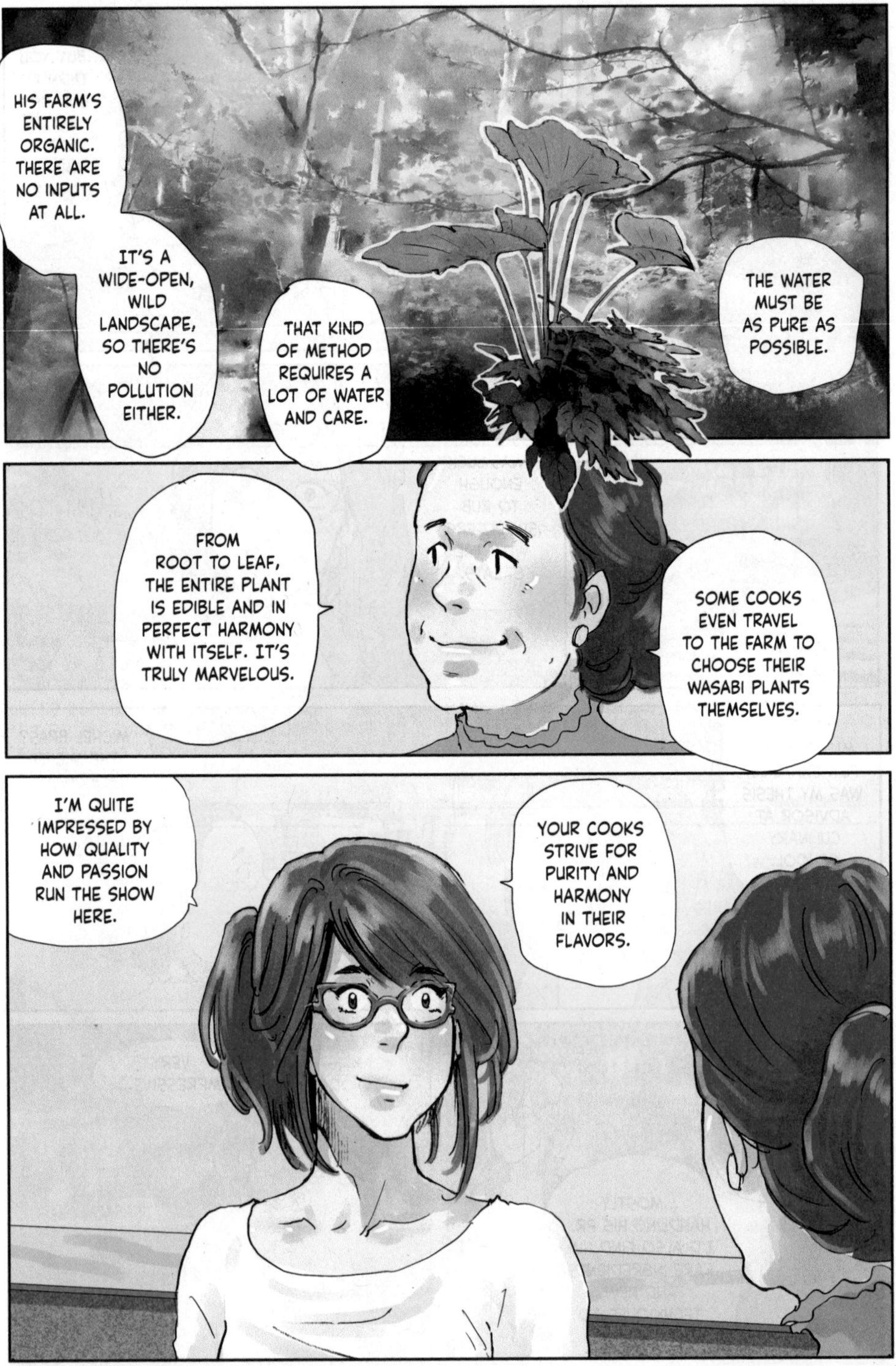
HIS FARM'S ENTIRELY ORGANIC. THERE ARE NO INPUTS AT ALL.
IT'S A WIDE-OPEN, WILD LANDSCAPE, SO THERE'S NO POLLUTION EITHER.
THAT KIND OF METHOD REQUIRES A LOT OF WATER AND CARE.
THE WATER MUST BE AS PURE AS POSSIBLE.
FROM ROOT TO LEAF, THE ENTIRE PLANT IS EDIBLE AND IN PERFECT HARMONY WITH ITSELF. IT'S TRULY MARVELOUS.
SOME COOKS EVEN TRAVEL TO THE FARM TO CHOOSE THEIR WASABI PLANTS THEMSELVES.
I'M QUITE IMPRESSED BY HOW QUALITY AND PASSION RUN THE SHOW HERE.
YOUR COOKS STRIVE FOR PURITY AND HARMONY IN THEIR FLAVORS.

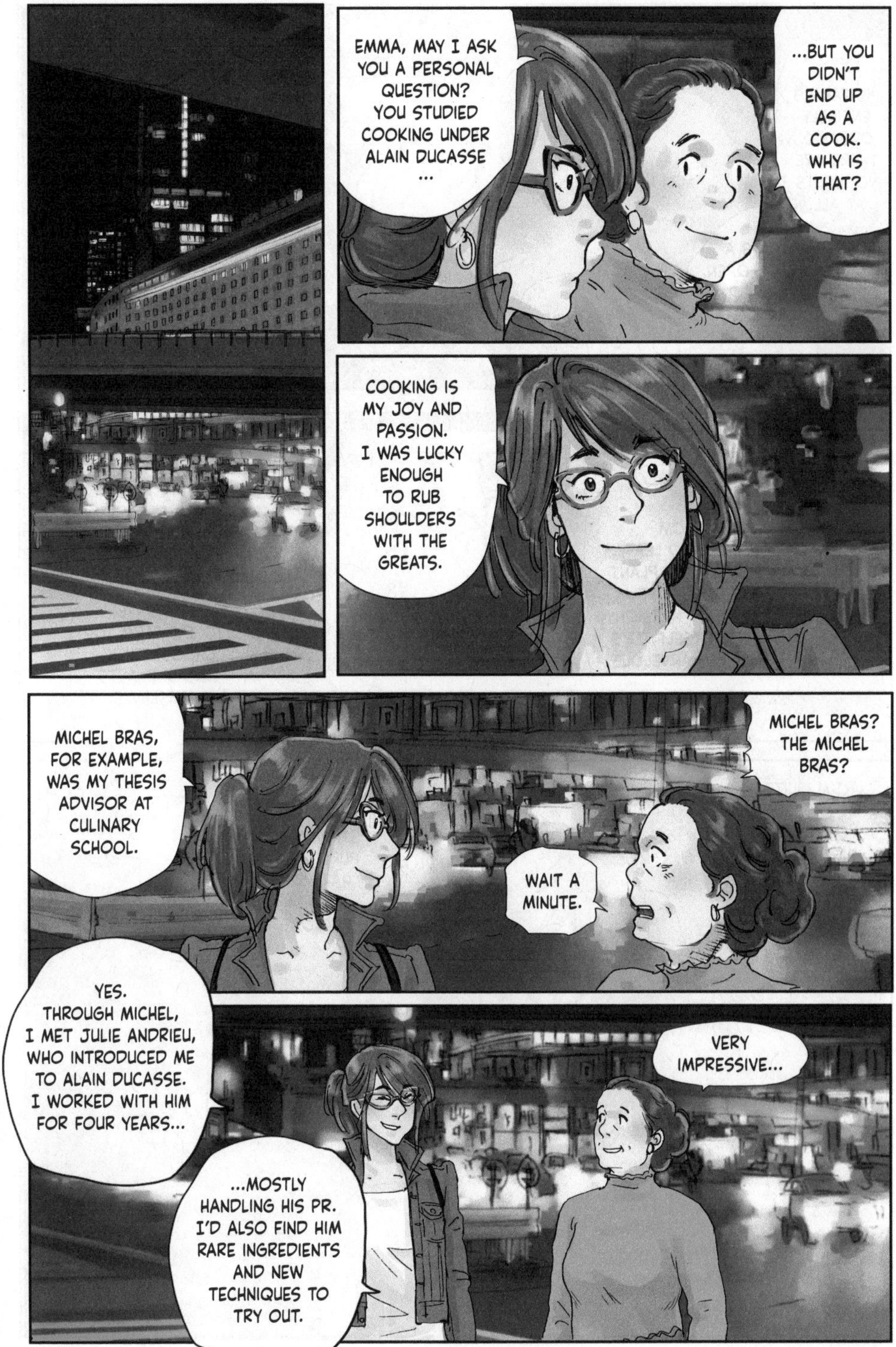
EMMA, MAY I ASK YOU A PERSONAL QUESTION? YOU STUDIED COOKING UNDER ALAIN DUCASSE ...
...BUT YOU DIDN'T END UP AS A COOK. WHY IS THAT?
COOKING IS MY JOY AND PASSION. I WAS LUCKY ENOUGH TO RUB SHOULDERS WITH THE GREATS.
MICHEL BRAS, FOR EXAMPLE, WAS MY THESIS ADVISOR AT CULINARY SCHOOL.
MICHEL BRAS? THE MICHEL BRAS?
WAIT A MINUTE.
YES. THROUGH MICHEL, I MET JULIE ANDRIEU, WHO INTRODUCED ME TO ALAIN DUCASSE. I WORKED WITH HIM FOR FOUR YEARS...
VERY IMPRESSIVE...
...MOSTLY HANDLING HIS PR. I'D ALSO FIND HIM RARE INGREDIENTS AND NEW TECHNIQUES TO TRY OUT.

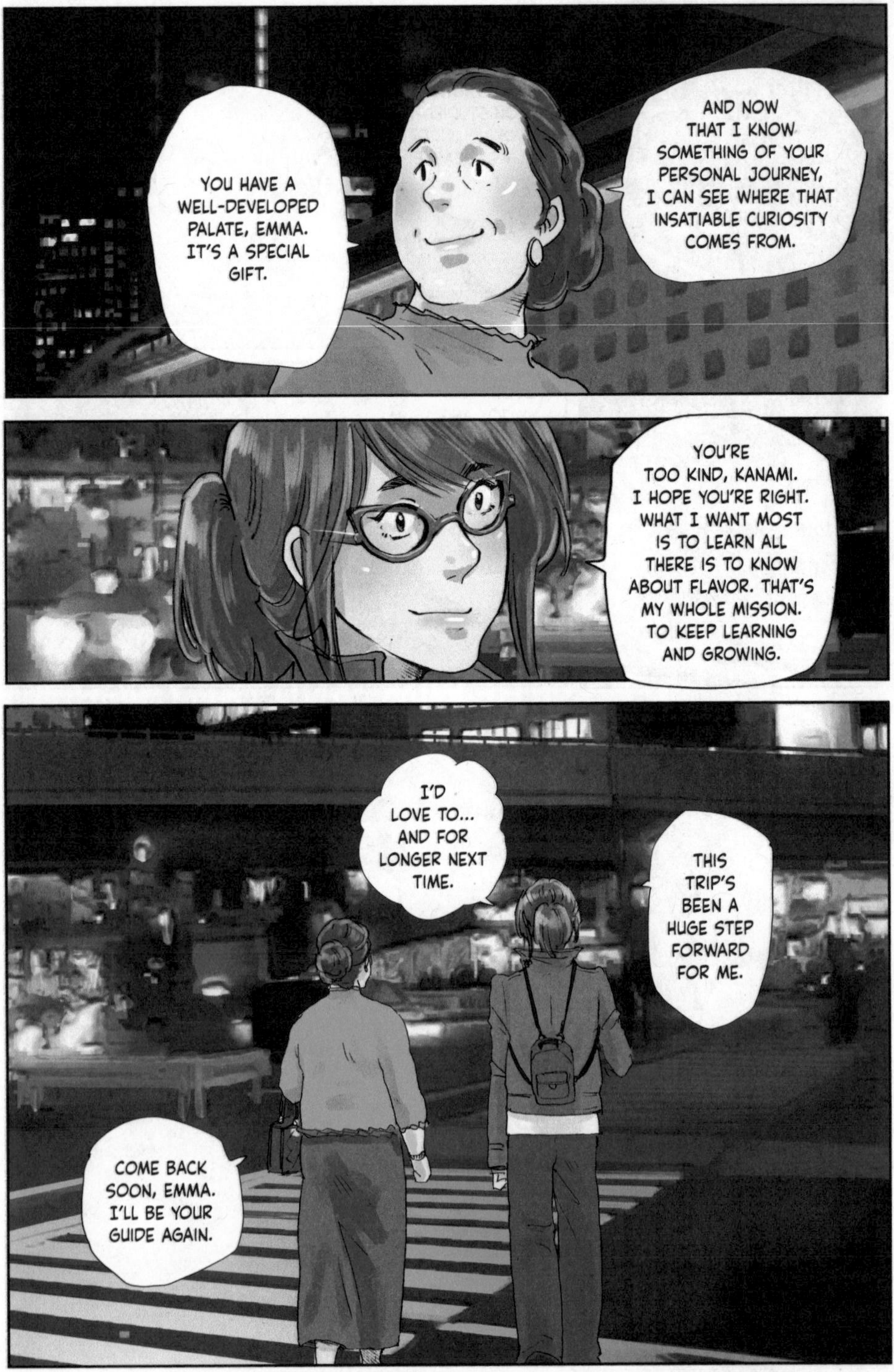
YOU HAVE A WELL-DEVELOPED PALATE, EMMA. IT'S A SPECIAL GIFT.
AND NOW THAT I KNOW SOMETHING OF YOUR PERSONAL JOURNEY, I CAN SEE WHERE THAT INSATIABLE CURIOSITY COMES FROM.
YOU'RE TOO KIND, KANAMI. I HOPE YOU'RE RIGHT. WHAT I WANT MOST IS TO LEARN ALL THERE IS TO KNOW ABOUT FLAVOR. THAT'S MY WHOLE MISSION. TO KEEP LEARNING AND GROWING.
I'D LOVE TO... AND FOR LONGER NEXT TIME.
THIS TRIP'S BEEN A HUGE STEP FORWARD FOR ME.
COME BACK SOON, EMMA. I'LL BE YOUR GUIDE AGAIN.

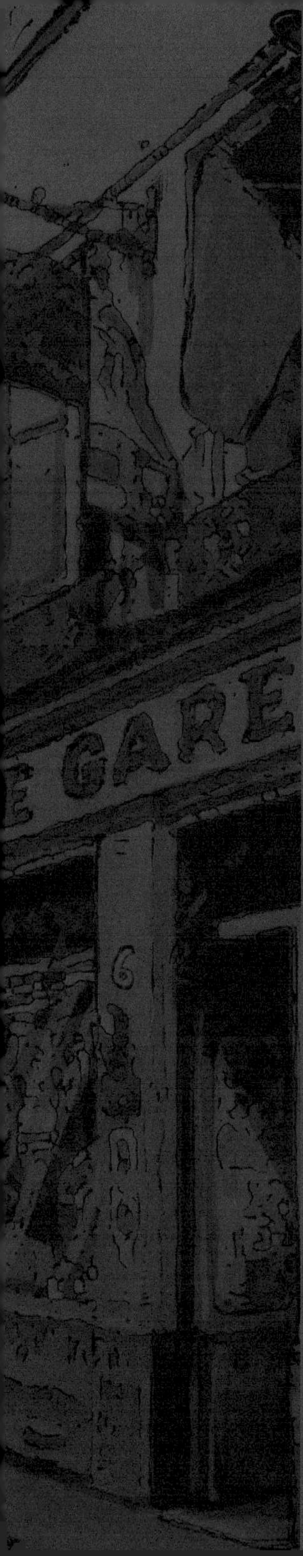

CHAPTER 7

THE WING AND THE THIGH

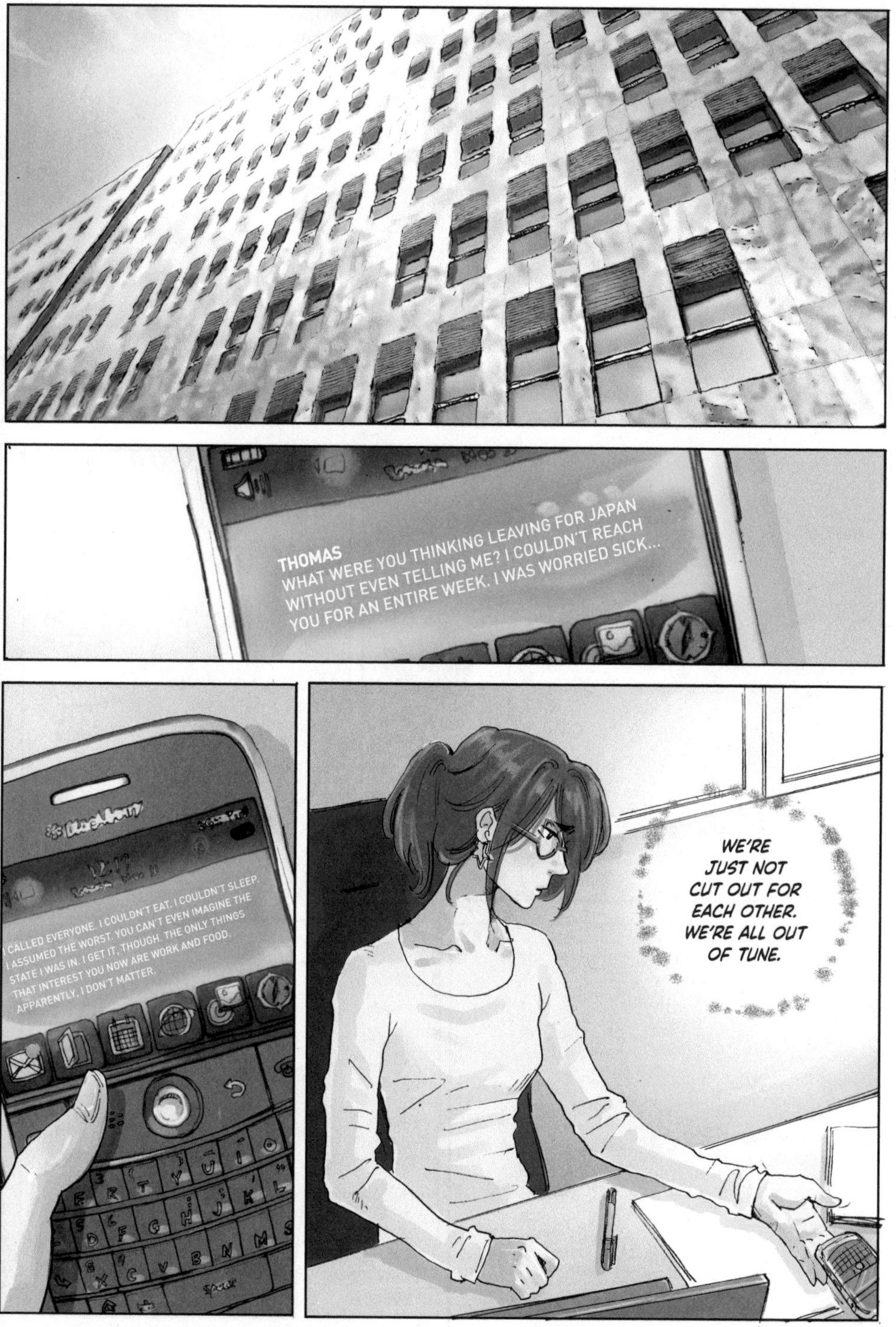
THOMAS
WHAT WERE YOU THINKING LEAVING FOR JAPAN WITHOUT EVEN TELLING ME? I COULDN'T REACH YOU FOR AN ENTIRE WEEK. I WAS WORRIED SICK...
I CALLED EVERYONE. I COULDN'T EAT, I COULDN'T SLEEP. I ASSUMED THE WORST. YOU CAN'T EVEN IMAGINE THE STATE I WAS IN. I GET IT, THOUGH. THE ONLY THINGS THAT INTEREST YOU NOW ARE WORK AND FOOD. APPARENTLY, I DON'T MATTER.
WE'RE JUST NOT CUT OUT FOR EACH OTHER. WE'RE ALL OUT OF TUNE.

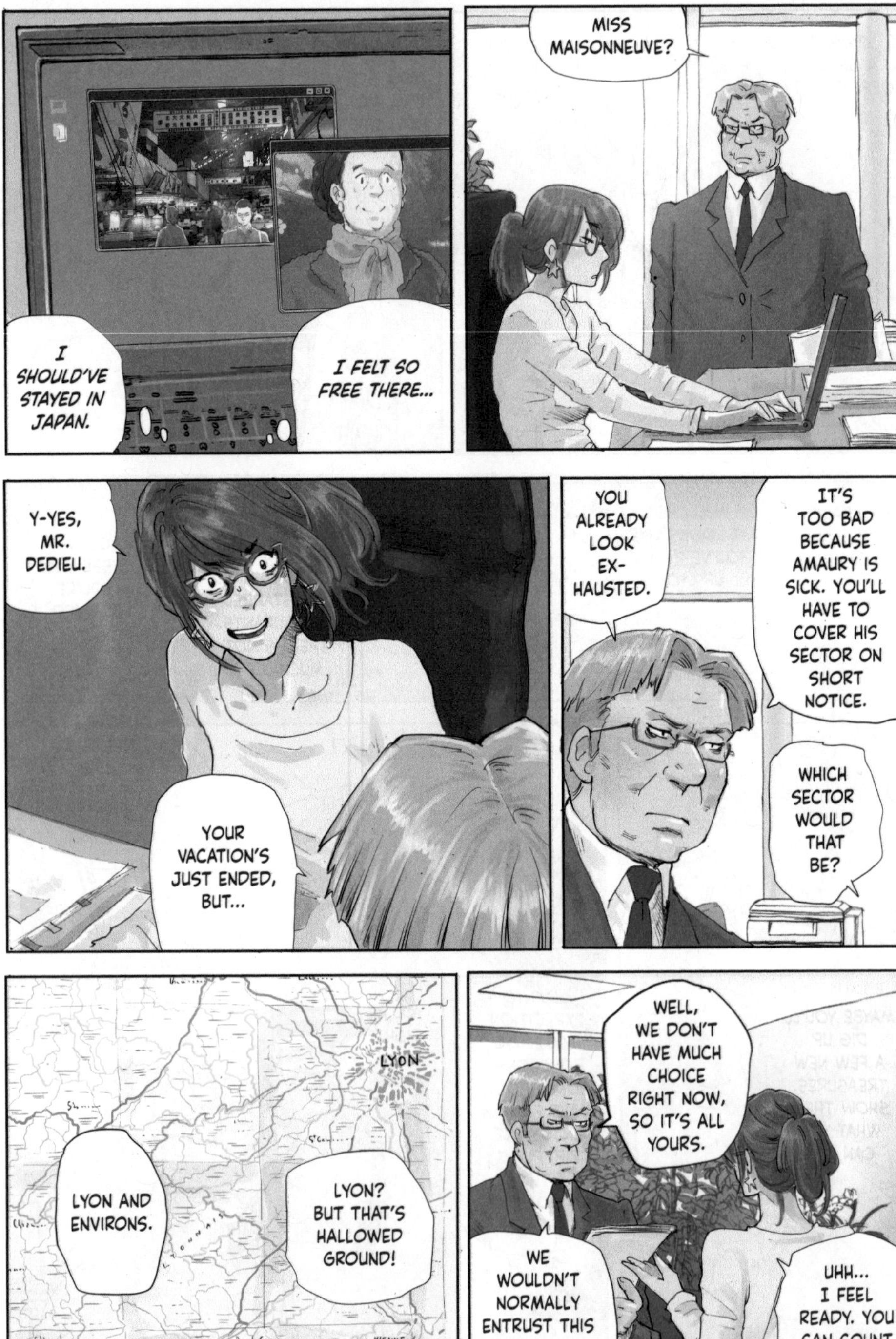
I SHOULD'VE STAYED IN JAPAN.
I FELT SO FREE THERE...
MISS MAISONNEUVE?
Y-YES, MR. DEDIEU.
YOUR VACATION'S JUST ENDED, BUT...
YOU ALREADY LOOK EX-HAUSTED.
IT'S TOO BAD BECAUSE AMAURY IS SICK. YOU'LL HAVE TO COVER HIS SECTOR ON SHORT NOTICE.
WHICH SECTOR WOULD THAT BE?
LYON
VIENNE
LYON AND ENVIRONS.
LYON? BUT THAT'S HALLOWED GROUND!
WELL, WE DON'T HAVE MUCH CHOICE RIGHT NOW, SO IT'S ALL YOURS.
WE WOULDN'T NORMALLY ENTRUST THIS TASK TO A BEGINNER.
UHH... I FEEL READY. YOU CAN COUNT ON ME.

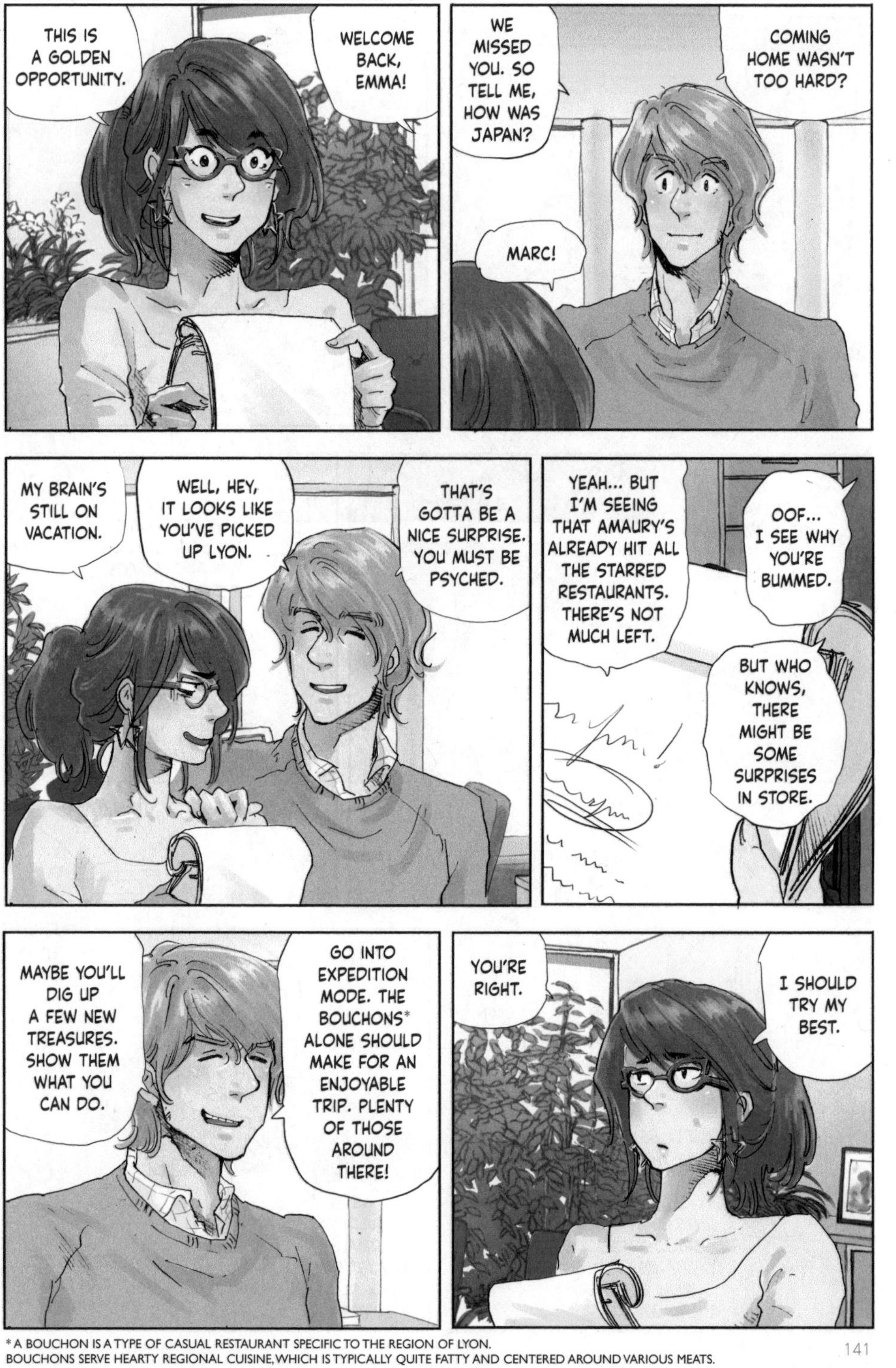
THIS IS A GOLDEN OPPORTUNITY.
WELCOME BACK, EMMA!
WE MISSED YOU. SO TELL ME, HOW WAS JAPAN?
COMING HOME WASN'T TOO HARD?
MARC!
MY BRAIN'S STILL ON VACATION.
WELL, HEY, IT LOOKS LIKE YOU'VE PICKED UP LYON.
THAT'S GOTTA BE A NICE SURPRISE. YOU MUST BE PSYCHED.
YEAH... BUT I'M SEEING THAT AMAURY'S ALREADY HIT ALL THE STARRED RESTAURANTS. THERE'S NOT MUCH LEFT.
OOF... I SEE WHY YOU'RE BUMMED.
BUT WHO KNOWS, THERE MIGHT BE SOME SURPRISES IN STORE.
MAYBE YOU'LL DIG UP A FEW NEW TREASURES. SHOW THEM WHAT YOU CAN DO.
GO INTO EXPEDITION MODE. THE BOUCHONS* ALONE SHOULD MAKE FOR AN ENJOYABLE TRIP. PLENTY OF THOSE AROUND THERE!
YOU'RE RIGHT.
I SHOULD TRY MY BEST.

* A BOUCHON IS A TYPE OF CASUAL RESTAURANT SPECIFIC TO THE REGION OF LYON.
BOUCHONS SERVE HEARTY REGIONAL CUISINE, WHICH IS TYPICALLY QUITE FATTY AND CENTERED AROUND VARIOUS MEATS.

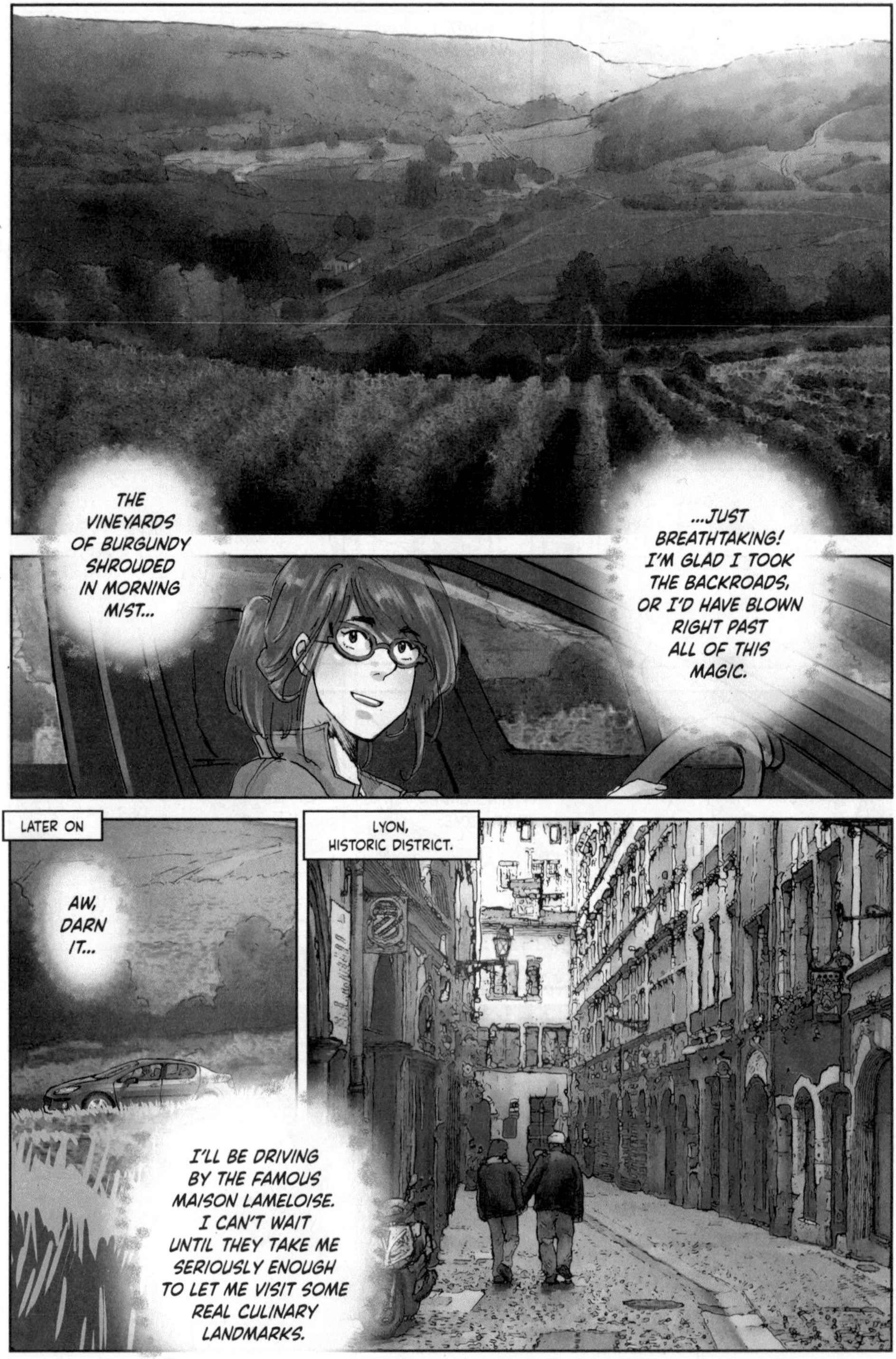
THE VINEYARDS OF BURGUNDY SHROUDED IN MORNING MIST...
...JUST BREATHTAKING! I'M GLAD I TOOK THE BACKROADS, OR I'D HAVE BLOWN RIGHT PAST ALL OF THIS MAGIC.
LATER ON
AW, DARN IT...
I'LL BE DRIVING BY THE FAMOUS MAISON LAMELOISE. I CAN'T WAIT UNTIL THEY TAKE ME SERIOUSLY ENOUGH TO LET ME VISIT SOME REAL CULINARY LANDMARKS.
LYON, HISTORIC DISTRICT.

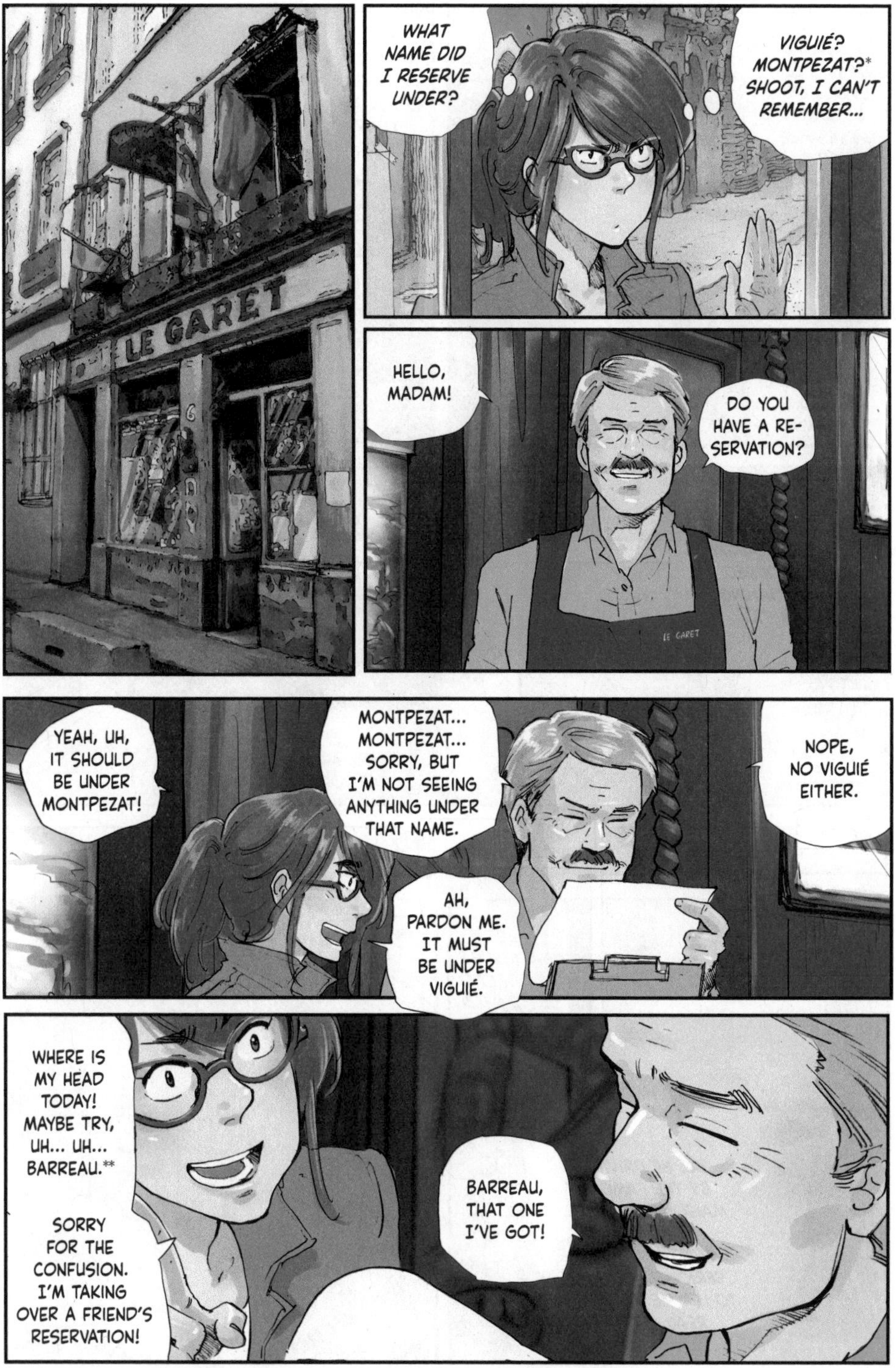
LE GARET
WHAT NAME DID I RESERVE UNDER?
VIGUIÉ? MONTPEZAT?* SHOOT, I CAN'T REMEMBER...
HELLO, MADAM!
DO YOU HAVE A RE-SERVATION?
LE GARET
YEAH, UH, IT SHOULD BE UNDER MONTPEZAT!
MONTPEZAT... MONTPEZAT... SORRY, BUT I'M NOT SEEING ANYTHING UNDER THAT NAME.
AH, PARDON ME. IT MUST BE UNDER VIGUIÉ.
NOPE, NO VIGUIÉ EITHER.
WHERE IS MY HEAD TODAY! MAYBE TRY, UH... UH... BARREAU.**
SORRY FOR THE CONFUSION. I'M TAKING OVER A FRIEND'S RESERVATION!
BARREAU, THAT ONE I'VE GOT!

* ÉTIENNE DE MONTPEZAT IS A WRITER AND JOURNALIST FROM CAHORS IN THE SOUTHWEST OF FRANCE.

** BARREAU IS THE NAME OF YET ANOTHER FRENCH WRITER.

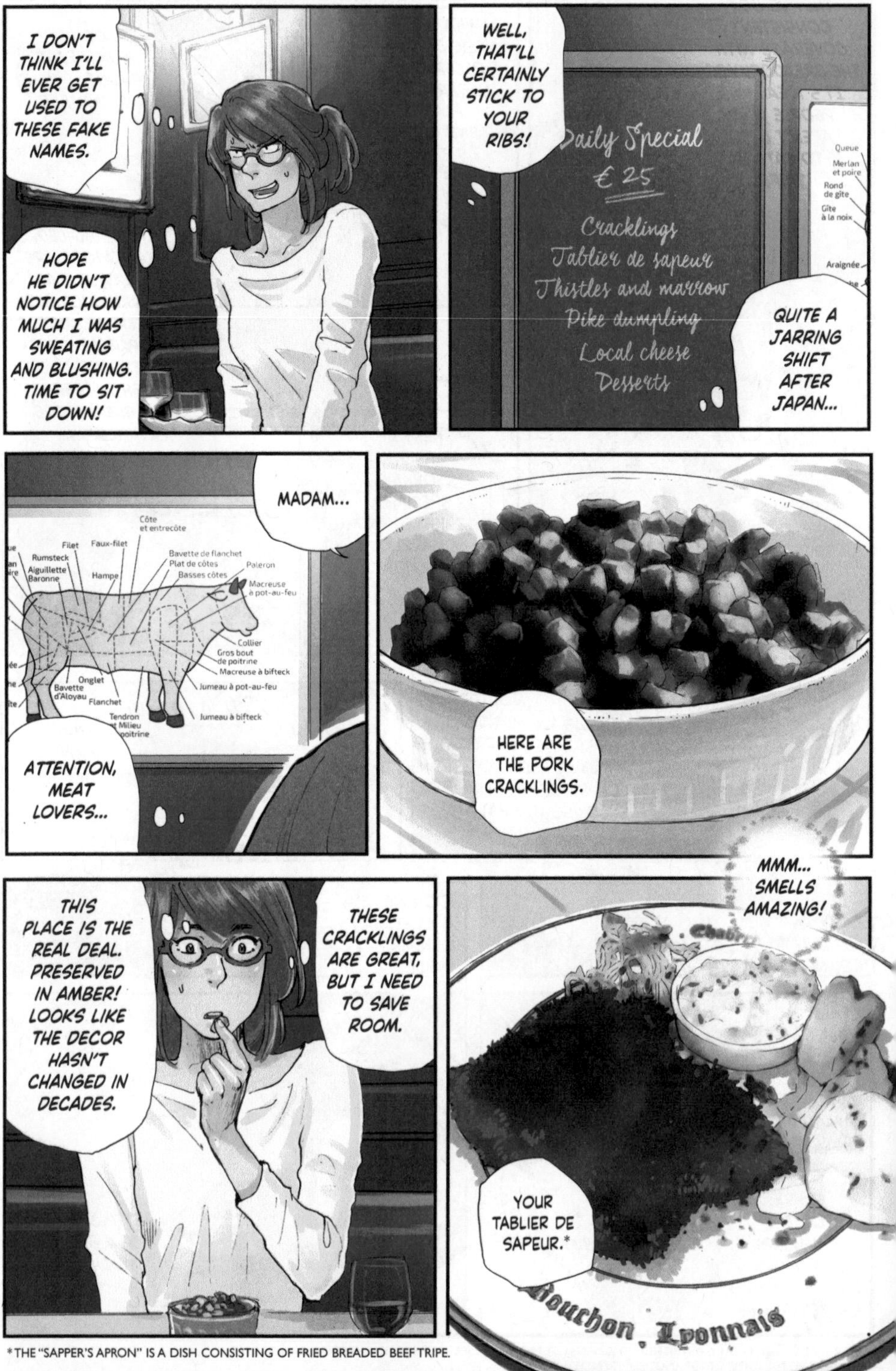
I DON'T THINK I'LL EVER GET USED TO THESE FAKE NAMES.
HOPE HE DIDN'T NOTICE HOW MUCH I WAS SWEATING AND BLUSHING. TIME TO SIT DOWN!
WELL, THAT'LL CERTAINLY STICK TO YOUR RIBS!
Daily Special
€ 25
Cracklings
Tablier de sapeur
Thistles and marrow
Pike dumpling
Local cheese
Desserts
Queue
Merlan et poire
Rond de gîte
Gîte à la noix
Araignée
QUITE A JARRING SHIFT AFTER JAPAN...
MADAM...
Côte et entrecôte
Filet
Faux-filet
Rumsteck
Aiguillette Baronne
Hampe
Bavette de flanchet
Plat de côtes
Basses côtes
Paleron
Macreuse à pot-au-feu
Collier
Gros bout de poitrine
Macreuse à bifteck
Jumeau à pot-au-feu
Jumeau à bifteck
Onglet
Bavette d'Aloyau
Flanchet
Tendron
ATTENTION, MEAT LOVERS...
HERE ARE THE PORK CRACKLINGS.
THIS PLACE IS THE REAL DEAL. PRESERVED IN AMBER! LOOKS LIKE THE DECOR HASN'T CHANGED IN DECADES.
THESE CRACKLINGS ARE GREAT, BUT I NEED TO SAVE ROOM.
MMM... SMELLS AMAZING!
YOUR TABLIER DE SAPEUR.*
Bouchon Lyonnais

*THE "SAPPER'S APRON" IS A DISH CONSISTING OF FRIED BREADED BEEF TRIPE.

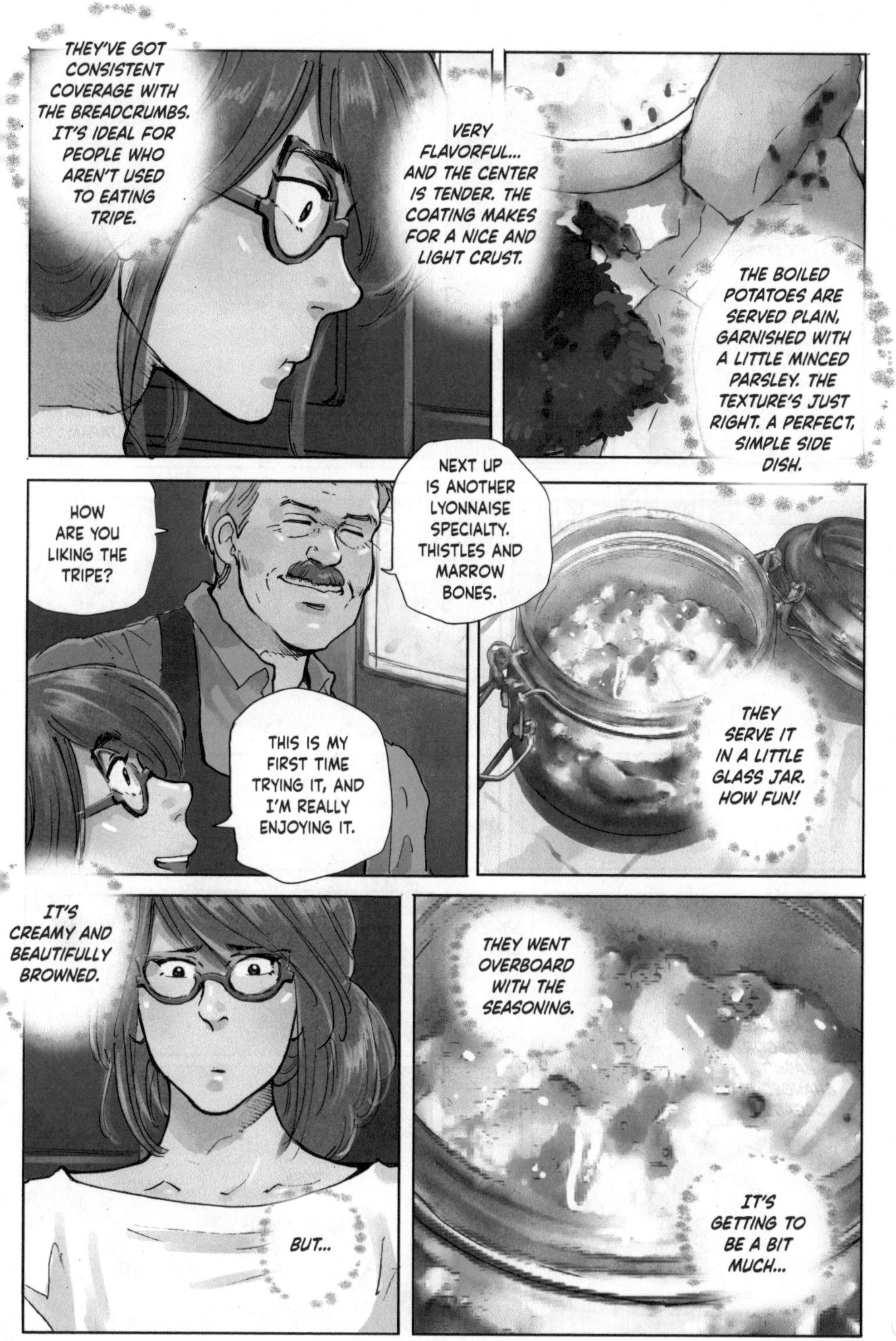
THEY'VE GOT CONSISTENT COVERAGE WITH THE BREADCRUMBS. IT'S IDEAL FOR PEOPLE WHO AREN'T USED TO EATING TRIPE.
VERY FLAVORFUL... AND THE CENTER IS TENDER. THE COATING MAKES FOR A NICE AND LIGHT CRUST.
THE BOILED POTATOES ARE SERVED PLAIN, GARNISHED WITH A LITTLE MINCED PARSLEY. THE TEXTURE'S JUST RIGHT. A PERFECT, SIMPLE SIDE DISH.
HOW ARE YOU LIKING THE TRIPE?
NEXT UP IS ANOTHER LYONNAISE SPECIALTY. THISTLES AND MARROW BONES.
THIS IS MY FIRST TIME TRYING IT, AND I'M REALLY ENJOYING IT.
THEY SERVE IT IN A LITTLE GLASS JAR. HOW FUN!
IT'S CREAMY AND BEAUTIFULLY BROWNED.
BUT...
THEY WENT OVERBOARD WITH THE SEASONING.
IT'S GETTING TO BE A BIT MUCH...

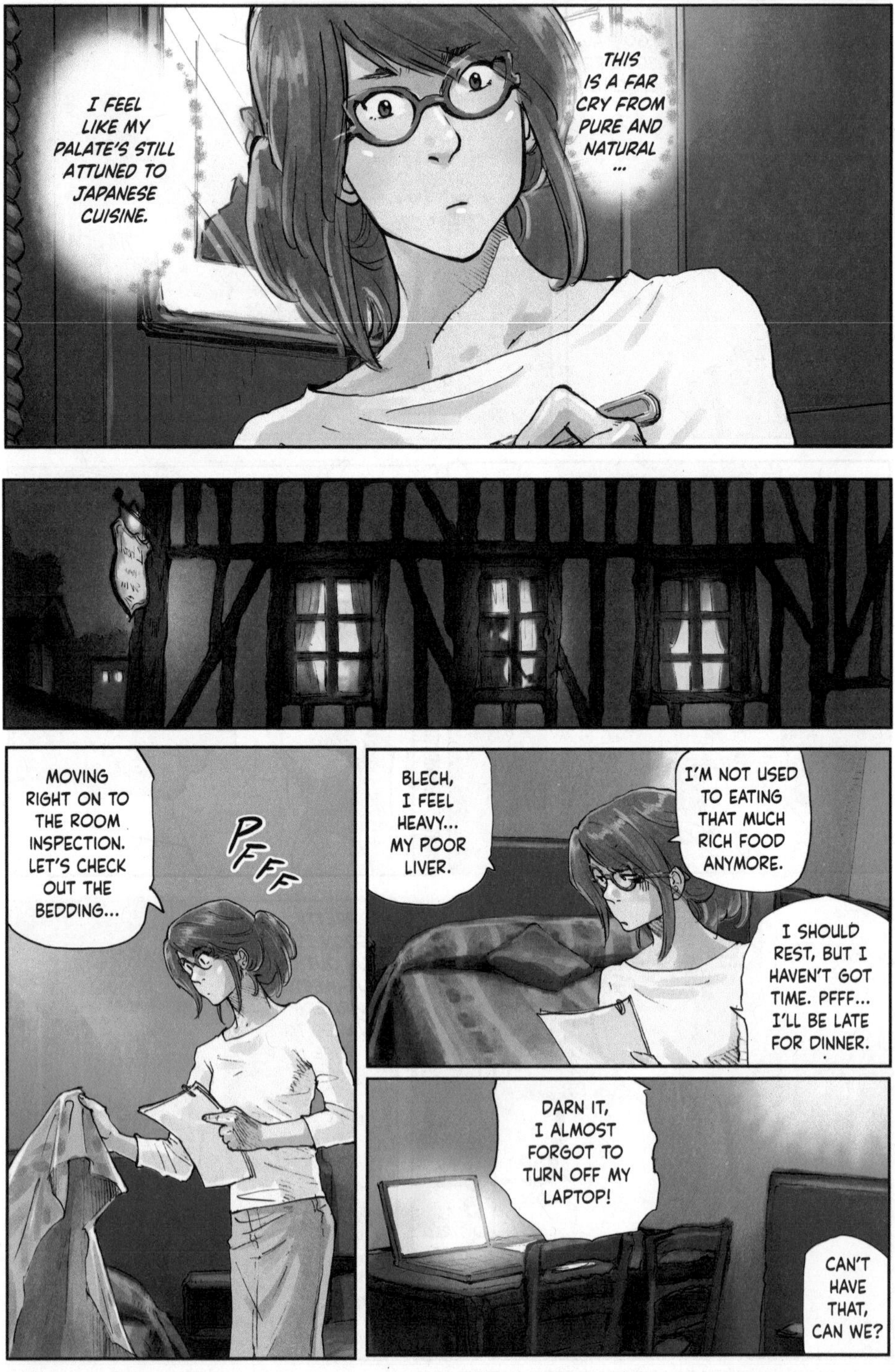
I FEEL LIKE MY PALATE'S STILL ATTUNED TO JAPANESE CUISINE.
THIS IS A FAR CRY FROM PURE AND NATURAL ...
MOVING RIGHT ON TO THE ROOM INSPECTION. LET'S CHECK OUT THE BEDDING...
PFFF
BLECH, I FEEL HEAVY... MY POOR LIVER.
I'M NOT USED TO EATING THAT MUCH RICH FOOD ANYMORE.
I SHOULD REST, BUT I HAVEN'T GOT TIME. PFFF... I'LL BE LATE FOR DINNER.
DARN IT, I ALMOST FORGOT TO TURN OFF MY LAPTOP!
CAN'T HAVE THAT, CAN WE?

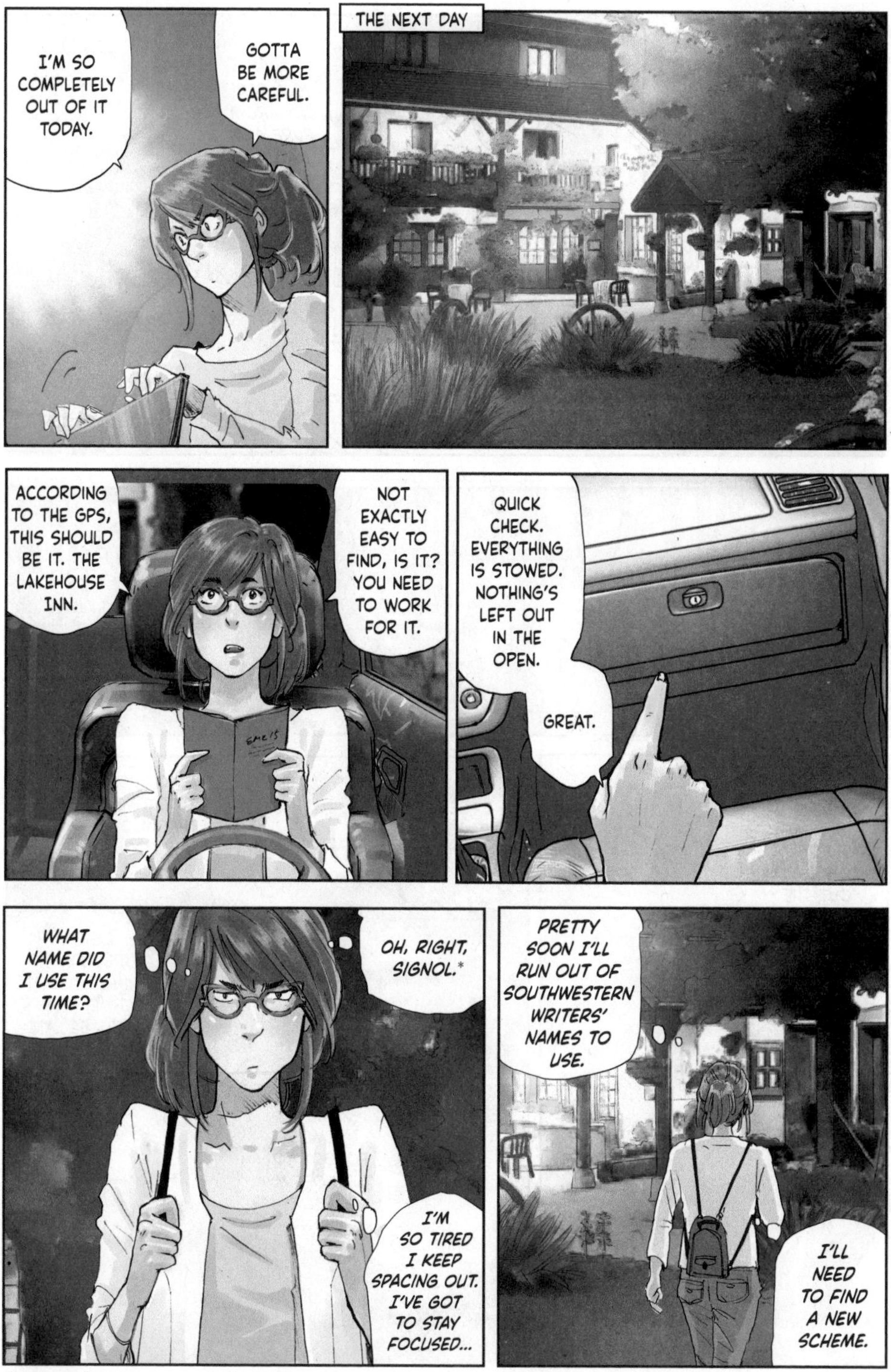
I'M SO COMPLETELY OUT OF IT TODAY.
GOTTA BE MORE CAREFUL.
THE NEXT DAY
ACCORDING TO THE GPS, THIS SHOULD BE IT. THE LAKEHOUSE INN.
NOT EXACTLY EASY TO FIND, IS IT? YOU NEED TO WORK FOR IT.
QUICK CHECK. EVERYTHING IS STOWED. NOTHING'S LEFT OUT IN THE OPEN.
GREAT.
WHAT NAME DID I USE THIS TIME?
OH, RIGHT, SIGNOL.*
I'M SO TIRED I KEEP SPACING OUT. I'VE GOT TO STAY FOCUSED...
PRETTY SOON I'LL RUN OUT OF SOUTHWESTERN WRITERS' NAMES TO USE.
I'LL NEED TO FIND A NEW SCHEME.

* CHRISTIAN SIGNOL IS A WRITER FROM QUERCY IN THE SOUTHWEST OF FRANCE.

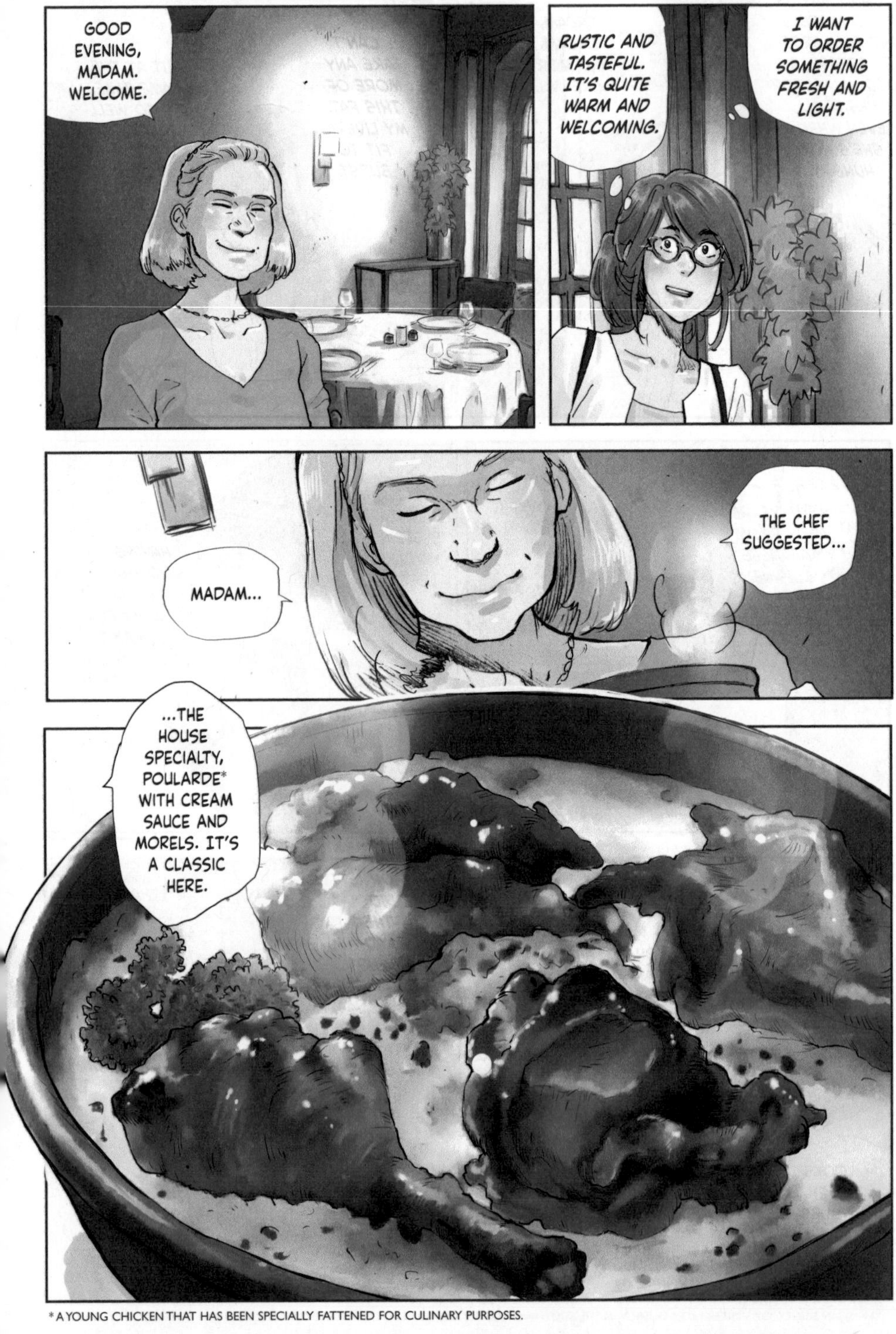
GOOD EVENING, MADAM. WELCOME.
RUSTIC AND TASTEFUL. IT'S QUITE WARM AND WELCOMING.
I WANT TO ORDER SOMETHING FRESH AND LIGHT.
MADAM...
THE CHEF SUGGESTED...
...THE HOUSE SPECIALTY, POULARDE* WITH CREAM SAUCE AND MORELS. IT'S A CLASSIC HERE.

* A YOUNG CHICKEN THAT HAS BEEN SPECIALLY FATTENED FOR CULINARY PURPOSES.

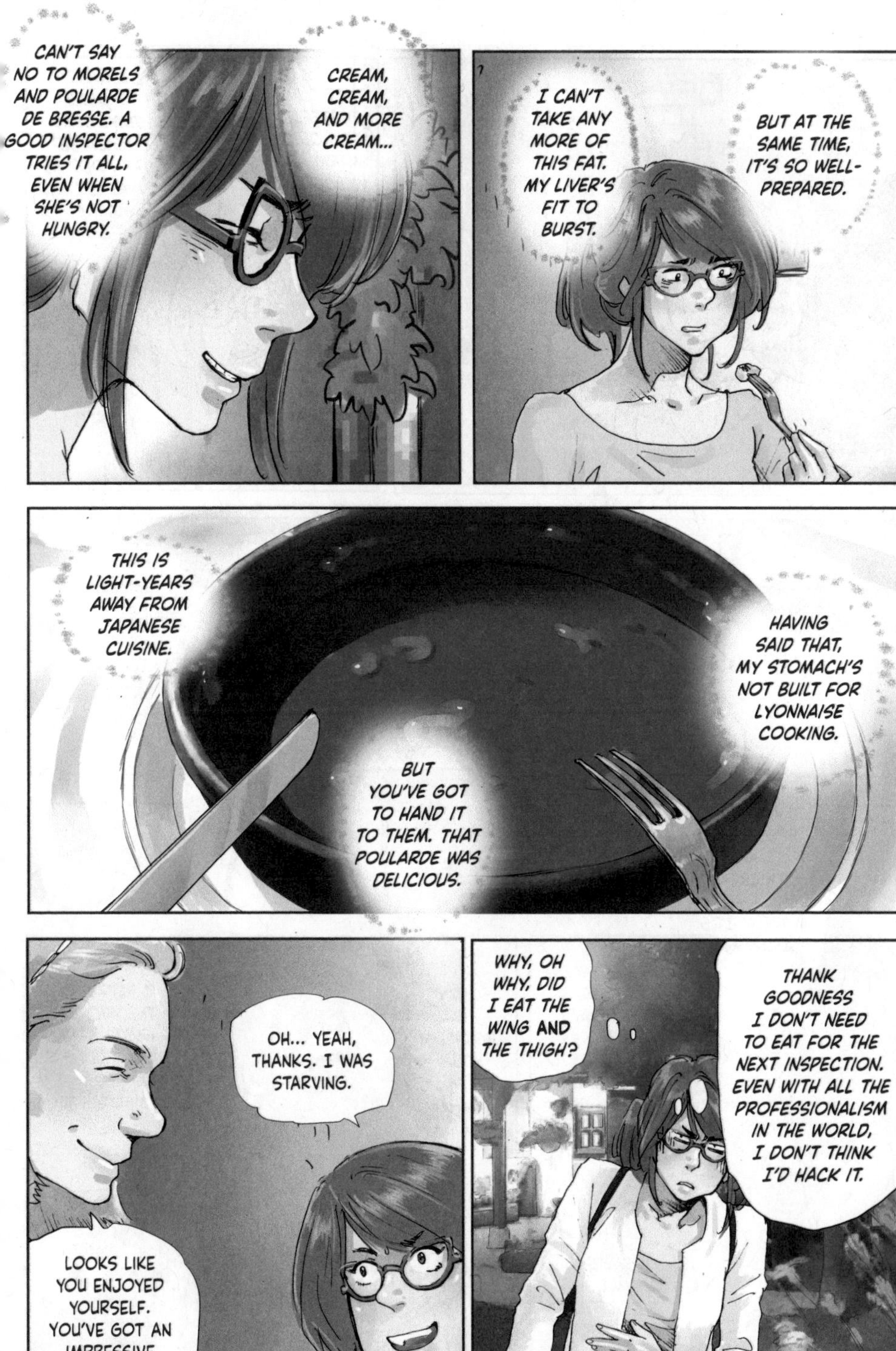

CAN'T SAY NO TO MORELS AND POULARDE DE BRESSE. A GOOD INSPECTOR TRIES IT ALL, EVEN WHEN SHE'S NOT HUNGRY.
CREAM, CREAM, AND MORE CREAM...
I CAN'T TAKE ANY MORE OF THIS FAT. MY LIVER'S FIT TO BURST.
BUT AT THE SAME TIME, IT'S SO WELL-PREPARED.
THIS IS LIGHT-YEARS AWAY FROM JAPANESE CUISINE.
HAVING SAID THAT, MY STOMACH'S NOT BUILT FOR LYONNAISE COOKING.
BUT YOU'VE GOT TO HAND IT TO THEM. THAT POULARDE WAS DELICIOUS.
OH... YEAH, THANKS. I WAS STARVING.
LOOKS LIKE YOU ENJOYED YOURSELF. YOU'VE GOT AN IMPRESSIVE APPETITE!
WHY, OH WHY, DID I EAT THE WING AND THE THIGH?
THANK GOODNESS I DON'T NEED TO EAT FOR THE NEXT INSPECTION. EVEN WITH ALL THE PROFESSIONALISM IN THE WORLD, I DON'T THINK I'D HACK IT.

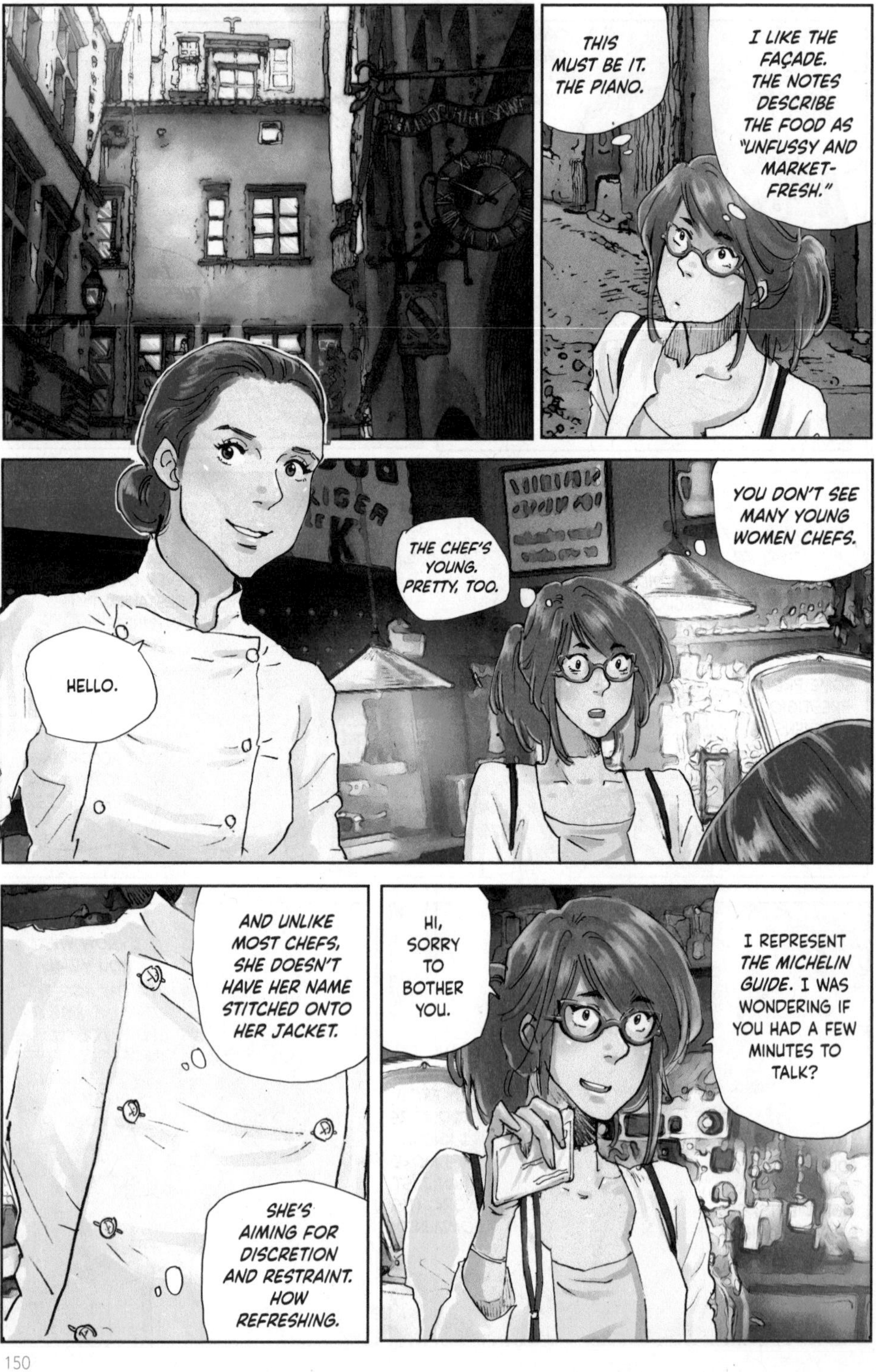
THIS MUST BE IT. THE PIANO.
I LIKE THE FAÇADE. THE NOTES DESCRIBE THE FOOD AS "UNFUSSY AND MARKET-FRESH."
HELLO.
THE CHEF'S YOUNG. PRETTY, TOO.
YOU DON'T SEE MANY YOUNG WOMEN CHEFS.
AND UNLIKE MOST CHEFS, SHE DOESN'T HAVE HER NAME STITCHED ONTO HER JACKET.
SHE'S AIMING FOR DISCRETION AND RESTRAINT. HOW REFRESHING.
HI, SORRY TO BOTHER YOU.
I REPRESENT *THE MICHELIN GUIDE*. I WAS WONDERING IF YOU HAD A FEW MINUTES TO TALK?

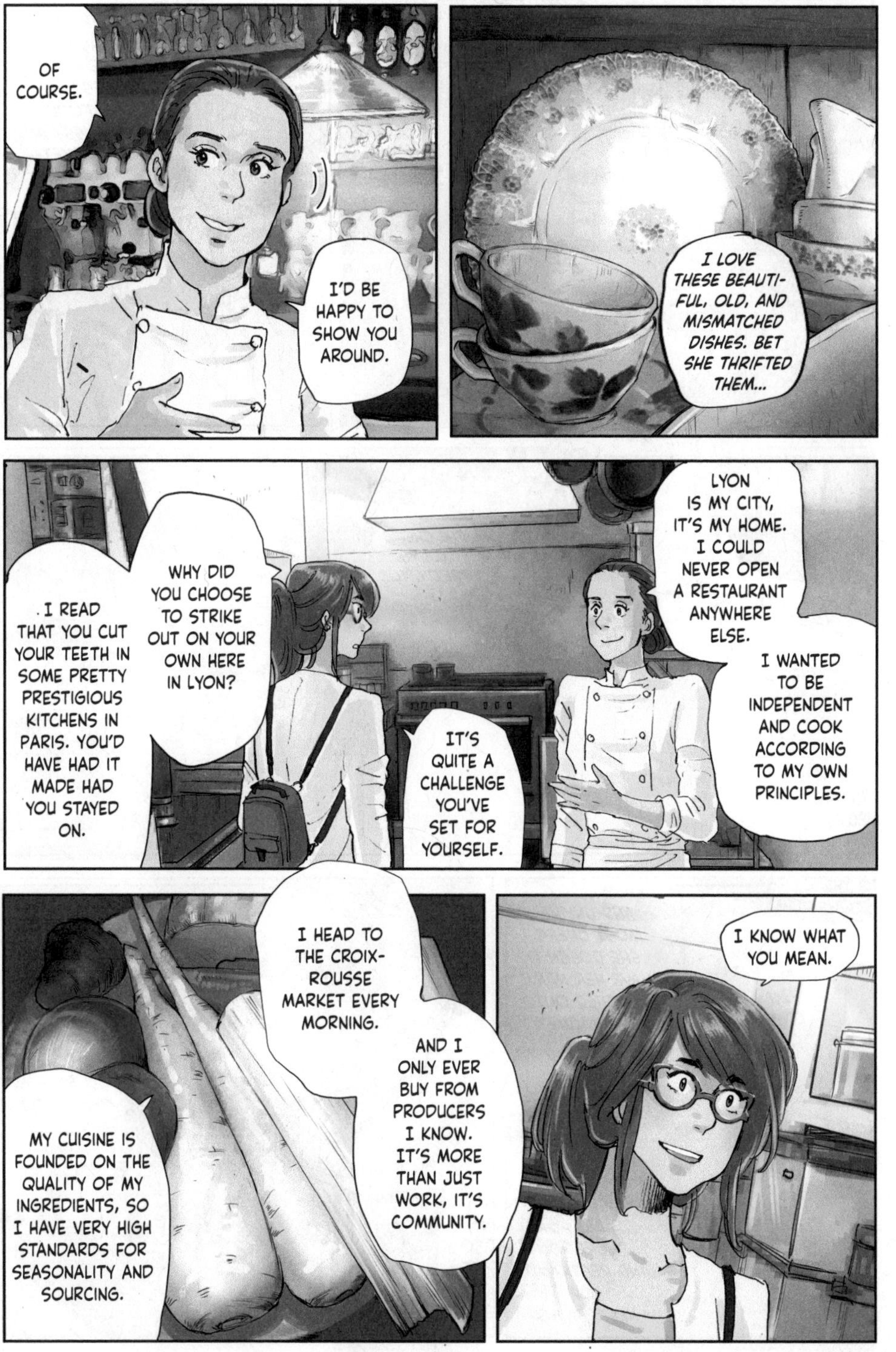
OF COURSE.
I'D BE HAPPY TO SHOW YOU AROUND.
I LOVE THESE BEAUTIFUL, OLD, AND MISMATCHED DISHES. BET SHE THRIFTED THEM...
I READ THAT YOU CUT YOUR TEETH IN SOME PRETTY PRESTIGIOUS KITCHENS IN PARIS. YOU'D HAVE HAD IT MADE HAD YOU STAYED ON.
WHY DID YOU CHOOSE TO STRIKE OUT ON YOUR OWN HERE IN LYON?
IT'S QUITE A CHALLENGE YOU'VE SET FOR YOURSELF.
LYON IS MY CITY, IT'S MY HOME. I COULD NEVER OPEN A RESTAURANT ANYWHERE ELSE.
I WANTED TO BE INDEPENDENT AND COOK ACCORDING TO MY OWN PRINCIPLES.
MY CUISINE IS FOUNDED ON THE QUALITY OF MY INGREDIENTS, SO I HAVE VERY HIGH STANDARDS FOR SEASONALITY AND SOURCING.
I HEAD TO THE CROIX-ROUSSE MARKET EVERY MORNING.
AND I ONLY EVER BUY FROM PRODUCERS I KNOW. IT'S MORE THAN JUST WORK, IT'S COMMUNITY.
I KNOW WHAT YOU MEAN.

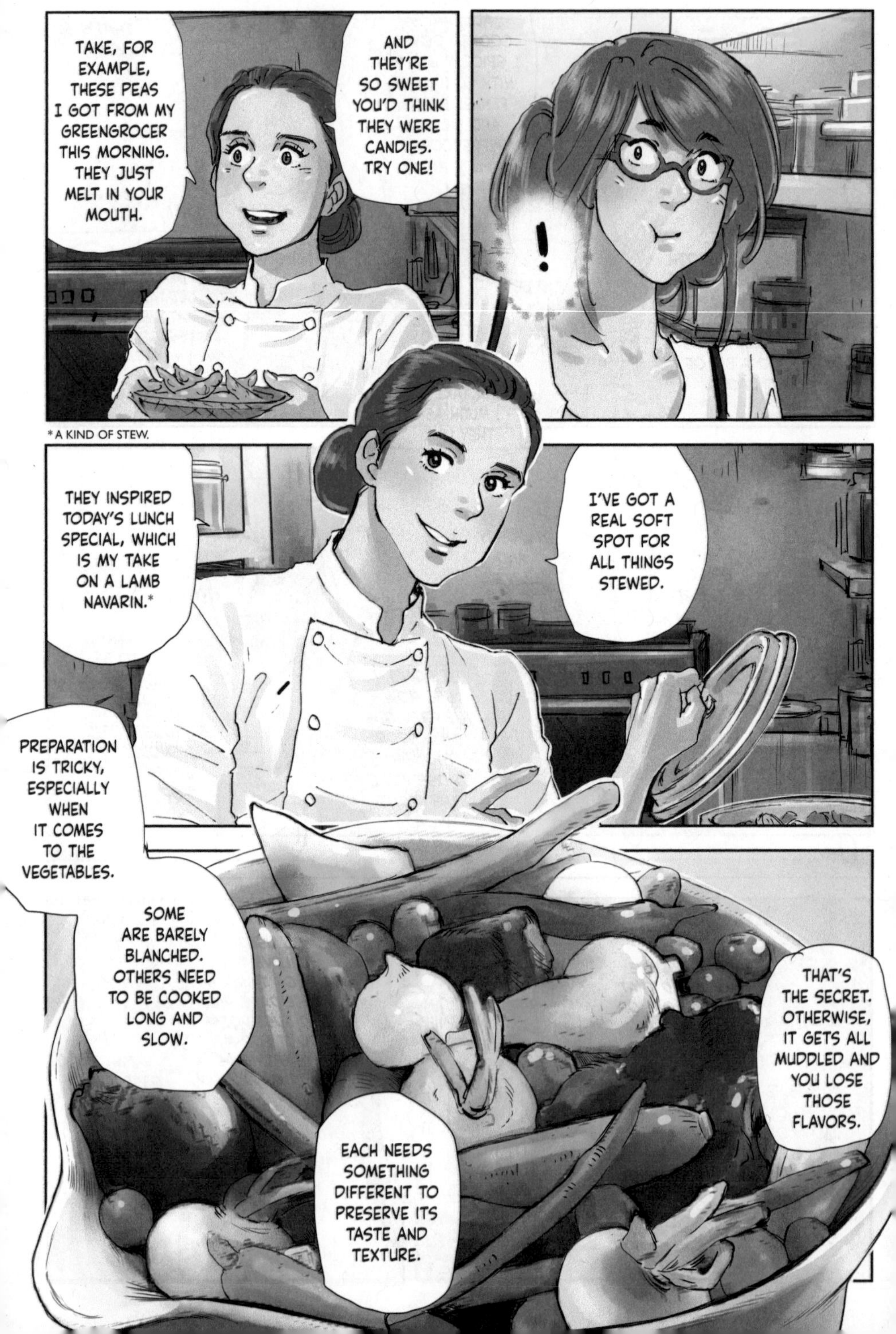
TAKE, FOR EXAMPLE, THESE PEAS I GOT FROM MY GREENGROCER THIS MORNING. THEY JUST MELT IN YOUR MOUTH.
AND THEY'RE SO SWEET YOU'D THINK THEY WERE CANDIES. TRY ONE!
!
THEY INSPIRED TODAY'S LUNCH SPECIAL, WHICH IS MY TAKE ON A LAMB NAVARIN.*
I'VE GOT A REAL SOFT SPOT FOR ALL THINGS STEWED.
PREPARATION IS TRICKY, ESPECIALLY WHEN IT COMES TO THE VEGETABLES.
SOME ARE BARELY BLANCHED. OTHERS NEED TO BE COOKED LONG AND SLOW.
EACH NEEDS SOMETHING DIFFERENT TO PRESERVE ITS TASTE AND TEXTURE.
THAT'S THE SECRET. OTHERWISE, IT GETS ALL MUDDLED AND YOU LOSE THOSE FLAVORS.

* A KIND OF STEW.

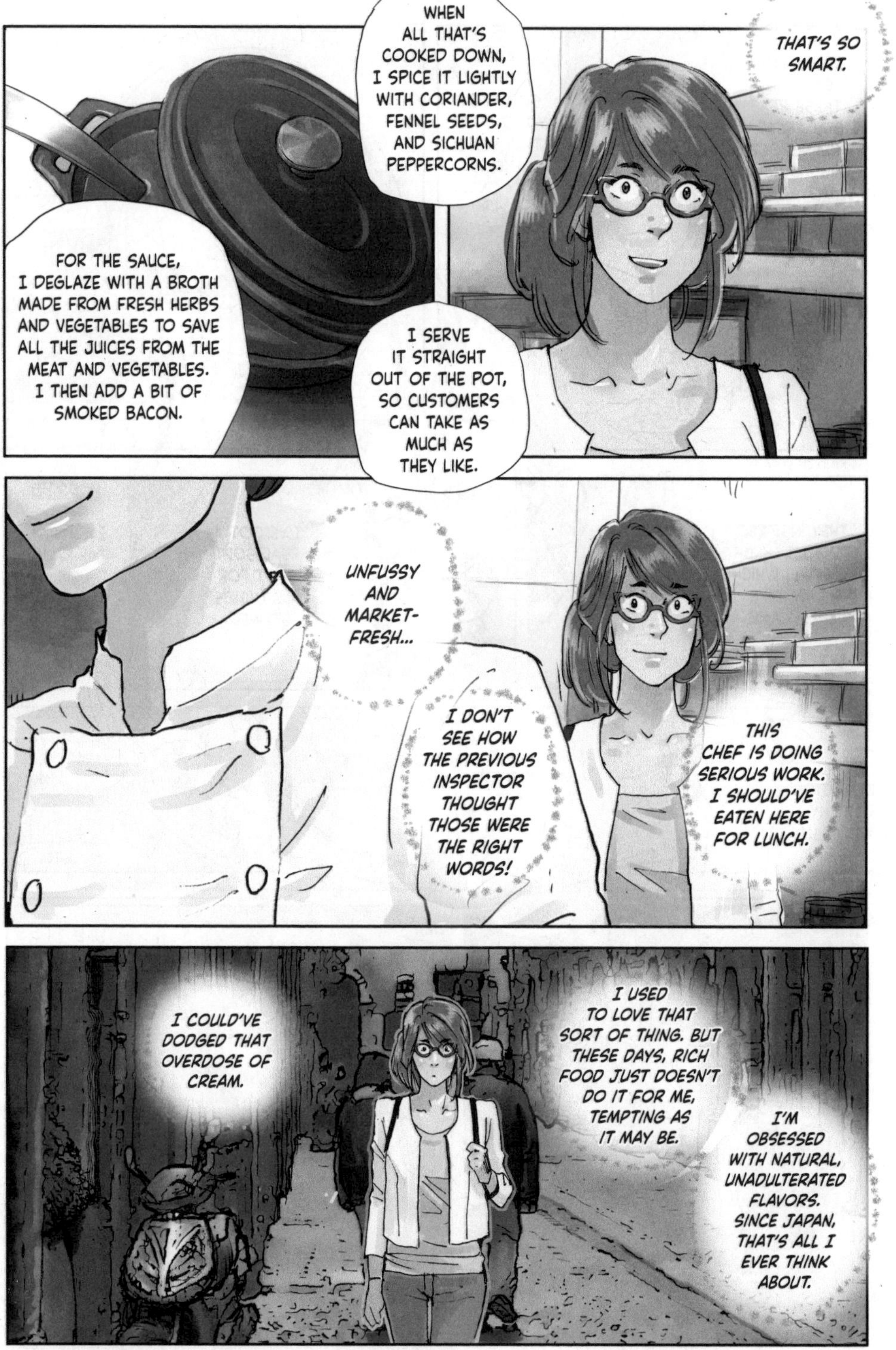
FOR THE SAUCE, I DEGLAZE WITH A BROTH MADE FROM FRESH HERBS AND VEGETABLES TO SAVE ALL THE JUICES FROM THE MEAT AND VEGETABLES. I THEN ADD A BIT OF SMOKED BACON.
WHEN ALL THAT'S COOKED DOWN, I SPICE IT LIGHTLY WITH CORIANDER, FENNEL SEEDS, AND SICHUAN PEPPERCORNS.
I SERVE IT STRAIGHT OUT OF THE POT, SO CUSTOMERS CAN TAKE AS MUCH AS THEY LIKE.
THAT'S SO SMART.
UNFUSSY AND MARKET-FRESH...
I DON'T SEE HOW THE PREVIOUS INSPECTOR THOUGHT THOSE WERE THE RIGHT WORDS!
THIS CHEF IS DOING SERIOUS WORK. I SHOULD'VE EATEN HERE FOR LUNCH.
I COULD'VE DODGED THAT OVERDOSE OF CREAM.
I USED TO LOVE THAT SORT OF THING. BUT THESE DAYS, RICH FOOD JUST DOESN'T DO IT FOR ME, TEMPTING AS IT MAY BE.
I'M OBSESSED WITH NATURAL, UNADULTERATED FLAVORS. SINCE JAPAN, THAT'S ALL I EVER THINK ABOUT.

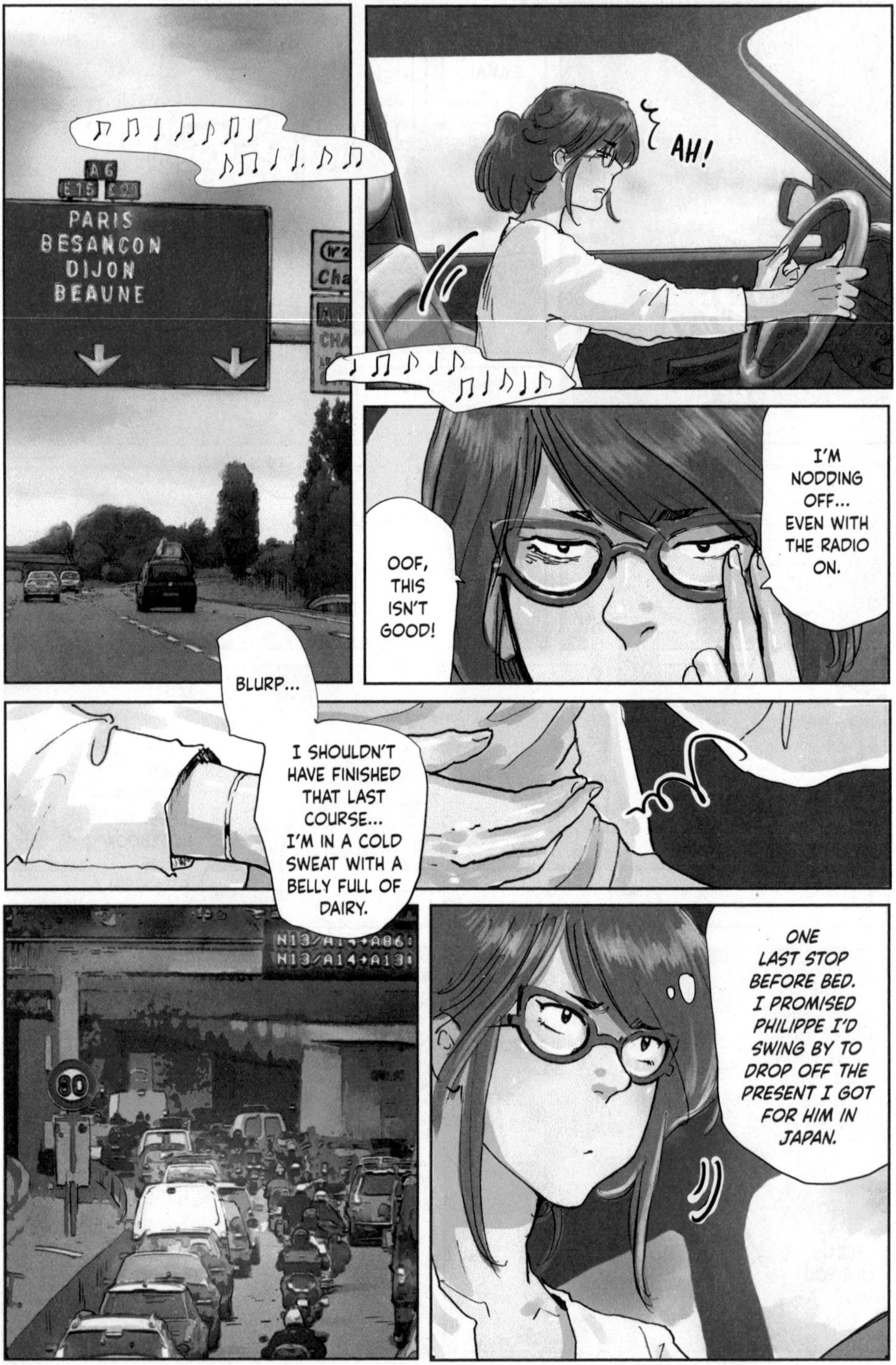
A6
E15 E21
PARIS
BESANCON
DIJON
BEAUNE
AH!
I'M NODDING OFF... EVEN WITH THE RADIO ON.
OOF, THIS ISN'T GOOD!
BLURP...
I SHOULDN'T HAVE FINISHED THAT LAST COURSE... I'M IN A COLD SWEAT WITH A BELLY FULL OF DAIRY.
N13/A14+A86
N13/A14+A13
80
ONE LAST STOP BEFORE BED. I PROMISED PHILIPPE I'D SWING BY TO DROP OFF THE PRESENT I GOT FOR HIM IN JAPAN.

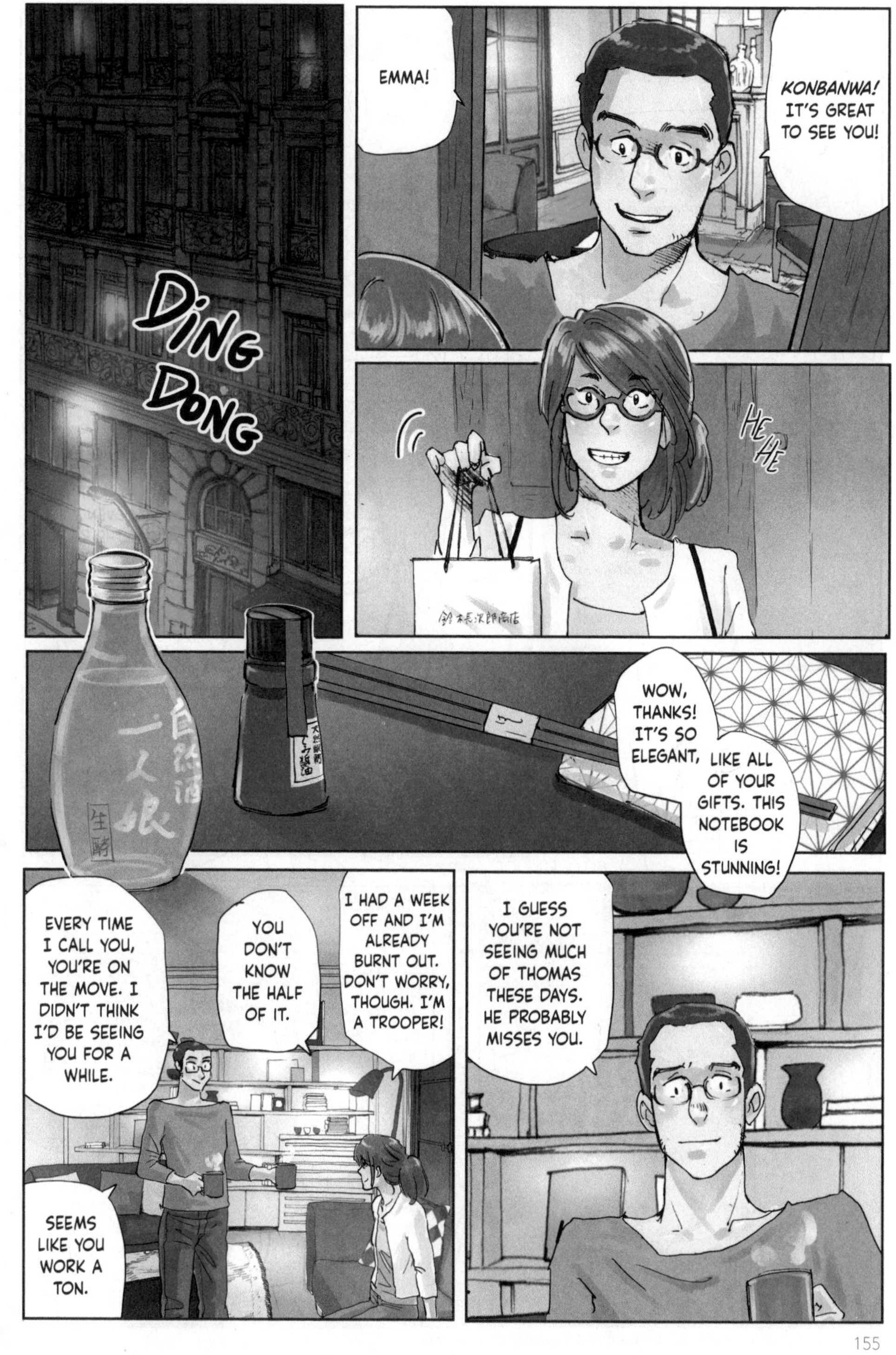
DING DONG
EMMA!
KONBANWA! IT'S GREAT TO SEE YOU!
HE HE
WOW, THANKS! IT'S SO ELEGANT,
LIKE ALL OF YOUR GIFTS. THIS NOTEBOOK IS STUNNING!
自然酒
一人娘
生酛
EVERY TIME I CALL YOU, YOU'RE ON THE MOVE. I DIDN'T THINK I'D BE SEEING YOU FOR A WHILE.
SEEMS LIKE YOU WORK A TON.
YOU DON'T KNOW THE HALF OF IT.
I HAD A WEEK OFF AND I'M ALREADY BURNT OUT. DON'T WORRY, THOUGH. I'M A TROOPER!
I GUESS YOU'RE NOT SEEING MUCH OF THOMAS THESE DAYS. HE PROBABLY MISSES YOU.

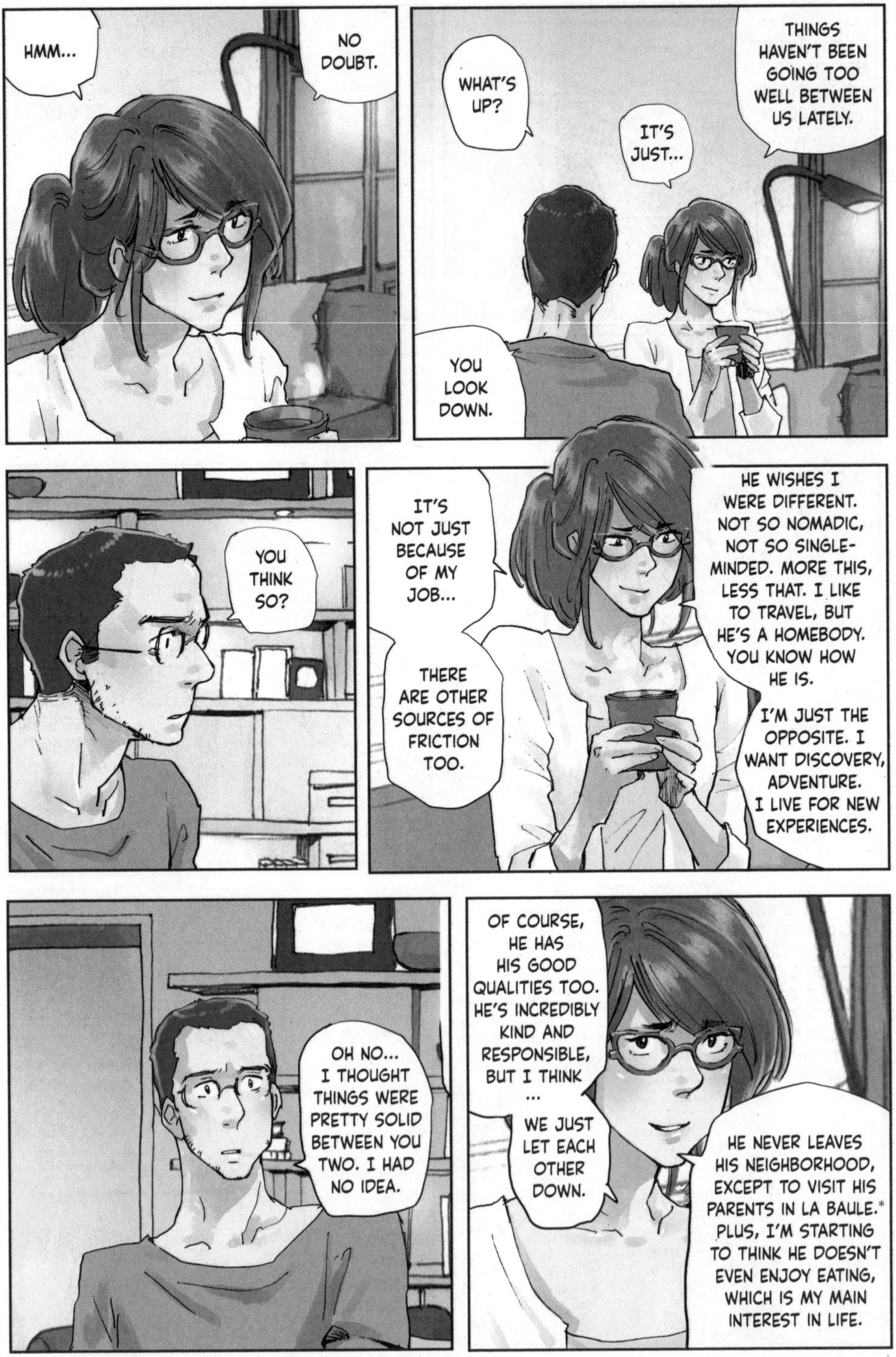
HMM...
NO DOUBT.
WHAT'S UP?
IT'S JUST...
THINGS HAVEN'T BEEN GOING TOO WELL BETWEEN US LATELY.
YOU LOOK DOWN.
YOU THINK SO?
IT'S NOT JUST BECAUSE OF MY JOB...
THERE ARE OTHER SOURCES OF FRICTION TOO.
HE WISHES I WERE DIFFERENT. NOT SO NOMADIC, NOT SO SINGLE-MINDED. MORE THIS, LESS THAT. I LIKE TO TRAVEL, BUT HE'S A HOMEBODY. YOU KNOW HOW HE IS.
I'M JUST THE OPPOSITE. I WANT DISCOVERY, ADVENTURE. I LIVE FOR NEW EXPERIENCES.
OH NO... I THOUGHT THINGS WERE PRETTY SOLID BETWEEN YOU TWO. I HAD NO IDEA.
OF COURSE, HE HAS HIS GOOD QUALITIES TOO. HE'S INCREDIBLY KIND AND RESPONSIBLE, BUT I THINK ...
WE JUST LET EACH OTHER DOWN.
HE NEVER LEAVES HIS NEIGHBORHOOD, EXCEPT TO VISIT HIS PARENTS IN LA BAULE.* PLUS, I'M STARTING TO THINK HE DOESN'T EVEN ENJOY EATING, WHICH IS MY MAIN INTEREST IN LIFE.

* LA BAULE-ESCOUBLAC IS A RESORT TOWN ON THE SOUTHERN COAST OF BRITTANY.

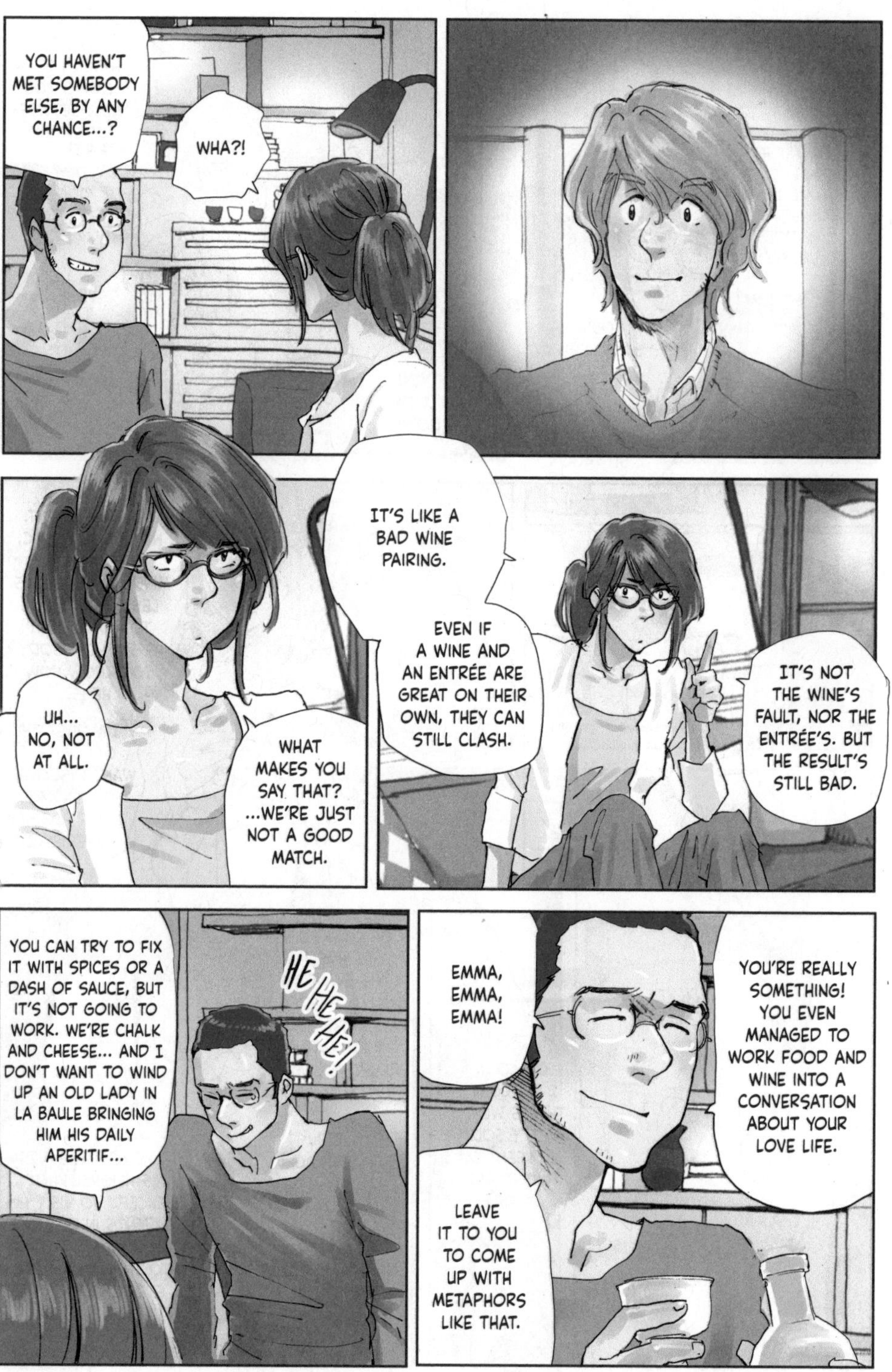
YOU HAVEN'T MET SOMEBODY ELSE, BY ANY CHANCE...?
WHA?!
UH... NO, NOT AT ALL.
WHAT MAKES YOU SAY THAT? ...WE'RE JUST NOT A GOOD MATCH.
IT'S LIKE A BAD WINE PAIRING.
EVEN IF A WINE AND AN ENTRÉE ARE GREAT ON THEIR OWN, THEY CAN STILL CLASH.
IT'S NOT THE WINE'S FAULT, NOR THE ENTRÉE'S. BUT THE RESULT'S STILL BAD.
YOU CAN TRY TO FIX IT WITH SPICES OR A DASH OF SAUCE, BUT IT'S NOT GOING TO WORK. WE'RE CHALK AND CHEESE... AND I DON'T WANT TO WIND UP AN OLD LADY IN LA BAULE BRINGING HIM HIS DAILY APERITIF...
HE HE HE!
EMMA, EMMA, EMMA!
YOU'RE REALLY SOMETHING! YOU EVEN MANAGED TO WORK FOOD AND WINE INTO A CONVERSATION ABOUT YOUR LOVE LIFE.
LEAVE IT TO YOU TO COME UP WITH METAPHORS LIKE THAT.

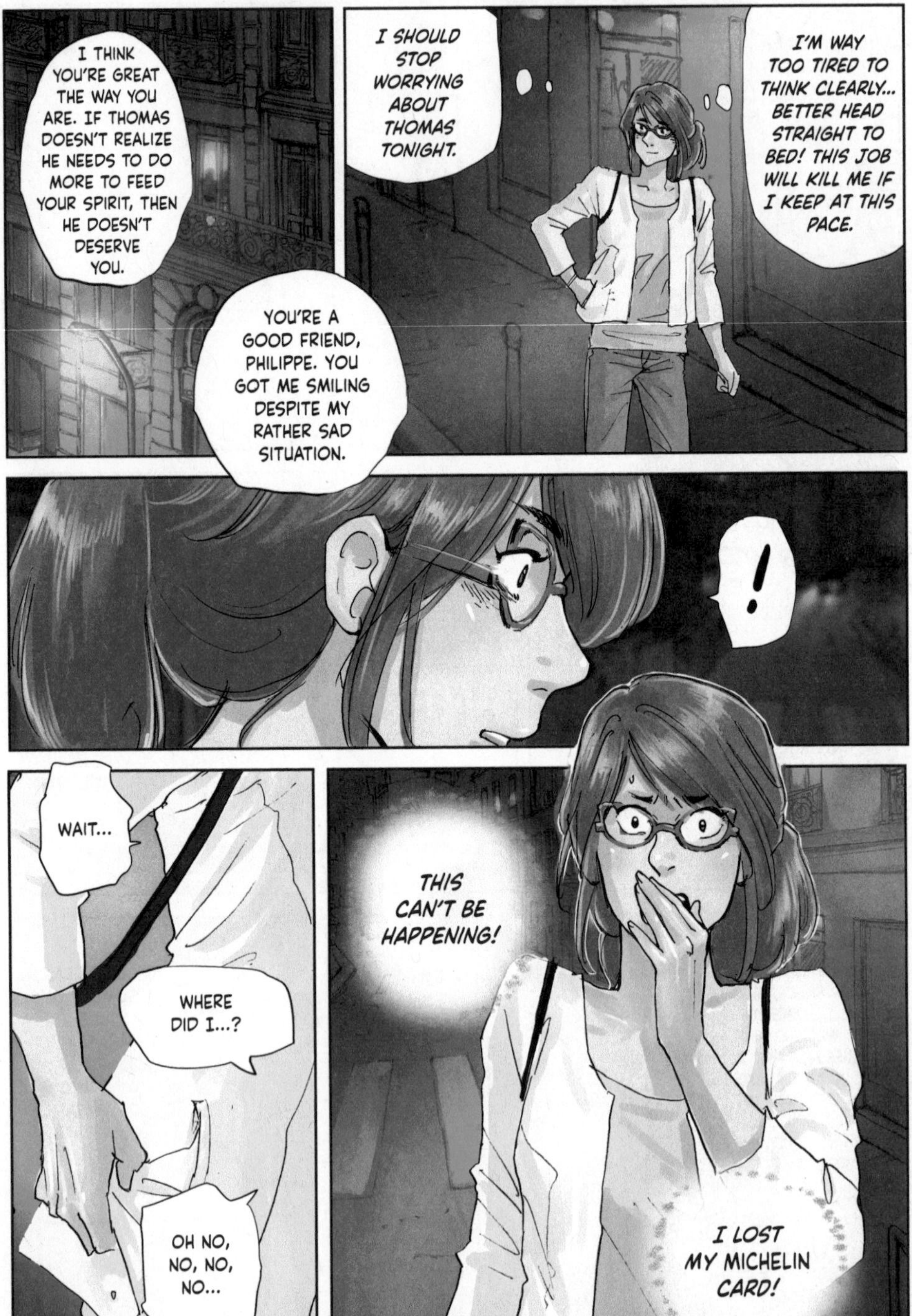
I THINK YOU'RE GREAT THE WAY YOU ARE. IF THOMAS DOESN'T REALIZE HE NEEDS TO DO MORE TO FEED YOUR SPIRIT, THEN HE DOESN'T DESERVE YOU.
YOU'RE A GOOD FRIEND, PHILIPPE. YOU GOT ME SMILING DESPITE MY RATHER SAD SITUATION.
I SHOULD STOP WORRYING ABOUT THOMAS TONIGHT.
I'M WAY TOO TIRED TO THINK CLEARLY... BETTER HEAD STRAIGHT TO BED! THIS JOB WILL KILL ME IF I KEEP AT THIS PACE.
!
WAIT...
WHERE DID I...?
OH NO, NO, NO, NO...
THIS CAN'T BE HAPPENING!
I LOST MY MICHELIN CARD!

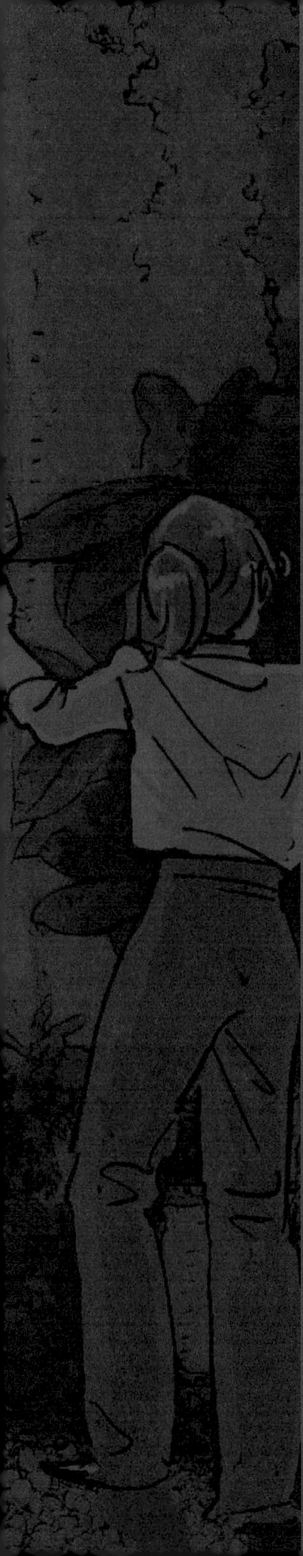

CHAPTER 8

ANTOINE’S PLACE

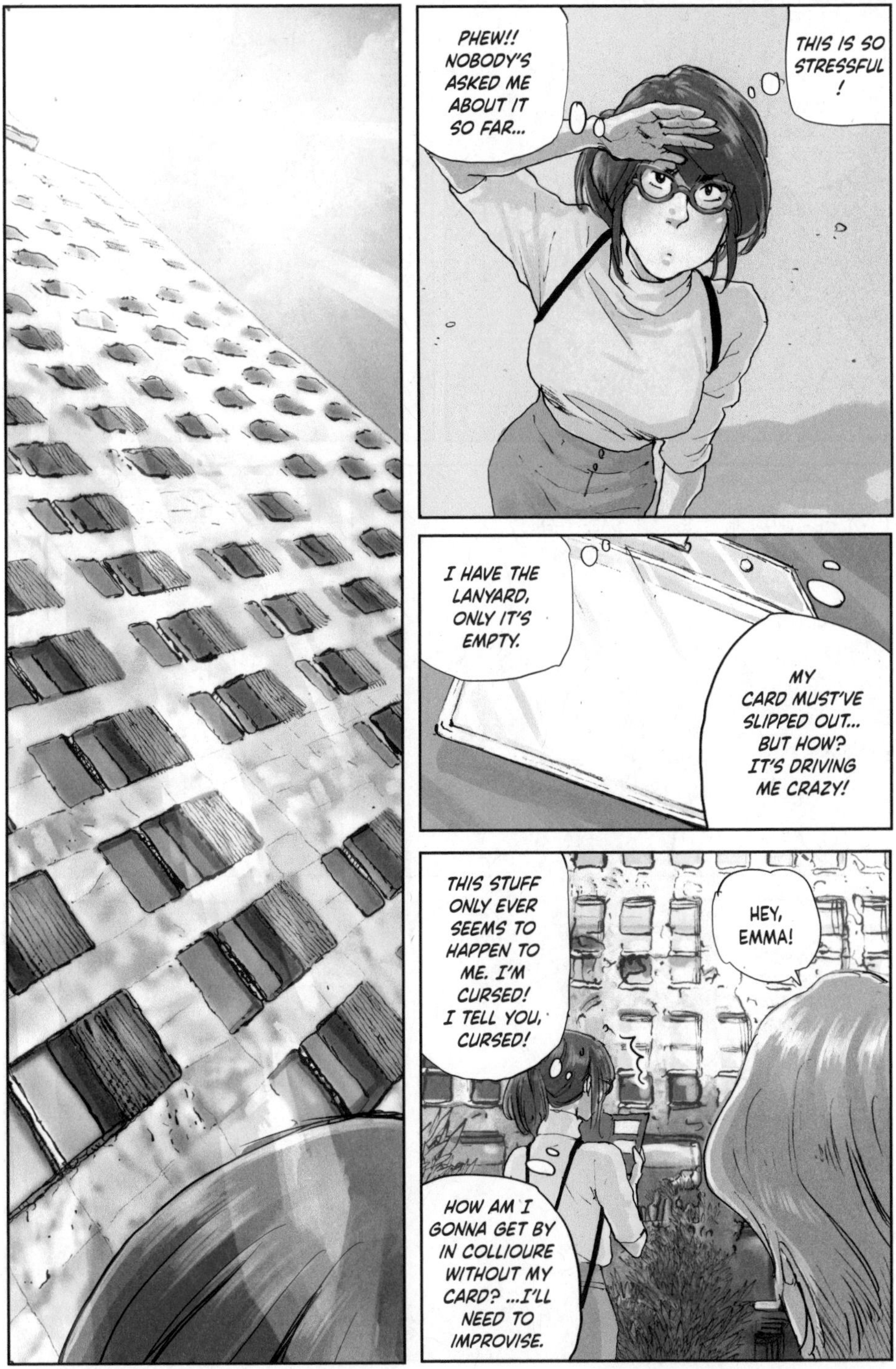
PHEW!! NOBODY'S ASKED ME ABOUT IT SO FAR...
THIS IS SO STRESSFUL!
I HAVE THE LANYARD, ONLY IT'S EMPTY.
MY CARD MUST'VE SLIPPED OUT... BUT HOW? IT'S DRIVING ME CRAZY!
THIS STUFF ONLY EVER SEEMS TO HAPPEN TO ME. I'M CURSED! I TELL YOU, CURSED!
HEY, EMMA!
HOW AM I GONNA GET BY IN COLLIOURE WITHOUT MY CARD? ...I'LL NEED TO IMPROVISE.

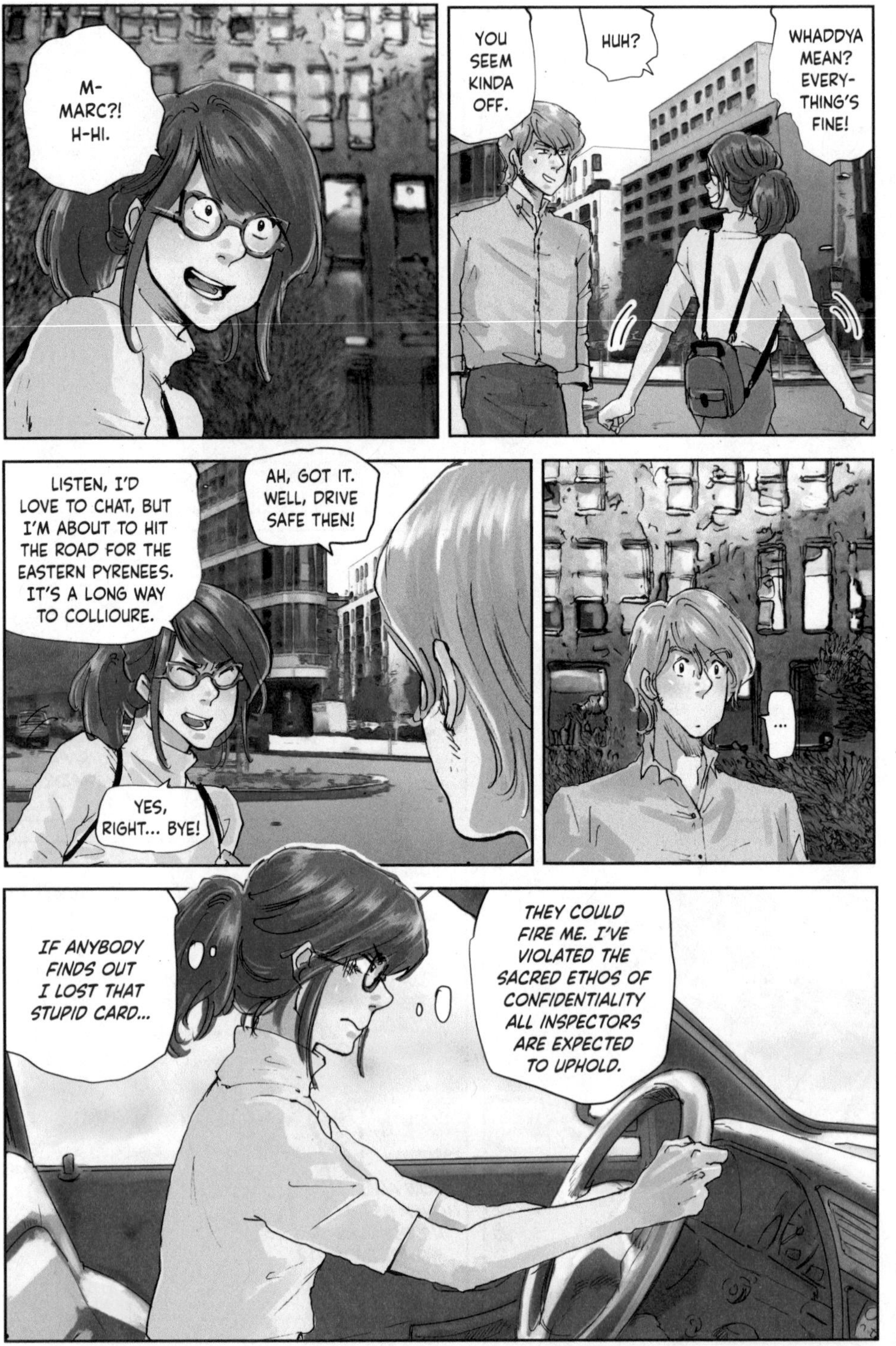
M- MARC?! H-HI.
YOU SEEM KINDA OFF.
HUH?
WHADDYA MEAN? EVERY-THING'S FINE!
LISTEN, I'D LOVE TO CHAT, BUT I'M ABOUT TO HIT THE ROAD FOR THE EASTERN PYRENEES. IT'S A LONG WAY TO COLLIOURE.
AH, GOT IT. WELL, DRIVE SAFE THEN!
YES, RIGHT... BYE!
...
IF ANYBODY FINDS OUT I LOST THAT STUPID CARD...
THEY COULD FIRE ME. I'VE VIOLATED THE SACRED ETHOS OF CONFIDENTIALITY ALL INSPECTORS ARE EXPECTED TO UPHOLD.

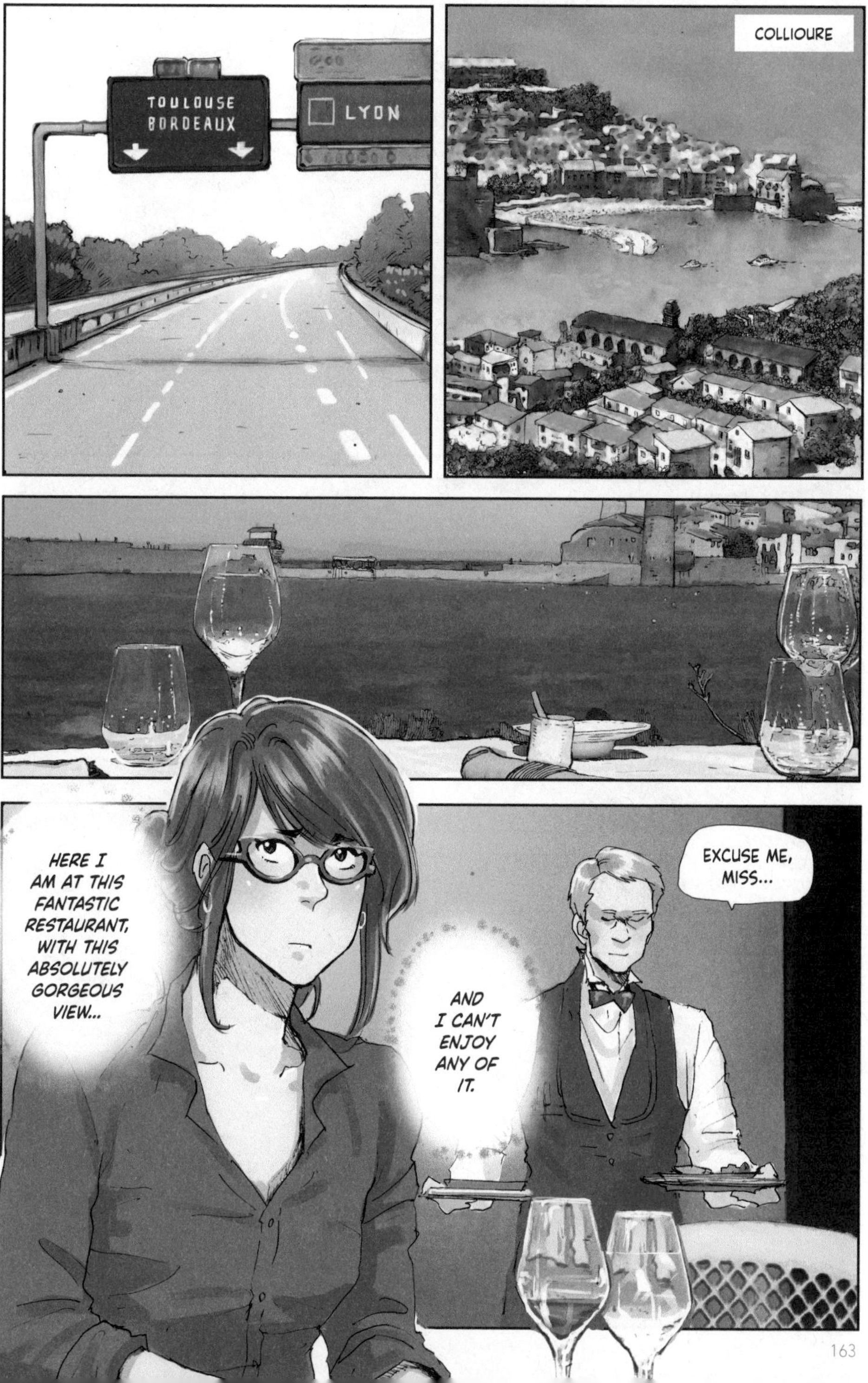
TOULOUSE
BORDEAUX
LYON
COLLIOURE
HERE I AM AT THIS FANTASTIC RESTAURANT, WITH THIS ABSOLUTELY GORGEOUS VIEW...
AND I CAN'T ENJOY ANY OF IT.
EXCUSE ME, MISS...

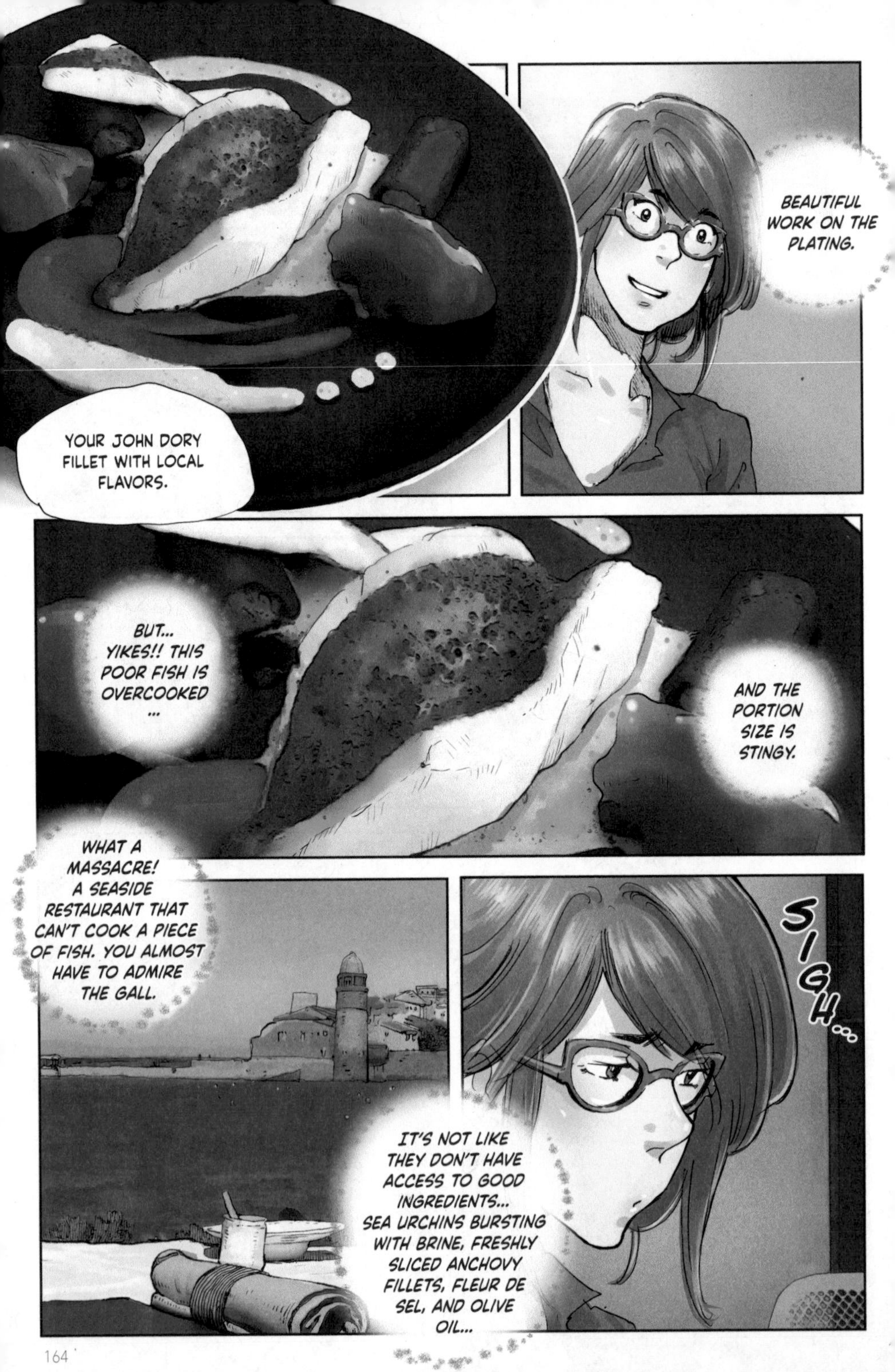
YOUR JOHN DORY FILLET WITH LOCAL FLAVORS.
BEAUTIFUL WORK ON THE PLATING.
BUT... YIKES!! THIS POOR FISH IS OVERCOOKED ...
AND THE PORTION SIZE IS STINGY.
WHAT A MASSACRE! A SEASIDE RESTAURANT THAT CAN'T COOK A PIECE OF FISH. YOU ALMOST HAVE TO ADMIRE THE GALL.
SIGH...
IT'S NOT LIKE THEY DON'T HAVE ACCESS TO GOOD INGREDIENTS... SEA URCHINS BURSTING WITH BRINE, FRESHLY SLICED ANCHOVY FILLETS, FLEUR DE SEL, AND OLIVE OIL...

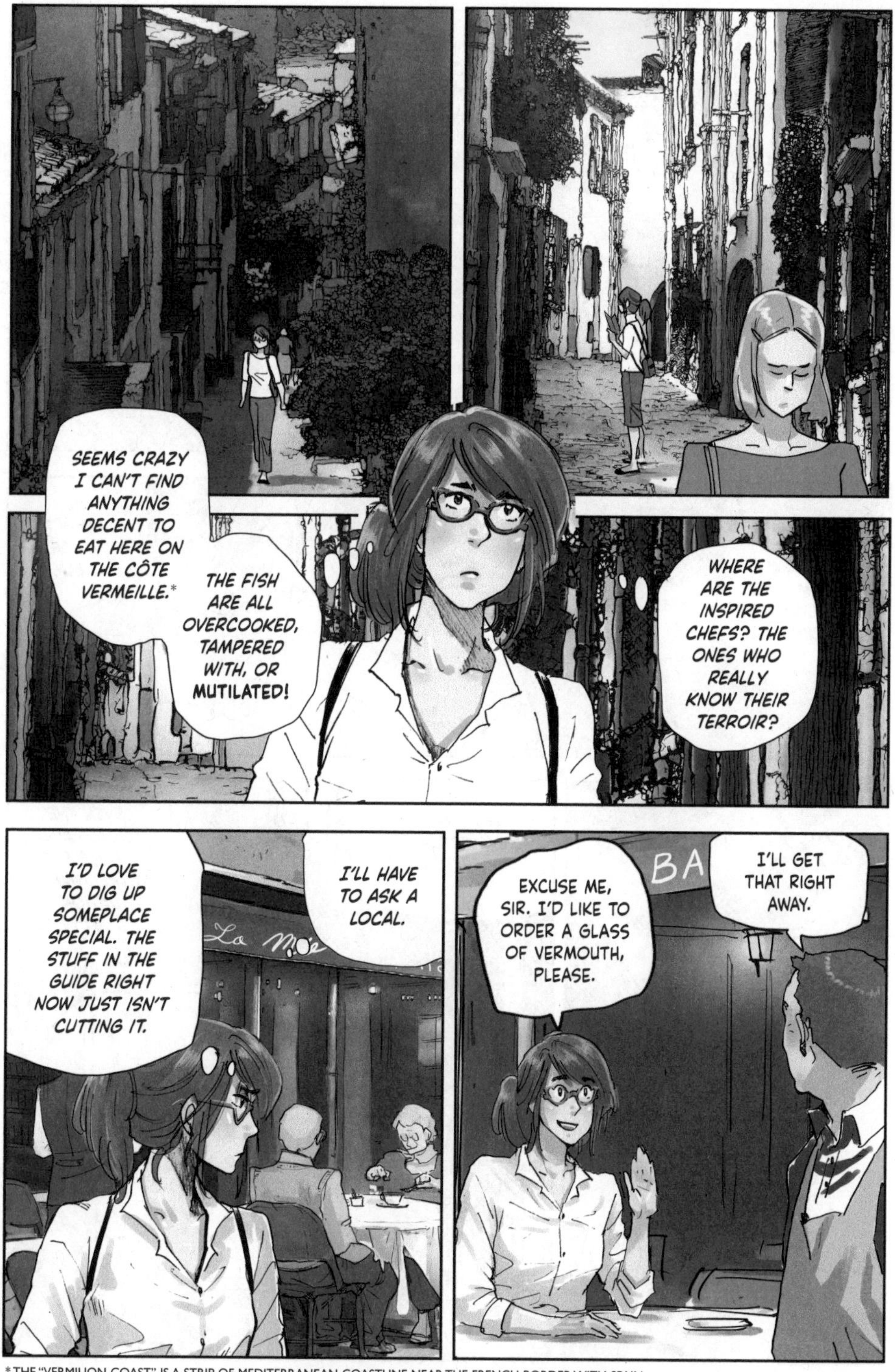
SEEMS CRAZY I CAN'T FIND ANYTHING DECENT TO EAT HERE ON THE CÔTE VERMEILLE.*
THE FISH ARE ALL OVERCOOKED, TAMPERED WITH, OR MUTILATED!
WHERE ARE THE INSPIRED CHEFS? THE ONES WHO REALLY KNOW THEIR TERROIR?
I'D LOVE TO DIG UP SOMEPLACE SPECIAL. THE STUFF IN THE GUIDE RIGHT NOW JUST ISN'T CUTTING IT.
I'LL HAVE TO ASK A LOCAL.
EXCUSE ME, SIR. I'D LIKE TO ORDER A GLASS OF VERMOUTH, PLEASE.
I'LL GET THAT RIGHT AWAY.

* THE "VERMILION COAST" IS A STRIP OF MEDITERRANEAN COASTLINE NEAR THE FRENCH BORDER WITH SPAIN.

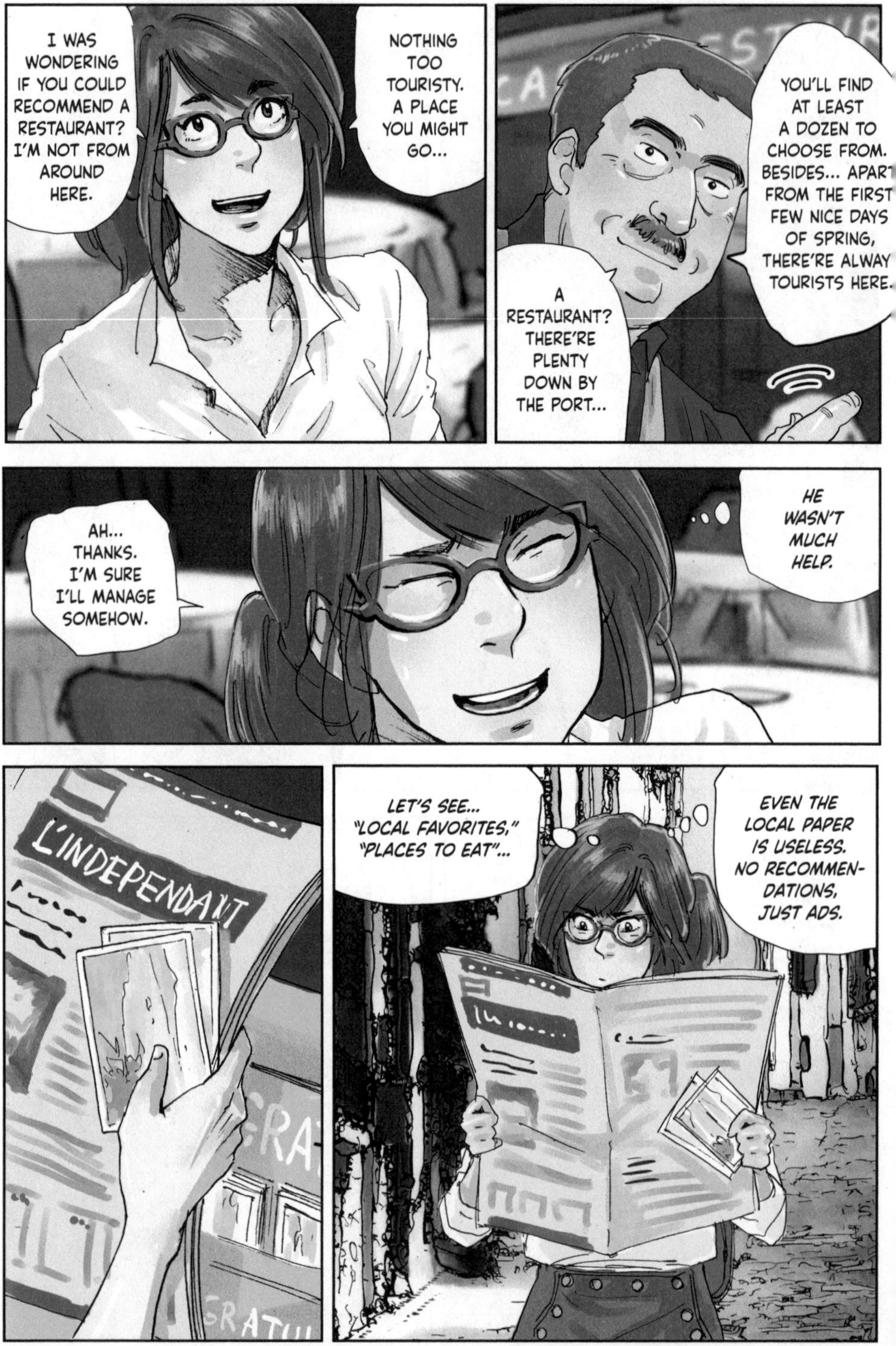
I WAS WONDERING IF YOU COULD RECOMMEND A RESTAURANT? I'M NOT FROM AROUND HERE.
NOTHING TOO TOURISTY. A PLACE YOU MIGHT GO...
A RESTAURANT? THERE'RE PLENTY DOWN BY THE PORT...
YOU'LL FIND AT LEAST A DOZEN TO CHOOSE FROM. BESIDES... APART FROM THE FIRST FEW NICE DAYS OF SPRING, THERE'RE ALWAY TOURISTS HERE.
AH... THANKS. I'M SURE I'LL MANAGE SOMEHOW.
HE WASN'T MUCH HELP.
L'INDEPENDANT
LET'S SEE... "LOCAL FAVORITES," "PLACES TO EAT"...
EVEN THE LOCAL PAPER IS USELESS. NO RECOMMEN-DATIONS, JUST ADS.

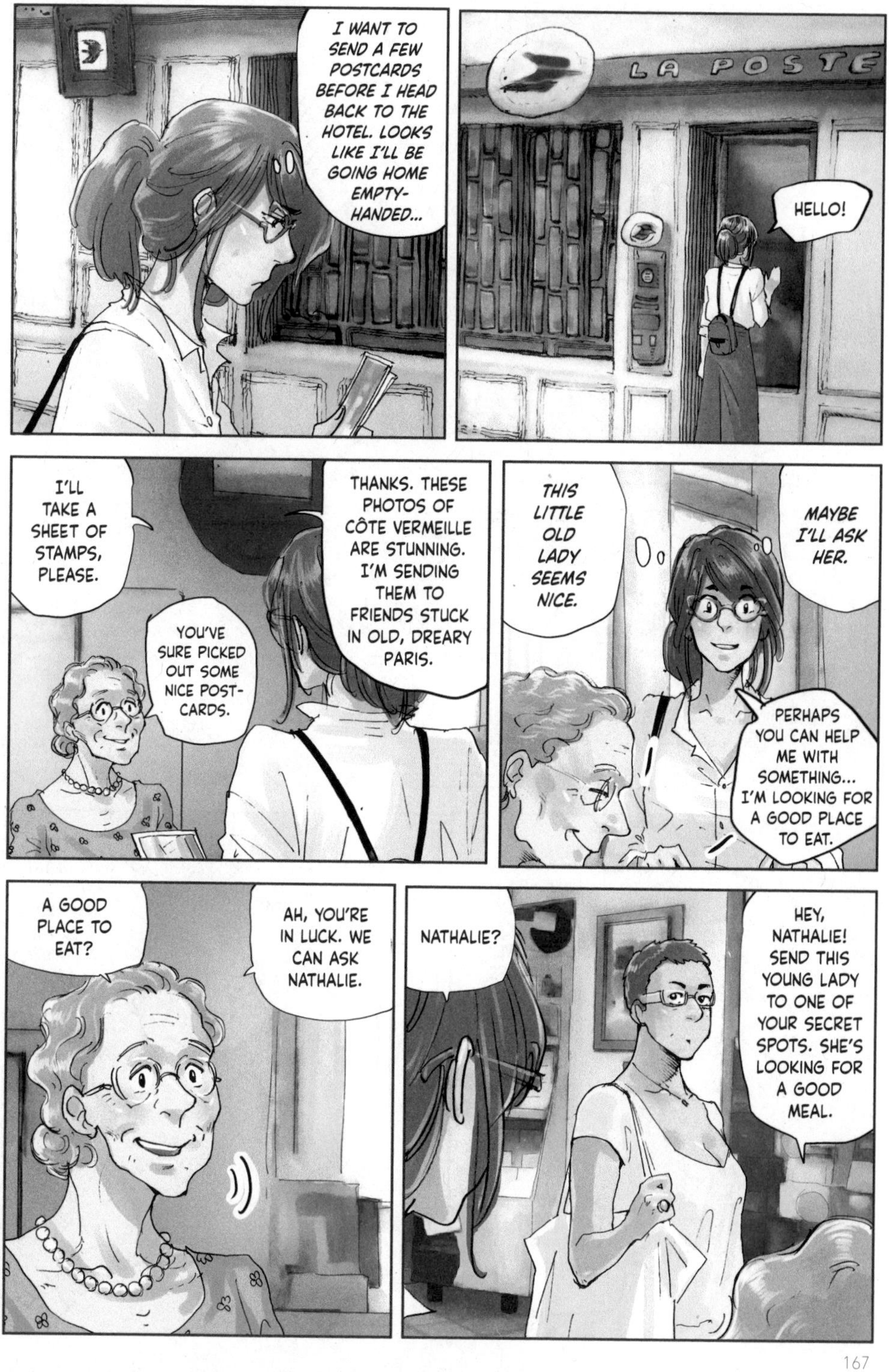
I WANT TO SEND A FEW POSTCARDS BEFORE I HEAD BACK TO THE HOTEL. LOOKS LIKE I'LL BE GOING HOME EMPTY-HANDED...
LA POSTE
HELLO!
I'LL TAKE A SHEET OF STAMPS, PLEASE.
THANKS. THESE PHOTOS OF CÔTE VERMEILLE ARE STUNNING. I'M SENDING THEM TO FRIENDS STUCK IN OLD, DREARY PARIS.
YOU'VE SURE PICKED OUT SOME NICE POST-CARDS.
THIS LITTLE OLD LADY SEEMS NICE.
MAYBE I'LL ASK HER.
PERHAPS YOU CAN HELP ME WITH SOMETHING... I'M LOOKING FOR A GOOD PLACE TO EAT.
A GOOD PLACE TO EAT?
AH, YOU'RE IN LUCK. WE CAN ASK NATHALIE.
NATHALIE?
HEY, NATHALIE! SEND THIS YOUNG LADY TO ONE OF YOUR SECRET SPOTS. SHE'S LOOKING FOR A GOOD MEAL.

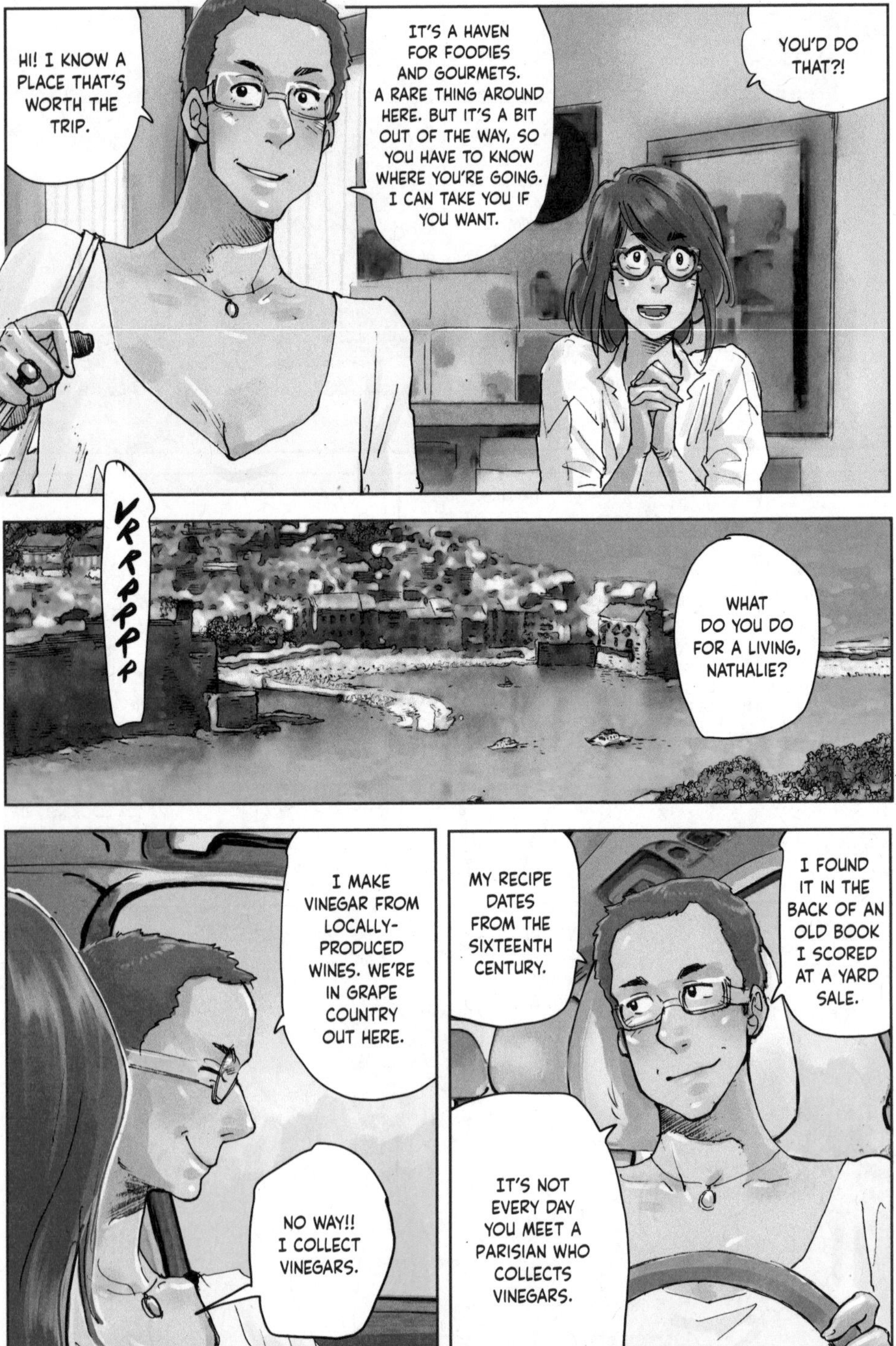
HI! I KNOW A PLACE THAT'S WORTH THE TRIP.
IT'S A HAVEN FOR FOODIES AND GOURMETS. A RARE THING AROUND HERE. BUT IT'S A BIT OUT OF THE WAY, SO YOU HAVE TO KNOW WHERE YOU'RE GOING. I CAN TAKE YOU IF YOU WANT.
YOU'D DO THAT?!
VRRRRRR
WHAT DO YOU DO FOR A LIVING, NATHALIE?
I MAKE VINEGAR FROM LOCALLY-PRODUCED WINES. WE'RE IN GRAPE COUNTRY OUT HERE.
NO WAY!! I COLLECT VINEGARS.
MY RECIPE DATES FROM THE SIXTEENTH CENTURY.
I FOUND IT IN THE BACK OF AN OLD BOOK I SCORED AT A YARD SALE.
IT'S NOT EVERY DAY YOU MEET A PARISIAN WHO COLLECTS VINEGARS.

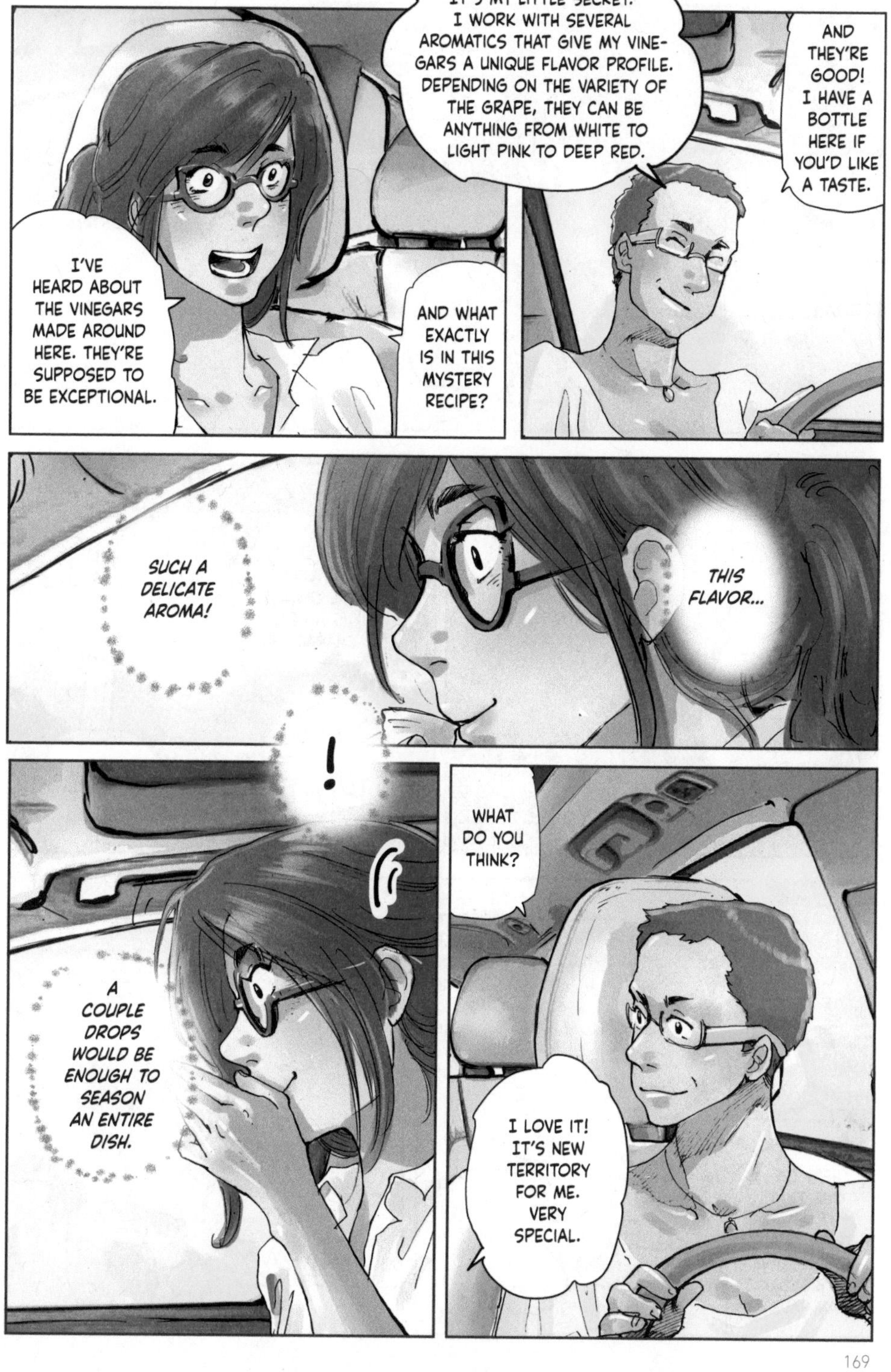
I'VE HEARD ABOUT THE VINEGARS MADE AROUND HERE. THEY'RE SUPPOSED TO BE EXCEPTIONAL.
AND WHAT EXACTLY IS IN THIS MYSTERY RECIPE?
IT'S MY LITTLE SECRET. I WORK WITH SEVERAL AROMATICS THAT GIVE MY VINEGARS A UNIQUE FLAVOR PROFILE. DEPENDING ON THE VARIETY OF THE GRAPE, THEY CAN BE ANYTHING FROM WHITE TO LIGHT PINK TO DEEP RED.
AND THEY'RE GOOD! I HAVE A BOTTLE HERE IF YOU'D LIKE A TASTE.
SUCH A DELICATE AROMA!
THIS FLAVOR...
!
A COUPLE DROPS WOULD BE ENOUGH TO SEASON AN ENTIRE DISH.
WHAT DO YOU THINK?
I LOVE IT! IT'S NEW TERRITORY FOR ME. VERY SPECIAL.

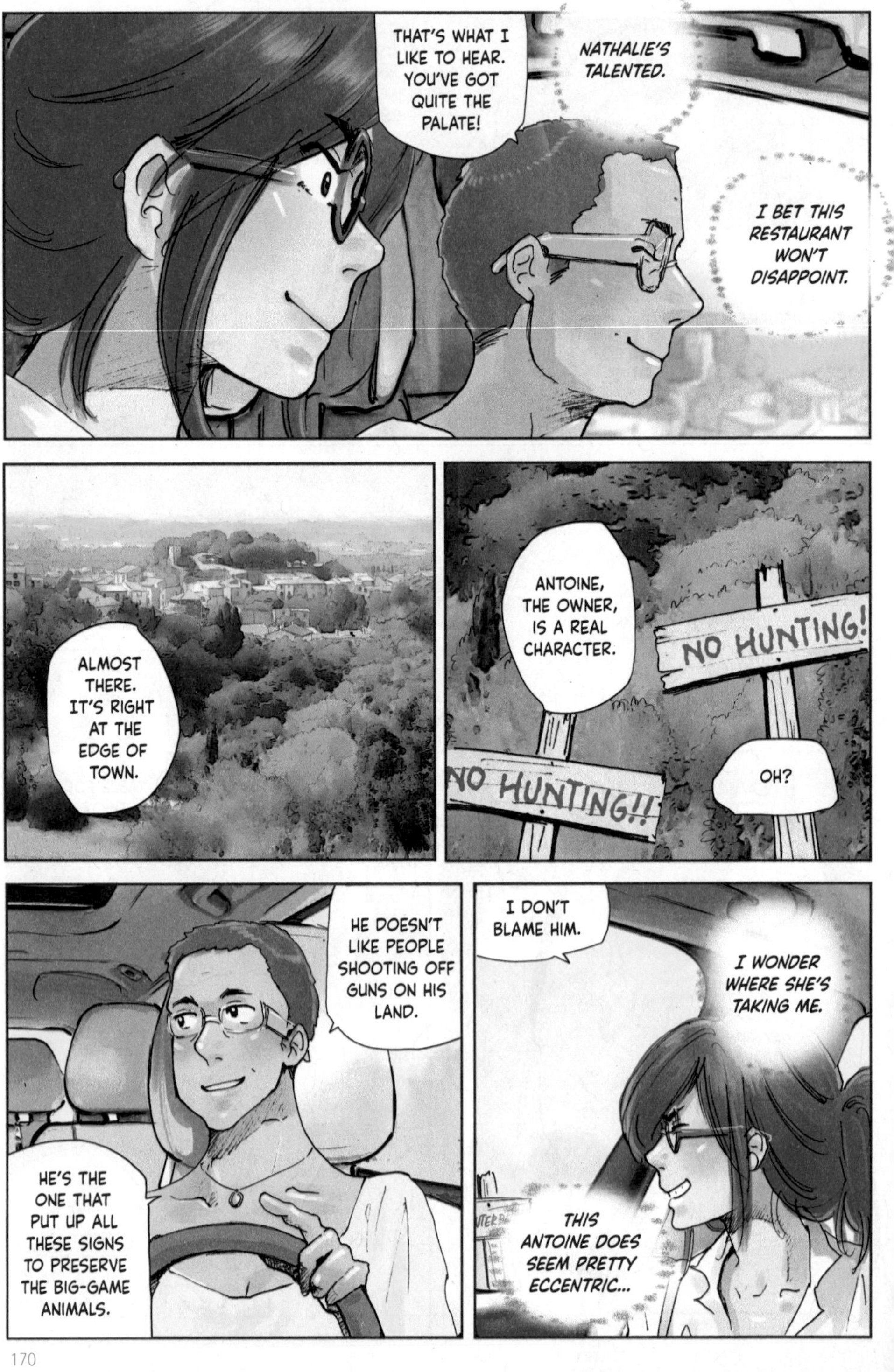
THAT'S WHAT I LIKE TO HEAR. YOU'VE GOT QUITE THE PALATE!
NATHALIE'S TALENTED.
I BET THIS RESTAURANT WON'T DISAPPOINT.
ALMOST THERE. IT'S RIGHT AT THE EDGE OF TOWN.
ANTOINE, THE OWNER, IS A REAL CHARACTER.
NO HUNTING!
NO HUNTING!!
OH?
HE DOESN'T LIKE PEOPLE SHOOTING OFF GUNS ON HIS LAND.
HE'S THE ONE THAT PUT UP ALL THESE SIGNS TO PRESERVE THE BIG-GAME ANIMALS.
I DON'T BLAME HIM.
I WONDER WHERE SHE'S TAKING ME.
THIS ANTOINE DOES SEEM PRETTY ECCENTRIC...

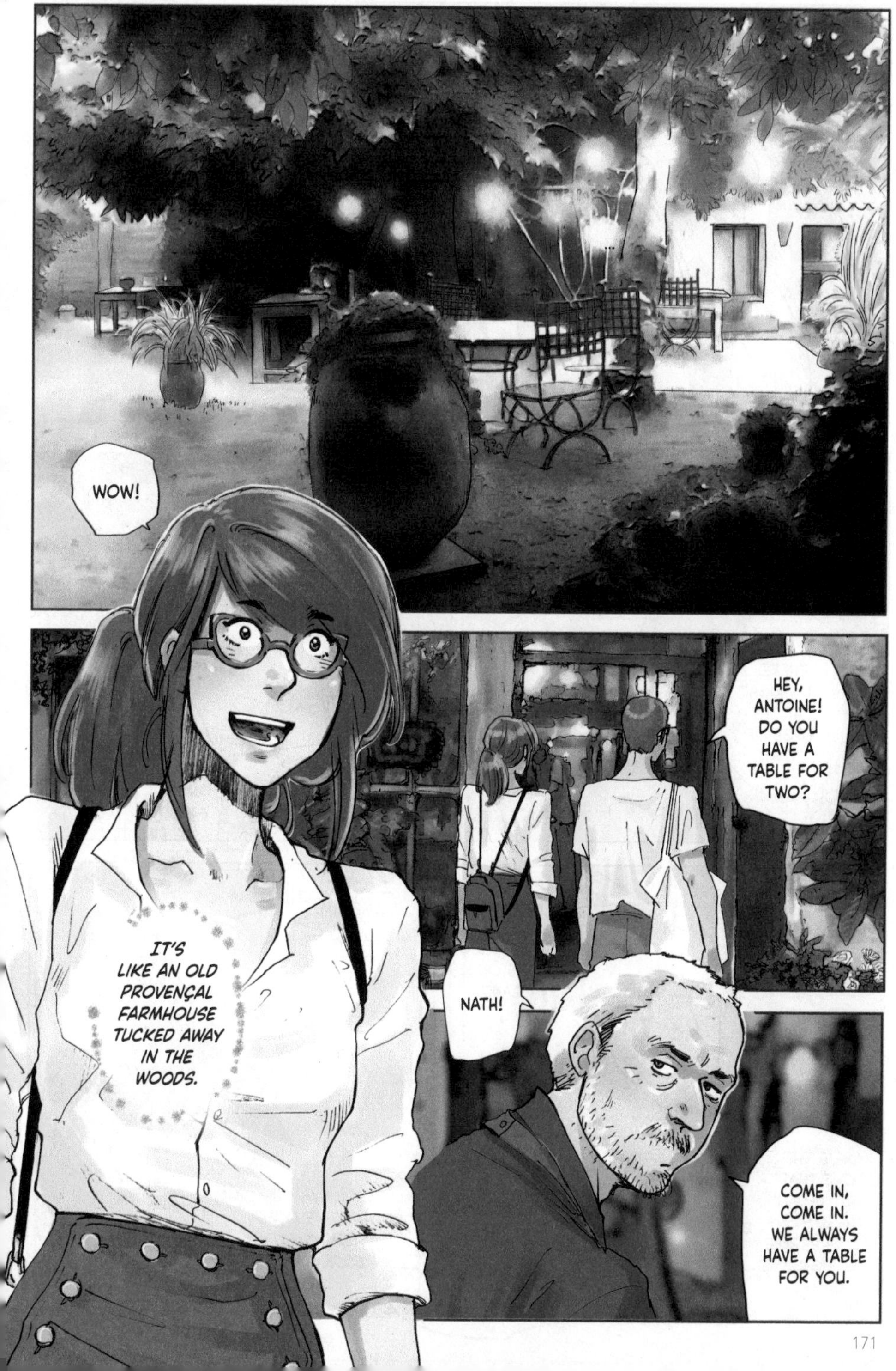
WOW!
IT'S LIKE AN OLD PROVENÇAL FARMHOUSE TUCKED AWAY IN THE WOODS.
HEY, ANTOINE! DO YOU HAVE A TABLE FOR TWO?
NATH!
COME IN, COME IN. WE ALWAYS HAVE A TABLE FOR YOU.

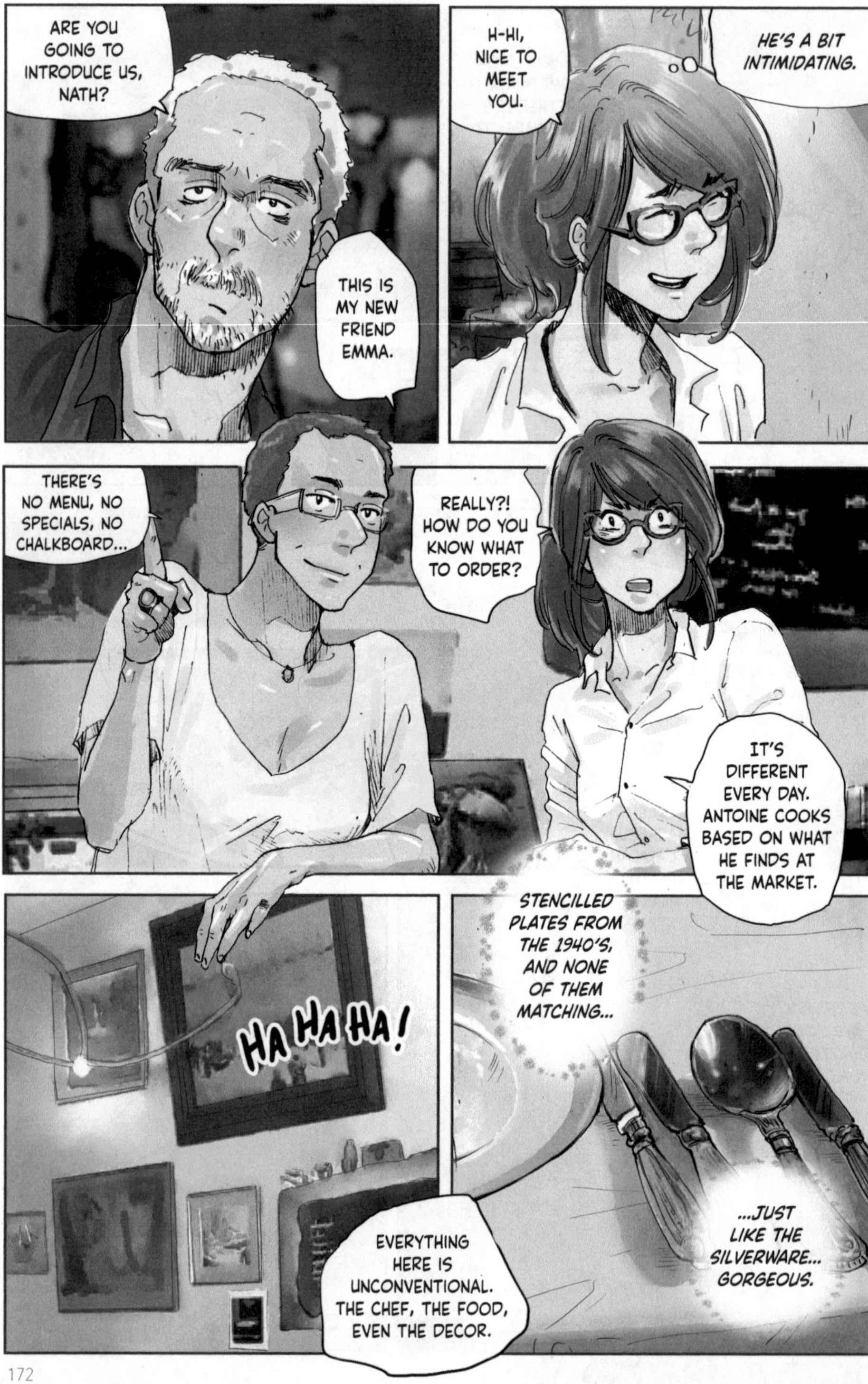
ARE YOU GOING TO INTRODUCE US, NATH?
THIS IS MY NEW FRIEND EMMA.
H-HI, NICE TO MEET YOU.
HE'S A BIT INTIMIDATING.
THERE'S NO MENU, NO SPECIALS, NO CHALKBOARD...
REALLY?! HOW DO YOU KNOW WHAT TO ORDER?
IT'S DIFFERENT EVERY DAY. ANTOINE COOKS BASED ON WHAT HE FINDS AT THE MARKET.
HA HA HA!
EVERYTHING HERE IS UNCONVENTIONAL. THE CHEF, THE FOOD, EVEN THE DECOR.
STENCILLED PLATES FROM THE 1940'S, AND NONE OF THEM MATCHING...
...JUST LIKE THE SILVERWARE... GORGEOUS.

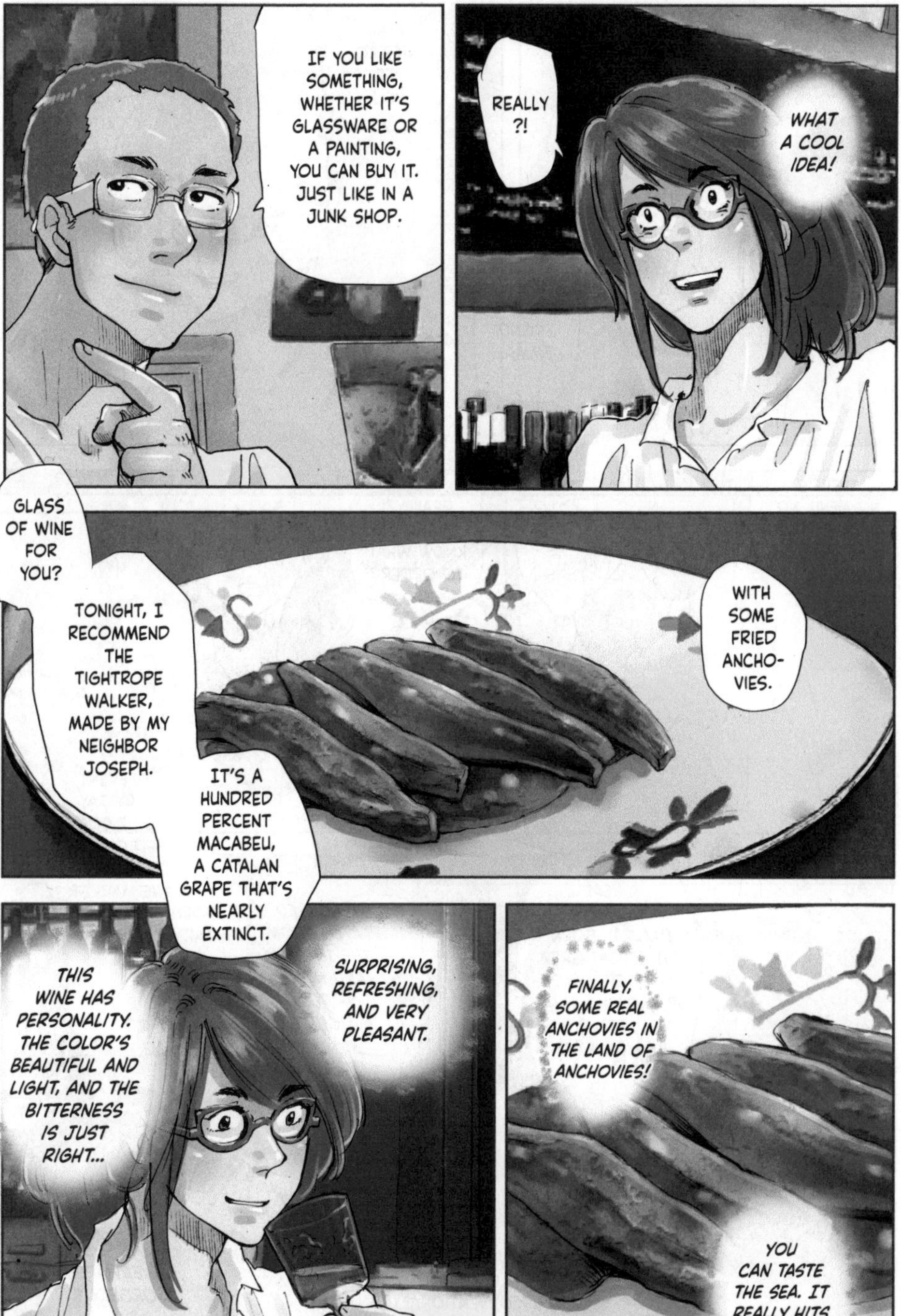
IF YOU LIKE SOMETHING, WHETHER IT'S GLASSWARE OR A PAINTING, YOU CAN BUY IT. JUST LIKE IN A JUNK SHOP.
REALLY ?!
WHAT A COOL IDEA!
GLASS OF WINE FOR YOU?
TONIGHT, I RECOMMEND THE TIGHTROPE WALKER, MADE BY MY NEIGHBOR JOSEPH.
IT'S A HUNDRED PERCENT MACABEU, A CATALAN GRAPE THAT'S NEARLY EXTINCT.
WITH SOME FRIED ANCHO-VIES.
THIS WINE HAS PERSONALITY. THE COLOR'S BEAUTIFUL AND LIGHT, AND THE BITTERNESS IS JUST RIGHT...
SURPRISING, REFRESHING, AND VERY PLEASANT.
FINALLY, SOME REAL ANCHOVIES IN THE LAND OF ANCHOVIES!
YOU CAN TASTE THE SEA. IT REALLY HITS THE SPOT!

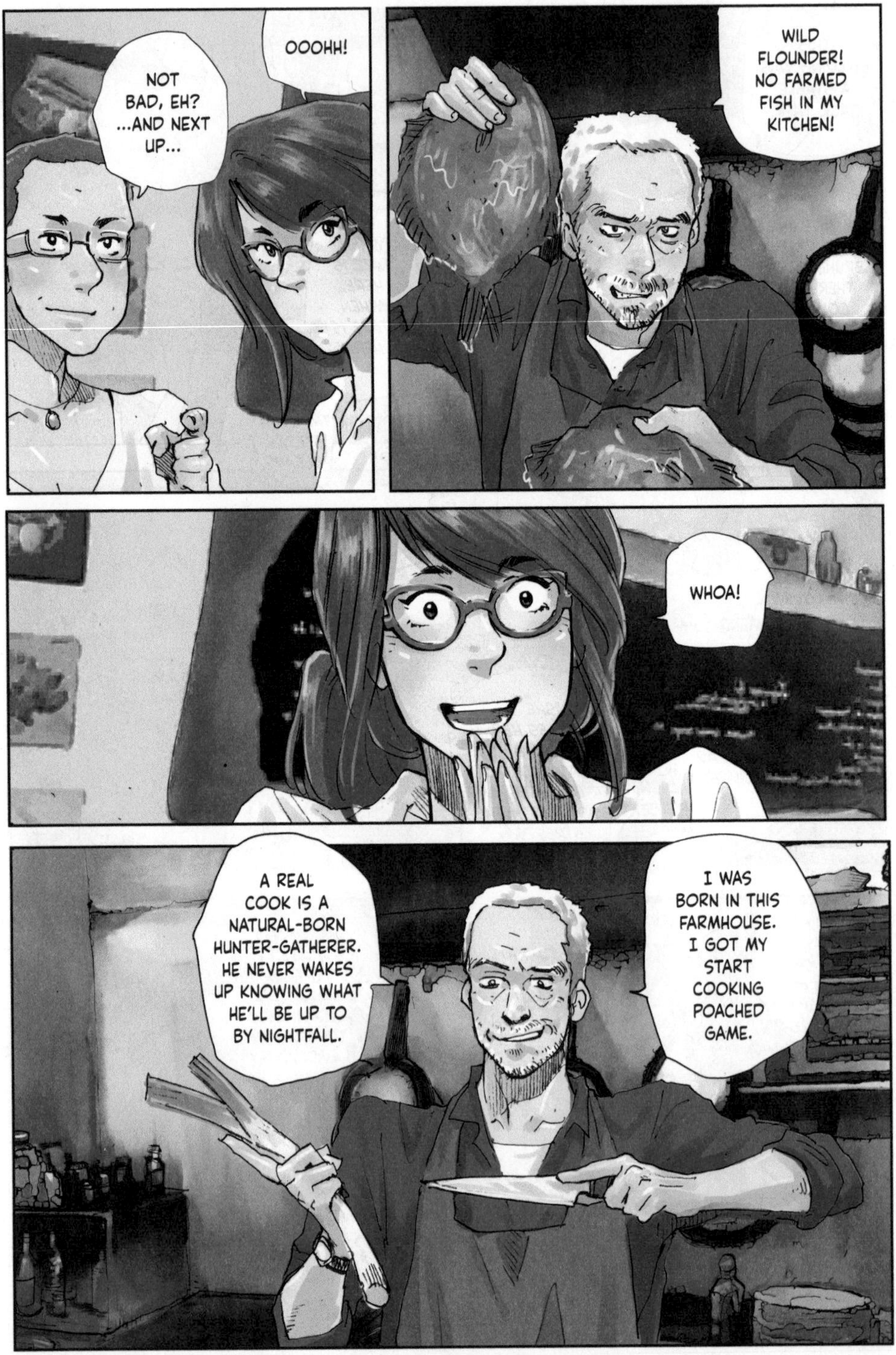
NOT BAD, EH? ...AND NEXT UP...
OOOHH!
WILD FLOUNDER! NO FARMED FISH IN MY KITCHEN!
WHOA!
A REAL COOK IS A NATURAL-BORN HUNTER-GATHERER. HE NEVER WAKES UP KNOWING WHAT HE'LL BE UP TO BY NIGHTFALL.
I WAS BORN IN THIS FARMHOUSE. I GOT MY START COOKING POACHED GAME.

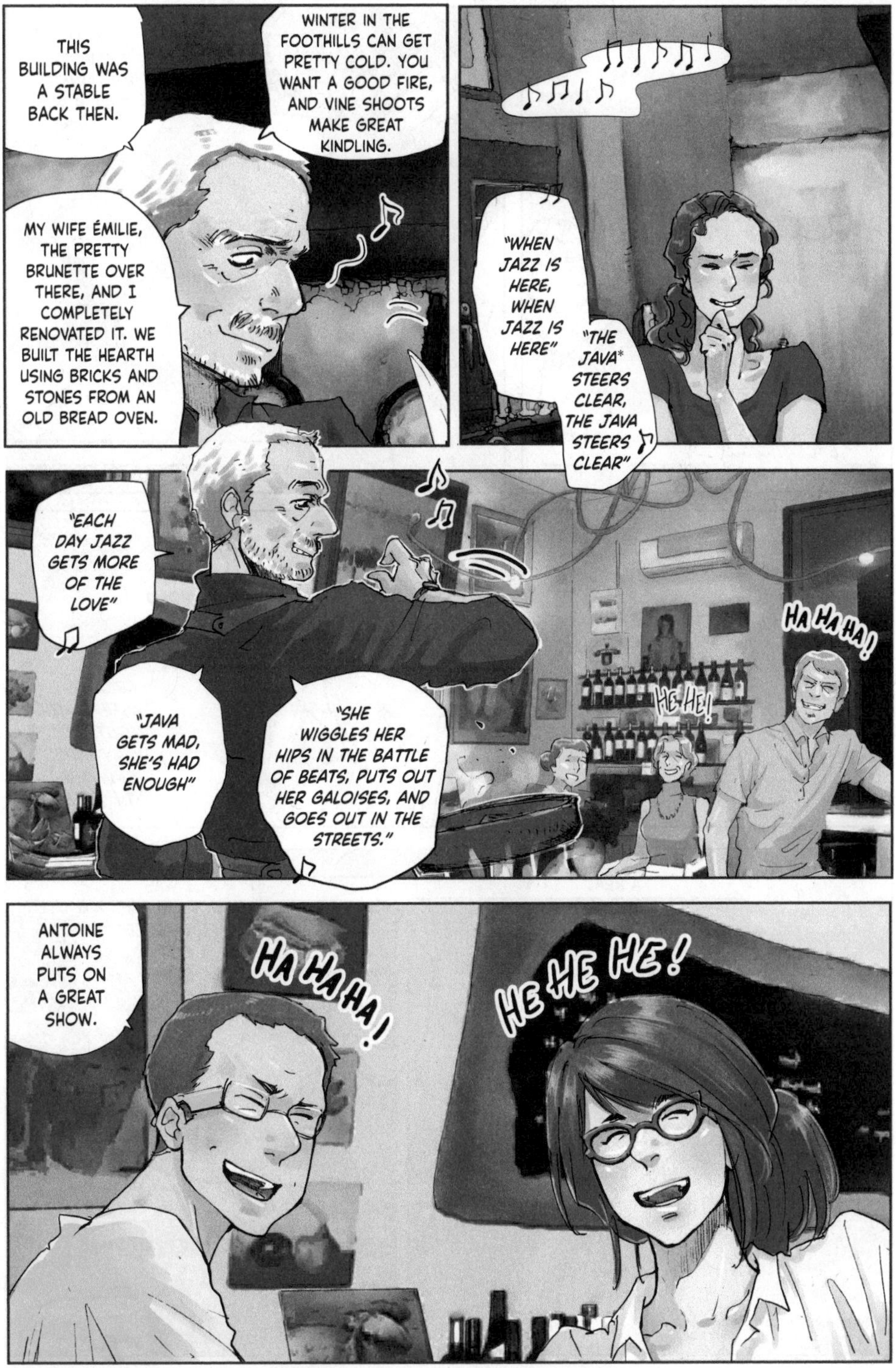
THIS BUILDING WAS A STABLE BACK THEN.
WINTER IN THE FOOTHILLS CAN GET PRETTY COLD. YOU WANT A GOOD FIRE, AND VINE SHOOTS MAKE GREAT KINDLING.
MY WIFE ÉMILIE, THE PRETTY BRUNETTE OVER THERE, AND I COMPLETELY RENOVATED IT. WE BUILT THE HEARTH USING BRICKS AND STONES FROM AN OLD BREAD OVEN.
"WHEN JAZZ IS HERE, WHEN JAZZ IS HERE"
"THE JAVA* STEERS CLEAR, THE JAVA STEERS CLEAR"
"EACH DAY JAZZ GETS MORE OF THE LOVE"
"JAVA GETS MAD, SHE'S HAD ENOUGH"
"SHE WIGGLES HER HIPS IN THE BATTLE OF BEATS, PUTS OUT HER GALOISES, AND GOES OUT IN THE STREETS."
HE HE!
HA HA HA!
ANTOINE ALWAYS PUTS ON A GREAT SHOW.
HA HA HA!
HE HE HE!

* THE JAVA IS A DANCE STYLE ASSOCIATED WITH PARISIAN MUSIC HALLS. IT BECAME POPULAR IN THE 1910'S.

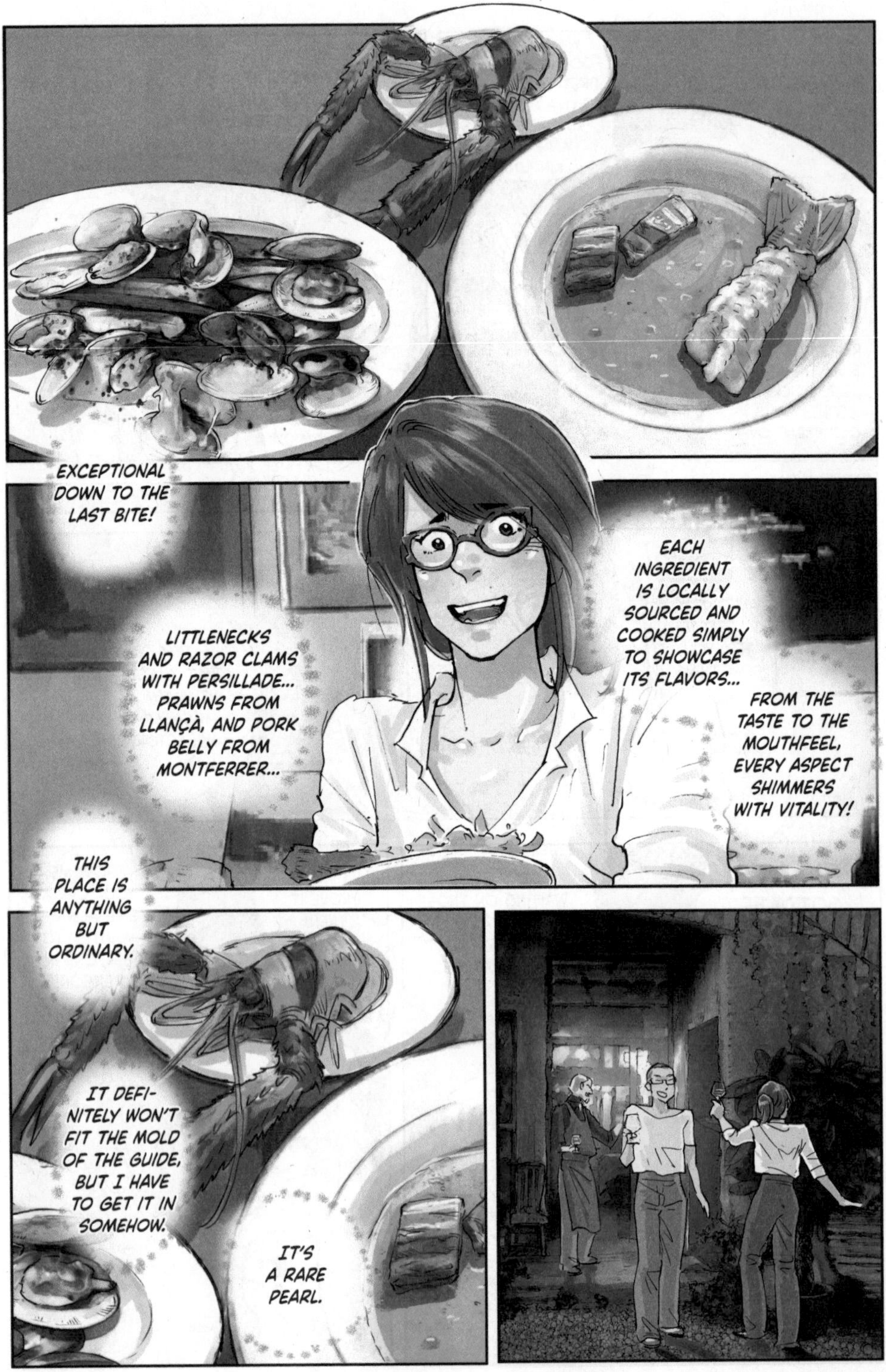
EXCEPTIONAL DOWN TO THE LAST BITE!
LITTLENECKS AND RAZOR CLAMS WITH PERSILLADE... PRAWNS FROM LLANÇÀ, AND PORK BELLY FROM MONTFERRER...
EACH INGREDIENT IS LOCALLY SOURCED AND COOKED SIMPLY TO SHOWCASE ITS FLAVORS...
FROM THE TASTE TO THE MOUTHFEEL, EVERY ASPECT SHIMMERS WITH VITALITY!
THIS PLACE IS ANYTHING BUT ORDINARY.
IT DEFI-NITELY WON'T FIT THE MOLD OF THE GUIDE, BUT I HAVE TO GET IT IN SOMEHOW.
IT'S A RARE PEARL.

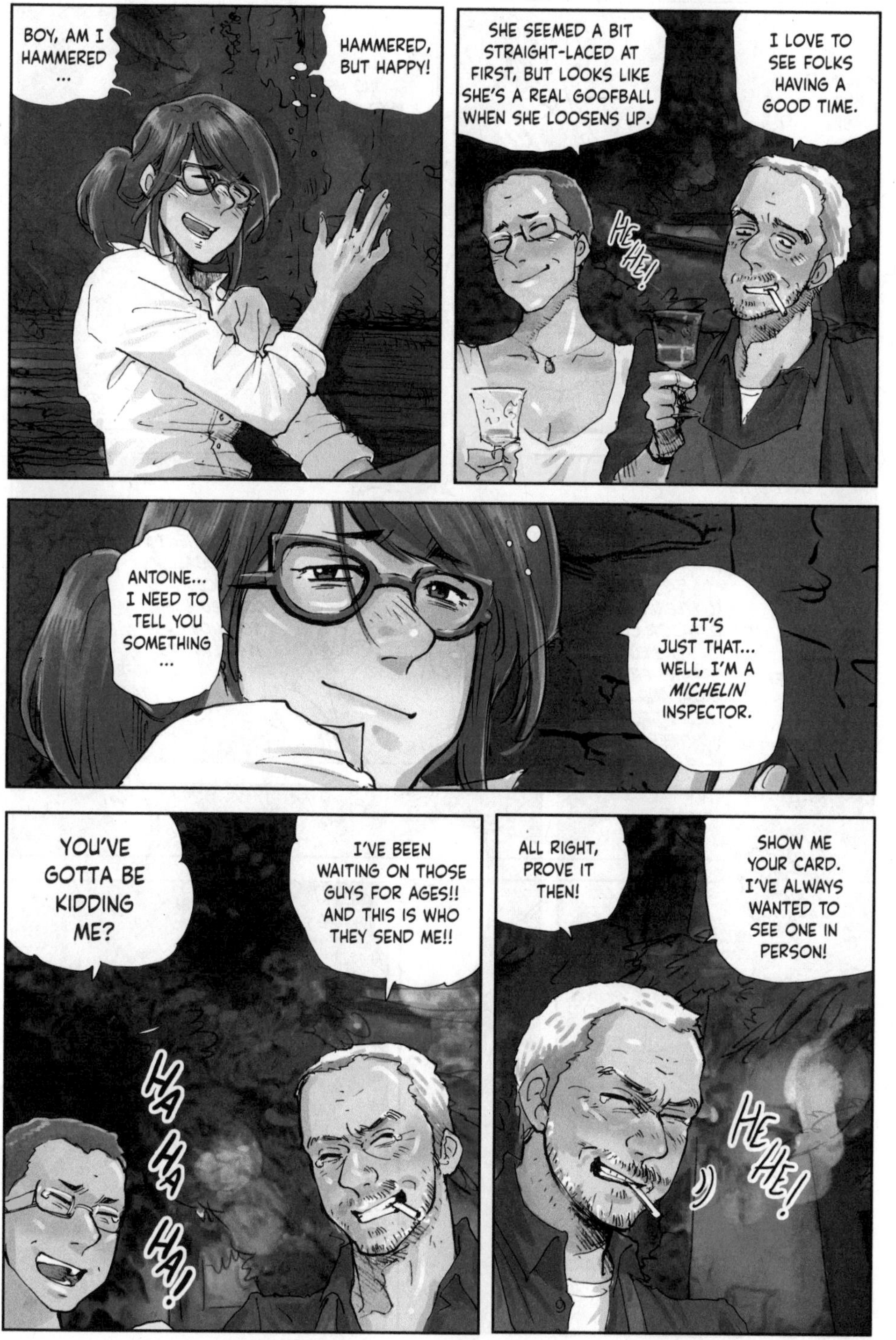
BOY, AM I HAMMERED ...
HAMMERED, BUT HAPPY!
SHE SEEMED A BIT STRAIGHT-LACED AT FIRST, BUT LOOKS LIKE SHE'S A REAL GOOFBALL WHEN SHE LOOSENS UP.
I LOVE TO SEE FOLKS HAVING A GOOD TIME.
HE HE!
ANTOINE... I NEED TO TELL YOU SOMETHING ...
IT'S JUST THAT... WELL, I'M A *MICHELIN* INSPECTOR.
YOU'VE GOTTA BE KIDDING ME?
I'VE BEEN WAITING ON THOSE GUYS FOR AGES!! AND THIS IS WHO THEY SEND ME!!
HA HA HA HA!
ALL RIGHT, PROVE IT THEN!
SHOW ME YOUR CARD. I'VE ALWAYS WANTED TO SEE ONE IN PERSON!
HE HE!

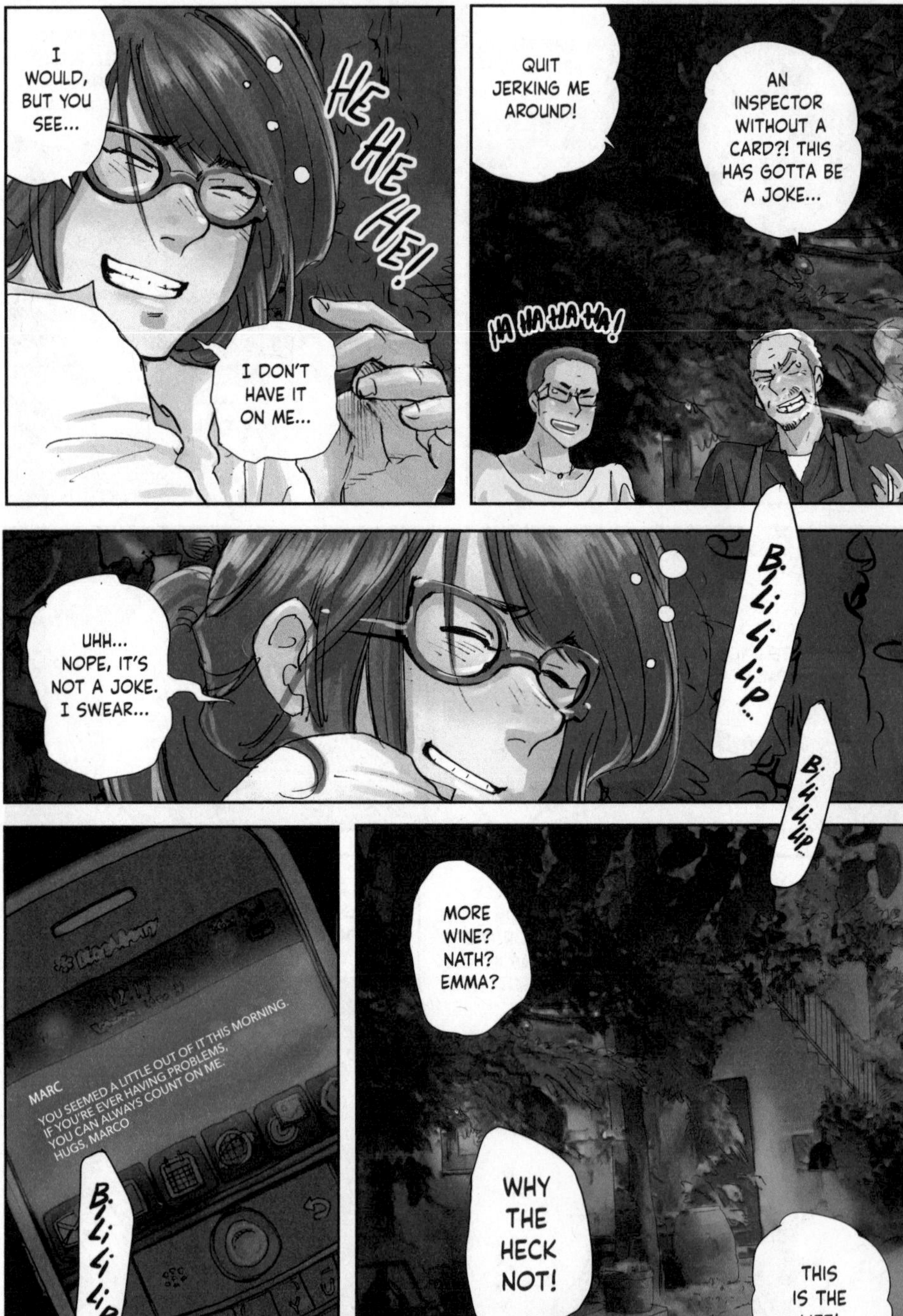

I WOULD, BUT YOU SEE...
HE HE HE!
I DON'T HAVE IT ON ME...
QUIT JERKING ME AROUND!
AN INSPECTOR WITHOUT A CARD?! THIS HAS GOTTA BE A JOKE...
HA HA HA HA!
UHH... NOPE, IT'S NOT A JOKE. I SWEAR...
BILILILIP...
BILILILIP
MARC
YOU SEEMED A LITTLE OUT OF IT THIS MORNING.
IF YOU'RE EVER HAVING PROBLEMS,
YOU CAN ALWAYS COUNT ON ME.
HUGS, MARCO
BILILILIP...
MORE WINE? NATH? EMMA?
WHY THE HECK NOT!
THIS IS THE LIFE!

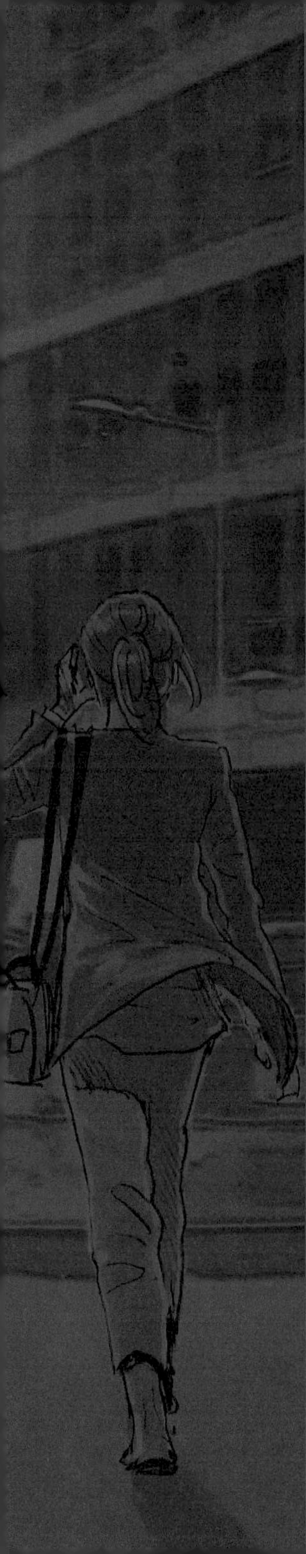

CHAPTER 9

THE BIG DAY

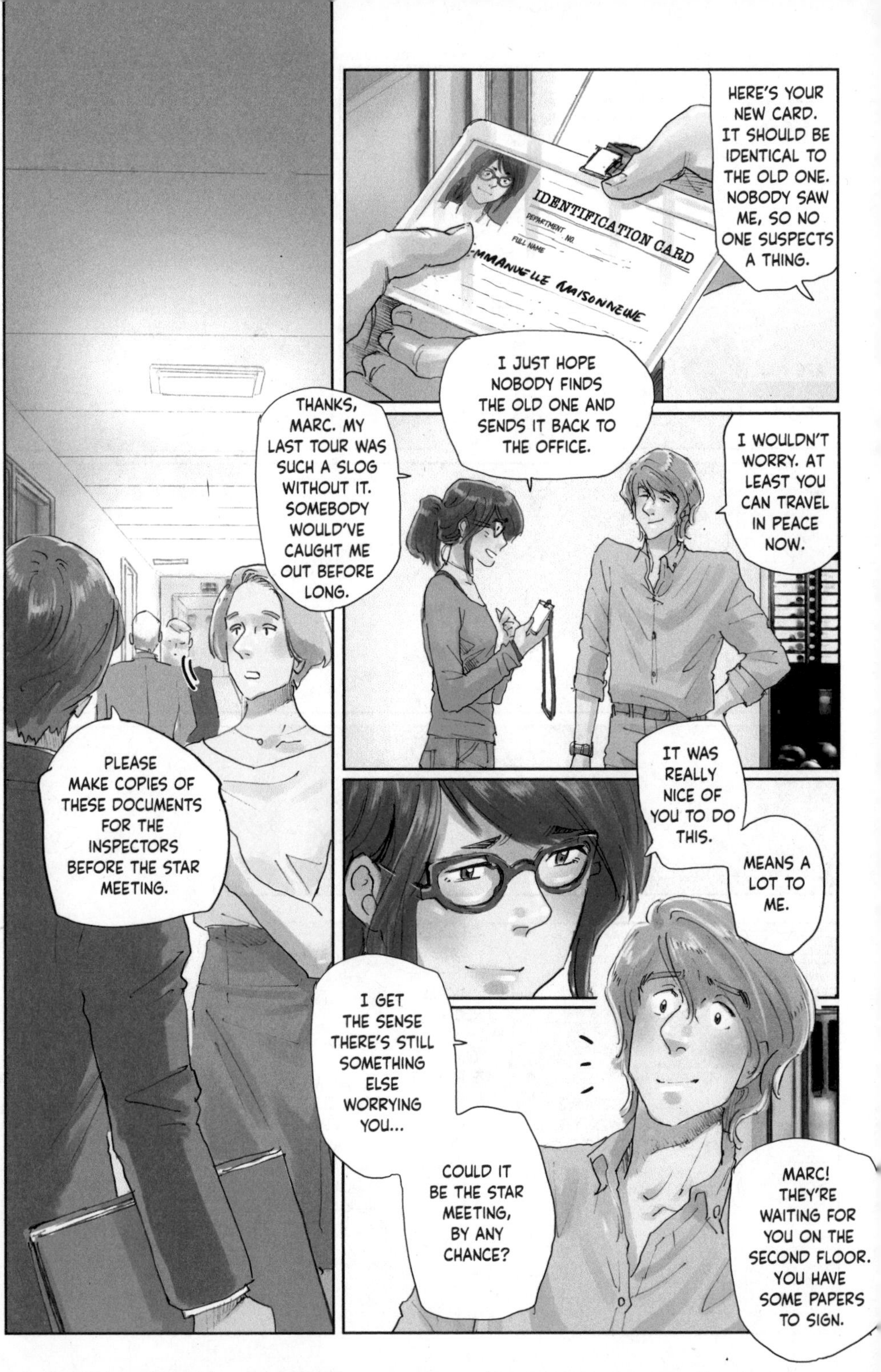
PLEASE MAKE COPIES OF THESE DOCUMENTS FOR THE INSPECTORS BEFORE THE STAR MEETING.
IDENTIFICATION CARD
DEPARTMENT NO.
FULL NAME
EMMANUELLE MAISONNEUVE
HERE'S YOUR NEW CARD. IT SHOULD BE IDENTICAL TO THE OLD ONE. NOBODY SAW ME, SO NO ONE SUSPECTS A THING.
THANKS, MARC. MY LAST TOUR WAS SUCH A SLOG WITHOUT IT. SOMEBODY WOULD'VE CAUGHT ME OUT BEFORE LONG.
I JUST HOPE NOBODY FINDS THE OLD ONE AND SENDS IT BACK TO THE OFFICE.
I WOULDN'T WORRY. AT LEAST YOU CAN TRAVEL IN PEACE NOW.
IT WAS REALLY NICE OF YOU TO DO THIS.
MEANS A LOT TO ME.
I GET THE SENSE THERE'S STILL SOMETHING ELSE WORRYING YOU...
COULD IT BE THE STAR MEETING, BY ANY CHANCE?
MARC! THEY'RE WAITING FOR YOU ON THE SECOND FLOOR. YOU HAVE SOME PAPERS TO SIGN.

* SPANNING A WIDE VARIETY OF TRADES, "BEST CRAFTSMAN IN FRANCE" AWARDS ARE GIVEN EVERY FOUR YEARS.

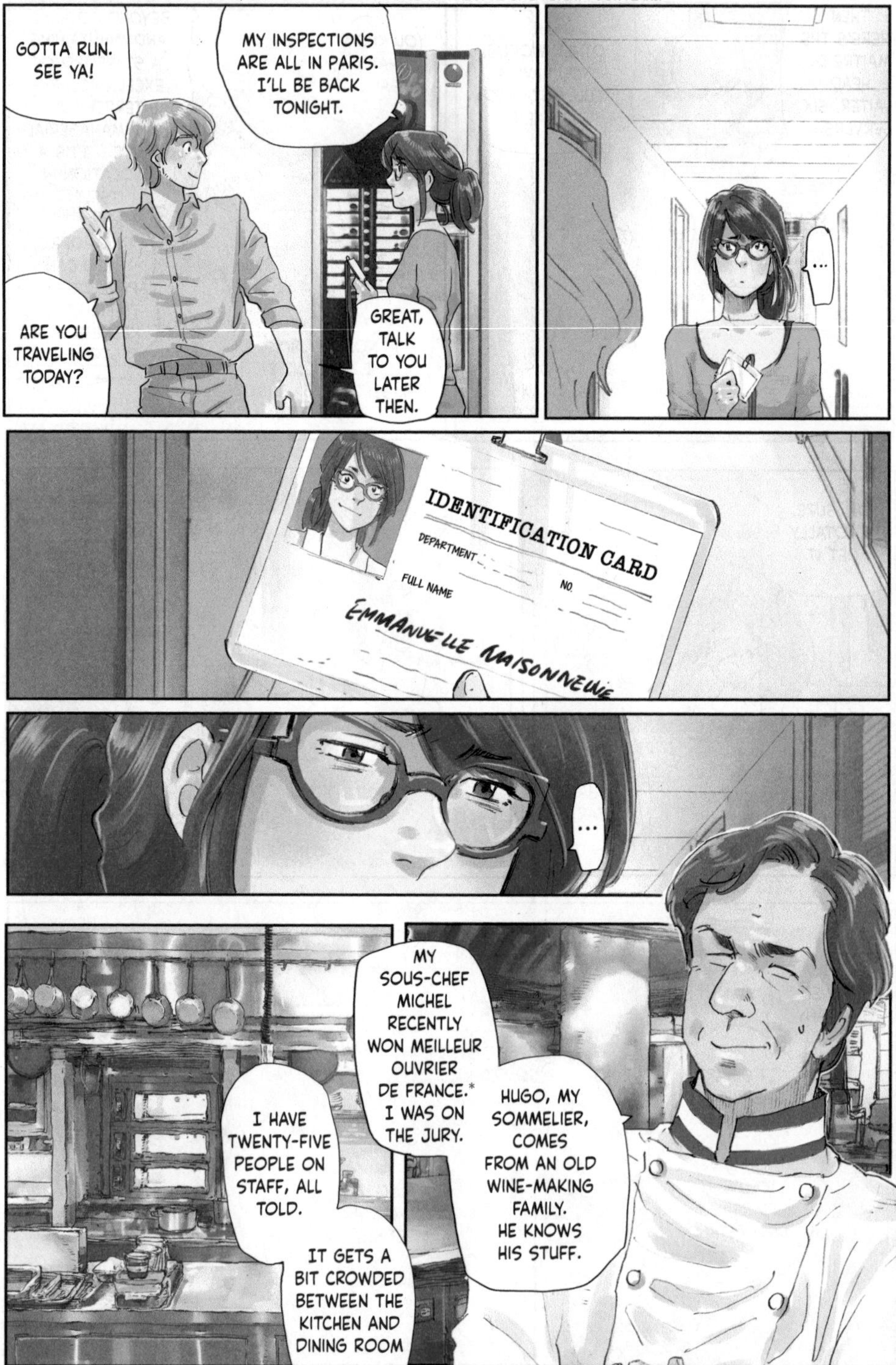
GOTTA RUN. SEE YA!
MY INSPECTIONS ARE ALL IN PARIS. I'LL BE BACK TONIGHT.
ARE YOU TRAVELING TODAY?
GREAT, TALK TO YOU LATER THEN.
...
IDENTIFICATION CARD
DEPARTMENT
NO.
FULL NAME
EMMANUELLE MAISONNEUVE
...
I HAVE TWENTY-FIVE PEOPLE ON STAFF, ALL TOLD.
IT GETS A BIT CROWDED BETWEEN THE KITCHEN AND DINING ROOM ...
MY SOUS-CHEF MICHEL RECENTLY WON MEILLEUR OUVRIER DE FRANCE.* I WAS ON THE JURY.
HUGO, MY SOMMELIER, COMES FROM AN OLD WINE-MAKING FAMILY. HE KNOWS HIS STUFF.

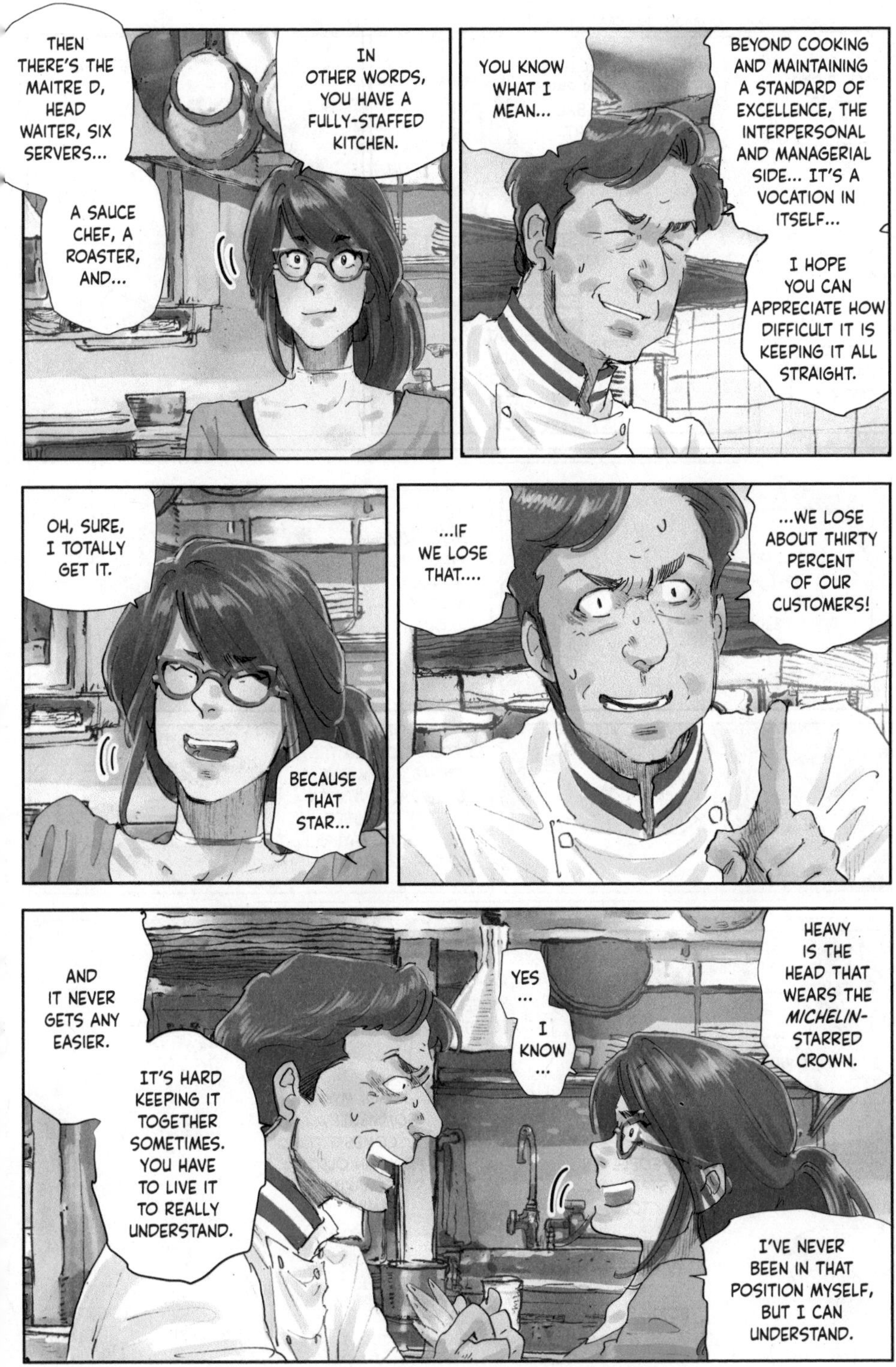
THEN THERE'S THE MAITRE D, HEAD WAITER, SIX SERVERS...
A SAUCE CHEF, A ROASTER, AND...
IN OTHER WORDS, YOU HAVE A FULLY-STAFFED KITCHEN.
YOU KNOW WHAT I MEAN...
BEYOND COOKING AND MAINTAINING A STANDARD OF EXCELLENCE, THE INTERPERSONAL AND MANAGERIAL SIDE... IT'S A VOCATION IN ITSELF...
I HOPE YOU CAN APPRECIATE HOW DIFFICULT IT IS KEEPING IT ALL STRAIGHT.
OH, SURE, I TOTALLY GET IT.
BECAUSE THAT STAR...
...IF WE LOSE THAT....
...WE LOSE ABOUT THIRTY PERCENT OF OUR CUSTOMERS!
AND IT NEVER GETS ANY EASIER.
IT'S HARD KEEPING IT TOGETHER SOMETIMES. YOU HAVE TO LIVE IT TO REALLY UNDERSTAND.
YES ... I KNOW ...
HEAVY IS THE HEAD THAT WEARS THE *MICHELIN*-STARRED CROWN.
I'VE NEVER BEEN IN THAT POSITION MYSELF, BUT I CAN UNDERSTAND.

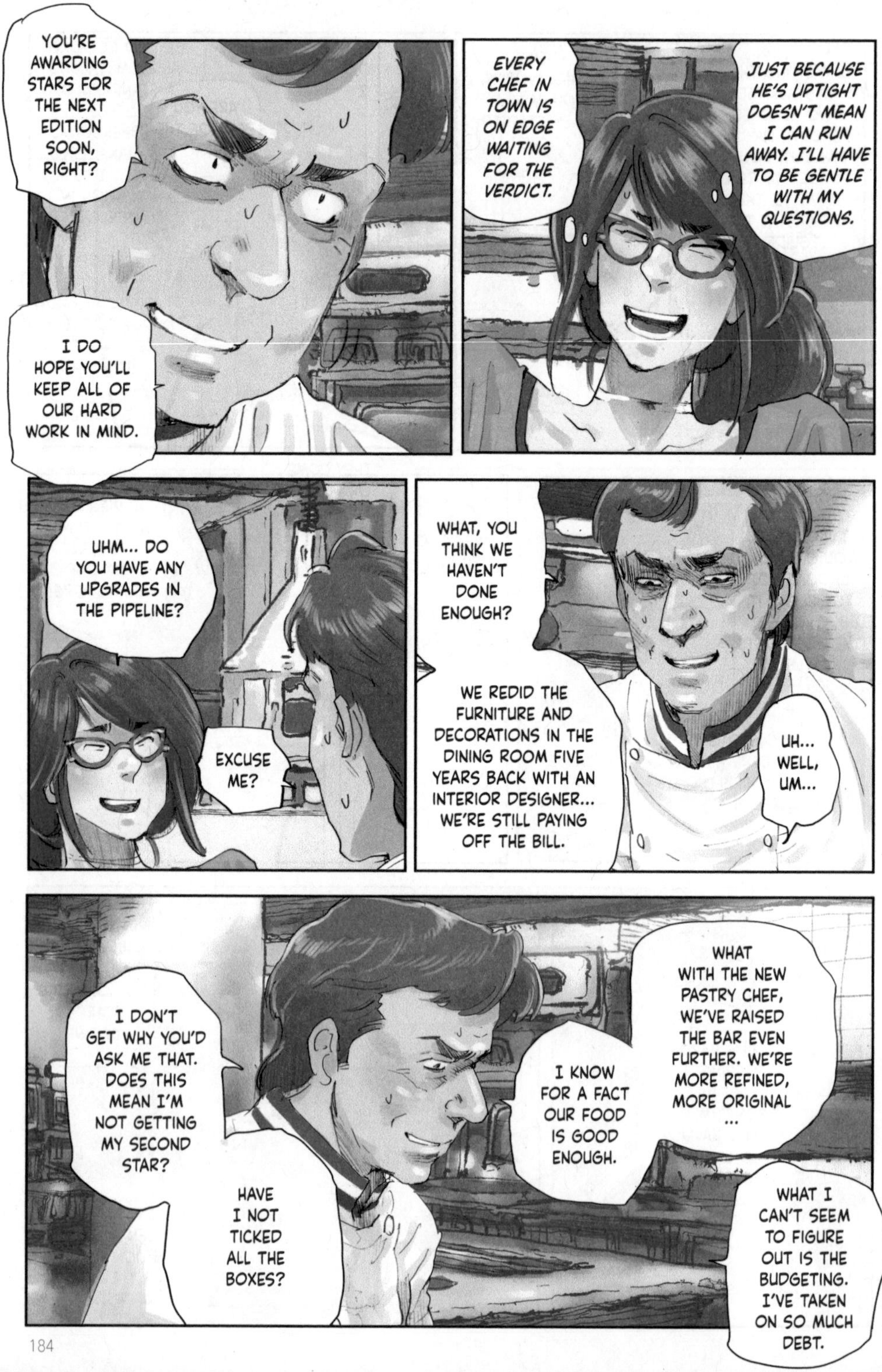
YOU'RE AWARDING STARS FOR THE NEXT EDITION SOON, RIGHT?
I DO HOPE YOU'LL KEEP ALL OF OUR HARD WORK IN MIND.
EVERY CHEF IN TOWN IS ON EDGE WAITING FOR THE VERDICT.
JUST BECAUSE HE'S UPTIGHT DOESN'T MEAN I CAN RUN AWAY. I'LL HAVE TO BE GENTLE WITH MY QUESTIONS.
UHM... DO YOU HAVE ANY UPGRADES IN THE PIPELINE?
EXCUSE ME?
WHAT, YOU THINK WE HAVEN'T DONE ENOUGH?
WE REDID THE FURNITURE AND DECORATIONS IN THE DINING ROOM FIVE YEARS BACK WITH AN INTERIOR DESIGNER... WE'RE STILL PAYING OFF THE BILL.
UH... WELL, UM...
I DON'T GET WHY YOU'D ASK ME THAT. DOES THIS MEAN I'M NOT GETTING MY SECOND STAR?
HAVE I NOT TICKED ALL THE BOXES?
I KNOW FOR A FACT OUR FOOD IS GOOD ENOUGH.
WHAT WITH THE NEW PASTRY CHEF, WE'VE RAISED THE BAR EVEN FURTHER. WE'RE MORE REFINED, MORE ORIGINAL ...
WHAT I CAN'T SEEM TO FIGURE OUT IS THE BUDGETING. I'VE TAKEN ON SO MUCH DEBT.

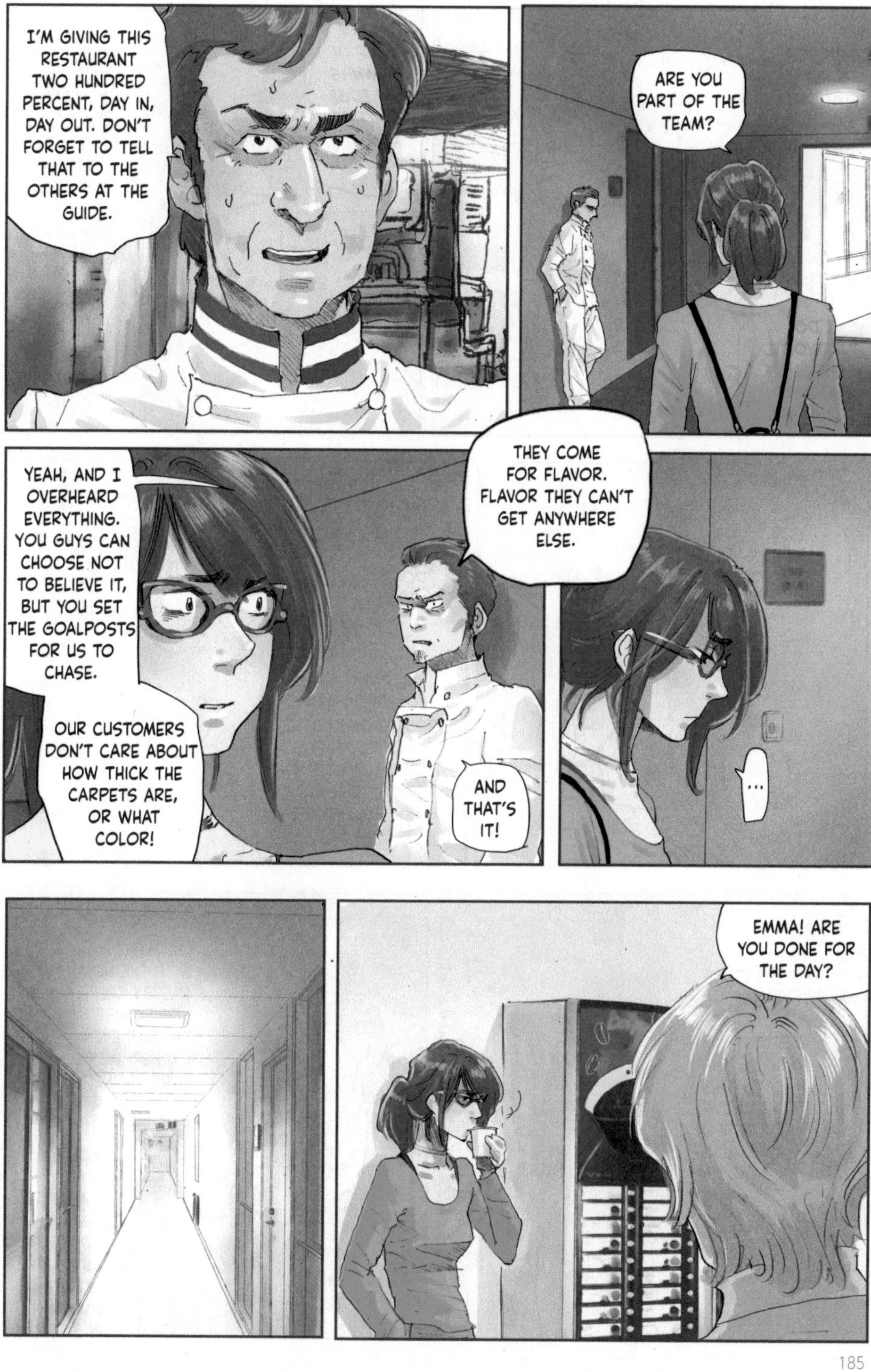
I'M GIVING THIS RESTAURANT TWO HUNDRED PERCENT, DAY IN, DAY OUT. DON'T FORGET TO TELL THAT TO THE OTHERS AT THE GUIDE.
ARE YOU PART OF THE TEAM?
YEAH, AND I OVERHEARD EVERYTHING. YOU GUYS CAN CHOOSE NOT TO BELIEVE IT, BUT YOU SET THE GOALPOSTS FOR US TO CHASE.
OUR CUSTOMERS DON'T CARE ABOUT HOW THICK THE CARPETS ARE, OR WHAT COLOR!
THEY COME FOR FLAVOR. FLAVOR THEY CAN'T GET ANYWHERE ELSE.
AND THAT'S IT!
...
EMMA! ARE YOU DONE FOR THE DAY?

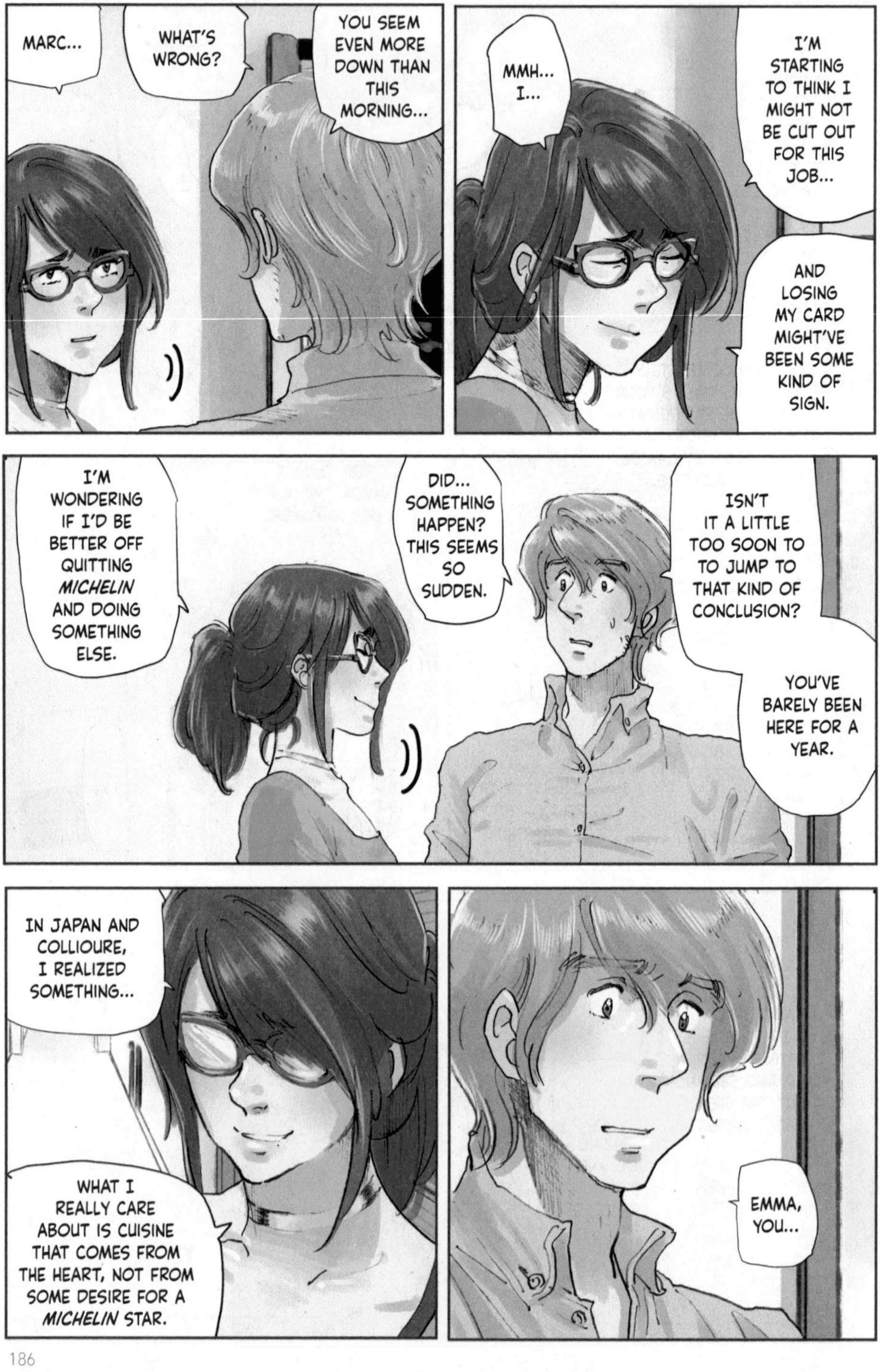
MARC...
WHAT'S WRONG?
YOU SEEM EVEN MORE DOWN THAN THIS MORNING...
MMH... I...
I'M STARTING TO THINK I MIGHT NOT BE CUT OUT FOR THIS JOB...
AND LOSING MY CARD MIGHT'VE BEEN SOME KIND OF SIGN.
I'M WONDERING IF I'D BE BETTER OFF QUITTING *MICHELIN* AND DOING SOMETHING ELSE.
DID... SOMETHING HAPPEN? THIS SEEMS SO SUDDEN.
ISN'T IT A LITTLE TOO SOON TO TO JUMP TO THAT KIND OF CONCLUSION?
YOU'VE BARELY BEEN HERE FOR A YEAR.
IN JAPAN AND COLLIOURE, I REALIZED SOMETHING...
WHAT I REALLY CARE ABOUT IS CUISINE THAT COMES FROM THE HEART, NOT FROM SOME DESIRE FOR A *MICHELIN* STAR.
EMMA, YOU...

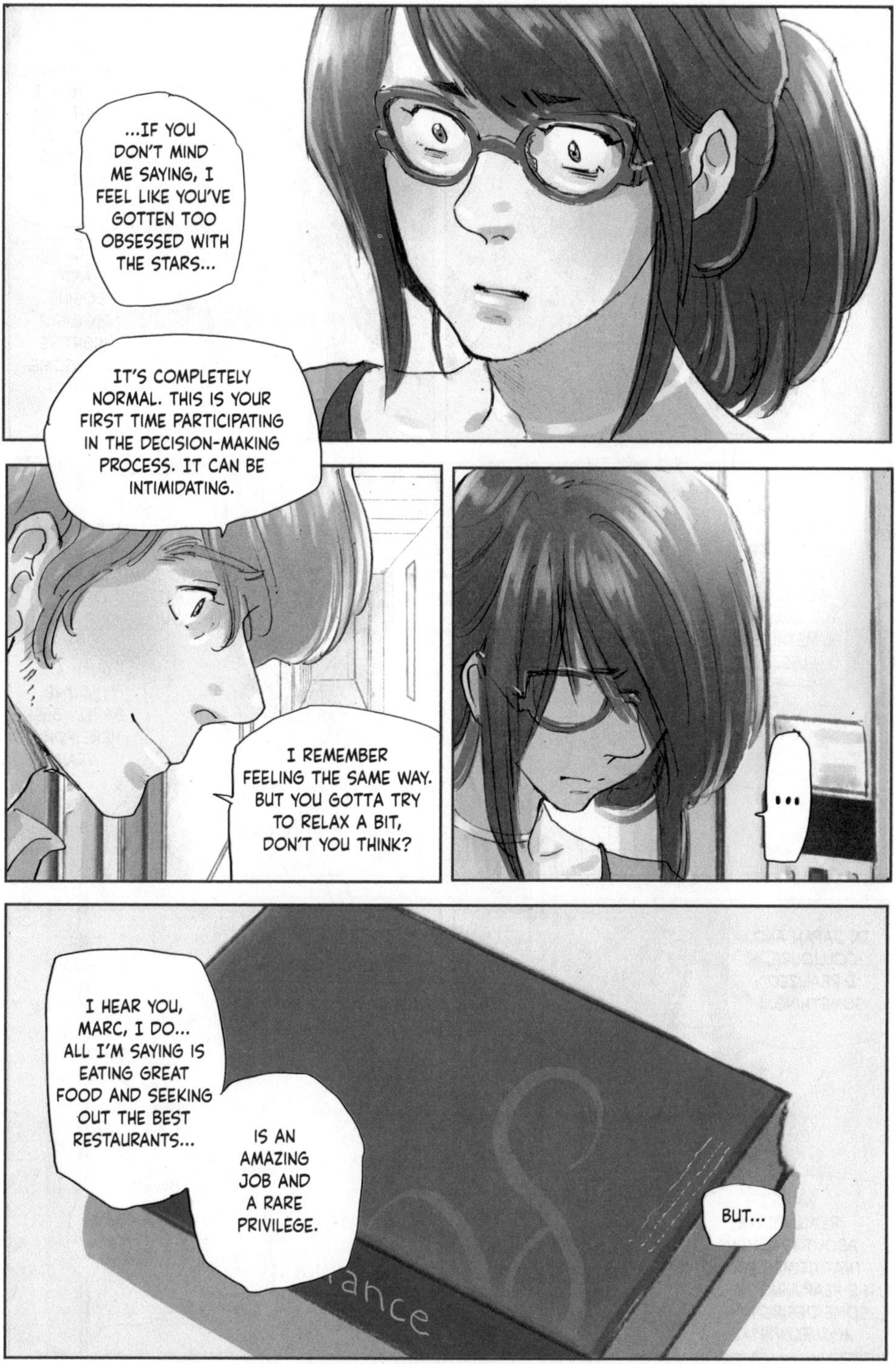

...IF YOU DON'T MIND ME SAYING, I FEEL LIKE YOU'VE GOTTEN TOO OBSESSED WITH THE STARS...
IT'S COMPLETELY NORMAL. THIS IS YOUR FIRST TIME PARTICIPATING IN THE DECISION-MAKING PROCESS. IT CAN BE INTIMIDATING.
I REMEMBER FEELING THE SAME WAY. BUT YOU GOTTA TRY TO RELAX A BIT, DON'T YOU THINK?
...
I HEAR YOU, MARC, I DO... ALL I'M SAYING IS EATING GREAT FOOD AND SEEKING OUT THE BEST RESTAURANTS...
IS AN AMAZING JOB AND A RARE PRIVILEGE.
BUT...

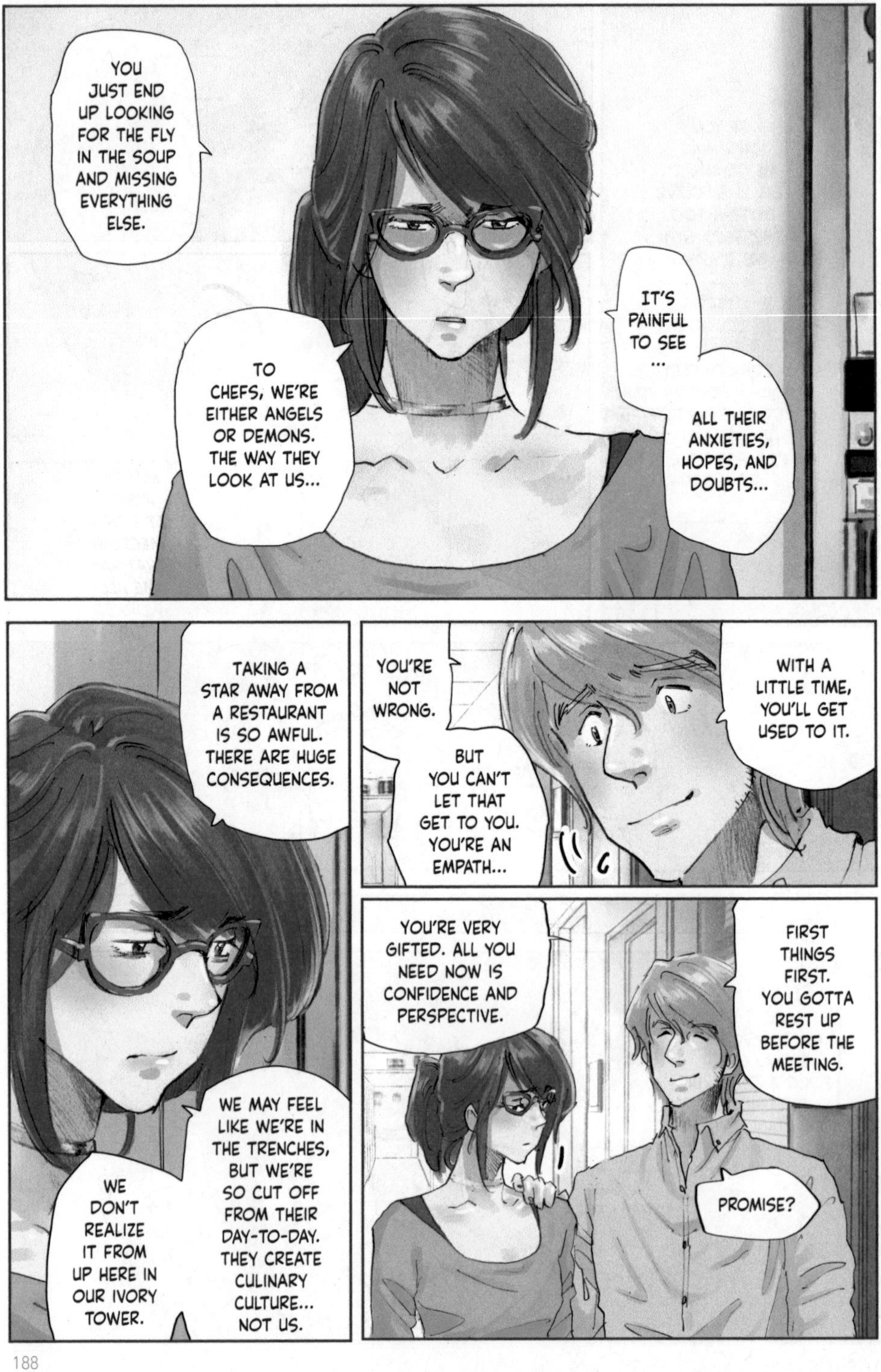
YOU JUST END UP LOOKING FOR THE FLY IN THE SOUP AND MISSING EVERYTHING ELSE.
TO CHEFS, WE'RE EITHER ANGELS OR DEMONS. THE WAY THEY LOOK AT US...
IT'S PAINFUL TO SEE ...
ALL THEIR ANXIETIES, HOPES, AND DOUBTS...
TAKING A STAR AWAY FROM A RESTAURANT IS SO AWFUL. THERE ARE HUGE CONSEQUENCES.
WE MAY FEEL LIKE WE'RE IN THE TRENCHES, BUT WE'RE SO CUT OFF FROM THEIR DAY-TO-DAY. THEY CREATE CULINARY CULTURE... NOT US.
WE DON'T REALIZE IT FROM UP HERE IN OUR IVORY TOWER.
YOU'RE NOT WRONG.
BUT YOU CAN'T LET THAT GET TO YOU. YOU'RE AN EMPATH...
WITH A LITTLE TIME, YOU'LL GET USED TO IT.
YOU'RE VERY GIFTED. ALL YOU NEED NOW IS CONFIDENCE AND PERSPECTIVE.
FIRST THINGS FIRST. YOU GOTTA REST UP BEFORE THE MEETING.
PROMISE?

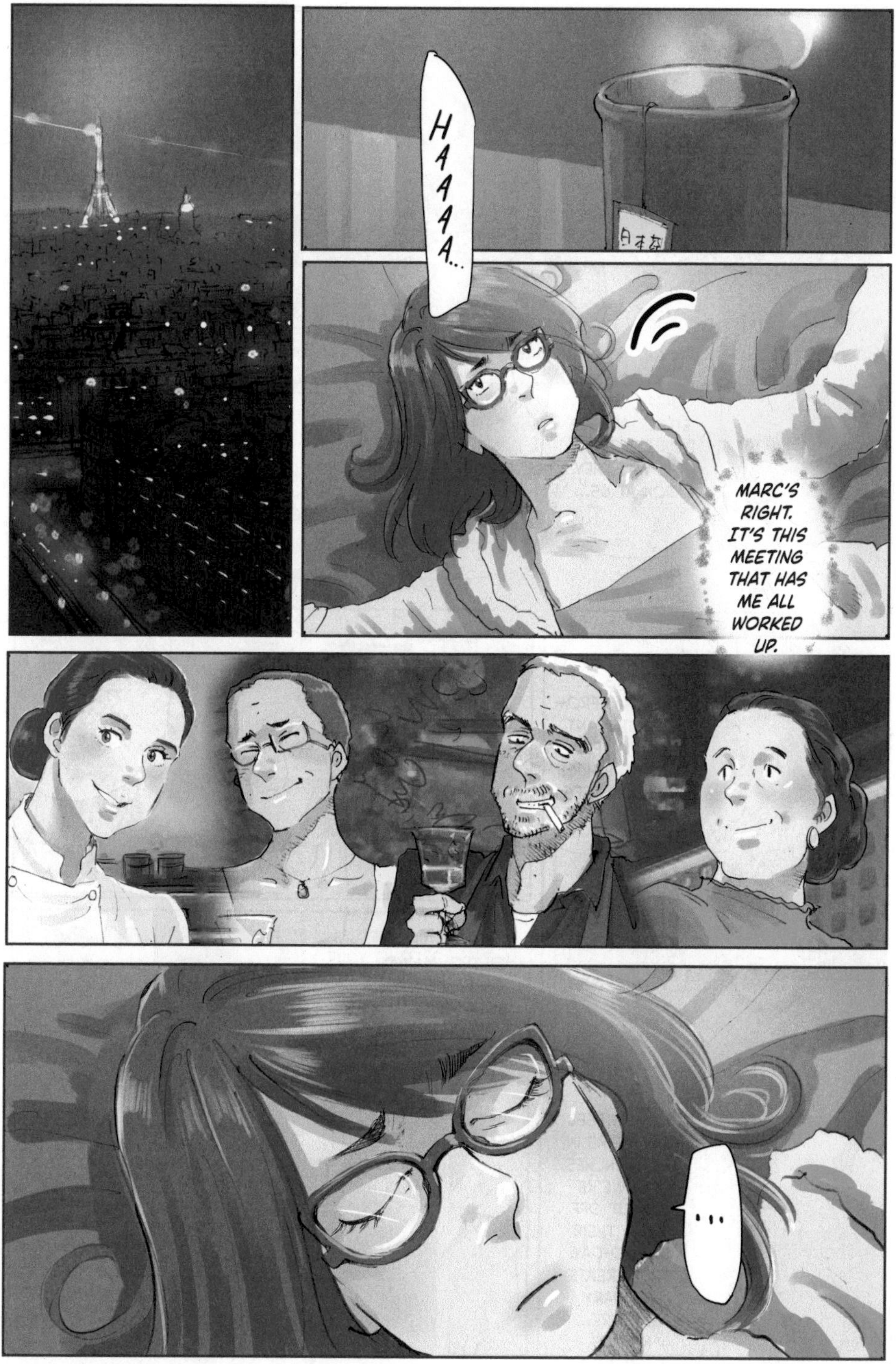
HAAAAA...
MARC'S RIGHT. IT'S THIS MEETING THAT HAS ME ALL WORKED UP.
...

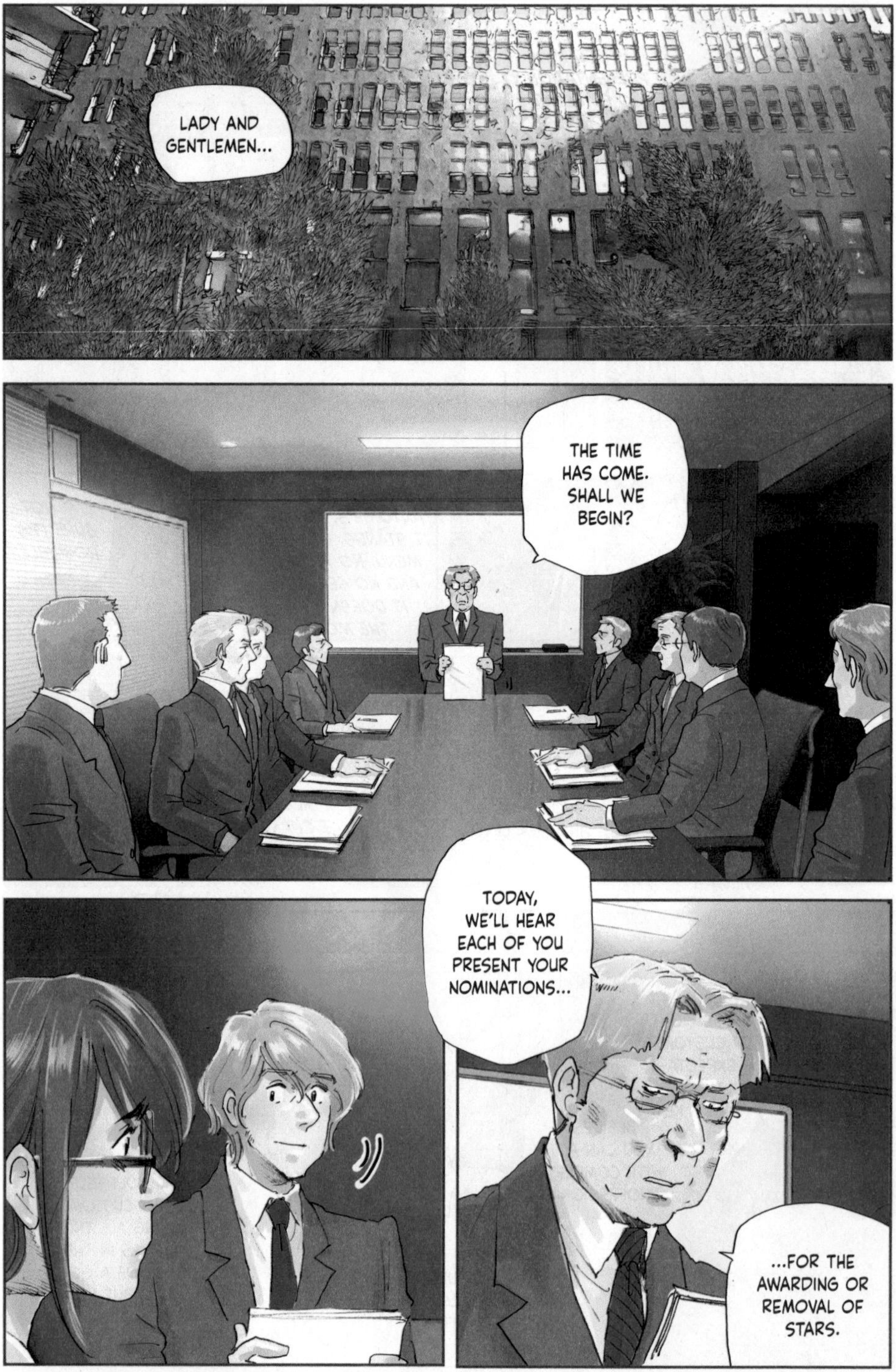
LADY AND GENTLEMEN...
THE TIME HAS COME. SHALL WE BEGIN?
TODAY, WE'LL HEAR EACH OF YOU PRESENT YOUR NOMINATIONS...
...FOR THE AWARDING OR REMOVAL OF STARS.

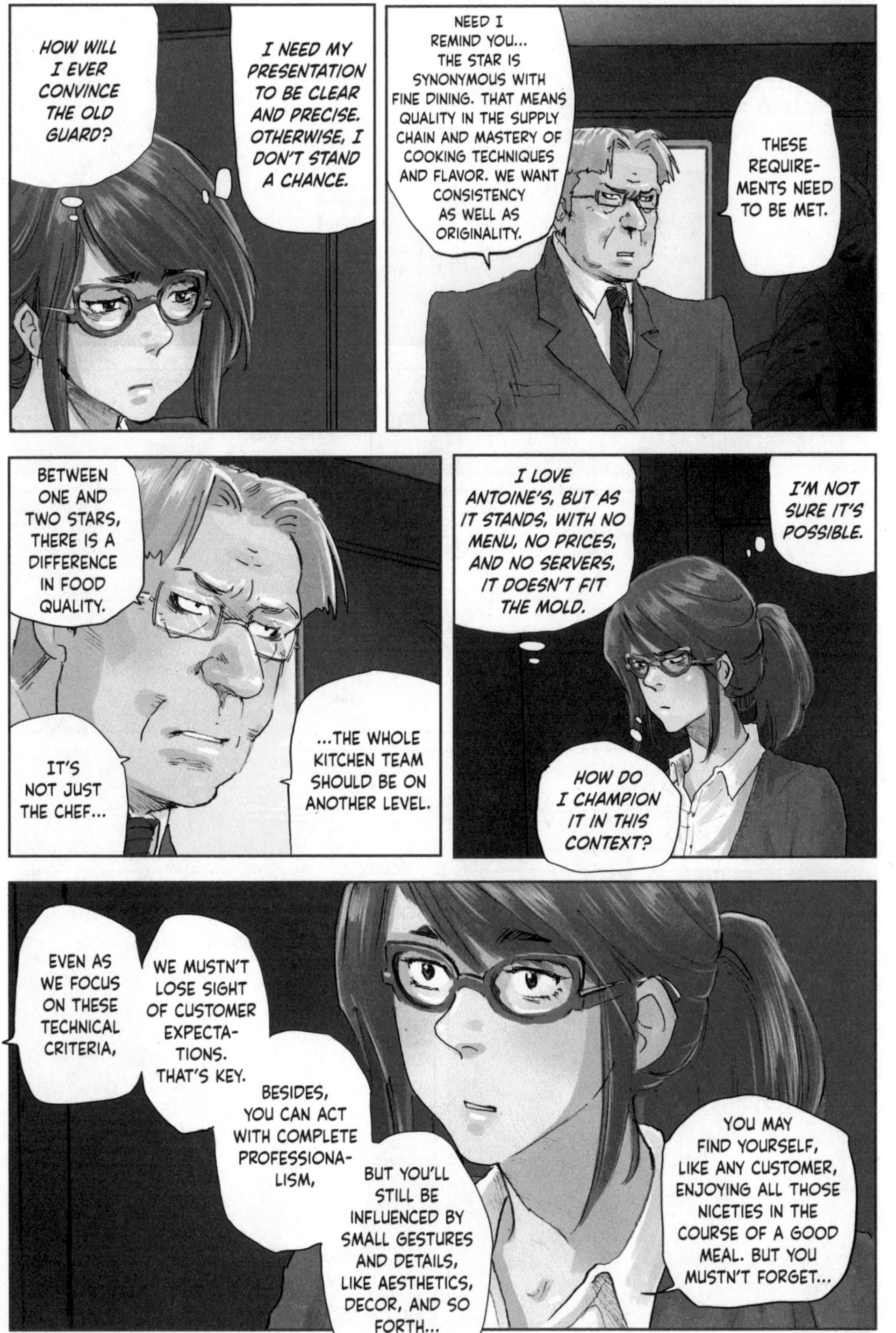
HOW WILL I EVER CONVINCE THE OLD GUARD?
I NEED MY PRESENTATION TO BE CLEAR AND PRECISE. OTHERWISE, I DON'T STAND A CHANCE.
NEED I REMIND YOU... THE STAR IS SYNONYMOUS WITH FINE DINING. THAT MEANS QUALITY IN THE SUPPLY CHAIN AND MASTERY OF COOKING TECHNIQUES AND FLAVOR. WE WANT CONSISTENCY AS WELL AS ORIGINALITY.
THESE REQUIRE-MENTS NEED TO BE MET.
BETWEEN ONE AND TWO STARS, THERE IS A DIFFERENCE IN FOOD QUALITY.
IT'S NOT JUST THE CHEF...
...THE WHOLE KITCHEN TEAM SHOULD BE ON ANOTHER LEVEL.
I LOVE ANTOINE'S, BUT AS IT STANDS, WITH NO MENU, NO PRICES, AND NO SERVERS, IT DOESN'T FIT THE MOLD.
I'M NOT SURE IT'S POSSIBLE.
HOW DO I CHAMPION IT IN THIS CONTEXT?
EVEN AS WE FOCUS ON THESE TECHNICAL CRITERIA,
WE MUSTN'T LOSE SIGHT OF CUSTOMER EXPECTA-TIONS. THAT'S KEY.
BESIDES, YOU CAN ACT WITH COMPLETE PROFESSIONA-LISM,
BUT YOU'LL STILL BE INFLUENCED BY SMALL GESTURES AND DETAILS, LIKE AESTHETICS, DECOR, AND SO FORTH...
YOU MAY FIND YOURSELF, LIKE ANY CUSTOMER, ENJOYING ALL THOSE NICETIES IN THE COURSE OF A GOOD MEAL. BUT YOU MUSTN'T FORGET...

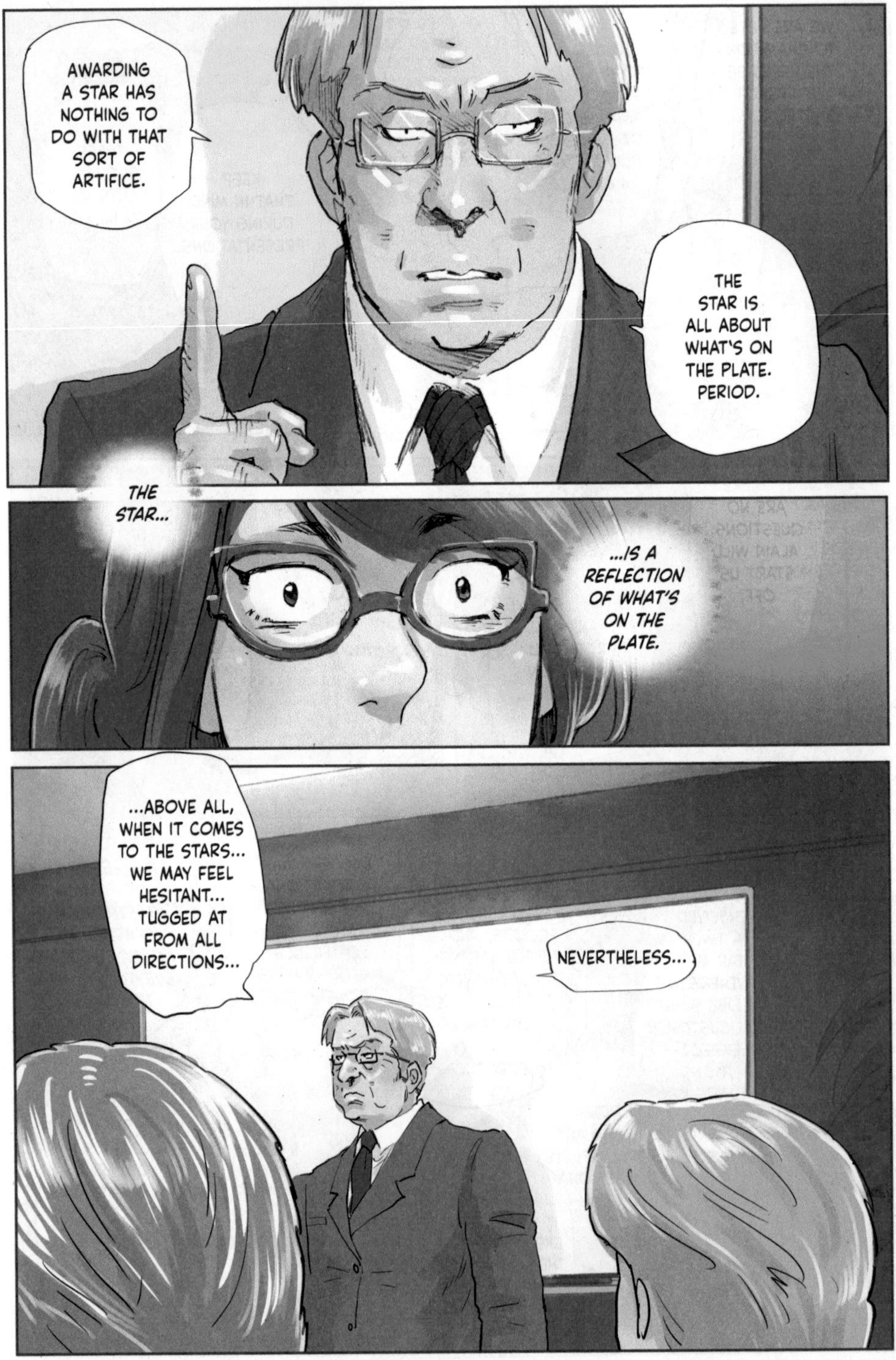
AWARDING A STAR HAS NOTHING TO DO WITH THAT SORT OF ARTIFICE.
THE STAR IS ALL ABOUT WHAT'S ON THE PLATE. PERIOD.
THE STAR...
...IS A REFLECTION OF WHAT'S ON THE PLATE.
...ABOVE ALL, WHEN IT COMES TO THE STARS... WE MAY FEEL HESITANT... TUGGED AT FROM ALL DIRECTIONS...
NEVERTHELESS...

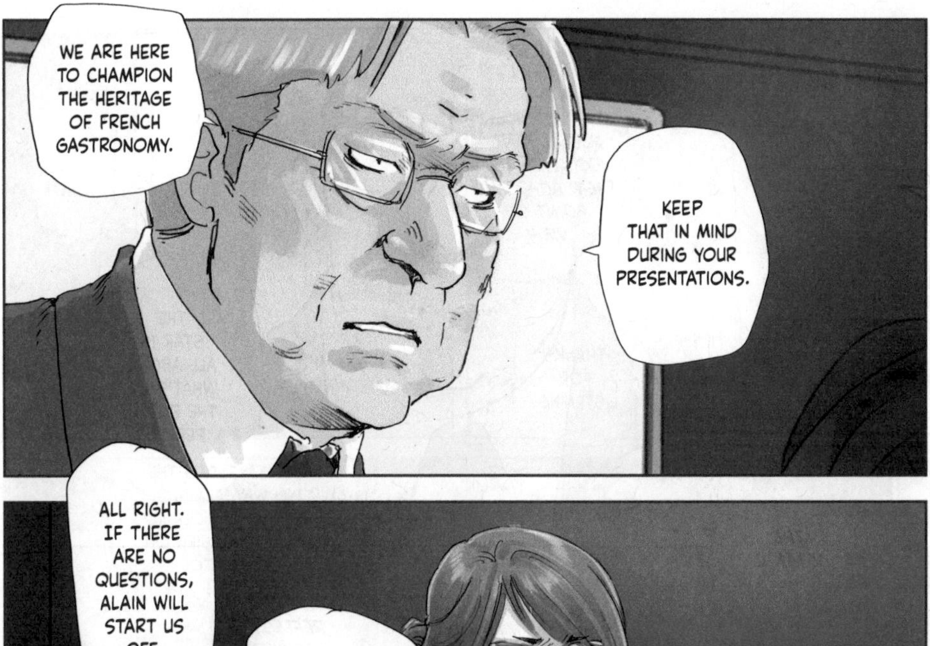
WE ARE HERE TO CHAMPION THE HERITAGE OF FRENCH GASTRONOMY.
KEEP THAT IN MIND DURING YOUR PRESENTATIONS.
ALL RIGHT. IF THERE ARE NO QUESTIONS, ALAIN WILL START US OFF.
THANK YOU, MR. DEDIEU. MY FELLOW INSPECTORS...
...

* A WHEEL OF CHOUX PASTRY CUT IN HALF AND FILLED WITH PRALINE CREAM, NAMED AFTER A BICYCLE RACE BETWEEN THOSE TWO CITIES.

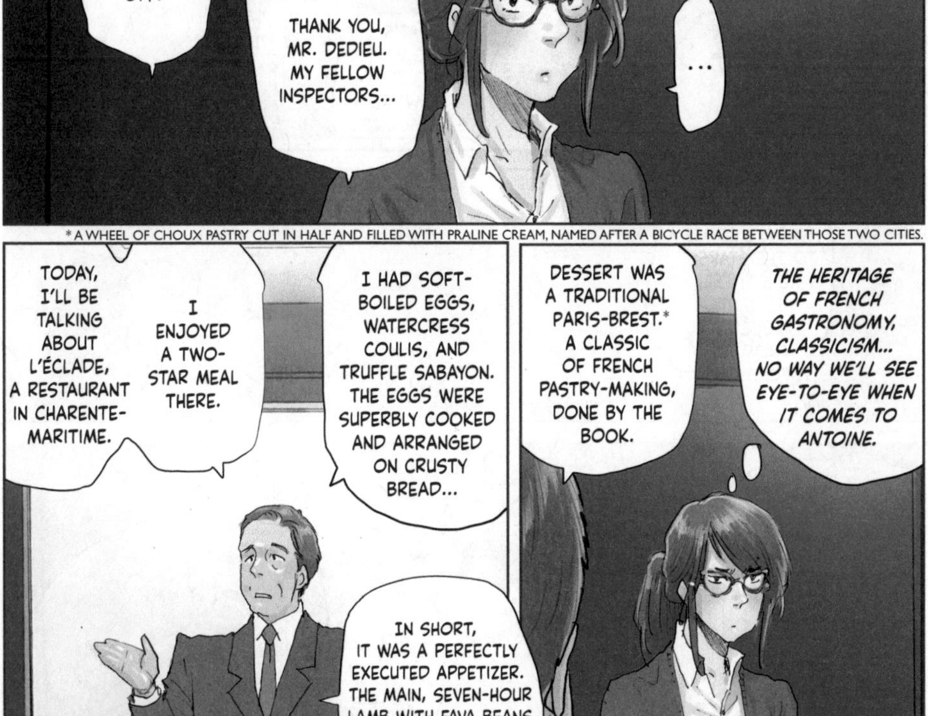
TODAY, I'LL BE TALKING ABOUT L'ÉCLADE, A RESTAURANT IN CHARENTE-MARITIME.
I ENJOYED A TWO-STAR MEAL THERE.
I HAD SOFT-BOILED EGGS, WATERCRESS COULIS, AND TRUFFLE SABAYON. THE EGGS WERE SUPERBLY COOKED AND ARRANGED ON CRUSTY BREAD...
IN SHORT, IT WAS A PERFECTLY EXECUTED APPETIZER. THE MAIN, SEVEN-HOUR LAMB WITH FAVA BEANS, WAS BURSTING WITH INTENSE FLAVORS...
DESSERT WAS A TRADITIONAL PARIS-BREST.* A CLASSIC OF FRENCH PASTRY-MAKING, DONE BY THE BOOK.
THE HERITAGE OF FRENCH GASTRONOMY, CLASSICISM... NO WAY WE'LL SEE EYE-TO-EYE WHEN IT COMES TO ANTOINE.

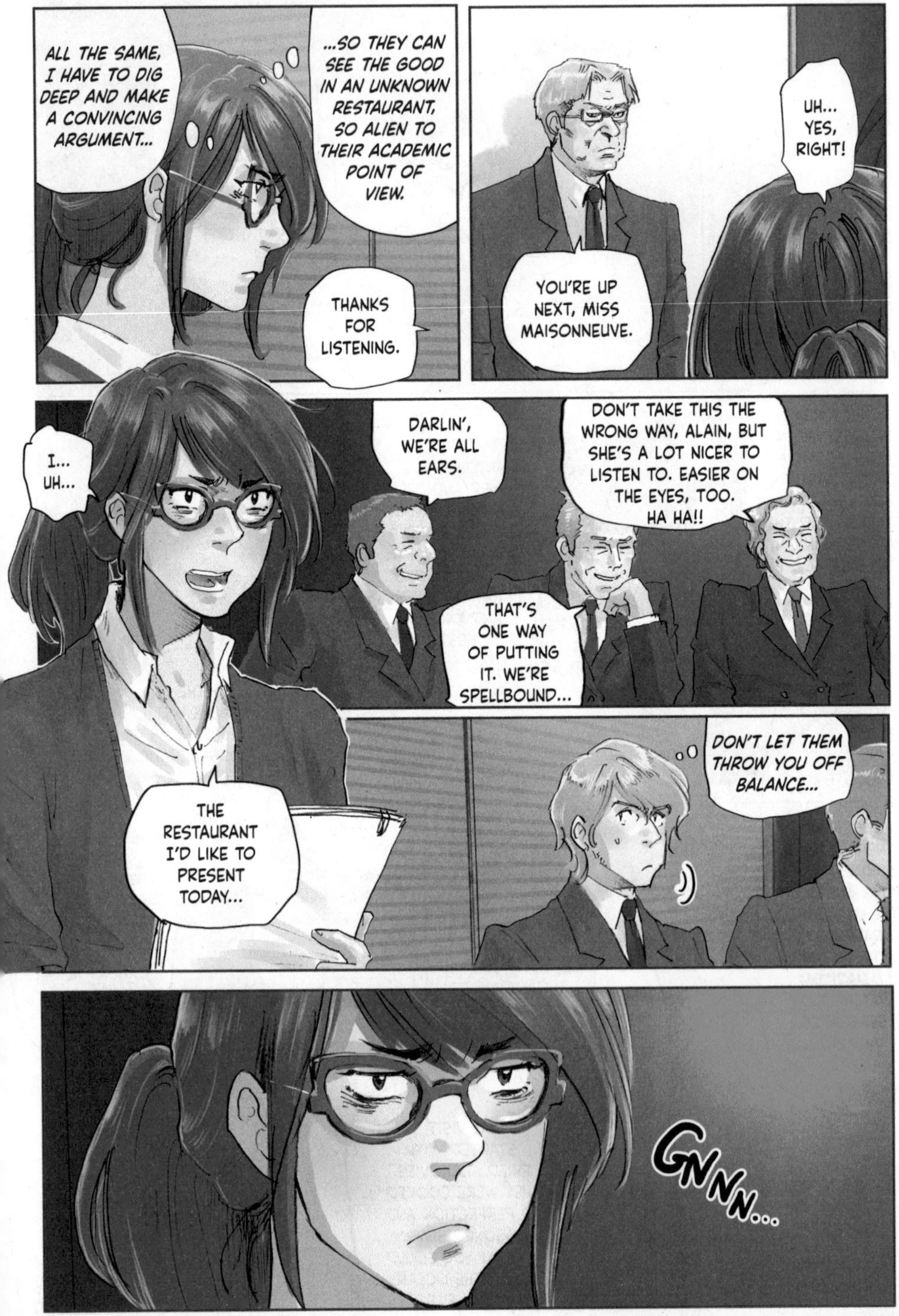

ALL THE SAME, I HAVE TO DIG DEEP AND MAKE A CONVINCING ARGUMENT...
...SO THEY CAN SEE THE GOOD IN AN UNKNOWN RESTAURANT, SO ALIEN TO THEIR ACADEMIC POINT OF VIEW.
THANKS FOR LISTENING.
YOU'RE UP NEXT, MISS MAISONNEUVE.
UH... YES, RIGHT!
I... UH...
DARLIN', WE'RE ALL EARS.
DON'T TAKE THIS THE WRONG WAY, ALAIN, BUT SHE'S A LOT NICER TO LISTEN TO. EASIER ON THE EYES, TOO. HA HA!!
THAT'S ONE WAY OF PUTTING IT. WE'RE SPELLBOUND...
THE RESTAURANT I'D LIKE TO PRESENT TODAY...
DON'T LET THEM THROW YOU OFF BALANCE...
GNNN...

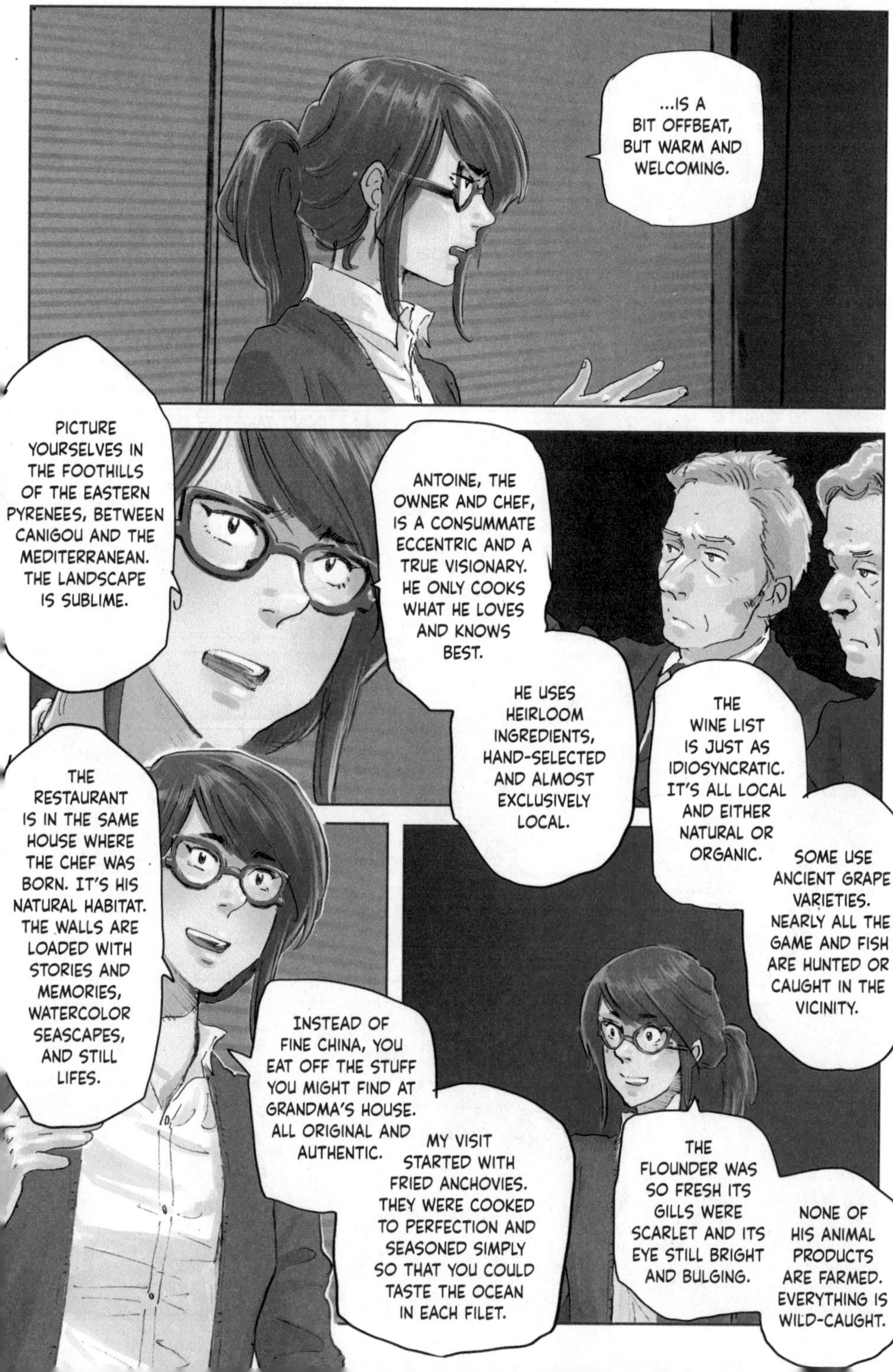
...IS A BIT OFFBEAT, BUT WARM AND WELCOMING.
PICTURE YOURSELVES IN THE FOOTHILLS OF THE EASTERN PYRENEES, BETWEEN CANIGOU AND THE MEDITERRANEAN. THE LANDSCAPE IS SUBLIME.
ANTOINE, THE OWNER AND CHEF, IS A CONSUMMATE ECCENTRIC AND A TRUE VISIONARY. HE ONLY COOKS WHAT HE LOVES AND KNOWS BEST.
HE USES HEIRLOOM INGREDIENTS, HAND-SELECTED AND ALMOST EXCLUSIVELY LOCAL.
THE WINE LIST IS JUST AS IDIOSYNCRATIC. IT'S ALL LOCAL AND EITHER NATURAL OR ORGANIC.
SOME USE ANCIENT GRAPE VARIETIES. NEARLY ALL THE GAME AND FISH ARE HUNTED OR CAUGHT IN THE VICINITY.
THE RESTAURANT IS IN THE SAME HOUSE WHERE THE CHEF WAS BORN. IT'S HIS NATURAL HABITAT. THE WALLS ARE LOADED WITH STORIES AND MEMORIES, WATERCOLOR SEASCAPES, AND STILL LIFES.
INSTEAD OF FINE CHINA, YOU EAT OFF THE STUFF YOU MIGHT FIND AT GRANDMA'S HOUSE. ALL ORIGINAL AND AUTHENTIC.
MY VISIT STARTED WITH FRIED ANCHOVIES. THEY WERE COOKED TO PERFECTION AND SEASONED SIMPLY SO THAT YOU COULD TASTE THE OCEAN IN EACH FILET.
THE FLOUNDER WAS SO FRESH ITS GILLS WERE SCARLET AND ITS EYE STILL BRIGHT AND BULGING.
NONE OF HIS ANIMAL PRODUCTS ARE FARMED. EVERYTHING IS WILD-CAUGHT.

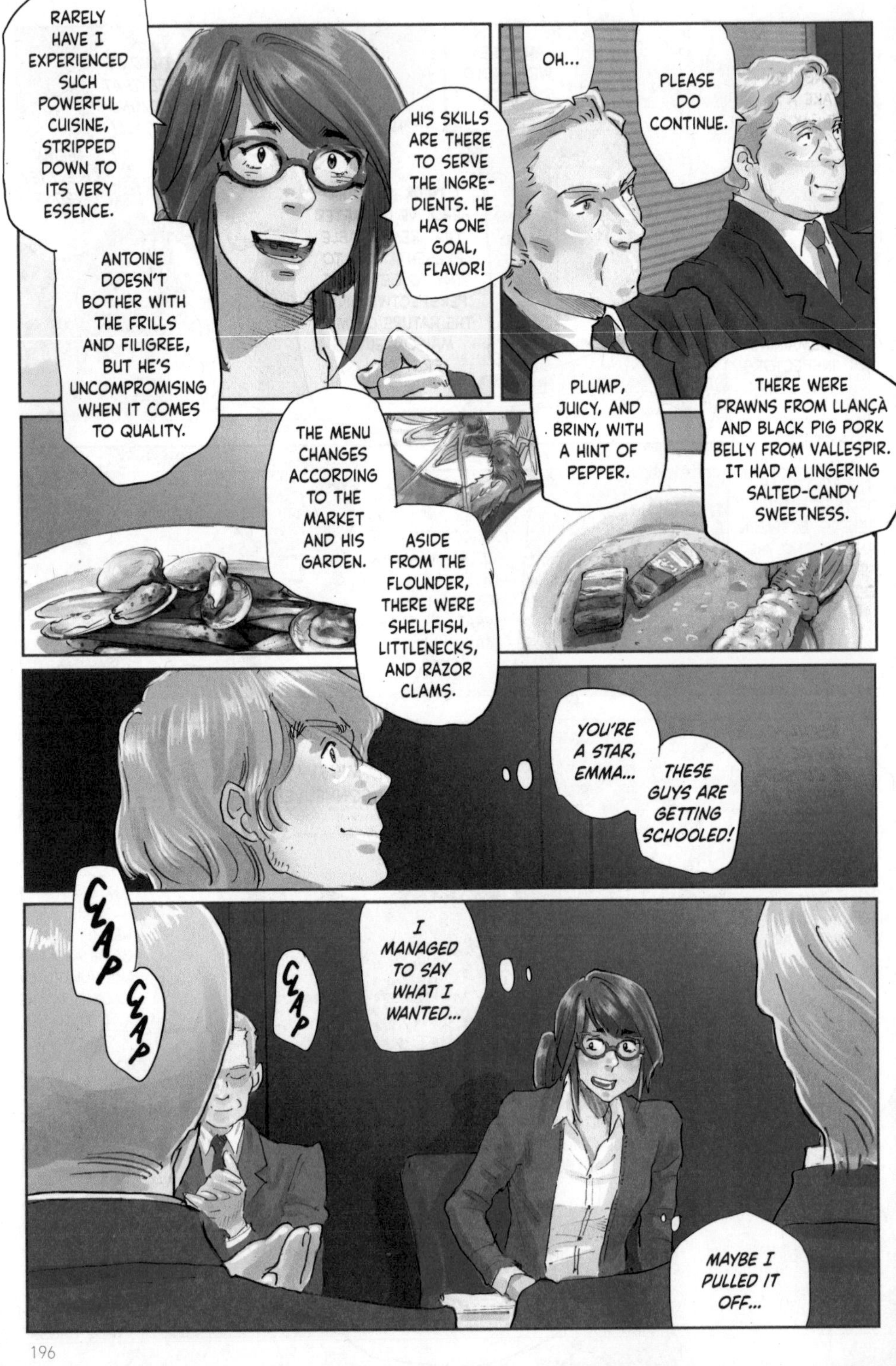
RARELY HAVE I EXPERIENCED SUCH POWERFUL CUISINE, STRIPPED DOWN TO ITS VERY ESSENCE.
ANTOINE DOESN'T BOTHER WITH THE FRILLS AND FILIGREE, BUT HE'S UNCOMPROMISING WHEN IT COMES TO QUALITY.
HIS SKILLS ARE THERE TO SERVE THE INGRE-DIENTS. HE HAS ONE GOAL, FLAVOR!
OH...
PLEASE DO CONTINUE.
THE MENU CHANGES ACCORDING TO THE MARKET AND HIS GARDEN.
ASIDE FROM THE FLOUNDER, THERE WERE SHELLFISH, LITTLENECKS, AND RAZOR CLAMS.
PLUMP, JUICY, AND BRINY, WITH A HINT OF PEPPER.
THERE WERE PRAWNS FROM LLANÇÀ AND BLACK PIG PORK BELLY FROM VALLESPIR. IT HAD A LINGERING SALTED-CANDY SWEETNESS.
YOU'RE A STAR, EMMA...
THESE GUYS ARE GETTING SCHOOLED!
CLAP CLAP
CLAP
I MANAGED TO SAY WHAT I WANTED...
MAYBE I PULLED IT OFF...

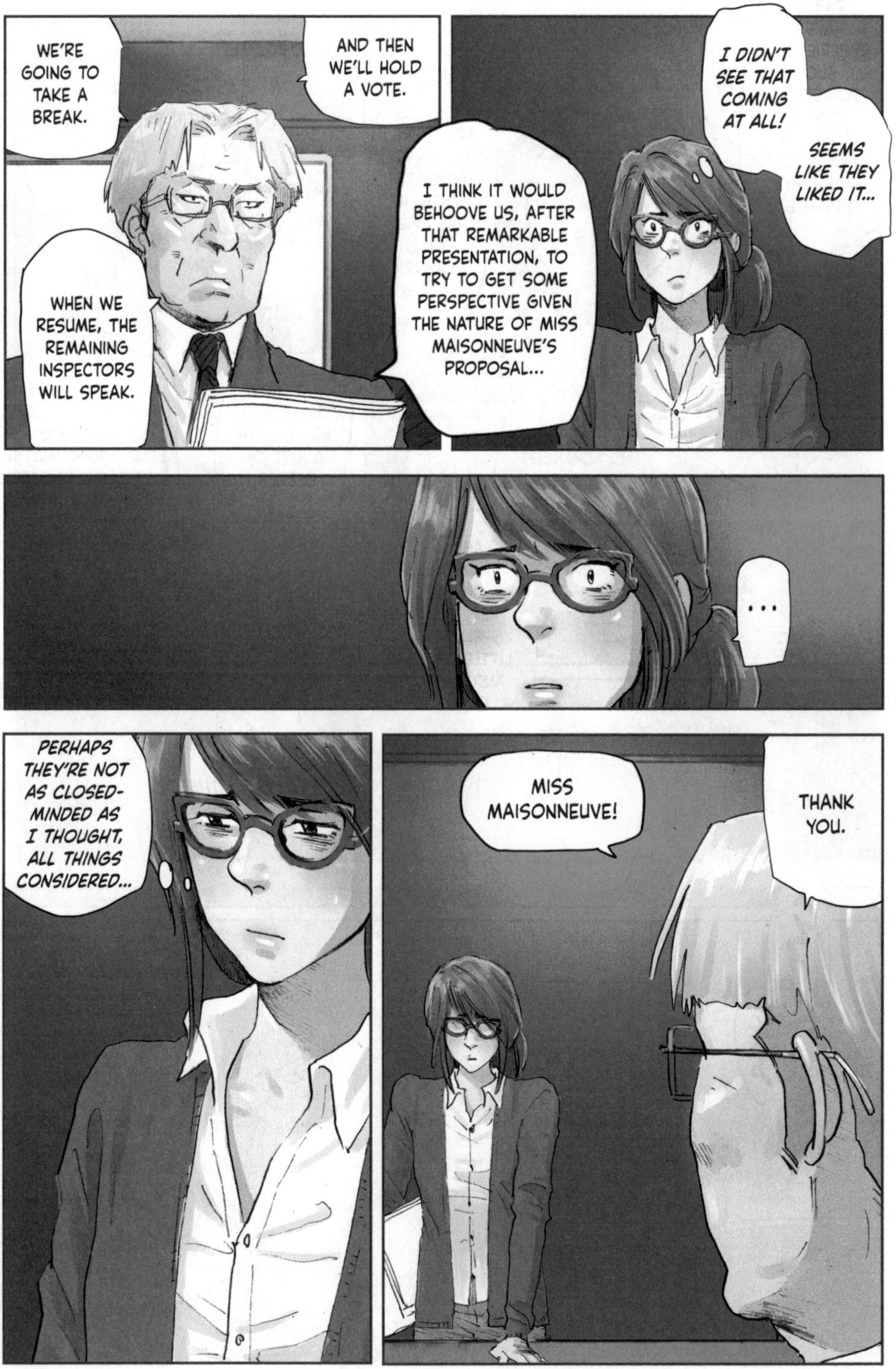
WE'RE GOING TO TAKE A BREAK.
AND THEN WE'LL HOLD A VOTE.
WHEN WE RESUME, THE REMAINING INSPECTORS WILL SPEAK.
I THINK IT WOULD BEHOOVE US, AFTER THAT REMARKABLE PRESENTATION, TO TRY TO GET SOME PERSPECTIVE GIVEN THE NATURE OF MISS MAISONNEUVE'S PROPOSAL...
I DIDN'T SEE THAT COMING AT ALL!
SEEMS LIKE THEY LIKED IT...
...
PERHAPS THEY'RE NOT AS CLOSED-MINDED AS I THOUGHT, ALL THINGS CONSIDERED...
MISS MAISONNEUVE!
THANK YOU.

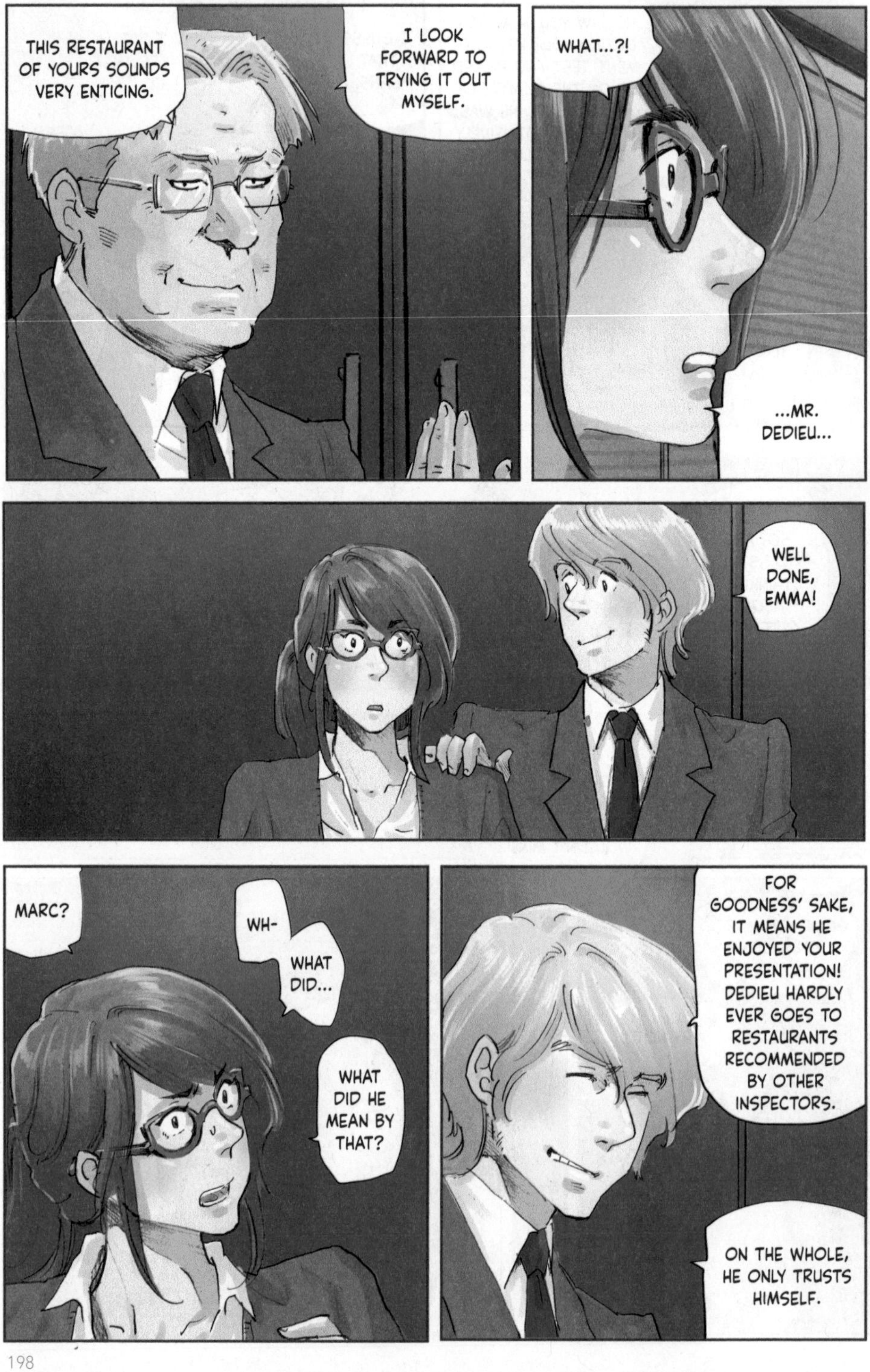
THIS RESTAURANT OF YOURS SOUNDS VERY ENTICING.
I LOOK FORWARD TO TRYING IT OUT MYSELF.
WHAT...?!
...MR. DEDIEU...
WELL DONE, EMMA!
MARC?
WH-
WHAT DID...
WHAT DID HE MEAN BY THAT?
FOR GOODNESS' SAKE, IT MEANS HE ENJOYED YOUR PRESENTATION! DEDIEU HARDLY EVER GOES TO RESTAURANTS RECOMMENDED BY OTHER INSPECTORS.
ON THE WHOLE, HE ONLY TRUSTS HIMSELF.

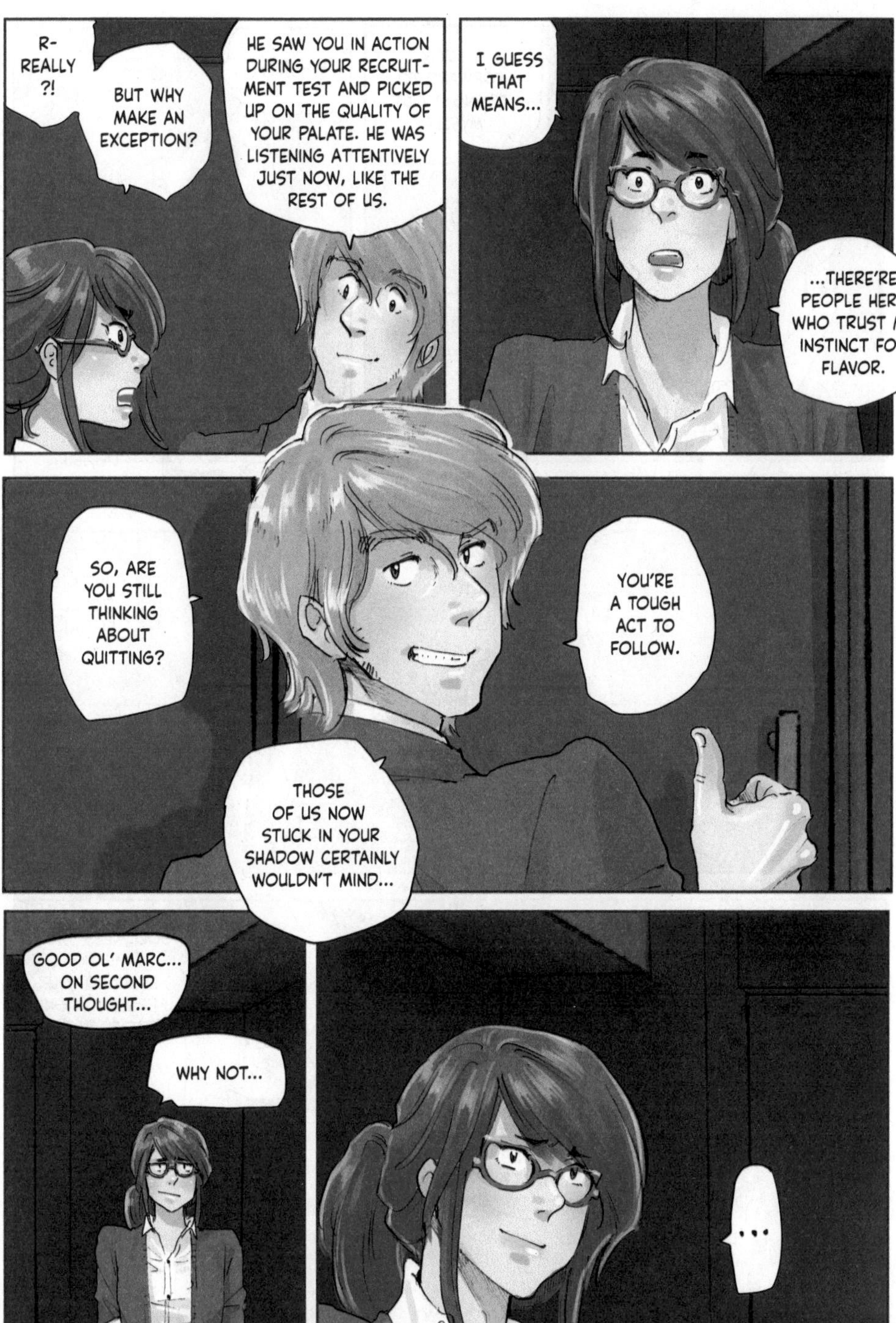
R-REALLY?!
BUT WHY MAKE AN EXCEPTION?
HE SAW YOU IN ACTION DURING YOUR RECRUIT-MENT TEST AND PICKED UP ON THE QUALITY OF YOUR PALATE. HE WAS LISTENING ATTENTIVELY JUST NOW, LIKE THE REST OF US.
I GUESS THAT MEANS...
...THERE'RE PEOPLE HERE WHO TRUST MY INSTINCT FOR FLAVOR.
SO, ARE YOU STILL THINKING ABOUT QUITTING?
YOU'RE A TOUGH ACT TO FOLLOW.
THOSE OF US NOW STUCK IN YOUR SHADOW CERTAINLY WOULDN'T MIND...
GOOD OL' MARC... ON SECOND THOUGHT...
WHY NOT...
...

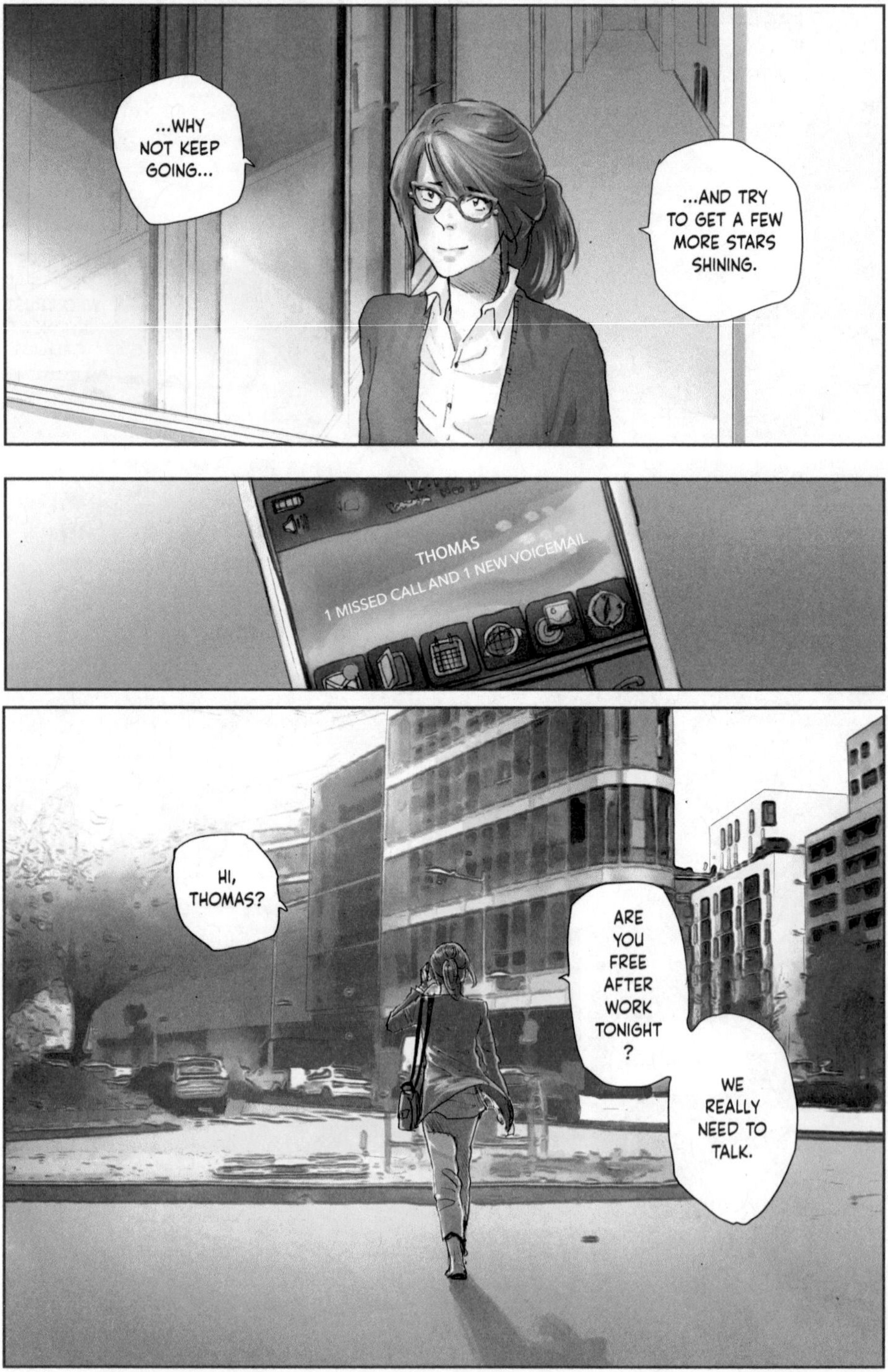
...WHY NOT KEEP GOING...
...AND TRY TO GET A FEW MORE STARS SHINING.
THOMAS
1 MISSED CALL AND 1 NEW VOICEMAIL
HI, THOMAS?
ARE YOU FREE AFTER WORK TONIGHT ?
WE REALLY NEED TO TALK.